Schopenhauer's Compass

East-West Discovery

Schopenhauer's Compass

An Introduction to Schopenhauer's Philosophy and its Origins

Urs App

UniversityMedia
2014

Copyright © 2014 UniversityMedia, Wil (Switzerland)
www.universitymedia.org
All rights reserved.
Printed on acid-free and lignin-free paper

Library of Congress Cataloging-in-Publication Data
App, Urs, 1949–
    Schopenhauer's Compass. An Introduction to Schopenhauer's
    Philosophy and its Origins. / Urs App.
    p. cm. — (UniversityMedia, East-West Discovery)
    Includes bibliographical references and index
    ISBN 978-3-906000-03-9 (acid-free paper)
    1. Arthur Schopenhauer (1788–1860).
    2. Philosophy—History—19th century—Study and teaching.
    3. Philosophy—Idealism—Monism—Materialism.
    4. Religion—Christianity—Buddhism—Hinduism—Islam
    5. Europe—Intellectual life—19th century.
    6. India—Philosophy—Religion.
    7. Orientalism—Europe—History—18th century—19th century.
    8. Mysticism—Sufism—Vedanta—Christianity.
I. Title.

ISBN 978-3-906000-03-9

To Monica Esposito

Nella vita e nella morte
quello che conta di più
è l'abbandonarsi

Contents

INTRODUCTION: Memory Gaps	1
CHAPTER 1. Suffering and Salvation	11
CHAPTER 2. Egotism and Selflessness	23
CHAPTER 3. Illusion and Ur-Knowledge	47
CHAPTER 4. Empirical and Better Consciousness	71
CHAPTER 5. Multiplicity and Oneness	101
CHAPTER 6. Ishq und Fanā	121
CHAPTER 7. Love and Unification	147
CHAPTER 8. Delusion and Awakening	173
CHAPTER 9. Willing and Contemplation	199
CHAPTER 10. Veil of Maya and Wisdom of Veda	221
CHAPTER 11. Affirmation and Abolition of Will	247
APPENDIX 1: Schopenhauer's Favorite Book	265
APPENDIX 2: Research Perspectives	301
Chronological Table	318
Abbreviations and References	320
Bibliography	321
Index	339

Memory Gaps

October 2008, Frankfurt city main cemetery. Did I not glance at a map of the cemetery yesterday at the Schopenhauer Archive in order to memorize the location of the philosopher's grave? I may have been a bit distracted, thinking that the grave of one of the city's most eminent men should be well marked and easy to find. It definitely was somewhere near the Western wall ... But my search along the endless wall is unsuccessful. Soon I find myself straying left and right in search of some marker and graves worthy of the man and his city. To no avail. Asking several visitors of the cemetery I find them equally ignorant about the resting place of Frankfurt's most eminent philosopher. Had I not seen a photo of the gravestone in some book? As I begin to lament my memory gap and get ready to abandon my search, an elderly couple kindly points the way to a plain, neglected grave. A modest stone plate, flat on the ground, bearing only Arthur Schopenhauer's name, and next to it a bundle of withered roses in a knocked-over plastic vase and two half-broken flower pots full of weeds. The area around the grave stone is overgrown and the neighboring tomb of the Schopenhauer scholar Arthur Hübscher equally neglected. Does Frankfurt am Main—one of the world's few cities whose name graces a current of philosophy (the Frankfurter Schule)—also suffer from a memory gap? In the heart of the old city J. W. Goethe (1749–1832) has his much-visited Goethehaus and a culture center named after him. As it should be, Frankfurt is proud of the man who had spent part of his youth in the city. By contrast, Arthur Schopenhauer who died here after a sojourn of almost three decades rests in a neglected grave covered with weeds. Yet the works of Frankfurt's greatest poet seem today far less widely read than those of Frankfurt's greatest philosopher. In a kiosk of a Sardinia ferry one searches in vain for any work by Goethe; but what did I find there a few summers ago among piles of holiday literature and bestselling thrillers? No less than five Italian translations of Schopenhauer!

From the cemetery I wandered to the Schöne Aussicht ("Beautiful View"), the street on the bank of the Main river where Schopenhauer used to live. His residences, the houses number 16 and 17, were damaged by aerial bombardment in 1943. The international German cultural institution named after Goethe (Goethe-Institut e.V.) recently proclaimed on its website that this is the very *address of philosophy*: "It may be grounds for surprise, but philosophy has an address—at least according to one of its most brilliant adepts. Arthur Schopenhauer arrived at final answers to the ultimate questions and claimed that philosophy had reached perfection in his own work. Philosophy is at home where he has his abode, in the 'true center of Europe.' The final address of philosophy is: Frankfurt am Main, Schöne Aussicht 16." (Volker Maria Neumann; www. goethe.de; August 2008).

When I visited this "address of philosophy" in October of 2008 I found a Pizzeria next to a huge gap shielded from view by eight-foothigh metal panels featuring not words of wisdom but huge publicity posters for American cigarettes, German beer, and free Christian Bibles.

Memory Gaps

Frankfurt, gap at Schöne Aussicht street (Photo by the author, 2008)

I was told that the present owner of this vacant property is a Persian investor, which reminds me of another memory gap: the oblivion of the philosopher's favorite book in Schopenhauer research. According to visitors, the *Oupnek'hat*—a two-volume Latin book containing fifty Upanishads translated from Persian—always lay open in Schopenhauer's apartment at the Schöne Aussicht, ready for the philosopher's vesperal devotion. Schopenhauer heaped the highest praise on it:

> How entirely does the Oupnekhat breathe throughout the holy spirit of the Vedas! How is every one who by a diligent study of its Persian Latin has become familiar with that incomparable book, stirred by that spirit to the very depth of his soul! How does every line display its firm, definite, and throughout harmonious meaning! From every sentence deep, original, and sublime thoughts arise, and the whole is pervaded by a high and holy and earnest

spirit. Indian air surrounds us, and original thoughts of kindred spirits.[1]

Sometimes one is asked what book one would take along to banishment on a solitary island if only a single work were allowed. For Schopenhauer the answer was clear: except for the original text, the Latin *Oupnek'hat* "is the most rewarding and uplifting reading possible in the world: it has been the consolation of my life and will be that of my death."[2]

But it was not only such gushing praise of the aged philosopher that should have made this Latin translation of fifty Upanishads an important research topic. Already in the latter half of the 19th century it was well known that young Schopenhauer in 1816, just when he started redacting his major work *The World as Will and Representation*, had jotted the following note in his philosophical notebook:

> I confess that I do not believe that my teaching could ever have come into being before the Upanishads, Plato, and Kant cast their rays simultaneously into one man's mind.[3]

---

[1] »Wie athmet doch der Oupnekhat durchweg den heiligen Geist der Veden! Wie wird doch Der, dem, durch fleißiges Lesen, das Persisch-Latein dieses unvergleichlichen Buches geläufig geworden, von jenem Geist im Innersten ergriffen! Wie ist doch jede Zeile so voll fester, bestimmter und durchgängig zusammenstimmender Bedeutung! Und aus jeder Seite treten uns tiefe, ursprüngliche, erhabene Gedanken entgegen, während ein hoher und heiliger Ernst über dem Ganzen schwebt. Alles athmet hier Indische Luft und ursprüngliches, naturverwandtes Daseyn.« *Parerga and Paralipomena* §184; SW5.421; Z10.437. English translation by Max Müller, *The Upanishads* (New York: Dover Publications, 1962, vol. 1: lxi).

[2] »Es ist die belohnendeste und erhebendeste Lektüre, die (den Urtext ausgenommen) auf der Welt möglich ist: sie ist der Trost meines Lebens gewesen und wird der meines Sterbens seyn.« *Parerga and Paralipomena* §184; SW5.421; Z10.437.

[3] »Ich gestehe übrigens daß ich nicht glaube daß meine Lehre je hätte entstehn können, ehe die Upanischaden, Plato und Kant ihre Strahlen zugleich in eines Menschen Geist werfen konnten« (HN1 #623). Schopenhauer first wrote: "...before an individual had in front of himself the Upanishads, Plato, and Kant" (»... ehe ein Individuum die Upanischaden, den Plato u. den Kant vor sich hatte«) (Handschriftlicher Nachlass Berlin 20.426).

In spite of this, the influence of the Upanishads on Schopenhauer remains nebulous even today.[4] Though some books, dissertations and numerous articles about Schopenhauer's early interest in Asian thought have been published, they unfortunately rely almost without exception on modern Upanishad translations from Sanskrit—that is, on texts that in 1816 did not exist. To my knowledge the entire research literature about oriental influences on Schopenhauer contains a single article in Italian (Piantelli 1986) that briefly discusses the question of influence using the source which Schopenhauer actually studied: the Latin text of the *Oupnek'hat*, his favorite book.

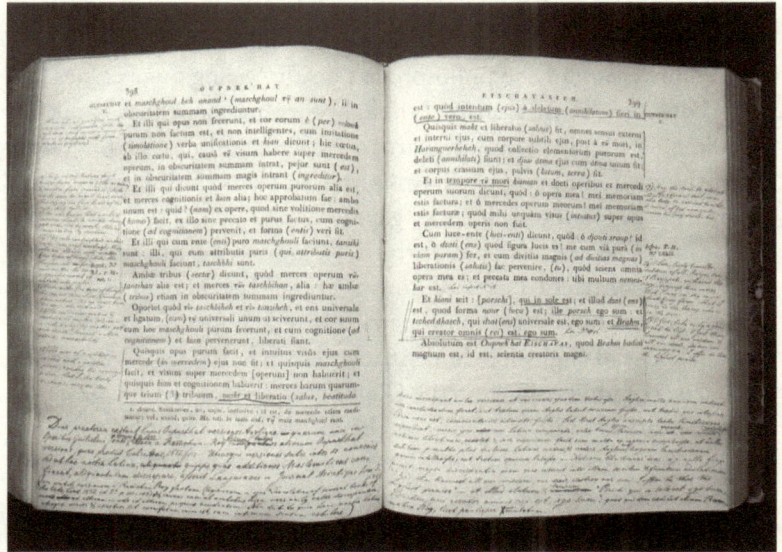

Marks and notes by Schopenhauer in his favorite book (OUP1:389-399)

---

[4] In 2011 Schopenhauer's most recent biographer, David Cartwright, was asked what Schopenhauer had learned from the Upanishads. He answered: "That is the million dollar question. He said that his doctrines could not have originated without the Upanishads, Plato, and Kant casting their rays of light simultaneously into a single mind. How to trace back one of these rays to the Upanishads is very difficult" (Skinner 2011).

Even more surprising is that not a single author has hitherto examined Schopenhauer's marks and handwritten notes in the extant copy of his *Oupnek'hat*. This is astonishing in light of the fact that the *Oupnek'hat* was without any doubt the most important Asian source for the birth of Schopenhauer's system. More than that: as I will show in this book, in the gestation period of Schopenhauer's metaphysics of will the *Oupnek'hat* was his most crucial single source *tout court*. No wonder that it became and remained his favorite book and was lauded as the "consolation" of his life and death.

After a lecture about Schopenhauer's favorite book at the Goethe-Haus in Frankfurt in December 2010, I once more took a walk along Frankfurt's Schöne Aussicht to find out what was happening around the so-called "address of philosophy" in the jubilee year marking the 150th anniversary of the philosopher's death. Seeing huge cranes and heavy construction machinery, I thought for a moment that Frankfurt is building a dignified counterpart to its stately House of Literature down the road: a House of Philosophy. No, I was told: it will be just another hotel. Frankfurt memory gaps.

It is my hope that his book furnishes a more adequate stopgap and represents a different onset of construction. The domain addressed here lay just as fallow as the property where Schopenhauer had lived and died: a dead angle of Schopenhauer research. In view of the praise heaped by the philosopher on the *Oupnek'hat* and his unequivocal pronouncements as to its influence on the formation of his philosophical system, one is left with the question why so far no Schopenhauer specialist has dared to set foot in this gap. In fact the *corpus delicti*, Schopenhauer's richly annotated copy of his favorite book, can be studied at the Schopenhauer Archive in Frankfurt's University library, just a few tram minutes from the so-called "address of philosophy." It is filled with the philosopher's underlines and handwritten comments stemming from the period between Schopenhauer's purchase of the *Oupnek'hat* in the summer of 1814 and his death in the fall of 1860.

Memory Gaps

Almost two decades ago, on February 22 of 1997, I said during a Schopenhauer Society lecture celebrating Schopenhauer's birthday that the genesis of Schopenhauer's philosophy cannot be understood without the study of his *Oupnek'hat*. This is just as true today. But this fascinating book is not the only available source. Indeed, there probably is no other philosopher in world history for whom we have such abundant and authentic material concerning the development of his thought. Apart from letters, notes from conversations, and library registers we have a complete set of Schopenhauer's lecture notes from his student years, books and articles containing his markings and handwritten notes, and most importantly his extremely interesting and rich philosophical notebooks. These were major sources used in this study.

Yet the present book does not only seek to throw light on the birth of *one* philosophy (that of Schopenhauer); rather, it also is a case study in the history of ideas that uncovers a variety of influences, some of them complex and exotic, that can be at play in the genesis of a philosophy. Moreover, the detailed study of the genesis of a philosophy may be the most natural introduction to a philosopher's thought. The reader may also discover that since Schopenhauer's lonely death at Frankfurt's Schöne Aussicht in 1860 his thought has lost little of its force and pertinence.

This book's original German version, written in 2008–9 and published in 2011 (see bibliography), was born in the context of my research project "Oriental influences on the genesis of Schopenhauer's philosophy" (Swiss National Science Foundation project 101511-116443). I wish to express my gratitude to the international jury that recognized the project's value, to the foundation's administrators who approved it, and to the Swiss tax payers who provided the funding. In the present English version I made a few corrections and added some remarks about recent publications. On the whole it is a literal translation of the German version; but since I was translating my own text I felt free to reformulate, shorten, or expand arguments when I felt this might be of help to the reader. I also included a new Appendix containing a description of Schopenhauer's favorite book based on the paper I presented at the international Schopenhauer conference (Frankfurt, 2010) in commemoration of the 150th anniversary of the philosopher's passing. For that earlier version see App 2013. Furthermore, I revised the German version's concluding chapter ("Perspektiven") and decided to include it here as Appendix 2.

Chapters 2 to 5 discuss in some detail Schopenhauer's early development and his study of European philosophy. Readers primarily interested in Oriental influences on the genesis of Schopenhauer's philosophy (discussed from Chapter 6) will find an introduction in Chapter 1 and a brief summary of early developments in Appendix 2 (pp. 304-6).

Unless otherwise specified, all translations from non-English sources are mine. Quotations from other languages are as a rule accompanied (in a footnote or column) by their original text. Readers of German, French or Latin can thus easily compare my translation with its source. Though the spelling of German, French, Latin, and Greek sources may occasionally seem mistaken to readers unfamiliar with historical orthography, it faithfully reproduces the originals. In-line page references always refer to the last full reference. Numbers preceded by a hashtag # refer to the note number in the first volume of Schopenhauer's Manuscript Remains. Due to my previous Schopenhauer-related publications (including transcriptions of the thinker's early notes on Asia-related subjects) and several books related to the history of Orientalism, I could unfortunately not avoid copiously referencing my own output; but do I hope that my work will inspire future researchers to make better use of manuscript and other primary sources and to study, in addition to modern Orient-related publications, the materials consulted by Schopenhauer himself.

Instead of using E.F.J. Payne's sometimes problematic English renderings of Schopenhauer's works I decided to furnish my own translations, accompanied in footnotes by the original German text from Arthur Hübscher's German editions of Schopenhauer's published works and Manuscript Remains. The new Cambridge edition that will soon supersede Payne's English translations is also based on Hübscher's editions and features Hübscher's page numbers in the margin. Thus Schopenhauer's paragraph numbers along with the numbers of Hübscher's editions should enable the reader to easily examine quotations in their context both in Payne's old translations and the new Cambridge edition whose first volumes are already in print. Square brackets mark explanatory text or ellipses added by me; in my English translations of Anquetil-Duperron's Latin *Oupnek'hat* parentheses and brackets follow Anquetil's use, as should be evident from the original text that I reproduced adjacent to my translation.

I wish to thank those readers of my German manuscript of 2009 whose feedback contributed to improvements in style and content, in particular Dr. Thomas Regehly whose repeated suggestions have been helpful. I am also grateful to the members of the steering committee of the Schopenhauer Society in Frankfurt am Main and to the personnel of the Schopenhauer Archive at Frankfurt University's Senckenberg library for their help, the permission to photograph and reproduce Asia-related materials in the archive, and the permission to use my photo of one of the archive's Schopenhauer portraits as an element of Alexander Huwyler's beautiful cover design.

My deepest thanks, however, go to the muse of this project, my beloved wife Monica Esposito (1962–2011). It is for her perusal that I translated chapters 1–5 and 11 into English in early 2009, shortly after completing the German manuscript, and she was very much looking forward to this book's publication. To my utmost regret she did not live to see it in print. It is to Monica and her memory that this book is dedicated. If anyone profoundly understood and sought to live what the "North Pole" of Schopenhauer's compass is all about, it was her. Witness the last sentence of her testament, a sentence that Schopenhauer would have wholeheartedly approved: "You must never forget: what counts most, both in life and in death, is to abandon self."

1. SUFFERING AND SALVATION

Unlike the hand of a watch, the needle of a compass does not point in a single direction. It must be lodged at its center and always indicates two diametrically opposed directions: South and North. Whichever way one may be tossed in one's life: the compass needle never changes its basic bearing.

In Schopenhauer's collected works there are two passages featuring a compass. The first describes the starting point indicated by one extremity of the compass needle: that of the human being holding the compass in hand, his position in the world, and his basic condition.

> In order to always have a secure compass in hand so as to find one's way in life, and to see life always in the correct light without going astray, nothing is more suitable than getting used to seeing this world as something like a penal colony. This view finds its theoretical and objective justification not only in my philosophy

but also in the wisdom of all times, namely, in Brahmanism, Buddhism, Empedocles, Pythagoras [...] Even in genuine and correctly understood Christianity, our existence is regarded as the result of a liability or a misstep [...] We will thus always keep our position in mind and regard every human, first and foremost, as a being that exists only on account of its sinfulness, and whose life is the expiation of the offence committed through birth. Exactly this constitutes what Christianity calls the sinful nature of man.[5]

In our metaphor this extremity of the compass needle points toward the letter "S." On Schopenhauer's compass this indicates sinfulness, guilt, penal colony and in the broadest sense existence (*Sein*). It is the realm of suffering. But every compass needle has two extremities and simultaneously points in the diametrically opposed direction, away from the person holding the compass.

Whereas the needle end pointing toward us indicates where we come from and our basic mode of existence, the letter "N" on the opposite side symbolizes the goal. Every compass in the world is fixated on this "N": but what does it signify for Schopenhauer? One might say that this goal is the subject of the famous passage at the very end of his major work, *The World as Will and Representation*:

---

[5] »Um allezeit einen sichern Kompaß, zur Orientirung im Leben, bei der Hand zu haben, und um dasselbe, ohne je irre zu werden, stets im richtigen Lichte zu erblicken, ist nichts tauglicher, als daß man sich angewöhne, diese Welt zu betrachten als einen Ort der Buße, also gleichsam als eine Strafanstalt, *a penal colony*—welche Ansicht derselben auch ihre theoretische und objektive Rechtfertigung findet, nicht bloß in meiner Philosophie, sondern in der Weisheit aller Zeiten, nämlich im Brahmanismus, im Buddhaismus, beim Empedokles und Pythagoras [...] selbst im ächten und wohlverstandenen Christenthum wird unser Daseyn aufgefaßt als die Folge einer Schuld, eines Fehltritts [...] wir werden stets im Sinne behalten, wo wir sind, folglich Jeden ansehn zunächst als ein Wesen, welches nur in Folge seiner Sündhaftigkeit existirt, dessen Leben die Abbüßung der Schuld seiner Geburt ist. Diese macht eben Das aus, was das Christenthum die sündige Natur des Menschen nennt.« (P2 §156; SW5.321; Z9:328–9)

In this manner—through the observation of the life and conduct of saints whom one might rarely encounter in one's own experience but who are brought before our eyes both through their recorded histories and through art vouchsafed by the mark of inner truth—we must thus banish the somber impression of that nothingness which hovers as the ultimate goal behind all virtue and saintliness and which we dread the way children fear darkness. Instead of evading it, as the Indian do, through myths and bland words such 'reabsorption into Brahman or the Nirvana of the Buddhists, we freely proclaim: for those who are still filled with the will, what remains after its complete abolition is indeed nothing. But conversely, for those in whom the will has turned and negated itself, this oh-so-real world of ours with all its suns and galaxies, is — nothing.[6]

The "N" of Schopenhauer's compass can thus be said to stand for "Nothing" or "Nothingness" and to correspond to the Nirvana of the Buddhists that is said to be a less radical term for the same thing.[7] This goal is the exact opposite of "S" and signifies release from the penal colony (saintliness, sinlessless), and in the broadest sense freedom from

---

[6] »Also auf diese Weise, durch Betrachtung des Lebens und Wandels der Heiligen, welchen in der eigenen Erfahrung zu begegnen freilich selten vergönnt ist, aber welche ihre aufgezeichnete Geschichte und, mit dem Stämpel innerer Wahrheit verbürgt, die Kunst uns vor die Augen bringt, haben wir den finstern Eindruck jenes Nichts, das als das letzte Ziel hinter aller Tugend und Heiligkeit schwebt, und das wir, wie die Kinder das Finstere, fürchten, zu verscheuchen; statt selbst es zu umgehn, wie die Inder, durch Mythen und bedeutungsleere Worte, wie Resorbtion in das Brahm, oder Nirwana der Buddhaisten. Wir bekennen es vielmehr frei: was nach gänzlicher Aufhebung des Willens übrig bleibt, ist für alle Die, welche noch des Willens voll sind, allerdings Nichts. Aber auch umgekehrt ist Denen, in welchen der Wille sich gewendet und verneint hat, diese unsere so sehr reale Welt mit allen ihren Sonnen und Milchstraßen—Nichts.« (W1 §71; SW2.487; Z2.508)

[7] Numerous authors misunderstood this passage as a critique of Buddhism. Based on this misunderstanding, Moira Nicholls (1999) claimed that Schopenhauer later on radically changed his opinion about Buddhism. See App 2010b.

CHAPTER ONE

suffering and even being: nothingness. This famous passage that so aptly expresses Schopenhauer's central bearing was first jotted down at the end of 1816 in one of his philosophical notebooks (HN1 #612) and was subsequently used with little change.

Part of the 1816 draft of Schopenhauer's final "nothingness" passage with source references (*Asiatick Researches, Oupnek'hat*) (HN1 #612)

This manuscript passage stems from the period when the main pillars of Schopenhauer's philosophical system had just been erected. The core of this system consists in the so-called "metaphysics of will" whose genesis I describe in this book. It furnishes in philosophical terms the diagnosis (suffering and its ultimate cause) and explains the therapy (the possibility of a temporary or permanent elimination of suffering).

The extremity of the compass needle pointing toward us thus signifies affirmation of will and being, whereas the opposite end unwaveringly points toward the abolition of will and toward nothingness. The understanding of this basic configuration is facilitated by information about the genesis of Schopenhauer's philosophy and by a better understanding of the process that led to the philosopher's conclusion that his diagnosis addresses the riddle of the entire world, starting with man—who holds the compass in his hand and regards himself as firmly positioned and upright while standing on a wildly gyrating globe racing through space—and extending to the most remote star nebulas of the universe.

How did the 28-year-old Schopenhauer arrive at the vision that, toward the end of 1816, had matured to such an extent that it was ready for systematic formulation in his major work of 1818, *The World as Will and Representation*? A hint is found in his 1816 draft of the "nothingness" note (see here above). This is the note that was later used in revised form for the concluding paragraph of *The World as Will and Representation*.

In the published version Schopenhauer decided to omit the note's reference to sources that had led him to believe that Brahmanism and Buddhism point in less drastic words to the same goal as his philosophy: "see *asiatick researches* and *Upnek'hat*" (#612). But forty-four years later, toward the end of his life, Schopenhauer added a handwritten gloss to the final word "nothingness" of his major work. This gloss, which in many editions figures as a footnote to the final word "Nichts," once more emphasized the Buddhist connection:

> Precisely this [nothingness] is also the Prajna paramita of the Buddhists, the 'beyond all knowledge,' i.e., the point where subject and object are no longer. (See J. J. Schmidt, About Mahayana and Prajna paramita).[8]

---

[8] »Dies ist eben auch das Pradschna-Paramita der Buddhaisten, das ›Jenseits aller Erkenntniß‹, d.h. der Punkt, wo Subjekt und Objekt nicht mehr sind. (Siehe J. J. Schmidt, ›Ueber das Mahajana und Pradschna-Paramita‹).« (SW2.487; Z2:508)

CHAPTER ONE

It is as if Schopenhauer had, shortly before his death, pasted an additional sticker on the all-important north side of his compass featuring the word *prajna paramita*: the supreme wisdom of Mahayana Buddhism as described by the Germano-Russian Isaac Jacob Schmidt (1779–1847) in his translation of the Diamond Sutra from Tibetan. Many stickers had been pasted on his compass over the years, as it were, and among them was also the Pali word *Nieban* (added in 1816) that later got replaced by its Sanskrit equivalent *Nirvana*. It is as if Schopenhauer had been on a life-long search for terms and explanations for this "N" pole of his compass.

In the *Parerga and Paralipomena*—the work that in the 1850s brought sudden fame to the hitherto practically unknown philosopher—Schopenhauer described this "N" pole in terms of "illuminism." He wrote that philosophy keeps swinging back and forth between rationalism and illuminism. Rationalism is said to have evolved from dogmatism to skepticism and to Kant's transcendental philosophy. Illuminism, by contrast, is "essentially directed toward the inside, inner enlightenment, spiritual vision [intellektuelle Anschauung], higher consciousness, immediately cognizing reason, consciousness of God, unification."[9] When illuminism grows on the soil of a religion it is, according to Schopenhauer, called *mysticism*. Illuminism's basic flaw is that "its knowledge is not communicable" and that therefore it cannot be proved. However, Schopenhauer insists that this does not mean that mystical experience plays no role in the work of philosophers.

> The presence of illuminism can at times be felt in Plato. It occurs more decisively in the philosophy of the Neoplatonics, the gnostics, of Dionysius Areopagita, of Scotus Eriugena, and also among Muslims in form of the doctrine of the Sufis. In India it reigns in Vedanta and Mimansa; and Jacob Böhme and all Christian mystics are most definitely its representatives. Illuminism al-

---

[9] »wesentlich *nach innen* gerichtet, innere Erleuchtung, intellektuelle Anschauung, höheres Bewußtseyn, unmittelbar erkennende Vernunft, Gottesbewußtseyn, Unifikation« (P2 §10; SW 5.10; Z9.17).

ways occurs when rationalism reaches a dead end after a period of dominance. This happened when, toward the end of Scholastic philosophy and in opposition to it, illuminism arose as mysticism, particularly that of Germans like Tauler and the author of the German Theology along with others; and again in most recent times as a reaction to Kant's philosophy in Jacobi, Schelling and in the latest phase of Fichte.[10]

In Schopenhauer's eyes the famous exponents of German idealism, Fichte and Schelling, were among the culprits who had smudged the limits between philosophy on one hand and illuminism or mysticism on the other, thus harming both. Schopenhauer claimed to have strictly avoided this pitfall:

> But philosophy should be communicable knowledge and must therefore be rationalism. For this reason I have, in the conclusion of my philosophy, pointed toward the realm of illuminism as something that is present, while consistently avoiding to encroach upon it even by a single step. As a consequence I did not venture to provide ultimate answers regarding the existence of the world but went only as far as the objective and rationalistic path allowed. I thus safeguarded the space of illuminism where it may, in its own way, come up with a solution to all riddles, and may do so without hindering my endeavor or having to polemicize against me.[11]

---

[10] »Illuminismus ist stellenweise schon im Plato zu spüren: entschiedener aber tritt er auf in der Philosophie der Neuplatoniker, der Gnostiker, des Dionysius Areopagita, wie auch des Skotus Erigena; ferner unter den Mohammedanern, als Lehre der Sufi: in Indien herrscht er in Vedanta und Mimansa: am entschiedensten gehören Jakob Böhme und alle christlichen Mystiker ihm an. Er tritt allemal auf, wann der Rationalismus ein Stadium, ohne das Ziel zu erreichen, durchlaufen hat: so kam er, gegen das Ende der scholastischen Philosophie und im Gegensatz derselben, als Mystik, zumal der Deutschen, im Tauler und dem Verfasser der deutschen Theologie, nebst Andern; und ebenfalls in neuester Zeit, als Gegensatz zur Kantischen Philosophie, in Jacobi und Schelling, gleichfalls in Fichtes letzter Periode.« (P2 §10; SW5.10; Z9.17)

[11] »Allein die Philosophie soll mittheilbare Erkenntniß, muß daher Ratio-

CHAPTER ONE

Schopenhauer here referred to the fourth book of his major work and in particular to the final "nothingness" passage whose early formulation was translated above. But according to Schopenhauer this strict confinement of philosophy to the boundary of rationality does not signify that philosophers should not be—or have not been—inspired by illuminism and mysticism. On the contrary: with the exception of Kant, precisely Schopenhauer's most highly esteemed philosophers are said to have made use of a hidden illuminist compass:. He explains:

> Often enough, however, rationalism may be rooted in a hidden illuminism that is used by the philosopher like a hidden compass while claiming to be guided exclusively by the stars—i.e., the external, clearly visible objects—and taking only these into account. This is admissible because he does not engage in relating incommunicable knowledge; on the contrary, he ensures that his communications remain purely objective and rational. This may have been the case with Plato, Spinoza, Malebranche, and numerous others; but it is nobody else's affair, and it is of no concern because these are the secrets of their bosom. By contrast, the clamorous reference to some spiritual vision [intellektuelle Anschauung] and the brazen-faced account of its content, coupled with the pretention of its objective validity—as seen in Fichte and Schelling— is insolent and reprehensible.[12]

---

nalismus seyn. Demgemäß habe ich, in der meinigen, zwar, am Schluß, auf das Gebiet des Illuminismus, als ein Vorhandenes, hingedeutet, aber mich gehütet, es auch nur mit Einem Schritte zu betreten; dagegen denn auch nicht unternommen, die letzten Aufschlüsse über das Daseyn der Welt zu geben, sondern bin nur so weit gegangen, als es auf dem objektiven, rationalistischen Wege möglich ist. Dem Illuminismus habe ich seinen Raum freigelassen, wo ihm, auf seine Weise, die Lösung aller Räthsel werden mag, ohne daß er dabei mir den Weg verträte, oder gegen mich zu polemisiren hätte.« (P2 §10; SW5.10; Z9.17)

[12] »Inzwischen mag oft genug dem Rationalismus ein versteckter Illuminismus zum Grunde liegen, auf welchen dann der Philosoph, wie auf einen versteckten Kompaß, hinsieht, während er eingeständlich seinen Weg nur nach den Sternen, d.h. den äußerlich und klar vorliegenden Objekten, richtet und

Arthur Hübscher has been correct in stating that Schopenhauer may be included without qualms in this line of philosophers inspired by illuminism (Hübscher 1973:48). But what kind of "hidden compass" Schopenhauer was using, and how he came up with his metaphysics of will, remains hazy even after the research efforts of the last half-century. Thanks to the work of Rudolf Malter and his successors, it has become ever more apparent that the question of suffering and its overcoming—the so-called soteriology—constitutes the central problematic of Schopenhauer's philosophy. But Schopenhauer's understanding of this also went through a gradual development process and did not from the outset match the view that Schopenhauer eventually presented in *The World as Will and Representation*. This is why it is essential to carefully examine the young man's notes and employ later pronouncements with prudence. Schopenhauer, too, was subject to the common tendency to portray one's development as far more streamlined than it really was. In the present book, the genesis of Schopenhauer's philosophical system is therefore mainly described on the basis of his contemporary notes and readings. It can be divided into the following phases (see also the table on p. 21):

1. The first phase is the time before the beginning of Schopenhauer's study of philosophy, i.e., before 1811. The significance of this phase has often been overlooked in previous studies.

2. The second phase covers the so-called "early philosophy," i.e. Schopenhauer's time as philosophy student until his doctorate in the fall of 1813. The detailed study by de Cian (2002) of this phase ends with Schopenhauer's doctoral dissertation.

---

nur diese in Rechnung bringt. Dies ist zulässig, weil er nicht unternimmt, die unmittheilbare Erkenntniß mitzutheilen, sondern seine Mittheilungen rein objektiv und rationell bleiben. Dies mag der Fall gewesen seyn mit Plato, Spinoza, Malebranche und manchem Andern: es geht niemanden etwas an: denn es sind die Geheimnisse ihrer Brust. Hingegen das laute Berufen auf intellektuelle Anschauung und die dreiste Erzählung ihres Inhalts, mit dem Anspruch auf objektive Gültigkeit desselben, wie bei Fichte und Schelling, ist unverschämt und verwerflich.« (P2 §10; SW5.10; Z9.17)

3. The third phase, which forms the main focus of the present book, encompasses the birth of Schopenhauer's metaphysics of will (1814) and the years 1815 and 1816, during which he worked out its implications, put it in words, and sought to situate it in the history of philosophy.

4. The fourth phase includes the redaction of Schopenhauer's main work, *The World as Will and Representation* (1816–1818). Not much research exists about this phase, and it lies outside our scope.[13]

Since this book is about the birth of Schopenhauer's metaphysics of will, its main focus will be on the third of these phases, that is, the period between 1814 and 1816. However, we will see that the preceding first and second phases are also of great importance. The table on page 21 situates these three phases in the larger context of Schopenhauer's life and work.

Rather than discussing *The World as Will and Representation* and later works, this book introduces the reader to hitherto neglected major influences on the genesis of his thought and makes copious use of manuscript sources. A fair amount of the presented materials were translated into English for the first time. For the convenience of multilingual readers and specialists, the original texts of almost all quotations are included in form of footnotes or columns. But this book is not only aimed at specialists. Readers who are little or not at all familiar with Schopenhauer will find that understanding what drove him and gave his thought its characteristic direction—his internal compass—may well be the most natural introduction to his philosophy.

---

[13] Kamata (1988:112–3) proposed a different periodization: an "early phase" (Frühphase) from 1809 to the end of 1814, and a "late phase" (Spätphase) from 1815 to 1816. Kamata's "Frühphase" is in turn divided into a "study phase" (Studienphase) (1809–13), the sojourn in Rudolstadt (1813), a first Weimar and Dresden period (1813–14), and a second Dresden period (1814). In terms of Kamata's periodization, the present book covers both the "early" and "late" phases of system genesis.

Suffering and Salvation

Phase	Time/Age	Writings
1. Early phase	1807–1811 (19–23 y.)	Travel diaries; Manuscript remains 1, #1–12
2. Student phase	1811–1813 (23–25 y.)	Manuscript remains 1, # 22–116 1813 Dissertation *Fourfold Root*
3A. Birth of the metaphysics of will	1814 (26 y.)	Manuscript remains 1, # 117–364
3B. Elaboration of the system	1815–1816 (27–28 y.)	Manuscript remains 1, # 365–509 1816 *On Seeing and Colors*
4. Redaction of the system	1817–1818 (29–30 y.)	Manuscript remains 1, # 510–716 1818 *The World as Will and Representation*
5. Didactic elaboration of the system	1819–1821 (31–33 y.)	Lecture manuscripts
6. Explanations; comments; additions; deletions; revisions; new contents	1822–1860 (34–72 y.)	1836 *Will in Nature* 1841 *Fundamental Problems of Ethics* 1844 *World as Will and Representation II* 1851 *Parerga and Paralipomena*

2. Egotism and Selflessness

When I hold a compass in my hand and adjust my position, one end of its needle points toward me and the other away from me. This expresses, I think, the fundamental tendency of Schopenhauer's entire philosophy. It found expression in countless variations, from the jottings of his youth to the latest notes of the old man, and of course also in the basic structure of his major work, *The World as Will and Representation*. Its first book shows the world as one perceives it: an object for a subject. The second unveils its essence as blind will that wants only itself and its propagation. This blind striving is perceived as bipolar and shows itself for example in the phenomenon of magnetism. Apart from countless other organisms, this striving will also took the form of one that—thanks to its brain and self-consciousness—became its mirror: the human being. Based on a note by Schopenhauer (HN1:462) Rudolf Malter called this Schopenhauer's 'single thought': "The world is the self-cognition of the will" (1988:14). Yet this captures only half of the compass needle and of Schopenhauer's single thought, namely, the nature of ourselves and the world. The third and fourth books of Schopenhauer's major work discuss the opposite pole to which the compass needle is invisibly yet ceaselessly attracted. The third book deals with the momentary forgetting of self in the artistic creation of the genius and in the experience of works of art by the public. The main subject of the fourth and last book is the permanent eclipse of the self: the selflessness of the saint and the extinction of all "I and mine" whose portrayal peaks in the Buddhist nirvana of the final passage and in "Nichts": our "N."[14]

Throughout his life Schopenhauer found confirmations of this compass-bearing in world literature. One year before his death he wrote:

> In the second and fourth chapter of the *German Theology* (sole ungarbled edition, Stuttgart 1851) it is stated that the fall both of the devil and of Adam consisted in their adoption of 'I' and 'to me', 'mine', and 'for me'; and on page 89 it is said: "In genuine love there remains neither I nor to me, mine, for me, you, yours, nor anything of the kind." According to this the 'Kural', translated by Graul from the Tamil language, states on page 8: "The outward-directed passion of mine and the inward-directed passion of I cease" (cf. verse 346). And in the *Manual of Buddhism* by Spence Hardy, page 258, Buddha says: "My followers reject the thought, this am I, or this is mine." On the whole, provided that one disregards the forms conditioned by external influences and is probing the essence of the matter, one will find that Shakyamuni [Buddha] and Meister Eckhart teach the same thing—with the difference that the former was able to express matters without encumbrance, whereas the latter had to wrap them in the robe of the Christian myth and was obliged to adapt his utterances to it.[15]

---

[14] John Atwell (1995:29–30) rightly noted that Schopenhauer's short-form version of his "single thought" ("The world is the self-cognition of the will" [»Die Welt ist die Selbsterkenntnis des Willens«, #662]) also points to the state, described in the fourth book of Schopenhauer's main work, where the will is completely known and abrogated.

[15] »In der *Deutschen Theologie* (alleinige unverstümmelte Ausgabe, Stuttgart

Egotism and Selflessness

That Schopenhauer regarded this teaching as the quintessence and goal of his own philosophy is shown in two remarks scribbled by the old man in a notebook he called "Senilia." In a paragraph about Meister Eckhart and his "wonderfully profound and correct view" Schopenhauer wrote: "In Buddhism one finds the same thought, unimpaired by such mythology and therefore simple and clear, as far as a religion can be clear. With me there is full clarity" (HN4b:28). While reading through this passage he apparently felt that the premise of this statement needed to be explicitly stated. So he added in the left margin: "Buddha, Eckhart and I teach essentially the same thing; Eckhart in the fetters of his Christian mythology."[16]

For Schopenhauer the teachings of the mystics were a fact that could not be subject to doubt. In the course of this book it will be seen that they constituted far more than just a confirmation of his philosophy. Certainly they were that, too, particularly in the period when his major work was almost totally ignored and hardly sold. Schopenhauer wrote nine years after its publication, in 1827:

> The *quietists* and *mystics* are not some sort of sect that maintains, transmits and defends a dogma that is theoretically agreeable to

---

1851) wird Kapitel 2 und 3 gesagt, daß sowohl der Fall des Teufels, als der Adams, darin bestanden hätte, daß der Eine, wie der Andere, sich das Ich und Mich, das Mein und Mir beigelegt hätte; und S. 89 heißt es: ›In der wahren Liebe bleibt weder Ich, noch Mich, Mein, Mir, Du, Dein, und desgleichen.‹ Diesem nun entsprechend heißt es im ›Kural‹, aus dem Tamulischen von Graul, S. 8: ›Die nach außen gehende Leidenschaft des Mein und die nach innen gehende des Ich hören auf‹ (vgl. Vers 346). Und im *Manual of Buddhism* by Spence Hardy, S. 258 spricht Buddha: ›Meine Schüler verwerfen den Gedanken, dies bin Ich, oder dies ist Mein.‹ Ueberhaupt, wenn man von den Formen, welche die äußern Umstände herbeiführen, absieht und den Sachen auf den Grund geht, wird man finden, daß Schakia Muni und Meister Eckhard das Selbe lehren; nur daß Jener seine Gedanken geradezu aussprechen durfte, Dieser hingegen genöthigt ist, sie in das Gewand des Christlichen Mythos zu kleiden und diesem seine Aussprüche anzupassen.« (W2 §48; SW 3.704; Z4.718)

[16] »Buddha, Eckhard u. ich lehren im Wesentl. das Selbe, Eckhard in den Feßeln seiner christl. Mythologie.« (HN4b.28)

and accepted by all its members who therefore are all connected to it. On the contrary, they often have no knowledge of each other; at least the Indian, Christian, and Muslim quietists are totally independent. And even the Christian ones seem to have had little knowledge of each other [...] Yet they express exactly the same thing. This great uniformity, coupled with the great authority and solidity of their pronouncements, confirms that their teaching is what they present it as: an *expression of their inner experience*. Since this *inner experience* is everywhere the same, quietists teach one and the same thing even though they are completely independent of each other and even separated by different centuries, parts of the world, and religions. This is true to such a degree that even great differences in education, historical time period, geographical origin, nationality, and sex do not cause any noticeable doctrinal difference.[17]

According to Schopenhauer, every philosophy worthy of its name must not only offer a cogent explanation of the "S" of sexuality—the most obvious expression of the blind and selfish striving of nature—but also of "N" which signifies its overcoming. This latter pole is intimately connected with metaphysics:

---

[17] »Die *Quietisten* und *Mystiker* sind nicht etwa eine Sekte, die ein theoretisch beliebtes und einmal ergriffenes Dogma festhält, fortpflanzt und vertheidigt, und deren Mitglieder daher alle zusammenhängen. Im Gegentheil sie wissen oft nicht von einander, wenigstens sind einander die Indischen, Christlichen und Muhammedanischen Quietisten völlig fremd. Und selbst die Christlichen werden oft wenig Kunde von einander gehabt haben ... Dennoch reden sie alle vollkommen übereinstimmend. Diese große Uebereinstimmung im Verein mit der großen Zuversicht und Festigkeit ihres Vortrages bestätigt ihre Lehre als das wofür sie sie geben: *Aussage über innre Erfahrung*. Da diese *innre Erfahrung* überall dieselbe ist, so lehren Quietisten, obwohl völlig unabhängig von einander, ja durch Zeitalter, Welttheile und Religionen von einander abgeschnitten, doch ganz und gar dasselbe, so sehr, daß sogar der große Unterschied in der Bildung ... keinen merklichen Unterschied in der Lehre verursacht, eben so wenig als die Verschiedenheit des Zeitalters, der Nation, des Geschlechts jenes vermag.« (HN3.351)

Therefore each system of metaphysics must either reject the quietists—which can only be achieved by regarding them either as impostors or as lunatics—or it must accept them and confirm their pronouncements. Hitherto, all systems of metaphysics had, in order to be consistent, to side with the former as soon as the subject came up. Mine is the first and only one that unequivocally takes the side of the second party, and I consider this fact a considerable sign of its truth.[18]

For centuries, educated Europeans had believed in a "consensus gentium:" a general agreement of all people that there is an omnipotent creator God. After Vasco da Gama opened the sea lane to India in 1498, ancient India was often adduced as the best confirmation of the original monotheism of all humankind (App 2010). But while rejecting such a monotheistic consensus, Schopenhauer saw a mystical one:

> A most remarkable example of this is found when comparing the *Torrens* by Madame Guyon with the teaching of the Vedas, in particular with the passage on page 63 of the first volume [of the *Oupnek'hat*] which concisely but exactly and even with identical imagery has the same content as the French book, even though it could not possibly have been known to Madame de Guyon around 1680.[19]

---

[18] »Daher hat jede Metaphysik die Quietisten entweder abzuweisen, welches nur geschehn kann indem sie solche entweder für Betrüger oder für Verrückte erklärt; oder sie muß sie gelten lassen und ihre Aussagen bestätigen. Alle bisherigen Metaphysischen Systeme müssen, um konsequent zu seyn, erstere Partei ergreifen, sobald der Gegenstand zur Frage kommt: das meinige ist das erste und einzige, welches entschieden die 2te Parthei ergreift, und ich halte diesen Umstand für kein unbedeutendes Merkmal seiner Wahrheit.« (HN3.351)

[19] »Ein höchst auffallendes Beispiel hievon liefert die Vergleichung der *Torrens* der Guion mit der Lehre der Veden, namentlich mit der Stelle im Oupnekhat, Bd. 1, S. 63, welche den Inhalt jener Französischen Schrift in größter Kürze, aber genau und sogar mit denselben Bildern enthält, und dennoch der Frau von Guion, um 1680, unmöglich bekannt seyn konnte.« (W2 §48; SW3:704; Z4.718)

CHAPTER TWO

Schopenhauer's awareness and understanding of this phenomenon increased in the course of his life, as is apparent in his growing collection of mystical literature and related notes. However, the basic tendency is already apparent in the young man's earliest reflections. In his travel diaries (1800 and 1803–4) enthusiastic descriptions of the beauty and power of nature alternate with thoughts about the misery and impermanence of life. During his visit to Westminster Abbey in London, the fifteen-year-old not only admired its mighty architecture but also copied an inscription gracing the bust of John Gay in Poet's Corner:

> Life is a jest and all things show it,
> I thought so once and now I know it (Lütkehaus 1988:69).

In the same year 1803 Schopenhauer translated Milton's poem *On Time* into German. It begins as follows:

> Fly, envious Time, till thou run out thy race:
> Call on the lazy leaden-stepping hours,
> Whose speed is but the heavy plummet's pace;
> And glut thyself with what thy womb devours,
> Which is no more than what is false and vain,
> And merely mortal dross ... (HN1 #1).

Milton's poem closes on an optimistic note since time's "greedy self" is consumed in the end:

> Then long Eternity shall greet our bliss
> With an individual kiss,
> And joy shall overtake us as a flood;
> When every thing that is sincerely good
> And perfectly divine,
> With Truth, and Peace, and Love, shall ever shine
> About the supreme throne
> Of Him, to whose happy-making sight alone
> When once our heavenly-guided soul shall climb,

Egotism and Selflessness

> Then, all this earthy grossness quit,
> Attired with Stars we shall for ever sit,
> Triumphing over Death, and Chance, and thee, o Time! (#1).

During his Hamburg years as a commerce clerk apprentice, young Schopenhauer encountered similar thoughts regarding the "blind monster of time" in the *Fantasies about Art for Friends of Art* by Ludwig Tieck and Wilhelm Wackenroder (Tieck 1799:126) and recommended the book to his friend Anthime. Tieck and Wackenroder wrote about ways to overcome the "feeling of general insignificance" and the "vanity and impermanence of all human affairs": the "eternity of art" and "highest and purest love" (pp. 124–6). In love and art there are moments when we forget ourselves: "a secret magical joy flows through us, and we think we awaken to ourselves" (p. 123). In such moments we can suddenly "cast, while in the rich and fresh presence of life, a dispassionate look at the world and our own heart" (p. 126). For Wackenroder, as later for Schopenhauer, music is the supreme art: "the ultimate breath of the spirits, the finest element from which the most recondite dreams of the soul draw their nourishment as from an invisible brook." Music "wants nothing and all, it is an organ more subtle than language and possibly more delicate than thought. The mind cannot use it any more as a means or organ; rather, it is the thing in itself [Sache selbst], which is why it lives and flourishes in its own magic circles" (pp. 120–1).

Wackenroder poured his vision of suffering and salvation into a "wonderful oriental tale of a naked saint" (pp. 135–46) that also illustrates the two compass poles of commerce apprentice Schopenhauer. Once upon a time in the Orient, the "homeland of all that is marvelous," a naked saint had lived for many years in a remote cave on a cliff overlooking a river. This man never found peace of mind: "it constantly seemed to him that in his ears he heard the whizz of the *wheel of time*." He was driven by a tremendous fear that drew him "without a second's rest ever deeper in the whirl of wild confusion." Day and night he found himself "in the most intensive and vehement agitation" like someone trying "to turn an immense wheel." He was totally caught up in his world and terrorized by the thought to lose time and himself. Sometimes, during beautiful moonlit nights, there were moments when he suddenly stopped. Then he sank to the ground, "flung about and whined out of desperation; he also bitterly wept like a child, saying that the whir of the mighty wheel of time did not give him the leisure to do anything else on earth such as acting, producing, and creating." In such moments he felt "an all-consuming yearning for unknown beautiful things." He was looking for a *"particular unknown"* (bestimmtes Unbekanntes) that he could grasp and hold on to; "he sought to save himself from himself through something outside or inside, but in vain!"

Wackenroder's tale treats of man's imprisonment in, and his liberation from, himself. A "beautiful moon-lit summer night," when the saint was once again crying on the floor of his cave and wringing his hands, finally brought the longed-for deliverance. On that night, two lovers on a small boat came upriver toward the cave of the naked saint. The penetrating ray of the moon "enlightened and dissolved the innermost, darkest depths of the lovers' souls," and from the boat "wafted an ethereal music into heavenly space: sweet horns and I do not know what other magical instruments produced a floating world of sounds," whereupon a love song resounded. "As soon as the music and the song began, the saint's whirring wheel of time vanished. These were the first sounds that penetrated into this wilderness; the obscure longing was satisfied, the spell broken, the stray genius freed from his mortal frame." The saint attained liberation from himself and his illusion: "The figure of the saint disappeared and a specter, beautiful like an angel and weaved of translucent mist, floated out of the cave and soared higher and higher into the sky": a "bright aerial figure" dancing "in heavenly delight" in the air until it "disappeared in the infinite firmament." Traveling caravans "were stunned by this beautiful nightly mirage, and the lovers imagined that they saw the genius of love and of music." (Tieck 1799:124–6).

This tale and other compositions and stories by Wackenroder and Tieck hold that art and religion, or art-religion, is the means of liberation from man's imprisonment in the illusion of "I" and "me." Tieck was a promoter of the German mystic Jacob Böhme (1575–1624) and introduced his writings to other protagonists of German romanticism such as Novalis and Friedrich Schlegel. In this tale, the ecstasies of music and love liberate man from his confinement in the "I" and his mortal frame: they free him from himself. For Tieck and Wackenroder who were both inspired by Böhme, true religion consisted in the liberation from the captivity in "I-ness" (Ichtung) and its illusory world. The "two great divine beings, religion and art, are said to be "the best guides of humanity" since they resemble "two magic concave mirrors ... which symbolically reflect all entities of the world, and through whose magical images one can get to know and understand the true spirit of all things" (p. 29).

One can imagine why seventeen-year-old Schopenhauer recommended books by Tieck and Wackenroder (1797, 1799) with so much insistence to his friend Anthime de Blésimaire. The bearing of his compass was similar to that of the two Böhme-inspired poets: from "I-ness" (Ichtung) to its abolition (Nichtung). Does not Schopenhauer's main work, written as it was only a few years after such reading, embrace a similar goal—to discover the true essence of all things in the magic images of representation—as well as similar paths toward it, namely art (the third book of *The World as Will and Representation*) and mystical annihilation (the fourth book)? But compared to Schopenhauer's fully elaborated philosophical system, Tieck's and Wackenroder's stories sound like the pell-mell of melodies during the tuning of orchestral instruments prior to a concert. The key is already there, and so are some themes—yet these disconnected fragments are still separated by a large gulf from the symphonic performance in Schopenhauer's major work.

From his last year in Hamburg, when 18-year old apprentice Schopenhauer was fascinated by such texts, we have a poem that shows both poles of his compass. It begins with the South pole:

> Voluptuous pleasure, oh hell,
> Oh sensuality, oh love,
> insatiable
> and invincible!

From the heights of heaven
Thou hast dragged me down
Into the dust of this earth
Where I lie fettered.[20]

This is immediately followed by the opposite pole:

How can I soar up
To the throne of the eternal,
Be mirrored in the imprint
Of the thought supreme,
Be cradled in fragrances,
And fly through space
Filled with devotion and awe,
Bursting out in jubilation,
Or wrapt in humility
and hearing only harmony?[21]

But the "bond of weakness" kept dragging Schopenhauer down from such soaring heights and rendered his efforts to rise "abortive and vain." Nevertheless his yearning for salvation did not abate:

What worthier aspiration
Than to triumph entirely
Over a life so hollow and vain
Unable to fulfill any wish
Though yearning breaks our hearts?[22]

---

[20] »O Wollust, o Hölle / O Sinne, o Liebe, / Nicht zu befried'gen, / Und nicht zu besiegen. / Aus Höhen des Himmels / Hast du mich gezogen / und hin mich geworfen / In Staub dieser Erde: / Da lieg' ich in Fesseln« (HN1 #2).

[21] »Wie wollt' ich mich schwingen / Zum Throne des Ew'gen, / Mich spiegeln im Abdruck / Des höchsten Gedankens, / Mich wiegen in Düften, / Die Räume durchfliegen, / Voll Andacht, voll Wunder, / Ausbrechend in Jubel, / In Demuth versinkend, / Den Einklang nur hörend« ... (HN1 #2).

[22] »Was wäre wünschenwerther wohl / Als ganz zu siegen / Ueber das leere und so arme Leben, / Was keinen Wunsch uns je erfüllen kann, / Ob Sehnsucht gleich uns auch das Herz zersprengt« (HN1 #2).

This victory of the "vain and empty life" is portrayed by the young thinker in ways that remind the reader of Tieck and Wackenroder:

> If we remove from life the few moments of religion, art and pure love: what is left except a sequence of trivial thoughts?[23]

In a famous passage penned a quarter-century later (1832, age 44), Schopenhauer described the South pole of his compass toward the end of his stint as a trade house apprentice in Hamburg:

> In my 17th year, without any advanced education, I was gripped by the *misery of life*, just like Buddha when in his youth he faced illness, old age, pain and death. Soon enough, the truth that expressed itself loudly and clearly through this world vanquished the Jewish dogmas I had been indoctrinated with, and I concluded that this world could not be the work of a perfectly good being but must rather be that of a devil who called creatures into being in order to gloat over their torments. The data indicated this, and the conviction of its truth gained the upper hand.[24]

Yet hope kept attracting Schopenhauer magnetically. At age 19 he drew it not only from Wackenroder's and Tieck's writings but also from the dramatic creations of Zacharias Werner (1768–1823) that he recommended to his mother (spring of 1807). Such recommendations are symptomatic of the young man's interests and merit all the more attention because in the same year young Schopenhauer actually met

---

[23] »Nehmen wir aus dem Leben die wenigen Augenblicke der Religion, der Kunst und der reinen Liebe, was bleibt als eine Reihe trivialer Gedanken?« (HN1 #12, section 8)

[24] »In meinem 17ten Jahre, ohne alle gelehrte Schulbildung, wurde ich vom *Jammer des Lebens* so ergriffen, wie Buddha in seiner Jugend, als er Krankheit, Alter, Schmerz u. Tod erblickte. Die Wahrheit, welche laut und deutlich aus der Welt sprach, überwandt bald die auch mir eingeprägten Jüdischen Dogmen, u. mein Resultat war, daß diese Welt kein Werk eines allgütigen Wesens seyn könnte, wohl aber das eines Teufels, der Geschöpfe ins Daseyn gerufen, um am Anblick ihrer Quaal sich zu weiden: darauf deuteten die Data, u. der Glaube, daß es so sei, gewann die Oberhand.« (HN4a.96; Cholerabuch 89)

CHAPTER TWO

Werner in Weimar and was, according to his own account, "positively influenced" by him.

Zacharias Werner. Drawing by E.T.A. Hoffmann

Decades later, Schopenhauer's admirer Becker read some works by Werner and was struck by the similarity of Werner's writings to core doctrines of Schopenhauer. Asked about this, the aged philosopher wrote in his letter of November 3, 1853:

> He was a friend of my youth and has definitely exerted influence on me, and a positive influence indeed. In my teens I was an admirer of his works and when, at the age of twenty, I could fully enjoy his company at the house of my mother in Weimar, I found myself extremely happy. He liked me and often spoke with me, even seriously and philosophically.[25]

---

[25] »[Werner] war ein Freund meiner Jugend u. hat gewiß Einfluß u. zwar

Around Christmas of 1807 Schopenhauer and Zacharias Werner arrived almost simultaneously in Weimar and frequently met during the first three months of 1808. Werner quickly became a regular member of the salon of Schopenhauer's mother Johanna where on two evenings per week the intellectual elite of Weimar including Goethe and Wieland met. During the first months of 1808 her house was also the place where Werner's drama *Wanda* was rehearsed, and when it was performed at the Weimar theater Schopenhauer was profoundly moved.

In turn, Werner was deeply influenced by Wackenroder and Tieck and showed just as much enthusiasm for love, art, and religion and for the "minutes of inspiration" they provided (Hitzig 1823:20). While Werner admired the "heroes of faith and art, Fichte, Schleiermacher, Schlegel, and Tieck," he was particularly smitten with Jacob Böhme. On March 18 of 1801 he wrote to his young friend Julius Hitzig:

> More than anything else, this pious spirit [of Böhme] pours healing oil into the wounded hearts. O dear, dear friend! If only I could convert you and convince you that *nothing* can console us other than *art* and *religion*; (why have we not yet found a common designation for these two synonyms?).[26]

Werner assured Hitzig that he "would gladly part with all poet's laurels if he could be not a founder, but only a member of a *genuine* religious sect;" and since he regarded all arts only as "entrance gates to *this* final goal" he proudly asserted that his dramas "could just as well

---

günstigen, auf mich gehabt. Im frühen Jünglingsalter schwärmte ich für seine Werke, u. als ich, im 20sten Jahre, seinen Umgang vollauf genießen konnte, im Hause meiner Mutter in Weimar, fand ich mich hochbeglückt. Er war mir gewogen u. sprach oft mit mir, sogar ernsthaft u. philosophisch.« (Gespräche 20)

[26] »Mehr aber als alles, gießt dieser fromme Geist Oel in die verwundeten Herzen. O, lieber, lieber Freund! Dass ich Dich doch bekehren, doch überzeugen könnte, daß uns *nichts* zu trösten vermag, als *Kunst und Religion*; (warum haben wir doch noch nicht *einen* Namen für diese beiden Synonyma).« (Hitzig 1823:24–5)

be called sermons" (p. 48). Werner had a pronounced missionary bent and loved to enthuse young men for his religion. He wrote to Hitzig:

> What could *ten* emotion-filled pure, enthusiastic young men, united for a *single purpose*, do *to the world in terms of religion* if they were to write less and do more, and if it were still possible to find *young* men.[27]

In letters to Hitzig Werner declared that he was looking for apostles and wanted "to make converts and gain brothers" (pp. 60, 119). Werner's "favorite relationship" pattern is said to have been the one between "master and disciple" (p. 118), and in the first years of the 19th century it was Hitzig who occupied the position of favorite disciple. A few years later, however, Schopenhauer was just as enthusiastic about Werner's dramas and enjoyed the poet's friendship. During three months he had many discussions with the man who was his senior by twenty years. The content of their "serious" and "philosophical" conversations is unknown, but since Werner's philosophy was drenched in Böhme's thought it appears likely that the mystic played an important role. In his student years Werner had heard Kant lecture in Königsberg, and later he had become enthusiastic about Schleiermacher, Tieck, and Wackenroder. But from 1801 onward he was completely smitten by Böhme and soon also by Schelling, another Böhme admirer. This must have been topics during the frequent discussions of Schopenhauer with Werner. But the teaching that Werner promoted with so much missionary fervor was also present in Werner's dramas that Schopenhauer had recommended even before meeting the poet. Their prolixity and sensual mysticism seems to have put off not only Goethe in Werner's time but also Schopenhauer researchers in our era. This may be why Werner has hitherto received little attention even though it is hard to find another man in direct contact with young Schopenhauer whose compass

---

[27] »Was könnten *zehn* gefühlvolle, reine, begeisterte Jünglinge, zu *einem* Zwecke verbündet, *mit der Welt in religiöser Hinsicht machen*, wenn sie weniger schreiben und mehr thun wollten, und wenn es möglich wäre, noch *junge* Leute zu finden« (Hitzig 1823:54).

had such a similar bearing and whose work anticipates the fundamental tendency of Schopenhauer's aesthetics and ethics so strikingly.

Werner's teaching found detailed artistic expression in the two-part drama *The Sons of the Thal* that he had revised just before his 1807–1808 stay in Weimar. Schopenhauer's mother read it on her son's recommendation (Lütkehaus 1998:151). Already in the prologue the core theme, inspired by mysticism, is announced: supreme renunciation in which "proud I-ness is nailed to the cross" (Werner 1823.1:iv). Werner's drama was originally conceived as a didactic presentation of freemasonry and describes the degeneration of an original teaching (the teaching of the brotherhood of the Thal) through the templars and the Christian church. This original teaching of course represented Werner's religion of the time. From the "pulpit of the theater stage" he wanted to flog the difference between genuine religion and degenerated templardom / Christianity into the public's mind. In this case, however, the pulpit was the book that Schopenhauer recommended to his mother even before the drama was staged. Werner appears to have studied the writings of a pioneer of Scottish and French freemasonry: the biographer of Fénelon and secretary of Madame Guyon, Chevalier Andrew Ramsay.[28] Ramsay's ur-religion was inspired by Fénelon and Guyon and Werner's by Guyon and Böhme. Werner's brotherhood of the Thal "has preserved the most ancient religion and is thus the root of that tree of which your templar's order is but a small branch;" and according to Werner shoots from this root are also found around "the Ganges, the Nile, the Indus, Tanais, and Oxus" (Werner 1823.2:272).

The climax of Werner's long-winded drama is a scene in the underground of Paris where "a colossal statue of a reclining Sphinx" represents the age-old Egyptian background of the teaching as well as the *hen kai pan* (One and All) that was so popular among German intellectuals and artists. It was for instance praised in Schiller's "Mission of Moses" (*Die Sendung Moses*) and sat framed on Beethoven's desk as his confession of faith:

---

[28] On Andrew Ramsay see App 2010c:254-296.

CHAPTER TWO

> I Am What there is
> I am all that is, that
> was, and will be,
> No mortal man has ever
> lifted my veil" (Assmann 2007:249).

Werner's interpretation of this *hen kai pan* forms the heart of the doctrine of the *Thal* and the climax of his drama. This teaching is proclaimed on one hand by the "old man of Carmel," who in the key scene sits behind the statue of the Sphinx, and on the other hand by "hidden voices" that keep wafting out of nowhere. The old man of Carmel explains the "riddle of existence"—and therewith the core of Werner's philosophy—as follows: The "illusion to become unique and something," i.e., the illusion of I-ness, is the reason why man forgets that he is one with all. This egotistical illusion led to his banishment "in a dungeon called *life*." Precisely this illusion, which makes man forget his true nature, must be dispelled "in order to become again Nothing and Everything" (Werner 1823.2:263–5). Werner's Sphinx thus reveals the meaning of its riddle of "One and All":

> All is yourself
> When you are everything rather than something.[29]

This is the content of the enlightenment that turns prisoners into kings:

> There and then the scales fell from his eyes:
> the illusion to become unique and something ceased;
> his nature was dissolved in the great all-in-all,
> a fresh breeze cooled him from above
> and his heart was leaping with joy.
> Garment and chain weighed on him no longer
> since he turned the garment into royal purple
> and his chain into jewelry.[30]

---

[29] »Alles bist du selber, / Wenn du Alles bist, nicht Etwas« (Werner 1823.2:271).

[30] »Da fiel es ihm wie Schuppen von den Augen: / Es schwand der Wahn, zu

Egotism and Selflessness

The egotistical illusion of being "unique and something" constitutes man's prison, and his deliverance consists in becoming Nothing and melting into the All.

Like Wackenroder's *Tale of the Naked Saint*, Werner's *Sons of the Thal* drama overtly bears the stamp of Jacob Böhme's mysticism. Just as important, however, is the influence on Werner by the French mystic Jeanne-Marie Bouvier de la Motte Guyon (1648–1717) or Madame Guyon. Her famous French autobiography had been published in 1720 in Cologne and its German translation 1727 in Leipzig. During the 18th century writings by Madame Guyon appeared in various European languages, and just when Werner wrote his *Sons of the Thal* drama, two volumes with German translations of Guyon's *Secrets of Esoteric Christianity Revealed in the School of Heavenly Wisdom* (1802–3) were published in Frankfurt and Leipzig. Madame Guyon's core teaching is perfectly mirrored in Werner's *Sons of the Thal*: proud I-ness must be nailed to the cross and completely eradicated. Only through absolute victory over self-attachment and through final liberation from all egotism and self-love in mystical death can this "Nothing" (by which one becomes "All") be reached. Madame Guyon's mysticism of love forms the heart of Werner's religion. But his interpretation of religion was also colored by his study of Schleiermacher's *Discourses on Religion*, Schelling's early writings, and Werner's own sensual and sexual mysticism. Self-forgetting in sexual ecstasy, in artistic and religious rapture, and in mystical death all have a common denominator: the release from the prison of one's "I." A representative of Werner's doctrine of the Thal explains:

> Man is capable of everything if only he
> Forgets himself and discards the realm of senses:
> The initial act of this relinquishment of self

---

werden Ein und Etwas; / Sein Wesen war in's große All zerronnen, / Und, wie ein Säuseln, kühlt es ihn von oben, / Dass ihm das Herz vor Lust zerspringen wollte, / Gewand und Kette drückten ihn nicht fürder; / Denn das Gewand schuf er zum Königs-Purpur, / Und seine Kette schuf er zum Geschmeide« (Werner 1823.2:270).

is *purification*, and the ultimate *death*;
And what reunites us with the All,
glorious *putrefaction*, is the crown.
For learning this we are here.[31]

Werner's "glorious putrefaction" (herrliche Verwesung) is one of the elements stemming from Madame Guyon. For the French mystic "death in the arms of love" is not the ultimate stage of relinquishment of self; rather, she writes of the "burial, putrefaction" and total "annihilation" of all self-love:

> The old Adam finally begins to decompose and putrefy ... Already the old human being is destroyed ... He has perished with all his evil desires ... Putrefaction is complete ... Through death he gained life, and in Nothingness he won All, through the cross resurrection![32]

This radical elimination of the illusion of I-ness and the awakening to its nihility in the experience of All-Oneness cannot be mediated because man can only know his own true nature when he kills and destroys all that is "I" and "mine" (Werner 1823.2:293). Thus the representative of the Thal community teaches entirely in the manner of Böhme and Madame Guyon: "Through loss of self you learn to see" (p. 294). The portrayal in the Thal drama of the protagonist's enlightenment furnishes the key to the philosophy that cast its spell over Werner's disciples including Schopenhauer. What is at stake is the dissolution of the illusion based on "I" through the self-relinquishment of the hero, the creative artist, and the saint—themes that, as we will see,

---

[31] »Der Mensch kann alles, wenn er nur sich selbst / Vergisst, und sich der Sinnenwelt entäußert: / Die erste Handlung dieser Selbstentäußrung / Ist *Reinigung*, die letzte ist der *Tod*; / Und das, was uns dem Ganzen wiedergibt, / die herrliche *Verwesung*, ist die Krone. / Um dieses zu erlernen, sind wir hier« (Werner 1823.2:292–3).

[32] »Der alte Adam fängt endlich an, in Fäulnis überzugehen und in Verwesung ... Schon ist der alte Mensch zerstört ... Er ist untergegangen mit allen seinen bösen Gelüsten ... Die Verwesung ist vollendet ... Sterbend hat er das Leben gewonnen, und im Nichts das All, im Kreuz die Auferstehung!« (Guyon 1978:76–9)

eventually became mainstays of Schopenhauer's philosophy. The young initiate in Werner's drama of the Thal expresses his living experience of this doctrine as follows:

> You cast me into a chaos of ideas;
> Yet I feel: they are intimately related to me:
> You have not created but only unfolded them.—
> Even the slightest egotism
> Is the death of all greatness; in ethical terms
> There never was a hero without self-annihilation—
> And what is true of the hero also applies to the creator;
> For is there a hero who is not a creator?—
> I have an inkling that death
> Which leaves behind nothing whatsoever of us
> Is a symbol of such self-denial
> Or perhaps even more—I understand, old man!
> Is it that wretched immortality,
> Which only extends to infinity
> Our own miserable I,
> Scraggy, pitiful and with all its filth:
> Is it that immortality must also die? So that we are
> Not in eternity nailed to our vapid self?
> We can, we *must* get rid of it
> So as to revel some day in the power of All![33]

---

[33] »Du wirfst mich in ein Chaos von Ideen; / Doch fühl' ich wohl—sie sind mir nah' verwandt: / Du hast sie nur entwickelt, nicht erschaffen.— / Der Egoismus, selbst der leiseste, / Ist aller Größe Tod; — im Sittlichen / War nie ein Held noch ohne Selbstverläugnung — / Und was vom Helden gilt, gilt auch vom Schöpfer; / Denn wer ist Held, wenn er nicht Schöpfer ist? — / Der Tod—so dämmert's mir—er soll vielleicht, / Er der von uns so gar nichts übrig lässt— / Vielleicht Symbol seyn dieser Selbstverläugnung— / Vielleicht noch mehr ...— vielleicht — Ich hab' es, Alter! / Die krüpplichte Unsterblichkeit—nicht wahr?— / Die unser eignes jämmerliches Ich / So dünn und kläglich—so mit allem Unrath / Nur fortspinnt in's Unendliche—nicht wahr?— / Auch sie muss sterben?—unser schales Selbst— / Wir sind in Ewigkeit nicht d'ran genagelt?— / Wir können es, wir müssen es verlieren, / Um einst in Aller Kraft zu schwelgen!« (Werner 1823.2:294–5)

On hearing these words of the initiate, the representative of the Thal brotherhood joyfully exclaims: "He has renounced—he found it on his own!"[34]

Werner's disciples appear to have embraced similar opinions and heeded the "hidden voices" that whisper out of nowhere during these key scenes of Werner's *Thal* drama. They murmur about the forgetting of self in the experience of art:

> Practice art with pure senses
> And you will gain the strength
> To dissolve in beauty![35]

Such dissolving can be triggered by the rapturous experience of natural beauty and music:

> I cannot withstand—in these sounds
> In these waves I must drown.
> My innermost core must melt—oh yearning—
> Unspeakable—is there still an I?[36]

As the Thal community's chalice of wisdom is transmitted, the hidden voices proclaim in tune with Wackenroder's naked saint:

> Only when you have escaped your self
> And floated into the great Universe
> Is the veil removed.[37]

We will never know how deeply such Böhme- and Guyon-inspired teachings of Werner influenced Schopenhauer. But is it not the case that some of these pronouncements could easily serve as mottos of the

---

[34] »Er hat entsagt—er hat es selbst gefunden!« (Werner 1823.2:295)

[35] »Uebe Kunst mit reinen Sinnen, / Dann wirst du die Kraft gewinnen, / Um in Schönheit zu zerrinnen!« (Werner 1823.2:256)

[36] »Ich halt's nicht aus—ich muss in diesen Tönen— / In diesen Wogen muss ich untergehn!— / Mein Innerstes—es muss zerfließen—Sehnsucht— / Unnennbar—bin ich noch?« (Werner 1823.2:256-7)

[37] »Nur, wenn du dir selbst entkommen, / Und in's große All geschwommen, / Ist die Binde dir entnommen« (Werner 1823.2:257).

third and fourth books of Schopenhauer's *The World as Will and Representation*? What did the young man learn from utterances of the *Thal* drama's hidden voices such as:

> Forms are generated and dissolve,
> Life must involve putrefaction,
> And the ray must lead to the ultimate source?[38]

How did Schopenhauer interpret Werner's assertion that this ultimate source (Urquell) is hidden to man because of his illusion of I-ness? Did such ideas become moorings for his later conceptions of Maya and *principium individuationis*? Was he convinced by Werner's argument that man's illusion of I-ness—or, as Böhme put it, man's "own-will" (Eigenwille) and his "I" and "mine"—are the true original sin, and that man's life is characterized by imprisonment in this illusion? Was the young man impressed by the thought that only self-denial and self-annihilation can offer an escape from the "prison called *life*"? Is it conceivable that during this Weimar period, when Schopenhauer was already twenty years old, his compass began to point to the "N" of Böhme, Madame Guyon and Zacharias Werner—"that you become again Nothing and All" (pp. 263–5)? At any rate, statements by Schopenhauer such as "I am what always is, always was, and always will be. And only I myself can lift my veil" (#654) indicate that the voice of Werner's Sphinx still echoed in 1817 while Schopenhauer redacted his major work. It is quite possible that already in 1808, at age twenty, the characteristic alignment was already in place that ten years later issued in the "Nothing" at the conclusion of his major work. It was the pole that magnetically attracted him until his last year (1860) when he added to "Nothing" and the other terms on the North side of his compass the words *prajna paramita*: the supreme wisdom "beyond subject and object" of Mahayana Buddhism.

At any rate: the polar constellation of self-infatuation / egotism versus selflessness appears to be the common denominator not only of

---

[38] »Formen werden und verwehen, / Leben muss Verwesung sehen, / Und der Strahl zum Urquell gehen« (Werner 1823.2:247).

Schopenhauer's early philosophy, to which we will presently turn, but also of his entire work in all of its dimensions, from his metaphysics to his aesthetics, and from his philosophy of nature to the crowning ethics. If Schopenhauer's philosophy, as he claims, explicates various dimensions of a "single thought," then this thought has its roots in the ground of egotism evident in nature as a whole and human beings in particular. But at the same time it points, like the opposite end of a compass needle, away from egotism toward the realm of selflessness: away from "I" and "mine." This constitutes man's inevitable yearning to overcome egotism and live selflessly, be it in the joys of love, in the act of creation, in the experience of nature and art, in the clarity of meditative concentration, or in the saintliness that according to Schopenhauer shows this pole most plainly and "is vouchsafed by the seal of inner truth."[39]

In one of the notes stemming from the period when twenty-year-old Schopenhauer frequented Zacharias Werner we find the following reflection about egotism and selflessness:

> When I shuffle off suffering from myself to someone else, its extent is thereby increased; hence the great mass of evil in the world that arose by man's egotistic shuffling onto others of the original positive evil (the guilt of the world). Only through voluntary shouldering and taking on of evil can it be reduced to the smallest possible, perhaps even infinitesimal amount, whereby the Kingdom of God will arrive.[40]

---

[39] W1 §71; SW 2.487; Z2.508.

[40] »Das Leiden, welches ich von mir weg und auf einen andern schiebe, wird dadurch vergrößert: darum die große Masse des Übels auf der Welt, die entstanden ist, indem das ursprüngliche positive Uebel (die Schuld der Welt) durch dies egoistische Weiterschieben vermehrt wurde. Nur durch freiwilliges Aufladen und Ansichziehn des Uebels wird es zur möglichsten, vielleicht unendlichen Verringerung gelangen und so das Reich Gottes kommen.« (HN1, #12, section 9)

> wirt geliebet von einem wåren volkomen gůt. In difem
> finne fpricht man und ift ouch wår 'got hat fich felber
> nicht lieb als fich felber.' Wan wêr icht beffers dan
> got, das hête got lieb und nicht fich felber, wan in di-
> fem wåren liechte und in difer wåren liebe ift oder
> blibt weder ich noch mich, mîn, mir, du, dîn und des
> glichen, funder das liecht bekennet und weiß ein gůt, das
> alle gůt und uber alle gůt ift und das alle gůt eins fint
> wefenlich in dem einen und âne das eine kein gůt ift.
> Und dar umb wirt ouch dâ nicht gemeinet dis oder das,
> ich noch du oder des glichen, funder allein das eine,
> das weder ich noch du, dis oder das ift, funder es ift

Manual of Buddhism p. 258

Theologia deutsch, ed. Pfeiffer (1851:89; see HN5:232) with Schopenhauer's markings and his reference in the margin to Spence Hardy's *Manual of Buddhism*, p. 258 (see p. 24 here above for the passage and its English translation)

3. Illusion and Ur-Knowledge

Why did Schopenhauer decide in the first place to study philosophy? He had promised to his father to become a merchant. When—after two unhappy years as an apprentice in Hamburg and his father's suicide—he decided to abandon a commercial career and become a university student, his mother urged him to specialize in law or medicine since that would guarantee prosperity. In 1809 his preparation for university was concluded and 21-year old Schopenhauer, equipped with a recommendation letter by Goethe, went to Goettingen to study medicine. But after only three semesters he changed his major to philosophy. What had happened? We have only a small number of diary notes from that period; but Schopenhauer-related entries in the university library's lending register as well as the student's extant lecture notes point to a growing interest in the history of nature and of mankind. It is as if the young man first wanted to understand his standpoint in nature and history. In this endeavor he had three famous guides: Professor Johann Friedrich Blumenbach (1752–1840) for natural history, Professor Arnold Hermann Ludwig Heeren (1760–1842) for human history, and Jean-André Deluc (1727–1817) for the history of the earth.

Though Deluc had already retired, the professor's published letters about the history of the earth were among Schopenhauer's main reading materials in the first two semesters. Deluc furnished a detailed description of the geological characteristics and fossil finds around Goettingen and Hamburg and thus explained, as it were, the history of the ground under Schopenhauer's feet. Deluc's letters were a continuation of his protracted discussion with Schopenhauer's admired teacher Professor Blumenbach. This discussion focused on a theme that fascinated all of Europe: fossils. Fossils may seem to be tiny, useless screws in the colossal machinery of the universe. But shark's teeth on the Alps, petrified unidentified creatures, and gigantic bones of tropical animals unearthed in the vicinity of London or in Siberia not only raised questions about the history of our earth but also fueled doubts about the accuracy of the biblical creation narrative, thus undermining people's trust in biblical authority. This was not a new development since already the discovery of the Americas with its peoples, animals and plants had fueled misgivings and inspired the idea of Isaac La Peyrère (1596–1676) that Preadamites must have been living long before Adam and Eve—an idea that reduced the biblical creation story to the status of last chapter of a far longer history and suggested that the author of the Book of Genesis had known only a tiny part of the real, far longer history of our world.

Schopenhauer's notes from Professor Blumenbach's lectures on mineralogy and natural history contain much information about fossils, prehistoric giant hyenas, "foot-long bird's claws" from Siberia, and the famous petrifications from Oeningen on Lake of Constance among which a scientist from Zürich, Johann Jakob Scheuchzer (1672–1733), thought he had found the only extant skeleton of an antediluvian man. During Schopenhauer's second year in Goettingen, however, Blumenbach's rival Georges Cuvier proved that what Scheuchzer had found was but the head and torso of a giant salamander. In his own manner, Blumenbach picked up La Peyrère's lead. Blumenbach's *Contributions to Natural History*, whose results the professor communicated in his lectures, began with an examination of Goettingen where "almost every pavement stone contains species and even entire generations of animals" that "must have become extinct":

> Our calcareous earth teems with numerous kinds of petrified sea creatures. But to my knowledge only a single species among them resembles an extant creature to the extent that we can regard it as its original ancestor.[41]

In his booklet *Specimen archaeologiae telluris*, which Schopenhauer borrowed just after the fifth volume of Deluc's letters, Blumenbach proposed a classification scheme for fossils and declared that theories by "physicotheologians" like Deluc, which attempted to trace back all fossils to a single gigantic inundation, were untenable.

Fossils in Blumenbach's *Specimen archaeologiae telluris* (1806)

---

[41] »Unser Kalkboden wimmelt gleichsam von den mannigfaltigsten Arten versteinter Seegeschöpfe, unter welchen aber meines Wissens nur eine einzige Gattung ist, wozu wir noch gegenwärtig ein derselben so sehr ähnelndes Geschöpf kennen, dass man es wohl für das Original dazu halten kann« (Blumenbach 1806:6).

CHAPTER THREE

The critical comparison of fossils and their surroundings suggested to Blumenbach that three main kinds of fossils exist: 1. the most recent ones such as the Oeningen petrifications that resemble creatures known to us; 2. older ones like the mammoths found in Siberia which somewhat resemble creatures from completely different climatic zones; and 3. the "most ancient and for the most part completely *unknown* creatures, which are monuments of a totally different creation prior to a catastrophe."[42]

Blumenbach deduced that there must have been several gigantic revolutions of which the youngest was only of a climatic nature and resulted in such fossils as the remains of tropical animals in Northern Europe and Russia. However, older fossils prove that "the solid crust of the earth itself must have undergone revolutions of such power that for example the sea bottom of the old world including complete deposits of sea-shells now covers high alps, and that conversely plants of former plains are now buried underneath the sea."[43] Such phenomena could only be explained by a series of catastrophes separated by very long intervals. Blumenbach concluded:

> All of this combined makes it in my opinion more than probable that our earth was once home not just to one or the other species that is now extinct, but rather to an entire pre-adamitic creation.[44]

---

[42] »die alerältesten, größtentheils von ganz *unbekannten* Geschöpfen, den Denkmahlen einer catastrophirten ganz fremdartigen Schöpfung« (Blumenbach 1806:115).

[43] »die feste Rinde der Erde selbst so mächtige Umkehrungen erlitten, dass zum Beispiel vormaliger Meeresboden der Urwelt nun mit sammt seinen ungestörten Conchylienlagern jetzt hohe Alpen deckt, und hingegen vormalige Landgewächse tief unter der jetzigen Meeresfläche vergraben sind« (Blumenbach 1806:121).

[44] »Alles dieß zusammen genommen, so wird es meines Bedünkens mehr als nur wahrscheinlich, dass schon einmal nicht nur eine oder die andre Gattung, sondern eine ganze organisirte präadamitische Schöpfung auf unserm Erdboden untergegangen ist« (Blumenbach 1806:13).

Illusion and Ur-knowledge

Whereas the different races of man and other animals could be explained by relatively minor changes, Blumenbach sought to account also for the extinction of entire species and the formation of new ones. Half a century later, Charles Darwin managed to explain this conclusively through his theory of evolution; but Blumenbach attempted to deduce it from an innate tendency in living beings toward self-formation (*Bildungstrieb*), whose discovery made him famous. This "Bildungstrieb" accounts, among other things, for the renewed growth of impaired or amputated organs, and according to Blumenbach this mechanism had been operating "in a similar but not identical way" (p. 21) in the course of the enormously long phases of earth history. In this manner Blumenbach was able to identify recent species as variants of older ones and account for a certain continuity of life forms across multiple gigantic catastrophes.

Schopenhauer's book lending record and his admiration for Blumenbach indicate that he was fascinated by such themes. Even the sole philosophy books borrowed during the first nine months of his stay in Goettingen point to his interest in the history of the earth and universe: they were the works of Lucretius, frequently mentioned by Blumenbach, which propagate Epicurus's vision of the universe as a mass of energized matter without any creator god that had found a recent echo in the works of French atheists such as Baron of Holbach's *Système de la nature* (1770). Only two professors saw Schopenhauer participate in their courses over the entire four Goettingen semesters: Blumenbach and Heeren. Blumenbach's lectures focused on aspects of the history of the earth and living creatures, whereas Heeren dealt with the history of humankind (European history, the history of the crusades, ancient history, and ethnography). In Heeren's ethnography course, the specialist of ancient history and India conveyed early information about Asian religions and cultures to Schopenhauer who hardly missed a lecture and took voluminous notes (App 2003, 2006a).

The young man's will to understand the larger picture appears also to be a reason for his interest in philosophy. Subsequent to the works of

Lucretius, the philosophical books checked out from the library were Schelling's *Of the World-Soul* (*Von der Weltseele*) and his *Ideas about a Philosophy of Nature* (*Ideen zu einer Philosophie der Natur*). Referring to Deluc's history of the earth, Goethe's metamorphosis of plants, Blumenbach's Bildungstrieb etc., Schelling attempted in his *World-Soul* (¹1798) to identify "a *common principle*" that "fluctuates between anorganic and organic nature and contains the ultimate reason for all changes in the former along with all activity in the latter, and appears to be *nowhere* because it is present *everywhere* and cannot be anything *definite* or *particular* because it is *everything*"[45] (Schelling 1798:iv). Even though Schelling considered it impossible to give a name to this principle of all organic and inorganic matter, he called it "world-soul" (*Weltseele*) on the basis of his conviction that just this had already been the theme of the oldest Greek philosophy, and that modern philosophy "is gradually returning to this after having completed the circle."[46] According to Schelling, "world-soul" thus refers to the principle of everything; and precisely this principle must be the core of genuine philosophy which therefore necessarily is *natural philosophy* (*Naturphilosophie*).

Astute readers may detect harbingers of Schopenhauer's metaphysics of will in the preface of Schelling's *World-soul*. Indeed, fifteen years after Schelling, Schopenhauer was also searching for the common essence of everything organic and inorganic; and like Schelling he also conceived it as a fundamental striving showing itself, among other modes, in magnetism and polarity. For Schelling, the magnetic force offered an apt explanatory model because he argued "that it could be inherent in *all* bodies of nature, though in infinitely small degrees."[47]

---

[45] »ein *gemeinschaftliches Princip*«, welches »zwischen anorgischer und organischer Natur fluctuirend die erste Ursache aller Veränderungen in jener, und den letzten Grund aller Thätigkeit in dieser enthält, das, weil es *überall* gegenwärtig ist, *nirgends* ist, und weil es *Alles* ist, nichts *Bestimmtes* oder *Besondres* sein kann« (Schelling 1798:iv).

[46] »zu welcher, nachdem sie ihren Kreislauf vollendet hat, die unsrige allmählich zurückkehrt« (Schelling 1798:iv).

[47] »dass sie *jedem* Körper der Natur, wenn auch in unendlich-kleinem Grade

Illusion and Ur-knowledge

A few pages later Schelling already presents this as a fact: "Since magnetism is a general force of nature, no body in the world can be totally non-magnetic, just as no body is totally transparent or opaque, absolutely warm or cold."[48] Like the magnetic force that seemingly by magic attracts the needle of the compass, the basic or "first force" (*erste Kraft*) appearing in the anorganic realm as formative force (*Bildungskraft*) and in the organic realm as a Blumenbachian formative drive (*Bildungstrieb*) (p. 298–9), was still a great unknown: "Hence the observation of anorganic as well as organic nature stops short of the great unknown that already in the most ancient philosophy was conjectured to be the first force of nature."[49] It is precisely this most basic force that maintains "the continuity of the anorganic and organic world" and binds "the whole of nature together to form a universal organism" (p. 305). It resembles magnetism:

> In the same way, the cause of magnetism is present everywhere yet acts only on a few bodies. The magnetic current finds the tiny needle in the open sea just as in a closed room, and wherever it finds it, it provides polar direction to it. So the stream of life, wherever it may originate from, meets organs receptive to it and conveys to them, where it encounters them, the activity of life.[50]

---

innewohnen könnte« (Schelling 1798:165).

[48] »Da der Magnetismus eine allgemeine Naturkraft ist, kein Körper der Welt absolut-unmagnetisch sey, eben so wie kein Körper absolut-durchsichtig, oder undurchsichtig, absolut-warm oder kalt ist« (Schelling 1798:169).

[49] »So steht die Betrachtung der anorgischen so gut wie der organischen Natur vor jenem Unbekannten stille, in welchem die älteste Philosophie schon die erste Kraft der Natur vermuthet hat« (Schelling 1798:303).

[50] »So ist die Ursache des Magnetismus überall gegenwärtig, und wirkt doch nur auf wenige Körper. Der magnetische Strom findet die unscheinbare Nadel auf dem offnen, freyen Meer so gut als im verschloßnen Gemach, und wo er sie findet, giebt er ihr die polarische Richtung. So trifft der Strom des Lebens, von wannen er komme, die Organe, die für ihn empfänglich sind, und giebt ihnen, wo er sie trifft, die Thätigkeit des Lebens« (Schelling 1798: 301).

CHAPTER THREE

This is the kind of reading matter that the student of medicine Schopenhauer borrowed from the university library in July of 1810. A week later he checked out two volumes of Plato, and after ten more days Schelling's above-mentioned *Ideas about a Philosophy of Nature*. Subsequently almost all books he borrowed from the Goettingen library were of a philosophical nature: the change of his major from medicine to philosophy was in the air. In the following winter semester Schopenhauer took his first course in philosophy: the lecture series on metaphysics by Gottlob Ernst Schulze (1761–1833) during which he informed his mother of the decision to devote his life to philosophy. Was he so taken with Schulze's metaphysics course? Perhaps initially; but though he later praised the professor's delivery, his notes exhibit increasing irritation after only a few months. Commenting on Schulze's statement that God's experiment with human nature was a success, Schopenhauer wrote: "O God, o God, have mercy upon the Lord!"[51] He was also incensed by the professor's assertion that saintliness and bliss are incompatible (HN2:12). In Schulze's psychology course, Schopenhauer remarked that "by his balderdash" the professor proved that he had "utterly failed to understand the divine in [Plato's] Philebos" (p. 14). As time went on, the student's expressions of indignation became increasingly stark—especially when things did not conform to the direction indicated by his compass. When Schulze claimed that contemplation is "the incapacity of directing attention focused on one object also to other things," Schopenhauer sarcastically remarked: "Socrates thus suffered from this mental retardation when he, as Alcibiades noted in the *Symposion*, once stood motionlessly in a field for twenty-four hours."[52]

After skipping a lecture by Gottlob ("Praise-the-Lord") Schulze, Schopenhauer punned: "Here, Praise-the-Lord, a lecture about loftiness is missing."[53] Loftiness and contemplation as well as saintliness

---

[51] »O Herre Gott o Herre Gott / Erbarme dich des Herrn!« (HN2:9)

[52] »An dieser Geistesschwäche hat also Sokrates stark laborirt, als er, wie Alkibiades im Symposion erzählt, ein Mal 24 Stunden unbeweglich auf dem Felde stand.« (HN2:15)

[53] »Hier fehlt Gottlob ein Diktat über das Erhabene« (HN2:14).

Illusion and Ur-knowledge

and beatitude were of particular concern to Schopenhauer since they pertained to the crucial North pole on his compass—and exactly in this respect the "sophist" Schulze happened to be lacking. But at least Schulze advised him not to waste time with such philosophers as Schelling and Spinoza and instead to concentrate on studying Plato and Kant. In Schulze's eyes, Schelling and Fichte were not much more than modern imitators of the Neoplatonics and mystics. In a segment of his metaphysics course entitled "On the attempt to reach the goal of metaphysics and to solve the riddle of the world by an intuitive vision of the absolute: or on Fichte's Wissenschaftslehre and Schelling's Naturphilosophie,"[54] the professor offered according to Schopenhauer's notes the following verdict about these new systems:

> This kind of perceptive power supposedly is a rationality beholding the absolute (capacity of intuitive vision), which is what Kant disclaimed. For Kant, all cognition is sensual or can only take place through the mediation of sensuality bound to the notion of space and time. The claim that the human mind is equipped with a capacity of intuitive or unmediated vision of the absolute is not new but as old as mysticism. It is also well known that for its doctrines about the true nature of the world and its relation to the Godhead, the Neoplatonic or Alexandrian school posited an intuitive vision of the one, supreme, ultimate Ur-Being, a creative power of all things, as the center around which all beings revolve and as the basis and ultimate ground of truth. They claimed to have discovered in the realm of inner feeling the source of the supreme realization that thinking man is not at all capable of reaching.[55]

---

[54] »Von dem Versuch vermittelst einer intellektuellen Anschauung des Absoluten den Zweck der Metaphysik zu erreichen u. das Räthsel der Welt zu lösen: oder von der Fichtischen Wissenschaftslehre u. der Schellingischen Naturphilosophie« (HNB2:100r).

[55] »Dergleichen Erkenntniskraft soll nun eine das Absolute anschauende Vernunft (intellektuelles Anschauungsvermögen) seyn, welche K[ant] leugnete, indem nach ihm alle Anschauung sinnlich ist, oder nur vermittelst der

CHAPTER THREE

When Schulze spoke of neoplatonic mysticism and its "intuitive vision" (intellektuelle / intellektuale Anschauung) that Schelling and Fichte had philosophically exploited, he sounded like a skeptic. Yet Schopenhauer was impressed by the challenging tenor of Schelling's *Ideas about a Philosophy of Nature* which proposed that mere reflection is "a mental illness of man" which "destroys all vision [Anschauung] in him" and makes the "division between man and the world permanent" (Schelling 1803:6). By contrast, "genuine philosophy" in Schelling's view takes intellectual reflection merely as a means (p. 7). Influenced by his study of Kant, Schelling regarded the entire world as representation: "We know things only through and in our representations. What they are prior to being represented in our mind cannot be imagined; of that we have no concept."[56] But the human being who ponders about the origin of these representations must, according to Schelling, be something more than just a reflection or object of thought:

> But insofar as I am free (and I am free when I rise above the connection of things and ask how this connection itself has become possible) I am no *thing*, no *object*. I live in a world of my own and am a being that is there not for others but for itself. In me there can only be deed and action.[57]

---

an die Vorstellung des Räumlich-Zeitlichen gebundenen Sinnlichkeit Statt finden kann. Das Vorgeben daß dem menschlichen Geist ein Vermögen der intellektuellen Anschauung oder unmittelbaren Betrachtung des Absoluten beywohne ist zwar nicht neu sondern so alt als die Mystik, auch hat bekanntlich die Neu-Platonische oder Alexandrinische Schule für ihre Lehren von der wahren Beschaftheit der Welt u. deren Verhältniß zur Gottheit die intellektuelle Anschauung des Einen, Höchsten, Ersten Urseyns dessen Schöpferkraft aller Dinge das Zentrum um das sich alle Wesen drehn als Fundament u. als höchsten Wahrheitsgrund aufgestellt u. in der Region des innern Gefühls die Quelle der höchsten Erkenntniß deren der denkende Mensch gar nicht fähig seyn soll entdeckt zu haben behauptet.« (HNB2:100v-101r)

[56] »Wir kennen die Dinge nur durch und in unsern Vorstellungen. Was sie also sind, in wie fern sie unserer Vorstellung vorangehen, also nicht vorgestellt werden, davon haben wir gar keinen Begriff« (Schelling 1803:9).

[57] »In so fern ich aber frey bin, (und ich bin es, indem ich mich über den Zusammenhang der Dinge erhebe und frage, wie dieser Zusammenhang selbst

Illusion and Ur-knowledge

Schelling had obviously digested Fichte's deed-action (Tathandlung) and was, like Fichte and later Schopenhauer, interested in post-Kantian metaphysics and the "thing in itself." His philosophy of nature sought to explain "the secret connection linking our mind to nature" (p. 63) which can only appear in an "absolute act of cognition":

> Absolute knowledge is only present when the subject-and-object dimensions are not merged as opposites but rather when the subjective is totally objective and vice-versa.[58]

Schelling saw Spinoza as a pioneer who "recognized subject-objectivity as the necessary and eternal character of the absolute," and he regarded himself and Fichte as heirs of such absolute knowledge and as the philosophers who had finally managed to conceive and formulate this identity in a scientific manner (pp. 85–6).

For Schopenhauer, such names and oracular pronouncements from the pen of a philosopher (who at Schopenhauer's age had already published the *World-soul* and the *Ideas about a Philosophy of Nature*) must have seemed like a harbinger of his own future output: a new philosophical system, absolute knowledge, understanding of the link of the human mind and nature, subject-objectivity ... The decision to change his major to philosophy seems a logical step. In the spring of 1811, when Schopenhauer related such happy tidings to his consternated mother in Weimar, he apparently had already a first system in mind. Wieland's niece Wilhelmine Schorcht described Schopenhauer's earliest philosophy as follows:

> Recently the young Schopenhauer was for a while in Weimar. He came filled with philosophical ideas and is totally devoted to a

---

möglich geworden?)—bin ich gar kein *Ding*, kein *Objekt*. Ich lebe in einer ganz eignen Welt, bin ein Wesen, das nicht für andere Wesen, sondern für sich selbst da ist. In mir kann nur That und Handlung seyn ...« (Schelling 1803:12).

[58] »Ein absolutes Wissen ist nur ein solches, worin das Subjektive und Objektive, nicht als Entgegengesetzte vereinigt, sondern worin das ganze Subjektive das ganze Objektive und umgekehrt ist« (Schelling 1803:71).

philosophy (which I am unable to name) that is exceedingly austere: any and all inclination, desire, and passion must be stamped out and battled against. I wish him all the necessary strength to win this war because a gigantic soul is needed to fulfill all these demands completely, as he is determined to do.[59]

Neither in Schulze's lectures nor in Schelling's books had a war been mentioned in which desire and passion are the enemy and their eradication the way to victory. It was due to a basic alignment of Schopenhauer's compass that was already in place when he began to study philosophy. This "war" did not concern puritan ideals but rather the very battle Böhme and Madame Guyon had written about: the war against all forms of egotism driven by self-centered desire. When the young student visited Wieland and explained to him why he wanted to change his major from medicine to philosophy, the old writer advised against this choice, arguing that philosophy is not a solid profession. Schopenhauer reportedly answered: "Life is a miserable affair and I have decided to spend it thinking about it."[60] This is precisely what he was to carry out in the remaining five decades of his life.

After some broadening of horizons during his last semester at Goettingen (particularly also through the ethnology lectures of Professor Heeren) and the continued study of Schulze, Plato, and Kant, Schopenhauer borrowed Schelling's *Lectures about the Method of Academic Study* from the Goettingen library to prepare himself for the study of philosophy under Fichte in Berlin. At the beginning of Schelling's fourth lecture Schopenhauer read: "The one thing from which all sci-

---

[59] »Neulich war der junge Schopenhauer auf einige Zeit in W[eimar]. Er kam ganz von filosofischen Ideen voll, er hat sich einer Filosofie mit Leib und Seele ergeben (ich weiß sie nicht namentlich zu sagen), die sehr streng ist; jede Neigung, Begierde, Leidenschaft müssen unterdrückt und bekämpft werden, dazu wünsche ich ihm nur die erforderliche Kraft, den Krieg zu bestehen, denn es gehört wohl eine Riesenseele dazu, die Forderungen alle ganz zu erfüllen, wie er den guten Willen hat.« (Gespräche p. 23, April 1811)

[60] »Das Leben ist eine missliche Sache, ich habe mir vorgenommen, es damit hinzubringen, über dasselbe nachzudenken.« (Gespräche p. 22)

ences spring and to which all of them return is ur-knowledge."[61] According to Schelling such "original knowledge" (Urwissen) is nothing other than "the ultimate ground and basis of possibility of all genuine absolute knowing."[62] Whereas the other sciences can show this ur-knowledge only in discrete appearances, Schelling held that there exists a mode of knowing that is "in all respects absolute" and "has ur-knowledge itself as ground and object": *philosophy*.[63] He distinguished such genuine and absolute knowledge from the delusory "discrete" kind that "in itself does not constitute true knowledge."[64] The absolute knowledge of philosophy is grounded in the "intuitive vision, which is absolutely one with its object—ur-knowledge itself."[65] This explains Schelling's battle-cry: "Without intuitive vision no philosophy!"[66]

But how could a young philosopher attain Schelling's "intuitive vision," the *sine qua non* (essential condition) of his profession? Schelling's answer is unambiguous:

> Those who do not have it also do not understand what is said about it; it can therefore not be taught at all. A negative condition of its presence is the clear and intimate insight into the nihility of all merely finite knowledge.[67]

---

[61] »Das schlechthin Eine, von dem alle Wissenschaften ausfließen und in das sie zurückkehren, ist das Urwissen« (Schelling 1803:83).

[62] »der letzte Grund und die Möglichkeit aller wahrhaft absoluten Erkenntnis« (Schelling 1803:86–7).

[63] Eine »schlechthin und in jeder Beziehung absolute Erkenntnisart«, welche »das Urwissen unmittelbar und an sich selbst zum Grund und Gegenstand hat«: die *Philosophie* (Schelling 1803: 96).

[64] »rein als solches ... kein wahres Wissen« ist (Schelling 1803: 85).

[65] »intellectuelle Anschauung, die mit ihrem Gegenstande, dem Urwissen selbst, schlechthin identisch ist« (Schelling 1803:97).

[66] »Ohne intellectuelle Anschauung keine Philosophie!« (Schelling 1803:97)

[67] »Wer sie nicht hat, versteht auch nicht, was von ihr gesagt wird; sie kann also überhaupt nicht gegeben werden. Eine negative Bedingung ihres Besitzes ist die klare und innige Einsicht der Nichtigkeit aller bloß endlichen Erkenntniß« (Schelling 1803:98).

At the end of his lecture Schelling nevertheless deigned to give a bit of advice to beginning philosophy students such as Schopenhauer:

> The task that each must set to himself at the very moment he engages in philosophy is to search for the One genuinely absolute comprehension, which by nature also is a comprehension of the absolute, until totality and perfect realization of the All in One is reached.[68]

This not only sounds like a recipe for Schopenhauer's philosophy but also like an echo of Zacharias Werner's sphinx in the *Sons of the Thal*. The 23-year-old student obviously thought that he possessed the essential condition for his chosen profession and mused during his journey from Goettingen to Berlin:

> Philosophy is a high altitude road and can only be reached via a steep path covered with sharp stones and prickly thorns. It is a remote path that turns ever more desolate the higher one ascends. Whoever walks on it must know no fear and needs to leave everything behind while confidently clearing his path through the freezing snow. Often he will suddenly face an abyss and gaze at the verdant valley below. Then dizziness wants to pull him over the edge, but he must hold on even if this involves bloodying his soles in order to cling to the cliffs. As reward he soon perceives the world far beneath; its sandy deserts and moors vanish, its uneven spots are leveled out, its jarring sounds no longer reach his ear, and its roundness is revealed to him. Always standing in the pure and cool mountain air, he already beholds the sun while everything beneath is still covered in the darkness of night.[69]

---

[68] »Die Aufgabe, die sich jeder setzen muß, unmittelbar, wie er zur Philosophie gelangt, ist: die Eine wahrhaft absolute Erkenntniß, die ihrer Natur nach auch eine Erkenntniß des Absoluten ist, bis zur Totalität und bis zum vollkommenen Begreifen des Allen in Einem zu verfolgen« (Schelling 1803:140).

[69] »Die Philosophie ist eine hohe Alpenstraße, zu ihr führt nur ein steiler Pfad über spitze Steine und stechende Dornen: er ist einsam und wird immer öder, je höher man kommt, und wer ihn geht, darf kein Grausen kennen, sondern muß alles hinter sich lassen und sich getrost im kalten Schnee seinen

Illusion and Ur-knowledge

As his Berlin notes and library records show, the young man first continued his intensive study of Schelling and natural science that seemed to be so deeply connected with philosophy. Had Schelling not stated that "nature is an objectification of ur-knowledge contained and resting in itself"?[70] In Schopenhauer's eyes, life often resembled a pitch-black night "replete with an long dream that often turns into a nightmare."[71] But fortunately he also experienced brighter moments: "From time to time there arises in me the most vivid awareness of having existed from time immemorial, and this greatly elates and invigorates me."[72]

The complex and often contradictory statements of Fichte and Schelling provoked Schopenhauer and stimulated his own thinking. What Schopenhauer staked out as his own philosophical enterprise during the two Berlin years was more or less in accord with Fichte's and Schelling's program. All three based themselves on Kant in adopting their basic idealistic position that "all objects exist only in relation to the subject, and the subject only in relation to the object."[73] All three also accept that our world with all its subjects and objects cannot mere-

---

Weg bahnen. Oft steht er plötzlich am Abgrund und sieht unten das grüne Thal: dahin zieht ihn der Schwindel gewaltsam hinab; aber er muß sich halten und sollte er mit dem eigenen Blut die Sohlen an den Felsen kleben. Dafür sieht er bald die Welt unter sich, ihre Sandwüsten und Moräste verschwinden, ihre Unebenheiten gleichen sich aus, ihre Mißtöne dringen nicht hinauf, ihre Rundung offenbart sich. Er selbst steht immer in reiner, kühler Alpenluft und sieht schon die Sonne, wenn unten noch schwarze Nacht liegt.« (HN1 #20).

[70] »Die Natur ist eine geschlossene in sich ruhende Objektivwerdung des Urwissens« (Schelling 1803:163).

[71] Eine rabenschwarze Nacht, »die ein langer Traum füllt, der oft zum drükkenden Alp wird« (HN1 #23).

[72] »Es entsteht in mir bisweilen das lebhafteste Bewußtseyn, daß ich von jeher dagewesen sey, und es wirkt große Erhebung und Stärkung in mir« (HN1 #22).

[73] »daß Objekte nur in Bezug auf das Subjekt und dies nur in Bezug auf jene existirt« (HN2:308).

ly be a dream, and that "something must definitely exist."[74] Along this line Schopenhauer wrote in his Schelling notebook:

> It depends on the question whether there is a difference between *being* [Seyn] and the *capacity to be perceived* [Erkanntwerdenkönnen], and whether after the subtraction of all perceptibility a *being* is left over, that is, whether there still *is* something for us beyond *subject* and *object*.[75]

At the end of the first book of *The World as Will and Representation*, Schopenhauer was to pose the same question: Is the world only representation or is it something more? In the second book he then furnished his answer: the world is essentially will. But in Berlin he was still far from such a conception. While both imitating and criticizing his predecessors Kant, Fichte, and Schelling, Schopenhauer's own philosophical perspective and method gradually took shape. In his notes about Schelling's *Of the I as Principle of Philosophy*, the student remarked that Fichte and Schelling called the basis of the world of representation an "absolute I" and identified this with God (p. 308). But at that time Schopenhauer was already a convinced atheist and believed that if a creator of our world existed he would be a sadistic demon rather than a benevolent God. Thus he regarded Schelling's glorious immortality as "no more than an infinite becoming and striving, i.e., unending torment."[76] In Schopenhauer's view, Schelling's God—disguised as the "form of all forms" or the "necessary and first form"—stems from never-never-land.[77] Schopenhauer's notes document his growing irritation which was in part due to the fact that Schelling's towering speculations

---

[74] Dass »doch etwas unbedingt seyn muß« (HN2:308).

[75] »Es kommt daher auf die Frage an, ob zwischen *Seyn* und *Erkanntwerdenkönnen* ein Unterschied sey, ob nach Abzug aller Erkennbarkeit noch ein *Seyn* übrig bliebe, ob jenseit *Subjekt* und *Objekt* für uns noch etwas *ist*.« (HN2:309)

[76] »doch nur unendliches Werden, Streben, d.h. unendliche Quaal« (HN2:307).

[77] »Form aller Formen«, »nothwendige und erste Form«, »aus Wolkenkuksheim« (HN2:305).

could not explain such basic phenomena such as hunger and sexuality (p. 307) nor the "own-will of I-ness" which, "like all things springing from selfhood," is for Schopenhauer nothing but "illusion and night."[78] Was philosophy good for anything if it could not even explain this basic bearing of Schopenhauer's compass?

But at least with regard to the pole of salvation Schopenhauer identified important common points. In his *Philosophical Letters about Dogmatism and Criticism* of 1795, the 20-year-old Schelling had written some paragraphs that Schopenhauer called the "great and pure truth."[79] There Schelling explained, as it were, Spinoza's hidden compass (1809:164–7). It was pointing, so Schelling claims, to the "intuitive vision of the absolute" that forms "the supreme, ultimate level of knowledge that can be reached by a finite being" and constitutes "the proper life of the spirit" fed by "its perception of itself."[80]

> All of us have a secret, wonderful ability to withdraw from the changes of time into our innermost being, stripped of everything external, and to see there in the form of changelessness the eternal in us. This view is the most intimate and personal experience on which everything that we know and believe about a suprasensual world depends.[81]

---

[78] »Eigenwillen der Selbstheit«, welcher »wie alles aus der Selbstheit entsprungene« nichts als »Trug und Nacht« ist (HN1 #28).

[79] »große lautre Wahrheit« bezeichnete (HN2:309).

[80] »intellektuale Anschauung des Absoluten« welche »das höchste, die letzte Stufe der Erkenntniß, zu der ein endliches Wesen sich erheben kann, das eigentliche Leben des Geistes« sei, was er »aus seiner Selbstanschauung« geschöpft habe (HN2:164–5).

[81] »Uns allen nämlich wohnt ein geheimes, wunderbares Vermögen bey, uns aus dem Wechsel der Zeit in unser Innerstes, von allem, was von aussenher hinzukam, entkleidetes Selbst zurückzuziehen, und da unter der Form der Unwandelbarkeit das Ewige in uns anzuschauen. Diese Anschauung ist die innerste, eigenste Erfahrung, von welcher allein alles abhängt, was wir von einer übersinnlichen Welt wissen und glauben« (HN2:165).

Schelling's description of Spinoza's "intuitive vision of the absolute" (intellektuale Anschauung des Absoluten) and of an "ultimate level of knowledge" matches the characterization of the "hidden compass" that Schopenhauer later ascribed to several philosophers including Spinoza. But the problem with Fichte and Schelling, Schopenhauer explains, is that they regarded intuitive vision as authoritative and made "insolent and reprehensible" claims regarding the objective validity of its contents.[82] Nevertheless Schelling's early portrayal of intuitive vision was labeled by Schopenhauer as "great pure truth" (große lautre Wahrheit). He referred to statements by Schelling such as:

> This intuitive vision occurs when we cease to be an *object* for ourselves and when in inner contemplation the seeing self is identical with the seen self. In this moment of vision, time and duration vanish: not we are in time, but time—or rather timeless, pure, absolute eternity—is *in us*.[83]

While Schopenhauer recognized a "better consciousness" in this, he harbored doubts about Schelling's and Fichte's capacity to come up with a rational deduction and philosophical explanation of this (as well as the opposite pole) of his compass. The intensity of his critique of the lectures and writings of his predecessors betrays how ardently he hoped to find such an explanation: this concerned his central problematic. His disappointment was thus enormous when he realized that neither of the two philosophers truly understood his deepest concern.

Whereas Kant had sought to keep philosophy within the boundary of rationality, Schopenhauer realized with growing dismay that Schelling and Fichte tried to transgress such limits through a pseudo-mysticism harmful both to philosophy and mysticism. Their attempt

---

[82] »unverschämt und verwerflich« (P2 §10; SW5.11; Z9.17).

[83] »Diese intellektuale Anschauung tritt dann ein, wo wir für uns selbst aufhören, *Objekt* zu seyn, wo in sich selbst zurückgezogen, das anschauende Selbst mit dem angeschauten identisch ist. In diesem Moment der Anschauung schwindet für uns Zeit und Dauer dahin: nicht wir sind in der Zeit, sondern die Zeit—oder vielmehr nicht sie, sondern die reine absolute Ewigkeit ist *in uns*« (Schelling 1809:166–7).

Illusion and Ur-knowledge

to capture the absolute in abstract concepts and to analyze its content philosophically seemed to him fundamentally misguided. He fought against this with all his might based on his conviction that philosophy must remain a rational enterprise. If illuminism played any role, as in Spinoza, that compass bearing had to remain hidden. Only in this way could philosophical argument remain in the sphere of rationality. If, on the other hand, the illuministic compass were to be openly displayed and intuitive vision were to take the place of philosophically stringent argumentation and be used as proof, the result could only be bad philosophy. This delimitation was of utmost importance for Schopenhauer and formed the foundation of his critique of Fichte's and Schelling's speculation and their underlying hidden theology. It also helped him define the boundary of his doctoral dissertation: the world as representation. In this work, published in 1813, Schopenhauer focused on the fundamental conditions of the appearance of objects to subjects and thus on phenomena rather than what Kant had called "thing-in-itself" (Ding an sich). Though Fichte and Schelling had attempted to explain the latter via intuitive vision, Schopenhauer held that it can *never* be an object to a subject. This boundary remained fundamental for Schopenhauer and was first unequivocally formulated in his Schelling notes in Berlin:

> I say: Philosophy is the conditioned knowledge of the absolute. Proof: If it were not conditioned it would be absolute; and the absolute is by definition only One, Being, not knowledge, and also not in need of knowledge. Where knowledge is necessary there is limitation. There can only be knowledge where there is comprehension [Verstand] and reason [Vernunft]; hence these are limited. They are the capacity of conceptualization and of the creation of new concepts from already existing ones. Therefore any concept is limited and can consequently never be adequate for the absolute. If the absolute were thus to be conceptualized, this could only be achieved within the limitations inherent in comprehension and the faculty of reason, i.e., in a limited way:

therefore all knowledge is limited. The supreme knowledge is that of the absolute, i.e., philosophy. But according to the foregoing, as knowledge, it necessarily must remain limited and hence is limited knowledge of the absolute. If a man approaches the absolute without limits, as he is able to and should, he does not *know* about the absolute but he *is* himself the absolute. But insofar as he philosophizes he does not do this.[84]

It is exactly Schopenhauer's clear understanding of the fundamental difference between the philosopher's rational comprehension and the mystic's existential realization which exacerbated his critique of Fichte and Schelling and propelled his estrangement. When in the winter of 1811/12 he read Schelling's famous *Philosophical Inquiries about the Essence of Human Freedom*, Schopenhauer already formulated this difference concretely:

> They [Schelling's *Philosophical Inquiries*] are almost entirely a recasting of Jacob Böhme's *Mysterium magnum*, in which practically every sentence and every expression can be identified. — But why do the same similes, forms and expressions that in Jacob Böhme's work I read with admiration and deep emotion, seem intolerable and ridiculous in Schelling's work? — Because I recognize that in Jacob Böhme it is realization of eternal truth that

---

[84] »Ich sage: Die Philosophie ist das bedingte Wissen vom Absoluten. Beweis: Wäre es nicht bedingt, so wäre es absolut, und das Absolute ist, seinem Begriffe nach, nur Eins, ein Seyn, kein Wissen, auch keines Wissens bedürftig. Wo also Wissen nöthig ist, da ist Bedingtheit. Wissen giebt es nur für Verstand und Vernunft, also sind diese bedingt. Sie sind die Vermögen der Begriffe und des Schaffens neuer Begriffe aus schon vorhandnen. Also ist der Begriff bedingt: folglich dem Absoluten nie adäquat. Soll daher das Absolute in den Begriff, so kann dies nur unter den Beschränkungen geschehn, die dem Verstand und [der] Vernunft ankleben, also bedingterweise: also ist alles Wissen bedingt. Das höchste Wissen ist das vom Absoluten, d.h. die Philosophie: doch bleibt, laut dem vorhergehenden, auch diese, als Wissen, nothwendig bedingt; ist also ein bedingtes Wissen vom Absoluten. Insofern der Mensch dem Absoluten sich unbedingt nähert (wie er kann und soll) *weiß* er nicht vom Absoluten, sondern *ist* das Absolute selbst. Sofern er aber philosophirt, thut er dies nicht.« (HN2:316–7)

is expressed in these similes, although it could also have been expressed just as aptly in many others if Jacob Böhme had not hit upon just these.— Schelling, however, adopts from him the same similes and expressions, which is all he can adopt, and takes the peel for the fruit or at least cannot distinguish one from the other. If the same divine realization as Jacob Böhme's had been actualized in him he would have found different, purer expressions in keeping with his own individual character.— Thus the imitation of a great artist's manner is repugnant even though the very same manner, in the original artist's works of art, is essential, i.e. inseparable from their beauty.[85]

Both Schopenhauer's attraction to Fichte and Schelling and his estrangement from them were fruitful processes without which his system would hardly have seen the day. The example of the youthful Schelling who at age 25 had already erected a philosophical system was also inspiring for other young philosophers such as Friedrich Schlegel and K.F.C. Krause. After his first few months in Berlin Schopenhauer already formulated "a little system" (Systemchen), fully conscious both of the need for the diminutive and of the difference to Schelling's and Fichte's abstract soufflés. Schopenhauer's "little system" furnishes, as it

---

[85] »Er [Schellings Aufsatz über die Freiheit] ist fast nur eine Umarbeitung von Jakob *Böhm's Mysterium magnum*, in welchem sich fast jeder Saz und jeder Ausdruck nachweisen lässt.— Warum aber sind mir bey S[chelling] dieselben Bilder, Formen und Ausdrücke unerträglich und lächerlich, die ich bey Jakob Böhm mit Bewunderung und Rührung lese?—Weil ich erkenne daß in Jakob Böhm die Erkenntniß der ewigen Wahrheit es ist, die sich in diesen Bildern ausspricht, obwohl sie auch mit gleichem Fug in vielen andern sich hätte aussprechen können, wenn J[akob] B[öhm] nicht grade auf diese gerathen wäre.— S[chelling] aber nimmt von ihm (was er allein von ihm nehmen kann) dieselben Bilder und Ausdrücke, hält die Schaale für die Frucht, oder weiß sie wenigstens nicht von der Frucht zu lösen. Wäre dieselbe göttliche Erkenntniß in ihm wirksam gewesen die in J[akob] B[öhm] lebte, so hätte sie nach seiner Individualität andre, reinere Ausdrücke gefunden.—So ist uns die Nachahmung der Manier eines großen Künstlers zuwider, welche Manier in seinen eignen Werken doch wesentlich, d.h. von der Schönheit unzertrennlich ist.« (HN2:314)

CHAPTER THREE

were, only raw food. Lacking any God and an absolute, it could almost stem from the pen of Baron d'Holbach, the notorious atheist and materialist of France's radical enlightenment. Schopenhauer wrote:

> Everywhere nature has a single purpose: to provide life and well-being, as much as possible. [...] Everywhere on earth life springs up and forges ahead; teleology is apparent in all respects and the aim of all aims is well-being and life. [...] Physical evil is nothing more than a symptom of the limits imposed on the attainment of this aim; it goes against the order and against the omnipresent intention of nature to avoid it. Nature wills life and well-being, as completely and protractedly as possible, and the many different species of creatures are but manifold paths to this end. [...] In man the highest degree of self-consciousness manifests itself. It is so elevated that man must achieve with consciousness what all other creatures achieve without, namely, to promote life and well-being. This 'ought' that manifests itself in his consciousness is the Categorical Imperative: he must will what nature wills. [...] The fact that our innermost being only aims at serving and fulfilling the purpose of nature and that our pure will is merely her will, explains our inner joy at the sight of her, about her forms that are clearly and purely depicted by art, and about music which imitates the unity and regularity of nature with the greatest variety and liveliness.[86]

---

[86] »Die Natur hat überall nur Einen Zweck: Leben und Wohlseyn zu bereiten; so viel als möglich [...] Auf der Erde drängt und quillt Leben überall hervor, die Teleologie ist überall kenntlich und der Zweck aller Zwecke ist Wohlseyn und Leben [..] Das physische Uebel ist auch nur eine Anzeige der Schranken die die Erreichung jenes Zwecks hat, es drängt sich ein gegen alle Ordnung, und gegen die überall kenntliche Absicht der Natur ihm vorzubeugen. Sie will Leben und Wohlseyn, möglichst vollkommen und möglichst lange, und die vielfältigen Gattungen der Geschöpfe sind nur vielfältige Wege zum Genuß [...]. Im Menschen offenbart sich der höchste Grad des Selbstbewusstseyns, ein so hoher Grad, dass er mit Bewusstseyn thun soll, was alle andren Geschöpfe ohne Bewusstseyn thun,—Leben und Wohlseyn befördern: dieses in seinem Bewusstseyn sich aussprechende *Soll* ist der Katego-

Illusion and Ur-knowledge

Whereas the philosophy which Schopenhauer in early 1811 had explained to Wieland's niece showed, as it were, the basic bearing of his compass—desires / passions and the liberation from them—his "little system" of early 1812 furnished the first philosophical explanation of the extremity of the compass needle pointing toward the origin of desire and of natural egotism: the will of nature and the inevitable striving for self-preservation and well-being.

But in the spring of 1812 a third system of Schopenhauer was already waiting in the wings: a system that for the first time presented both poles in a unified philosophical framework (even if it could not yet fully explain it). This was Schopenhauer's so-called philosophy of double consciousness (Duplizitätsphilosophie). In secondary literature it is often called "philosophy of better consciousness" (Philosophie des besseren Bewusstseins) and portrayed as Schopenhauer's one and only early philosophy. Since the publications of Hans Zint and Rudolf Malter, the soteriological intention of Schopenhauer's philosophical venture has received increasing attention, and recently the presence of soteriological intention has also been demonstrated in Schopenhauer's early philosophy (de Cian 2002). Nevertheless it remains unclear what was at stake here. What kind of soteriology did Schopenhauer propose? Salvation or redemption from what? And what was his view of the role of philosophy in this?

---

rische Imperativ—er soll wollen was die Natur will [...] Weil unser innerstes Wesen nur darauf hinausgeht den Zweck der Natur zu befördern, unser reiner Wille nur ihr Wille ist, so erklärt sich unsre innige Freude bey ihrem Anblick, bey ihren Formen die die Kunst rein darstellt, bey der Musik die die Einheit und Regelmässigkeit in der grössten Mannigfaltigkeit und Lebendigkeit,— der Natur nachahmt.« (HN1 #34)

4. Empirical and Better Consciousness

After the introductory course in the regional league of philosophy with "Gottlob Ernst Schulze, professor of misosophy [hate of wisdom] in Göttingen" (HN2.26), the 23-year-old student found himself suddenly in the champions league in Berlin. At last he could drink the essence of philosophy from a pure fount: a man who did not just react, ruminate on the ideas of true philosophers, and criticize them like Schulze, but a system-builder in person: Fichte, the famous author of a modern system of transcendental philosophy (the Wissenschaftslehre)!

In the fall of 1811 Schopenhauer sat attentively in the auditorium of the famous professor. With his shrill voice, Fichte had prohibited beginning students to take notes during his introductory lectures: they were required to think, not to write! For Schopenhauer this exercise was as stimulating as it was frustrating. He was not used to Fichte's vocabulary and mode of thinking; and when, in spite of his effort, he could not manage to follow a train of thought he began to doubt his qualification for the philosopher's trade. His notebook contains critiques that show both the student's extreme thirst for knowledge and rising level of frustration:

> During this hour he said things other than what I wrote down here that made me wish that I could point a pistol at his chest and exclaim: Now you must die without mercy; but for the sake of your poor soul, tell me if your nonsensical gibberish meant anything or if you simply uttered it to fool us?[87]

Returning home after Fichte's lectures, Schopenhauer summarized their content from memory and soon began adding his own comments. Fortunately the high-altitude road of philosophy features not only sharp rocks bloodying one's soles but also moments of elation when the sun's rays suddenly break through the clouds and the thick haze clears, as in Fichte's explanations about the "flash of evidence." In his notes to Fichte's second lecture Schopenhauer wrote:

> That flash of evidence exists, as all experience proves. There comes a moment where the entire world of phenomena fades away under the radiance of the I that recognizes the reality of itself and of a suprasensory world, as a shadow play fades away when a lamp is lighted. This moment may arrive for few people, only for true philosophers. Hence Plato says: Πολλοι μεν ναρθηκοφοροι, βακχοι δε γε παυροι [Wielders of the staff of Bacchus are numerous, but Bacchants are few].[88]

---

[87] »In dieser Stunde hat er außer dem hier Aufgeschriebenen Sachen gesagt die mir den Wunsch auspressten, ihm eine Pistole auf die Brust sezzen zu dürfen und dann zu sagen: Sterben mußt du jetzt ohne Gnade; aber um deiner armen Seele Willen, sage ob du dir bey dem Gallimathias etwas deutliches gedacht hast oder uns blos zu Narren gehabt hast?« (HN2:41)

[88] »Jenen Bliz der Evidenz giebt es, über alle Erfahrung. Es kommt ein Augenblick wo die ganze Welt der Erscheinung verbleicht, überstrahlt von dem Ich das seine Realität und die einer übersinnlichen Welt erkennt; wie ein Schattenspiel verschwindet wenn ein Licht angezündet wird. Der Augenblick mag Wenigen kommen, den ächten Philosophen. Platon spricht daher: Πολλοι μεν ναρθηκοφοροι, βακχοι δε γε παυροι.« (HN2:23).

Fichte explained that teachers and books cannot communicate the truth and explained: "If the student realizes it through the said flash of evidence and thus attains true knowledge, it is due to himself and not to the teacher. Once the student has grasped it in that manner, he will keep it forever as his own."[89] The professor's third introductory lecture began with his detailed explanations about the "flash of evidence." Schopenhauer wrote in his notebook that it consists in the realization that "the insight and the ground are one" and that "each is seen in the other."[90] Professor Fichte also addressed the question about the origin of this flash by explaining that Wissenschaftslehre in the literal sense signifies "the science that indicates the ground of all knowledge."[91]

This was meant to encourage the overwhelmed philosophy freshmen who were happy to be allowed to take notes during the subsequent lectures about the "facts of consciousness." Schopenhauer was certainly inspired by Fichte's explanations about the basic drive or instinctive desire (Trieb) and its "visibility" or appearance: the world (p. 66). According to Fichte, the I evident in reflection does not come first. Rather, he regarded "the I of the drive" as the original "I"—which is why the entire Fichtean system sets out "from the ground of the drive."[92] But what did Fichte mean by this "I of the drive" or "I of instinctive desire" that he regarded as more basic than the reflective, self-conscious I? And when he claimed that the world is "nothing other than the visibility of I," did he speak about the "perceiving I," the "desiring I," or both at once? At any rate, according to Schopenhauer's notes, Fichte's explanations about the "facts of consciousness" began with this "I of instinctive

---

[89] »Daß indeß der Schüler sie erkennt durch jenen Bliz der Evidenz, und so zum wahren Wissen gelangt, ist nur sein eignes Werk und das kann´ der Lehrer nicht bewirken. Hat der Schüler sie also erfaßt, so behält er sie auf immer« (HN2:24).

[90] »die Wahrnehmung und der Grund eins sey, in diesem jene, in jener diesen sehn« (HN2:25).

[91] »die Wissenschaft welche den Grund angiebt alles Wissens« (HN2:26).

[92] »das Ich des Triebs«, »vom Grund des Triebs« (HN2:68).

desire" (Ich des Triebs). According to Fichte, the world as representation can only arise when "the drive is given an image: perception."[93] But for Fichte it all forms part of a "system of lower consciousness" and represents "inferior knowledge" as distinct from "genuine knowledge,"[94] "higher consciousness," or "higher knowledge"[95] whose origin Fichte went on to explain from his fifth lecture in the fall of 1811.

The main theme of the fifth lecture was the transition from the drive as "fundamental principle of actual knowledge" to the superior, driveless (trieblos) knowledge actualized through realization or comprehension (Wissen oder Erkenntnis). Fichte's explanation could almost stem from Schopenhauer's pen:

> Knowledge tears itself away from this drive and the entire system of perception; it pulls itself away from the drive as the dominant ground of its perception. [...] Only when the drive ceases to be law can the entire perception become empty: an empty receptacle for the higher. This state of transition is established as follows: perception, the subjective, tears itself away from the objective. Rather than abandoning one system or another, it liberates itself from the entire system. The subjective perception (subjektive Anschauung) thus becomes empty, and one cannot really grasp how it still can be a perception.[96]

---

[93] »dem Trieb ein Bild gegeben werde, die Wahrnehmung« (HN2:70).

[94] »im System des niedern Bewußtseyns«; »das niedre Wissen« welches »gar nicht das rechte Wissen« ist (HN2:70).

[95] Das »höhere Bewußtseyn« oder »höhere Wissen« (HN2:70).

[96] »Von diesem Trieb und dem ganzen System der Anschauung reißt das Wissen sich los; es reißt sich los vom Triebe als dem bestimmenden Grund seiner Anschauung. ... Nur unter der Bedingung daß der Trieb aufhört Gesez zu seyn, wird die ganze Anschauung leer, und wird leer für das Höhere. Der Zustand des Uebergangs steht so: die Anschauung, das Subjektive, reißt sich los vom Objektiven; sie reißt sich nicht los von diesem oder jenem System, sondern vom ganzen System. Die Subjektive Anschauung wird also leer, man kann nicht recht begreifen wie sie noch eine Anschauung ist« (HN2:73).

Empirical and Better Consciousness

Once Fichte's "higher knowledge"—which arises "through the I's abandonment of all these determinations"—is reached, there are neither concepts nor multiplicity: "in one word, higher knowledge has no form. ... It is the original form of being" and "the only true *vision* that alone expresses the entire reality."[97] Such statements were admired by Schopenhauer and matched the direction of his compass; hence his rapturous comment in the margins about Fichte's "higher consciousness": "*Ego*. That's the truth!"[98] But Schopenhauer's enthusiasm about Fichte's portrayal of moments when one "liberates oneself from the drive" and rises in "pure vision" to the sphere of "higher consciousness"[99] was severely dampened as soon as the professor spoke about the content of such higher consciousness: "We call the absolute being *God.*"[100] Fichte's subsequent lectures became increasingly complex, and soon expressions of Schopenhauer's frustration and critique took the upper hand.[101] Nevertheless, various ideas of Fichte were integrated in Schopenhauers thinking, for example the concept of "empirical consciousness."[102] At

---

[97] »mit Einem Wort die höhere Anschauung hat keine Gestalt. ... Sie ist die ursprüngliche Form des Seyns«; »das allein wahre und alle Realität ausdrükkende *Gesicht*« (HN2:74–5).

[98] »*Ego*. Wahr gesprochen!« (HN2:74)

[99] »losreißt vom Trieb«; Erhebung »zum reinen Anschauen« (HN2:77); Erreichen der Sphäre des »höheren Bewußtseyns« (HN2:79).

[100] »Das absolute Seyn nennen wir *Gott*« (HN2:81).

[101] One year later, in a note written in Rudolstadt (1813; HN1 #112), Schopenhauer was to dismiss this entire doctrine (Lehre) by spelling it »Leere« (vacuousness), stating that Fichte had become a philosopher only because of Kant's Thing in itself (Ding an sich) and that his philosophy suffered the consequences, having become a "vacuousness of science" (»blos über Kants Ding an sich zum Philosophen geworden«; es sei »denn auch eine Philosophie danach geworden, eine Wissenschaftsleere.«)

[102] F. Chenet's opinion (1997) that Schopenhauer's term has its origin in Jacobi appears baseless since there is no evidence for Schopenhauer's study of Jacobi at this early stage.

times Fichte used this expression in lieu of "factual consciousness" to refer to knowledge tied to desire or drive (Trieb).[103]

While Schopenhauer struggled with Fichte's philosophy he also immersed himself in intensive study of the works by Kant and Schelling. In the fall of 1811 he borrowed three books of Kant (the Metaphysical Foundations of Natural Science, of Ethics, and of Jurisdiction) and read more than a dozen of Schelling's publications while taking extensive notes. He thought he found the clearest expression of Schelling's system (HN2:325) in the booklet entitled *Philosophy and Religion* of 1804; his related notes and comments fill almost seven tightly written pages that also illustrate Schopenhauer's main objections to Schelling's and Fichte's systems. Most vexing was their claim of a *philosophical* conception of the "absolute" and the God whom they hid behind this term. Schopenhauer wrote:

> I fight against your absolute, as I fight against the God of the deists. Yet I do not say to either group that their concept ('the absolute' and 'God') is as lacking of a referent as a centaur, but rather that it is the effect of transcendent reason and was born because man did not want to distinguish his highest inner essence and capacity from reason (which is the task of true philosophical criticism).[104]

In Schopenhauer's eyes the systems of both idealists constituted philosophically disguised theology rather than genuine philosophy: "Schelling does with his absolute what all pious and enlightened theists did with their God: they assert logical impossibilities about it."[105]

---

[103] »faktisches Bewußtseyn«, »triebgebundenes Erkennen« (HN2: 84).

[104] »Ich streite gegen euer Absolutes grade wie gegen den Gott der Deisten: sage aber keinem von Beyden, daß ihr Begriff (das Absolute und Gott) so grundlos ist als der vom Hippokentauren: sondern daß er ein Werk des transcendenten Verstandes ist, entstanden indem der Mensch sein höchstes innerstes Wesen und Vermögen vom Verstande nicht trennen will (was eben der wahre Kriticismus soll).« (HN2:326)

[105] »Schelling thut mit seinem Absoluten was alle frommen und erleuchteten Theisten mit ihrem Gott thaten—sie sagten logische Unmöglichkeiten von

Empirical and Better Consciousness

And Fichte—instead of "learning from Kant's great discoveries that the world of reason is separate and locked into the cage of sensuality" and that there is "an entirely different world"[106] which shows itself, for instance, in the categorical imperative of Kant's ethics—fused these two heterogenous worlds to form a monster. For Schopenhauer this was the exact opposite of philosophy because genuine philosophy can only be "perfect and pure criticism," i.e., the unambiguous distinction between a "higher world"—which sends "rays into the prison night of reason" and thus manifests its existence—and the ordinary sphere of understanding and reason.[107] He noted: "We philosophize only for our faculty of understanding (Plato); the other world itself has no need for any philosophy in order to become aware of itself."[108]

Schopenhauer had personally experienced the irruption of this "other world" in moments of ecstasy in nature and art, and he had seen it described in the works of Plato and the mystics: in the world of the sun in Plato's metaphor of the cave, in Böhme's enlightenment, and later also in Madame Guyon's absolute selflessness.[109] This was what he called "the better consciousness in me"—the consciousness that lifted him "up into a world where there is neither personality nor causality

---

ihm aus« (HN2:326).

[106] » aus Kant's großen Entdeckungen zu erkennen: daß die Welt des Verstandes eine für sich bestehende und im Käfig der Sinnenwelt eingeschlossene ist« und dass es überdies »eine ganz andre Welt giebt« (HN2: 356).

[107] »vollkommner reiner Kriticismus«; »wahre Philosophie« die »Strahlen in die Kerkernacht des Verstandes sendet« (HN2:356).

[108] »Denn nur für ihn, den Verstand, philosophieren wir (Plato), die andre Welt selbst bedarf keiner Philosophie, um sich zu erkennen.« (HN2:356)

[109] Schopenhauer's familiarity with writings of Jakob Böhme is already evident in the winter of 1811–12 (HN2:314) and possibly dates from his high school days in Weimar. His earliest mention of Guyon does not stem, as Hübscher claims, from the year 1817 (Hübscher 1973:46) but is found in a note from late autumn of 1815 when Schopenhauer adduced Guyon's autobiography as a good example of a saint's life (HN1 #496). Of course this does not preclude that Schopenhauer had, under the influence of Zacharias Werner, read or heard about writings by Böhme and Guyon at a much earlier point in time..

nor subject and object."[110] This was precisely the direction indicated by his inner compass:

> As soon as we ... *behold* the things of the world *objectively*, i.e., when we *contemplate*, then *subjectivity* and therewith the source of all misery ceases for a moment and we are free.[111]

A philosophy deserving its name must be able to rationally explain both of these poles. Whenever Schopenhauer in his notes about Schelling and Fichte used words like "full" or "complete truth," he referred to their "pure view" (reine Schau) or "intuitive vision" (intellektuale Anschauung); and his harshest critique often concerned the same subject. Based on his own experience and reports by mystics such as Böhme, Schopenhauer thought he was in a position to judge the accuracy of philosophers' pronouncements; and Fichte's and Schelling's failure to meet his expectation of a conclusive philosophical explanation seems to have been a main reason for his increasingly acerbic critique. Their claim to have philosophically penetrated into this "higher world" seemed to him not only disingenuous but also unphilosophical and incompatible with trustworthier authorities. He concluded:

> Schelling's Intellektuale Anschauung is, as it turns out, something different from the better consciousness that I ascribe to man. [According to Schelling] the reader should always maintain it, which is only possible with a theoretical concept. [By contrast,] what I mean is beyond time and is not subject to free choice according to concepts.[112]

---

[110] »das beßre Bewußtseyn in mir«; eine Welt »wo es weder Persönlichkeit und Kausalität noch Subjekt und Objekt mehr giebt« (HN1 #81).

[111] »Sobald wir ... die Dinge der Welt *objektiv betrachten, d.h. kontempliren*, ist für den Augenblick die *Subjektivität* und somit die Quelle alles Elends geschwunden, wir sind frei« (HN1 #86).

[112] »Schelling's Intellektuale Anschauung ist doch etwas andres als das *beßre Bewußtseyn* das ich dem Menschen zuspreche. Denn der Leser soll sie immer gegenwärtig erhalten, und das kann man nur [durch] einen Verstandesbegriff: was ich meyne ist außerzeitlich und steht nicht in unsrer Willkühr nach Begriffen.« (HN2:326)

Empirical and Better Consciousness

This is Schopenhauer's earliest documented use of the term "better consciousness." What is at stake is the experience of a sphere that can neither be attained by study nor willfully entered. Like a ray of sunlight it may suddenly break the darkness of the "prison night of reason" (Kerkernacht des Verstandes), which is why it is different from Schelling's intuitive vision (intellektuelle or, as Schopenhauer often spelled it, intellektuale Anschauung):

> I absolutely reject an intellektuale Anschauung that depends upon empirical will and cultivation of mind. This does not imply that I deny—like Schelling—what the enthusiasts have called 'enlightenment from above' and Plato (*Res publica* VII) 'elevation to the spiritual sun.' [Such enlightenment] is neither conditioned by empirical will (though it is one with pure will) nor by cultivation of mind which in comparison appears totally insignificant; it is the inner essence of the genius.[113]

For Schopenhauer such unmediated intuitive vision occurred in moments of absolute clarity produced by grace rather than willful desire. They could not be arbitrarily prolonged. Schopenhauer also rejected the view aired by Schleiermacher in his 1812 lecture about the history of philosophy in the Christian era. When Schleiermacher said that one possesses a vision of God either permanently or not at all, Schopenhauer was incensed and jotted in the margin of his lecture notes:

> Nego ac pernego [I reject, absolutely reject this!]. I either totally reject the term 'vision of God' or interpret it as man's highest consciousness of himself that is as independent as possible from his sensual nature. It is in this way that I also interpret Jacob Böhme's

---

[113] »Eine solche vom empirischen Willen und der Verstandesbildung abhängige intellektuale Anschauung leugne ich schlechthin; wiewohl nicht (was eben Schelling leugnet) dasjenige was die Schwärmer Erleuchtung von Oben genannt haben, Plato (*Respublica* VII) das Aufsteigen zur geistigen Sonne, was nicht abhängt vom empirischen Willen (obwohl es mit dem reinen Willen Eins ist) noch von der Verstandeskultur, deren Werk dagegen verbleicht und schwindet; was das innre Wesen des Genies ist.« (HN2:311-2)

enlightenment: he reportedly got enlightened for the first time as an apprentice, the second time at age 25, and the third time at age 35. The intervals are substantial: but all those who are capable of a suprasensory consciousness of self know that such consciousness is not permanently available but breaks through only on rare occasions.[114]

On Schopenhauer's compass, the pole of destination (marked here by "better consciousness" and "better will") stands opposed to the pole of origin that he from the spring of 1812 labeled "empirical consciousness" and "empirical will." He regarded the central task of genuine philosophy as "criticism" (Kritizismus), that is, the clear distinction and rational deduction of these two poles. In this sense the position of the philosopher lies exactly at the hub of the compass. Though he feels magnetically attracted by one side and repulsed by the other and directs his path accordingly, he must analyze this fact and its reasons rationally and with detachment. This appears to be the stance of genuine criticism that Schopenhauer considered identical with genuine philosophy.

The genuine, i.e., critical philosopher must do theoretically what the virtuous man does in practice. The virtuous man does not fashion an absolute of the desire that sticks to him by virtue of his sensual nature. Rather, he follows the better will in himself without linking this to any desire, for example in form of a recompense, and thus avoids striving for the good only in a relative rather than an absolute sense. Likewise, the genuine philosopher distinguishes his better consciousness from the conditions of em-

---

[114] »Nego ac pernego [Nein und nochmals nein!]. Den Begriff ›Anschauung Gottes‹ lasse ich entweder gar nicht zu oder er muß bedeuten das höchste von seiner sinnlichen Natur möglichst unabhängige Selbstbewußtsein des Menschen. In diesem Sinne nehme ich auch des erhabnen Jakob Böhm's Erleuchtung: von ihm wird uns gemeldet er sey in seinen Lehrjahren zum ersten Mal, in seinem 25sten Jahr zum 2ten und im 35sten zum 3ten Mal erleuchtet. Die Zwischenräume sind zwar groß:—aber Jeder der eines übersinnlichen Selbstbewußtseyns fähig ist, weiß daß es nicht immer ihm offensteht, sondern nur selten durchbricht.« (HN2:226)

pirical consciousness and does not mix up the two (in the manner of a sensual believer in need of recompense as a bridge toward virtue). Detachedly and steadfastly he leaves behind him the conditions of his empirical consciousness and is content to neatly separate better consciousness from empirical consciousness, and thus to have recognized the two-fold nature of his being.[115]

In Schopenhauer's eyes Schelling's system lacked such detachment and overstepped the boundary of philosophy. "In one word, it presents to us the whole world as a *phenomenon* that flows in accordance with ultimate laws from an *action* of God and that has a *final aim*."[116] Rather than critical philosophy, this is dogmatism and mythology:

> Schelling's entire system is nothing but mythology, possibly the most abstract mythology one can arrive at. But this is not an essential characteristic [of philosophy] and has the same nature as utmost sensuality. In fact it is his mistake, and also that of all dogmatic philosophers, to regard philosophy as an abstract mythology. Philosophy is an art, and its means is reason. And since that is the case it is thoroughly prosaic.[117]

---

[115] »Statt dessen soll der wahrhafte d.h. der kritische Philosoph, theoretisch thun, was der tugendhafte Mensch praktisch thut. Dieser nämlich macht das ihm durch seinen sinnliche Natur anklebende Begehren nicht zum absoluten, sondern folgt dem bessern Willen in ihm, ohne ihn mit jenem Begehren, als z.B. mit einer Belohnung, in Verbindung zu sezzen und so nur relativ nicht absolut das Gute zu wollen. Eben so löst der ächte kritische Philosoph sein beßres Erkennen ab von den Bedingungen des empirischen, trägt diese nicht hinüber in jenes (wie der sinnliche Gläubige die Belohnung als eine Brücke zur Tugend) sondern läßt kalt und unerschüttert die Bedingungen seiner empirischen Erkenntniß hinter sich, zufrieden, die beßre Erkenntniß rein von jener gesondert zu haben, die Duplicität seines Seyns erkannt zu haben.« (HN2:329)

[116] »stellt uns mit einem Wort die ganze Welt dar als eine *Begebenheit* nach endlichen Gesezzen die aus einer *Wirkung* Gottes fließt und eine *Endabsicht* hat« (HN2:329).

[117] »Schellings ganzes System ist nichts als Mythologie, vielleicht die abstrakteste zu der man gelangen kann. Doch ist dies nur eine unwesentliche Eigenschaft und sie hat mit der allersinnlichsten dieselbe Natur. Philosophie für

Toward the end of his Fichte notes, Schopenhauer offers a description of the ideal position of the philosopher and for the first time sketches the course of his future philosophy:

> Thus genuine criticism will distinguish better consciousness from empirical consciousness like gold from ore. It will present better consciousness purely and without any admixture of sensuality or judgment: it will present it entirely, collect every sign of its manifestation in consciousness, and form a unity of it. In this way empirical consciousness will also be seen in its pure form and one will be able to classify it according to its characteristics. This undertaking will in the future be perfected, worked out in more and finer detail, and presented for easier comprehension; but there is no possibility of it ever being overturned.[118]

This enterprise of distinguishing, describing, and classifying continued in Schopenhauer's philosophical notes of 1812. From the outset he realized that better consciousness cannot be the object of positive description:

> If it is *better consciousness* then we cannot say anything about it positively because our statement lies within the realm of reason. Hence we can only say what happens in that realm [of reason] and make merely negative statements about better consciousness.[119]

---

abstrakte Mythologie zu halten ist eben sein und aller Dogmatiker Irrthum. Philosophie ist Kunst, und ihr Material der Verstand. Aus letzterem Grund ist sie durchaus Prosa« (HN2:330).

[118] »So wird der wahre Kriticismus das beßre Bewußtseyn trennen von dem empirischen, wie das Gold aus dem Erz, wird es rein hinstellen ohne alle Beimengung von Sinnlichkeit oder Verstand,—wird es ganz hinstellen, Alles wodurch es sich im Bewußtseyn offenbart, sammeln, vereinen zu einer Einheit; dann wird er das empirische auch rein erhalten, nach seinen Verschiedenheiten klassifiziren: solches Werk wird in Zukunft vervollkommnet, genauer und feiner ausgearbeitet, faßlicher und leichter gemacht,—nie aber umgestoßen werden können.« (HN2:360)

[119] »Will es *bessres Bewußtseyn* seyn so können wir positiv von ihm nichts weiter sagen, denn unser Sagen liegt im Gebiet der Vernunft; wir können also nur sagen was auf diesem vorgeht, wodurch wir von dem bessern Bewußtseyn

Empirical and Better Consciousness

Better consciousness is said to be "beyond all experience and thus beyond all reason."[120] On the other hand, "empirical consciousness" signifies representation (Vorstellung), and representation is nothing other than being an object for a subject. It is precisely because of this that Schopenhauer chose empirical consciousness and subject-object relationship as the topic of his doctoral dissertation of 1813. By contrast, intuitive vision (intellektuale Anschauung), in which subject and object are one, is "beyond all reason" and thus not subject to positive, philosophical description (#45). Schopenhauer's compass and his intention of building a system manifested themselves, for example, in the association of these two poles with central concepts of famous philosophers. Early on, the "divine Plato" and the two worlds of his cave metaphor (shadows and sun, or what we hold for real and what is real) had caught Schopenhauer's attention. In 1812, Kant and Schelling joined the club: Kant's phenomenon was seen as corresponding to Schelling's real aspect of the absolute, and Kant's thing in itself (Ding an sich) to Schelling's ideal aspect of the absolute (#50). We will encounter other associations until Schopenhauer's basic system was completed in 1816 when he felt able to sketch in a table the structure of his major work.[121]

The sphere of "illusion and night sprung from selfhood,"[122] empirical consciousness, affirms temporality and being and is fundamentally subject-centered:

> If I consider myself as temporal, then only the present moment is mine (for in time only it is real, and past and future are nothing at all); I must use it, for only in it am I real and do I exist.[123]

---

nur negativ sprechen« (HN1 #35).

[120] »jenseits aller Erfahrung also aller Vernunft« (HN1 #35).

[121] HN1 #577; see below pp. 244–245.

[122] Die »aus Selbstheit entsprungne« Sphäre von »Trug und Nacht« (HN1 #28).

[123] »Betrachte ich mich als zeitlich so ist nur der Augenblick, die Gegenwart mein, (denn in der Zeit ist nur sie real, Vergangenheit und Zukunft sind gar nichts) sie muß ich nuzzen denn nur in ihr bin ich real und existirend« (HN1 #72).

By contrast, better consciousness affirms what is beyond time and negates temporal being:

> As soon as we cease to be in space and time ... we shall no longer be at all: our being (the opposite of nothingness) therefore ceases with death. ... On the other hand, if we become conscious of ourselves as not in time and space, then we rightly call all that is in time and space *nothing*. [...] The ability of one and the same I to become conscious of itself (to posit itself) as temporal and spatial, or conversely as non-temporal and non-spatial, constitutes *freedom*.[124]

Such remarks around the beginning of the dissertation year 1813 show that Schopenhauer was not trying to philosophically adjust his compass bearing. Rather, this basic bearing was firmly set but needed to be understood and philosophically elaborated. In this vein the role of asceticism was gradually better defined:

> *Virtue* is the affirmation of the extratemporal existence, indeed it is the direct expression of awareness as such: pure affirmation.—But with *asceticism* there is in addition an intentional negation, the formal denial and rejection of everything temporal as such.[125]

The basic idea of asceticism as a way to salvation had not undergone any change since Schopenhauer had spoken to Wieland's niece at the very beginning of his philosophy studies, and it is quite possible that

---

[124] »Sobald wir aufhören werden in Raum und Zeit zu seyn [...] so werden wir gar nicht mehr seyn: unser Seyn (das Gegentheil des Nichts) hört also auf mit dem Tode [...] Dagegen, wenn wir uns unserer bewußt werden als nicht in Zeit und Raum,—dann nennen wir eben das was in diesen ist mit Recht *Nichts* [...] Das Vermögen aber des einigen und selben Ichs, als Zeitlichen und Räumlichen oder auch als Nicht-Zeitlichen und Nicht-Räumlichen sich seiner bewußt zu werden (sich zu sezzen) ist die *Freiheit*.« (HN1 #66)

[125] »Die *Tugend* ist die Affirmation des Außerzeitlichen Seyns, sie ist ja der unmittelbare Ausdruck des Bewußtseyns eines solchen: reine Affirmation.—Bey der *Asketik* aber ist noch eine absichtliche Negation hinzugekommen, die förmliche Verleugnung, Zurückweisung alles Zeitlichen als solchen« (HN1 #72).

already at age twenty Schopenhauer agreed about this with his friend Zacharias Werner. Throughout, morality and asceticism run counter to the fundamental impulse of selfishness which already in the "little system" of 1812 appeared as a law of nature. Only virtue and asceticism can open the door of this prison. But of all living organisms, this possibility is only open to human beings:

> When we compare that which is moral and ascetic and tears itself away from everything earthly—in other words, *freedom* in man—with animals fettered to the law of nature, then one is tempted to compare the entire long, graduated series of animals to the unripe fruits of a tree, which cling to it more or less firmly and absorb the sap. Man, by contrast, resembles the ripe fruits which, at the point of highest perfection, drop off by themselves.[126]

What occurs with the compass in our hand—namely, that the "wrong" end of the needle always points toward us and the "right" end away from us—is also the case with Schopenhauer's empirical and better consciousness. Our "empirical, sensual, and rational consciousness in space and time" that forms the realm of "illusion and night" is "the wrong direction, from which virtue and asceticism constitute the return journey; and their result, blissful death, the release."[127]

The role of the philosopher, then, is to objectively discern and rationally describe the basis of both the problem and its resolution. This endeavor is aided by the experience of selfless contemplation:

---

[126] »Wenn man das Moralische, Asketische, von allem Irdischen sich losreißende,—mit einem Wort *die Freiheit* im Menschen vergleicht mit dem Gebundenseyn an Naturgesezze der Thiere; so liegt der Vergleich nah, daß die sämmtliche, lange, abgestufte Reihe der Thiere, den unreifen, mehr oder minder festsitzenden und Säfte saugenden Früchten des Baums gleiche, der Mensch aber den reifen, die auf dem Punkt der höchsten Vollendung sich von selbst ablösen.« (HN1 #74)

[127] Unser »empirisches, sinnliches, verständiges Bewußtseyn in Raum und Zeit« bildet das Reich von »Trug und Nacht« und ist »die verkehrte Richtung, von der Tugend und Asketik die Rückkehr und ein, in Folge dieser, seeliger Tod die Ablösung ist« (HN1 #79).

But as soon as we objectively *observe* the things of the world, i.e. *contemplate*, then for a moment subjectivity, and hence the source of all misery, has vanished. We are free, and the consciousness of the world of the senses stands before us as something strange and foreign which no longer torments us and is no longer an object of self-serving consideration within the nexus of space, time and causality. Rather, we see the Platonic Idea of the object. ... What remains after liberation from the temporal consciousness is the better, eternal consciousness.[128]

Schopenhauer criticized Schelling for having provided a mythological instead of a philosophical deduction of the world's suffering and evil. In his view it is a central task of philosophy to come to grips not only with the origin of evil and suffering but also with the possibility of their eradication. Schopenhauer's search is evident in the philosophical notes of 1812 where "self-will" (Eigenwillen) and "selfhood" are designated as the source of the totality of illusion and night (#28). The opposite pole is represented by their annihilation (HN2:349). One year later, in 1813, we have the "solely subjective interest of the sensual individual" and the entirely self-serving view of all things from the viewpoint of "the advantage and disadvantage of the subject" which forms "the source of all evil."[129] In the self-serving perspective typical of "empirical consciousness," we see in things nothing but "their relation to our individual self and its needs."[130]

---

[128] »Sobald wir aber dagegen die Dinge der Welt *objektiv betrachten*, d.h. *kontempliren*, ist für den Augenblick die *Subjektivität* und somit die Quelle alles Elends geschwunden, wir sind frei und das Bewußtsein der Sinnenwelt steht vor uns als ein fremdes uns nicht mehr Bedrängendes, auch nicht mehr in der für unser Individuum nützlichen Betrachtung des Nexus von Raum, Zeit und Kausalität, sondern wir sehn die Platonische Idee des Objekts. [...] Diese Befreiung vom Zeitlichen Bewußtseyn läßt das bessre ewige Bewußtseyn übrig.« (HN1 #86)

[129] »das blos subjektive Interesse des sinnlichen Individuums« und das exklusive, egoistische Betrachten aller Gegenstände in Hinsicht auf »das Wohl und Weh des Subjekts«, welches »die Quelle alles Uebels ist« (HN1 #86).

[130] Wir sehen in den Dingen nichts »als ihre Beziehung auf unser Individu-

Empirical and Better Consciousness

In the spring of 1814 the "basic error" and "all our sinfulness" is said to consist in our desire "to force eternity into the framework of time"[131] and in our greedy attempt to prolong temporal existence. Hence the will to live itself is moving into the cross hairs: "Life means to crave temporal existence and to continuously desire it."[132] Shortly afterwards it is indeed "life itself" that is identified as the fundamental error (#146), which is why radical therapy consists in letting go of the will to live (#158). Then, at the beginning of Schopenhauer's stay in Dresden in the summer of 1814, the foundation stone of Schopenhauer's metaphysics of will was finally laid: "That we *will* at all is our misfortune."[133] From that point on, neither this nor the opposing pole—liberation from willing "through better knowledge"—ever changed: Schopenhauer had found his philosophical bearing, and it is exactly at this point in time that he for the first time cited his favorite book, the *Oupnek'hat*: "Liberation from will ... through better consciousness."[134]

But we have gotten ahead of ourselves by more than a year. In 1812 and 1813 Schopenhauer was still preparing the ground for such later developments and was busy with the characterization of empirical and better consciousness. Among other things he associated empirical or temporal consciousness with the satisfaction of the sexual drive that he regarded as "the greatest affirmation of temporal consciousness;"[135] and the opposite pole, chastity, was seen as the first step toward asceticism.

The moral dimension of two-fold consciousness also gained profile: vice is the "negation of extratemporal consciousness"[136] (#88), and

---

um und dessen Bedürfnisse« (HN1 #86).

[131] »Der Grundirrthum« und »alle unsere Sündhaftigkeit« bestehen darin, dass wir »die Ewigkeit durch die Zeit ausmessen wollen« (HN1 #143).

[132] »Zeitliches Daseyn wollen und immerfort wollen ist Leben« (HN1 #143).

[133] »Daß wir überhaupt *wollen* ist unser Unglück« (HN1 #213).

[134] »Befreiung vom Wollen ... durch die bessre Erkenntniß« (HN1 #213).

[135] »Die größte Affirmation des zeitlichen Bewußtseyns« (HN1 #88).

[136] »Negation des außerzeitlichen Bewußtseyns« (HN1 #88).

better consciousness manifests itself in love / humaneness (#87) and asceticism (#88), both of which constitute merely different modes of selflessness. In this context Schopenhauer again refers to Jacob Böhme as witness:

> Jesus says: 'Blessed are the poor in spirit,' and Jacob Böhme says in magnificent and noble words: "He who is as free of own-will as a child in the mother's womb and lets his inner mainspring, whence man has emanated, guide and lead him: he is the noblest and wealthiest on earth.[137]

Just as every compass needle is a magnetic dipole, the better consciousness and its opposite pole, empirical consciousness, are also "knitted together into the identity of *a single* I."[138] As much as man's 'I' may long for liberation: originally and by nature it is chained to the opposite pole.

> With the empirical consciousness we necessarily have not only sinfulness, but also all the evils that follow from this kingdom of error, chance, wickedness and folly, and finally death. Death is, so to speak, a debt contracted through life, as are also the other evils [...]. Therefore through the fall of man, the Bible and Christianity rightly introduce into the world death and the distress and miseries of life.[139]

---

[137] »Jesus sagt ›seelig sind die armen am Geist.‹ Und Jakob Böhm sagt herrlich und erhaben: ›Der also stille lieget in eigenem Willen als ein Kind im Mutterleibe, und lässet sich seinen inwendigen Grund, daraus der Mensch entsprossen ist, leiten und führen: der ist der Edelste und Reicheste auf Erden.‹ 37stes Sendschreiben« (HN1 #87). In present-day editions this is found in Sendschreiben 41, paragraph 13.

[138] »in die Identität *Eines* Ichs verknüpft« (HN1 #99).

[139] »Mit dem empirischen Bewußtsein ist nicht nur Sündhaftigkeit, sondern auch alle Uebel die aus diesem Reich des Irrthums, des Zufalls, der Bosheit und Thorheit folgen, und endlich der Tod nothwendig gesetzt: der Tod ist gleichsam eine durch das Leben kontrahirte Schuld, die andern minder gewiß bestimmten Uebel eben so. ... Die Bibel und das Christenthum lassen daher mit Recht durch den Sündenfall den Tod in die Welt kommen und die Beschwerden und Noth des Lebens.« (HN1 #99)

Empirical and Better Consciousness

In thinking about the "two-fold nature of our consciousness" (#99), Schopenhauer conceived the role of aesthetics and ethics in terms of liberation from egocentricity. Better consciousness is activated in the "contemplation of objects that are called beautiful" and especially by music which, according to Schopenhauer, "most immediately stimulates the better consciousness but is also furthest removed from the empirical [consciousness]." As does the contemplation of nature and architecture, music "rescues us from subjectivity; but it achieves more and acts positively."[140] Whereas the artistic genius can in the act of creation only temporarily rise above the self-centeredness of empirical consciousness, the saint liberates himself permanently:

> In morality *better consciousness*, which lies *far above all reason*, expresses itself in conduct as saintliness, and is the true salvation of the world. This same consciousness expresses itself in art as genius, as a consolation for the temporal and earthly state.[141]

In the cited paragraph, Schopenhauer for the first time made use of the label "salvation" (Erlösung) for the destination or "N" pole of his compass. However, this was already implied in earlier notes, for example:

> In this temporal and sensuous world of our understanding there are indeed personality and causality; in fact they are even necessary.—The better consciousness in me lifts me into a world where there is no longer personality and causality nor subject and object. My hope and belief is that this better (suprasensory and extratemporal) consciousness will become my sole one, and for that reason I hope that it is no God.—But if anyone wants to use the

---

[140] »am unmittelbarsten das Bessre Bewußtseyn anregt, aber auch am fernsten vom Empirischen liegt«; die Musik »entreißt ... uns der Subjektivität: aber sie thut mehr und wirkt positiv (was wie gesagt auch jene thun)« (HN1 #86).

[141] »Im Moralischen spricht sich das *bessre Bewußtseyn* aus, das *hoch über alle Vernunft* liegt, sich im Handeln als Heiligkeit äußert, und die wahre Welterlösung ist: dasselbe äußert sich, zum Trost für die Zeitlichkeit, in der Kunst als Genie«. (HN1 #85)

term God symbolically for that better consciousness itself or for things he is unable to distinguish and name, so be it; but I should think this ought not to happen among philosophers.[142]

It is clear that Schopenhauer had experienced moments of such "better consciousness" in which the desiring subject together with its objects had vanished. He was no saint, yet as a philosopher he felt challenged to explain such experiences. What is the connection between this "better consciousness" and "empirical consciousness"—the sphere of personality, causality, subject and object? And how ought one to conceive the transition from empirical to better consciousness? Schopenhauer mused:

> The *change* of direction, the transition from the realm of darkness, of need, desire, illusion, of that which becomes but never is, to the kingdom of light, repose, joy, amiability, harmony and peace, is *infinitely difficult* and *infinitely easy*.—This realization forms the basis of the poem of the knight who is to enter a castle surrounded by a rapidly rotating wall with a single narrow gate in it. The valiant knight applies his spur, gives rein to his steed, and gallops full tilt straight ahead, his eyes closed—and breaks through the gate. This is the symbol of virtue, the path of light. To achieve the immensely difficult and impossible, we need only to *will*, but *will* we must.[143]

---

[142] »In dieser Zeitlichen, Sinnlichen, Verständlichen Welt giebt es wohl Persönlichkeit und Kausalität, ja sie sind sogar nothwendig.—Das bessre Bewusstseyn in mir erhebt mich in eine Welt wo es weder Persönlichkeit und Kausalität noch Subjekt und Objekt mehr giebt. Meine Hoffnung und mein Glaube ist daß dieses bessre (übersinnliche ausserzeitliche) Bewusstseyn mein einziges werden wird: darum hoffe ich es ist kein Gott.—Will man aber den Ausdruck Gott symbolisch gebrauchen für jenes bessre Bewußtseyn selbst, oder für manches das man nicht zu sondern und zu benennen weiß; so mags seyn: doch dächte ich nicht unter Philosophen.« (HN1 #81)

[143] »Das *Ändern* der Richtung, der Uebergang vom Reich der Finsterniß, des Bedürfnisses, Wunsches, der Täuschung, des Werdenden und nie Seyenden,—zum Reich des Lichts, der Ruhe, Freude, Lieblichkeit, Harmonie und Friedens ist *unendlich schwer* und *unendlich leicht*. — Diese Erkenntniß

Empirical and Better Consciousness

At a later point Schopenhauer added in the margins:

> To will! great word! Needle on the balance of the Last Judgment! Bridge between heaven and hell! The faculty of reason is not the light shining from heaven but only a signpost set up by ourselves that we direct toward the chosen goal so that it may indicate the direction when the goal itself is concealed. But one can just as easily point it toward hell as toward heaven.[144]

This view is still very different from Schopenhauer's later metaphysics of will where no such willful twisting of directionality is possible and where the *overcoming of all willing* forms the sole bridge to salvation. In the spring of 1813, reason was still called "the link between temporal and better consciousness."[145] At this point Schopenhauer still had not found the fundamental idea that would soon allow him to turn his twofold-consciousness framework into a unified philosophical system. But as he was searching for that bond between empirical and better consciousness he already felt pregnant with a system:

> Under my hands, or rather in my mind, a work, a philosophy is developing which is to be ethics and metaphysics in one. Hitherto these were as falsely separated as was man into body and soul. The work expands, and the parts take form slowly and by degrees like

---

hat der Dichtung zu Grunde gelegen, vom Ritter der in ein Schloß soll das eine Mauer mit einer einzigen engen Thür umgiebt, welche Mauer wirbelnd schnell sich dreht: der tapfre Ritter spornt das Roß, läßt den Zügel los, Kopf voran, Augen zu,— und sprengt die Pforte. Dies ist das Symbol der Tugend, des Wegs des Lichts; um das ungeheuer Schwere, Unmögliche zu vollenden, braucht man nur zu wollen, aber wollen muss man.« (HN1 #91)

[144] »Wollen! grosses Wort! Zunge in der Waage des Weltgerichts! Brücke zwischen Himmel und Hölle! Vernunft ist nicht das Licht das aus dem Himmel glänzt, sondern nur ein Wegweiser den wir selbst hinstellen[,] nach dem gewählten Ziel ihn richtend, dass er die Richtung zeige wenn das Ziel selbst sich verbirgt. Aber richten kann man ihn nach der Hölle wie nach dem Himmel.« (HN1 #91)

[145] Vernunft als »Band zwischen zeitlichem und bessern Bewußtseyn« (HN1 #91).

a child in the womb: I do not know which developed first and which last, just as happens with a child in its mother's womb.[146]

In the margins of his notebook he added:

> I am becoming aware of *one* limb, *one* blood vessel, *one* part after another, that is to say, I write things down without worrying how they will fit into the whole because I know that everything has sprung from a single foundation. This is how an organic whole is formed, and only such [an organic whole] can *live*.[147]

The bearing of Schopenhauer's compass had been set for a long time; now the task was to improve its philosophical understanding. At the end of his Fichte-related notes Schopenhauer had written that genuine criticism must "separate the better consciousness from the empirical one, just like gold from ore" and that this would allow to present the two in their pure form, as well as to separately "classify empirical consciousness according to its differences."[148] In 1813 he realized part of this endeavor in the form of his doctoral dissertation *On the Fourfold Root of the Principle of Sufficient Reason* (*Ueber die vierfache Wurzel des Satzes vom zureichenden Grunde*). This dissertation, which he submitted at the University of Jena in the fall of 1813, was a thin book that exclusively discussed the most fundamental law of human thinking and knowing: the principle of sufficient reason. What was at stake were

---

[146] »Unter meinen Händen und vielmehr in meinem Geiste erwächst ein Werk, eine Philosophie, die Ethik und Metaphysik in Einem seyn soll, da man sie bisher trennte so fälschlich als den Menschen in Seele und Körper. Das Werk wächst, concrescirt allmälig und langsam wie das Kind im Mutterleibe: ich weiß nicht was zuerst und was zulezt entstanden ist, wie beym Kind im Mutterleibe« (HN1 #92).

[147] »Ich werde *ein* Glied, *ein* Gefäß, *einen* Theil nach dem andern gewahr d.h. ich schreibe auf, unbekümmert wie es zum Ganzen passen wird: denn ich weiß es ist alles aus einem Grund entsprungen. So entsteht ein organisches Ganzes und nur ein solches kann *leben*.« (HN1 #92)

[148] »das beßre Bewußtseyn trennen von dem empirischen, wie das Gold aus dem Erz« ; »rein hinstellen« und »nach seinen Verschiedenheiten klassifiziren« (HN2:360).

thus the fundamental mechanisms of the sphere that Schopenhauer later called "the world as representation" (die Welt als Vorstellung).

> Our consciousness, insofar as it appears as sensuality, understanding and reason, is divided into subject and object and contains, up to that point, nothing else. To be an object for the subject and to be our representation [Vorstellung] signify the same thing. All our representations are objects of a subject, and all objects of the subject are our representations.[149]

While limiting the discussion to the world as representation did facilitate the relatively speedy redaction of the dissertation, it also had its price. Several times Schopenhauer almost apologizes for this and makes veiled references to a larger work:

> What the inner essence of the artist and of the saint is, and whether they could possibly be the same, are questions that cannot be discussed here since that would go against my intention of not touching upon questions of ethics and aesthetics in this treatise. However, this might at some point possibly become the topic of a larger work whose content, when compared to the present one, would be like the waking state compared to a dream.[150]

In order to avoid reducing his doctoral dissertation to the status of a dream, he immediately added the words of Seneca: *Somnia narrare vigilantis est* (Talking about dreams is something for those who are awake). The said "dream" is the world as representation (and thus the

---

[149] »Unser Bewußtseyn, so weit es als Sinnlichkeit, Verstand, Vernunft erscheint, zerfällt in Subjekt und Objekt, und enthält, bis dahin, nichts außerdem. Objekt für das Subjekt seyn, und unsre Vorstellung seyn, ist dasselbe. Alle unsre Vorstellungen sind Objekte des Subjekts, und alle Objekte des Subjekts sind unsere Vorstellungen« (SW7:18).

[150] »Was denn aber das innerste Wesen des Künstlers, das innerste Wesen des Heiligen sey, ob vielleicht eines und dasselbe—darüber mich hier auszulassen, wäre gegen meinen Vorsatz, das Ethische und Aesthetische in dieser Abhandlung nicht zu berühren. Vielleicht aber könnte mir jenes ein Mal Gegenstand einer größern Schrift werden, deren Inhalt sich zu dem der gegenwärtigen sich verhalten würde wie Wachen zum Traum.« (SW7:91)

realm of subject and object and the principle of sufficient reason), and it is the philosopher's task to account for it and to analyze it. But the dream and waking states are deeply connected and cannot be discussed discretely. Thus it was inevitable that some content of the mentioned "larger work" would get mentioned. This larger work would treat of "the best within man, that is to say, that which appears like a solid body, while in comparison the entire rest of the world resembles a shadow in a dream."[151] Schopenhauer explained that his dissertation can be likened to an anatomical preparation of a single body part featuring "spots where it is severed from other portions of the whole, of which it necessarily forms part," and where "the natural connection is forcibly and arbitrarily removed."[152]

What did Schopenhauer at that time regard as "the whole"? On the basis of his notes it is extremely likely that already in 1813 he discerned the outlines of a system in which better consciousness and the awakening after the dream set the tone. But in his dissertation Schopenhauer decided to focus on a single aspect: the fundamental structure and mechanisms of subject-object-based knowledge. While parts of the dissertation were of course used and discussed in the first book of Schopenhauer's major work, the junctures are of particular interest for our study of the genesis of his metaphysics of will.

One such juncture plays an important role in system genesis and concerns Schopenhauer's view of the body. "Only *one* object is *immediately* given to us: our own body."[153] This "un-mediated object" is mentioned several times in his dissertation, for example in the discussion of feelings: "The immediate object of willing and of cognition, the body, is almost constantly affected by them [the motives], and bodily feelings

---

[151] »das Beste im Menschen, ja dasjenige wogegen die ganze übrige Welt sich verhält wie ein Schatten im Traum zum wirklichen, soliden Körper« SW7:84).

[152] »wo sie von andern Theilen des Ganzen zu dem sie nothwendig gehört, abgeschnitten und der natürliche Zusammenhang durch bloße Willkühr gewaltsam aufgehoben ist« (SW7:84).

[153] »Nur *ein* Objekt ist uns *unmittelbar* gegeben, der eigne Leib.« (SW7:36)

accompany them and mix with them."¹⁵⁴ This statement is found in the last part of the dissertation which discusses "the immediate object of the inner sense, the subject of the will."¹⁵⁵ Even though being a subject signifies "nothing other than cognizing," and being an object means "being cognized,"¹⁵⁶ our "I" not only knows but also wills. This points to the second important cut of Schopenhauer's dissertation preparation.

> The identity of the subject of willing with that of knowing, based on which [identity] the word 'I' (necessarily) includes and signifies both, is totally inconceivable because only relations of objects are conceivable. ... But since what is at issue here is the subject, the rules determining the knowledge of objects no longer apply since an actual identity of the knowing [subject] with what is known as willing, i.e. of the subject and the object, is *immediately given*. Those who properly envisage the inconceivability of this identity will call it, as I do, the miracle κατ' εξοχην [par excellence].¹⁵⁷

The human body as immediate object and this inconceivable identity of the willing and knowing "I" were bound to play a central role in the construction of Schopenhauer's system. They constitute two "im-

---

¹⁵⁴ »Das unmittelbare Objekt des Wollens, wie des Erkennens, der Leib, wird fast immer von ihnen [den Motiven] affiziert und körperliche Gefühle begleiten sie und vermischen sich mit ihnen.« (SW7:77)

¹⁵⁵ »das unmittelbare Objekt des innern Sinnes, das Subjekt des Willens« (SW7:68).

¹⁵⁶ »weiter nichts als Erkennen« ; »nichts weiter als Erkanntwerden« (SW7:69).

¹⁵⁷ »Die Identität aber des Subjekts des Wollens mit dem erkennenden Subjekt, vermöge welcher (und zwar nothwendig) das Wort ›Ich‹ beide einschließt und bezeichnet, ist schlechthin unbegreiflich. Denn nur die Verhältnisse der Objekte sind begreiflich ... Hier aber, wo vom Subjekt die Rede ist, gelten die Regeln für das Erkennen der Objekte nicht mehr und eine wirkliche Identität des Erkennenden mit dem als wollend Erkannten, also des Subjekts mit dem Objekt, ist *unmittelbar gegeben*. Wer aber das Unbegreifliche dieser Identität sich recht vergegenwärtigt, wird sie mit mir das Wunder κατ' εξοχην nennen.« (SW7:72–3)

mediate" facts, which also means that each in its own way transcends the framework of the world as representation. The origin of such willing could not be discerned in that subject-object framework, which is why Schopenhauer wrote of a "universal act of will":

> Maybe I explain what I mean better, though more metaphorically, if I call it an a-temporal universal act of will of which all temporal acts are only the emergence or appearance. Kant called this the *intelligible character* (which should probably be called 'unintelligible', and on pp. 560–586 of the *Critique of Pure Reason* he offers a discussion of the difference between the intelligible character and the empirical character as well as of the entire relationship of freedom and nature. I regard this discussion as a most admirable, unequalled masterpiece of profound human thoughtfulness. In the first volume of his writings, pp. 465–473, Schelling gave a very valuable account and explanation of it.[158]

Such junctures in Schopenhauer's dissertation point in two major directions. Those concerning the "innermost essence of the artist and the saint" (which "possibly are one and the same" SW7:91) point toward the pole of salvation and thus toward the third and fourth book of Schopenhauer's main work. Schopenhauer saw their common denominator in better consciousness and specifically in temporary or permanent selflessness. In the opposite direction, the possibility of empirical consciousness with its subject-object matrix and the "intelligible character" were waiting to be explained. This investigation later formed the

---

[158] »Vielleicht bezeichne ich das Gemeinte besser, obwohl auch bildlich, wenn ich es einen außer der Zeit liegenden universalen Willensakt nenne, von dem alle in der Zeit vorkommenden Akte nur das Heraustreten, die Erscheinung sind. Kant hat dieses den *intelligiblen Karakter* genannt (vielleicht hieße es richtiger der inintelligible) und von dem Unterschied zwischen ihm und dem *empirischen*, wie auch vom ganzen Verhältniß der Freiheit zur Natur, in der Kritik der reinen Vernunft pp. 560–586, eine Auseinandersetzung gegeben, die ich für ein unvergleichliches, höchst bewundrungswerthes Meisterstück des menschlichen Tiefsinns halte. Schelling hat im ersten Bande seiner Schriften, pp. 465–473 eine sehr schätzbare erläuternde Darstellung davon gegeben.« (SW7:76–7)

content of the first and second book of Schopenhauer's *The World as Will and Representation*. As Schopenhauer remarked, Kant might well have spoken of the "unintelligible character" because what is meant here is exactly what accounts for the possibility of subject- and objecthood and thus lies beyond "consciousness caught up in subject-and-object" (SW7:92) and consequently beyond any representation. It is this ground of the willing-knowing "I" that Schopenhauer in his dissertation called "a universal act of will outside of time."[159] Already around the end of 1811 he had noticed that Schelling's book about freedom was in substance a reformulation of Böhme's *Mysterium magnum* (HN2:314), and his reference to Schelling regarding the "universal act of will" also applied to Böhme. In the presentation that Schopenhauer called "very valuable," Schelling based everything on an "original and basic willing" (Ur- und Grundwollen) and wrote:

> The I, says Fichte, is its own act (Tat), and consciousness is self-positing—but the I is not something different from this but rather consists in the very positing of oneself (Selbstsetzen). But this consciousness, insofar as it is conceived only as a grasping or cognition of the I, is not what is primary because it already presupposes, like all mere knowledge, Being in its proper sense. But this Being that is supposedly prior to knowledge is as little being as it is knowledge. It is an actual self-positing, an original and basic willing [Ur- und Grundwollen] that turns itself into something and forms the ground and basis of any essential entity [Wesenheit].[160]

---

[159] »einen außer der Zeit liegenden universalen Willensakt« bezeichnete (SW7:76).

[160] »Das Ich, sagt Fichte, ist seine eigne That; Bewußtseyn ist Selbstsetzen—aber das Ich ist nichts von diesem verschiedenes, sondern eben das Selbstsetzen selber. Dieses Bewußtseyn aber, inwiefern es bloß als Selbst-Erfassen, oder Erkennen des Ich gedacht wird, ist nicht einmal das erste, und setzt wie alles bloße Erkennen das eigentliche Seyn schon voraus. Dieses vor dem Erkennen vermuthete Seyn ist aber kein Seyn, wenn es gleich kein Erkennen ist; es ist reales Selbstsetzen, es ist ein Ur- und Grundwollen, das sich selbst zu

CHAPTER FOUR

From this perspective the knowing and willing "I" (the discussion of whose identity was the topic of Schopenhauer's reflection) is in reality nothing but an expression of this "original and basic willing" beyond all being and knowing: a fundamental willing that "turns itself into something."[161] The objectification process of this basic willing forms the central theme of Schelling's book and also, as Schopenhauer well knew, of Jacob Böhme's *Mysterium magnum*. In Schelling's words:

> In the ultimate and highest instance there is no other being at all than willing. Willing is original being [Urseyn], and to it alone apply all the predicates that characterize it: groundlessness, eternity, independence of time, self-affirmation. All of philosophy aims at nothing other than to find this supreme expression.[162]

Though philosophy may also have other aims, this statement certainly rings true for Schelling, Schopenhauer, and their mentor Jacob Böhme. Their compasses had a remarkably similar bearing. Apart from their ideas about a "fundamental willing" (Grundwollen) they were quite in accord about the path to salvation. On one of Schelling's pages that was praised by Schopenhauer one reads that man, "caught in I-ness and egotism," committed an "original sin."[163] Schelling held that this "somber principle of selfhood and own-will," the "hunger of egotism," and the "misuse of own-will that was elevated to selfhood (Selbstseyn)"[164] can be overcome by way of "the true death of own-

---

Etwas macht und der Grund und die Basis aller Wesenheit ist.« (Schelling 1809:467–8)

[161] Ein »Ur- und Grundwollens« das »sich selbst zu etwas macht«. (Schelling 1809:468)

[162] »Es giebt in der letzten und höchsten Instanz gar kein andres Seyn als Wollen. Wollen ist Urseyn und auf dieses allein passen alle Prädikate desselben: Grundlosigkeit, Ewigkeit, Unabhängigkeit von der Zeit, Selbstbejahung. Die ganze Philosophie strebt nur dahin, diesen höchsten Ausdruck zu finden.« (Schelling 1809:419)

[163] »in der Eigenheit und Selbstsucht ergriffen« ; »ursprüngliche Sünde« (Schelling 1809:471–2).

[164] Das »finstre Prinzip der Selbstheit und des Eigenwillens« (Schelling

being [Eigenheit] through which all human will must pass as through a fire in order to be purified."[165]

In spite of the deliberate limitation to the structural laws of empirical consciousness, Schopenhauer's dissertation must be seen in the context of his compass. It forms part of a larger project aiming at the separation of the gold of better consciousness from the ore of empirical consciousness, and at the analysis and classification of the latter (HN2:360). But the inexplicable identity of the knowing and willing subject made the difficulty of this task paradigmatically apparent. Schelling's and Böhme's "original willing" and Kant's "intelligible character" seemed to point to an "original ground [Urgrund] or rather non-ground [Ungrund]" prior to any duality (Schelling 1809:497) that resists all classification. How is it at all possible to gain philosophical access to this "original willing" or "non-ground," the very condition of possibility of all thinking and being? The answer may lie not in the "yonder" but in the most immediate "hither." As the junctures at crucial places of Schopenhauer's dissertation show, the needle of his compass already pointed toward the entirely incomprehensible being that holds the compass in his hand—the willing and knowing I—and its equally singular "immediate object": the body. But the developments of 1814 were also influenced by other factors to which we will turn in the following chapters.

1809:474); der »Hunger der Selbstsucht« (p. 475); der »Misbrauch des zum Selbstseyn erhobenen Eigenwillens« (p. 476).

[165] Mittels »des wirklichen Absterbens der Eigenheit, durch welches aller menschliche Wille als ein Feuer hindurchgehen muss, um geläutert zu werden«. (Schelling 1809: 463)

5. Multiplicity and Oneness

When the young doctor of philosophy Arthur Schopenhauer returned to Weimar at the end of 1813, the ghost of Benedict Spinoza (1632–1677) still haunted its narrow lanes. In 1785, Friedrich Heinrich Jacobi's (1743–1819) letters about Spinoza had attracted renewed attention to the Dutch thinker and his attempt to prove the Oneness of everything, which he called "God." All things that appear to be separate, and even we who observe them, are only modalities of the One. In his letters, Jacobi had revealed that Gotthold Ephraim Lessing (1729–1781) was a believer in this doctrine of All-Oneness. In his talks about God of 1787, J. G. Herder (1744–1803) defended Spinoza against Jacobi's attacks, and after Goethe seconded Herder the small town of Weimar became the cradle of a "Spinoza Renaissance" (Timm 1974) that involved a surprising number of people. Goethe, the poets' king, not only called the ill-reputed Spinoza his favorite philosopher but even hailed him as "the most theistic and most Christian"

CHAPTER FIVE

(*theissimus* and *christianissimus*). The "One-and-All" (*hen kai pan*) of Lessing's Spinozism led to an "enthusiastic faith in the unified ground of spirit and nature, individuality and totality;" and for a while Herder's and Goethe's Weimar wallowed in the amalgamation of "God = nature = life = love = fate = beauty" (p. 275). Pierre Bayle's and Jacobi's "Maledictus" Spinoza, the proverbial atheist or pantheist, was rechristened "Benedictus" Spinoza. Around this time the polarity of the magnet became a symbol for a main characteristic of Neo-Spinozism: the link of repulsion and attraction, expansion and contraction, extraversion and introversion, multiplicity and oneness, selfhood and liberation from self. The oneness of opposites, the unfolding of God in creation etc. were of course old themes of mystics such as Nicolaus of Cusa (1401–1464) and Jacob Böhme (1575–1624). But now such linked opposites were also discovered in phenomena such as electricity, galvanism, and magnetism.

A second major characteristic of German Neospinozism was the notion of the tiered character of beings (p. 288). One of its echoes in Weimar was Goethe's idea of an original plant (Urpflanze) that exemplified Spinoza's "modifications" of the One. The theme was eminently metaphysical since it turned around the question why there are beings at all and not rather nothing. How could the multiplicity of our world arise out of oneness? Is such multiplicity possibly only an illusion of man who, from sexual desire to the most devout religiosity, seems to seek nothing other than union and return to unity? Such questions were posed, for example by the Dutch Platonist François Hemsterhuis (1721–1790) whose *Lettre sur les désirs* (Letter about desires) was translated by one of the fathers of German Neospinozism, Herder, who commented on it in *Love and Selfhood* (Herder 1781).[166] The question of desire and the origin of multiplicity involved, as Timm noted, also that about the origin of evil: "Who has unfolded the cosmos and imposed on it the forced separation and mutually conflicting selfhood of

---

[166] Schopenhauer borrowed the two volumes of Hemsterhuis's philosophical works (in French) from the Dresden library in the second half of July, 1814.

multiple individualities? Unde malum [whence evil]?"[167] For Hemsterhuis, the buck stopped with God: "By nature everything strives for unity. An external force has thus separated the unity of the whole into particularities, and this force is God. The attempt to penetrate to the essence of this inconceivable being would constitute the most extravagant folly."[168]

Jacob Böhme had engaged in precisely this kind of folly, and one more look at Schelling will show that such folly was not only flourishing among romantic poets like Novalis and Zacharias Werner but also in the garden of German philosophy. In the *Bruno* dialogues of 1802, which Schopenhauer had read and commented upon in 1811 in Berlin, Schelling extended his doctrine of science in direction of the "absolute" by adopting Spinoza's philosophy. In his eyes, Plato's *Timaeus* and Giordano Bruno had presented an attractive conceptual model for All-Oneness: the world as a single organism. In *Bruno*, Schelling discussed on this backdrop the question "how the finite could emerge from the infinite."[169] The supreme oneness from which everything emerges is called "sacred abyss" (heiliger Abgrund; p. 66) and Schelling invokes the oneness of the world-organism: "You will thus refrain from entertaining the notion that individual things, the manifold forms of living beings, or whatever else it is that you distinguish, are really contained in the universe as separate unities by and for themselves in the manner that you see them."[170] According to Schelling there is only a single for-

---

[167] »Wer hat den Kosmos gespannt, ihm die zwangshafte Trennung, die widerständige Selbstheit der mannigfachen Individualitäten auferlegt? Unde malum?« (Timm 1974:292)

[168] »Alles strebt seiner Natur nach zur Einheit. Eine fremde Kraft also hat die Einheit des Ganzen in Einzelheiten zerlegt, und diese Kraft ist Gott. Bis zu dem Wesen dieses unbegreiflichen Wesens hindringen zu wollen, wäre der ausschweifendste Wahnsinn.« (Timm 1974:292)

[169] »wie das Endliche aus dem Unendlichen heraustritt« (Schelling 1834:65).

[170] »Du wirst also nicht glauben, daß die einzelnen Dinge, die vielfältigen Gestalten der lebenden Wesen, oder was du sonst unterscheidest, wirklich so getrennt, als du sie erblickst, im Universum an und für sich selbst erhalten seyen.« (Schelling 1834:68)

mula for knowing all beings from stones to animals and humans: the understanding of the connection between the infinite and the finite. In his view the sole entrance gate to such knowledge lies in the mirroring of the infinite in the 'I':

> *Bruno*: The infinite thus awakens to the infinite; and how, in your opinion, does this awakening of the infinite to itself express itself? Is there a word for it?
> *Lucian*: I.
> *Bruno*: You named the concept through which, as if by a magic spell, the entire world opens up.[171]

The 'I' is the place "where the finite enters into oneness and, as it were, into the immediate community with the infinite."[172] In the parts of *Bruno* that according to Schopenhauer represent the "core of Schelling's doctrine," Schelling associated the phenomenal world of "relative I-ness" with "relative truths" and "relative knowledge." The opposite pole was formed by absolute I-ness or intuitive vision (intellektuelle Anschauung):

> *Bruno*: However, in absolute I-ness or intuitive vision things are not qualified according to their appearance, even if it is infinite, but rather according to their eternal character or as they are in themselves. What is generated is absolute knowledge.[173]

---

[171] »*Bruno*: Das Unendliche kommt also zu dem Unendlichen, und wie denkst du nun, daß dieses zu sich selber Kommen des Unendlichen sich ausspreche, oder welcher Ausdruck dafür sei?
Lucian: Ich.
Bruno: Du hast den Begriff genannt, mit dem als einem Zauberschlag die Welt sich öffnet. «(Schelling 1834:111–2)

[172] »wo das Endliche in die Einheit und gleichsam die unmittelbare Gemeinschaft mit dem Unendlichen tritt« (Schelling 1834: 113).

[173] »*Bruno*: In der absoluten Ichheit aber, oder in der intellektuellen Anschauung werden die Dinge nicht für die Erscheinung, obzwar unendlich, sondern dem ewigen Charakter nach, oder wie sie an sich sind, bestimmt. Es entsteht absolutes Wissen.« (Schelling 1834:168)

Through the "absolute knowledge" of intuitive vision, the true essence of the universe is recognized: the things "as they are in themselves," in their fundamental oneness. By contrast, relative knowledge is only able to grasp objects as phenomenal appearances or representations in multiplicity. The similitude to Schopenhauer's "empirical consciousness" (which is also bound to the world of subject and object and hence of multiplicity) and his "better consciousness" (where even the most basic duality of subject and object vanishes) is obvious.

In *Philosophy and Religion* of 1804, studied by Schopenhauer in early 1812, Schelling further explained this view and skillfully combined Platonism, Kant, and Spinoza with elements of Jacob Böhme. Schopenhauer's notes from his first philosophy course in early 1811 prove that Professor Schulze took pains to explain how deeply Platonism and Neoplatonism had influenced Fichte and Schelling. He discussed, for example, their dependence with regard to the true character of the world and its relationship with God. Already the Neoplatonics, he explained, had reached views like Fichte's and Schelling's through "the intuitive vision (intellektuelle Anschauung) of the One, Supreme, First Original Being."[174] In this respect Schulze regarded their teachings not as new but rather "as old as mysticism." Furthermore, according to Schulze, Fichte and Schelling posited this One as "the supreme basis of truth," claimed that it could exclusively be known "in the realm of inner feeling," and regarded it as "the source of supreme knowledge."[175] Here, too, Schulze detected a link to Neoplatonism. In the course of his explanations about Neoplatonic philosophy and major figures like Ammonius Saccas and his disciple Plotinus, Schulze often referred to his own main source: the volume about Neoplatonism by the historian of philosophy Tennemann (published in 1807).[176]

---

[174] »intellektuelle Anschauung des Einen, Höchsten, Ersten Urseyns« (HNB2:100v).

[175] »als höchsten Wahrheitsgrund«; »in der Region des innern Gefühls«; »die Quelle der höchsten Erkenntniß« (HNB2:100v-101r).

[176] Schopenhauer had already borrowed Tennemann's *Geschichte der Philosophie* (History of Philosophy) in the fall of 1810; it was through the first and second

CHAPTER FIVE

In that volume Tennemann explained some of the central traits of Neoplatonism, a movement that began to spread around the Mediterranean in the third century of the common era and counted Plotinus (c. 204–270) and Proclus (412–485) among its noted representatives. With the Neoplatonics, "the summit of speculation, the infinite and absolute" had become "almost the sole objective of philosophizing":

> They believed that this original being (Urwesen) could only be truly known when such knowledge was gained directly from it, when the act of knowing and its object coincide, or when their identity and non-difference are recognized. *Oneness of knowing and known established through immediate vision*: this was the highest summit that speculation could ever attain.[177]

---

volume of this work that he was introduced to early Greek and Platonic philosophy. In the second volume, which mainly discusses Socrates and Plato, the young man read in the chapter »Dinge an sich und Erscheinungen« (Things-in-themselves and Representations) that Plato clearly distinguished these two things. According to Tennemann, Plato's "thing-in-itself is not an object of perception, not in space, not composite, and indestructible" (Platos »Ding an sich [ist] kein Gegenstand der Anschauung, nicht im Raume, nicht zusammengesetzt, nicht veränderlich, nicht zerstörbar«). Tennemann argues that this signifies that "the thing-in-itself is characterized by unity, totality, and absolute being at all times" (»dem Dinge an sich [kommt] Einheit, Totalität, absolutes Seyn zu aller Zeit [zu]«, Tennemann 1799:365–6). On the other hand, representation (Erscheinung) signifies "the thing insofar as it is seen and perceived" and is "mutable" (»das Ding, insofern es angeschauet und wahrgenommen wird. Es ist veränderlich«, p. 367). Plato is said to regard the "mutable" merely as an "image of the immutable" (»Bild von dem Unveränderlichen«, p. 368) because "the things-in-themselves, i.e., the divine ideas, constitute the intelligible world (*noêtos topos*), the archetype of the actual world (»Dinge an sich, das ist, die göttlichen Ideen machen die intelligibele Welt [*noêtos topos*] aus, das Archetypon der wirklichen Welt«, p. 372).

[177] »Man glaubte nur dann dieses Urwesen mit Wahrheit erkannt zu haben, wenn die Erkenntniß desselben aus ihm selbst geschöpft sey, der Erkenntnißact und das Object sich berührten, oder beide in ihrer Identität und Indifferenz erkannt würden. *Einheit des Erkennens und des Erkannten durch unmittelbare Anschauung gegeben*, dies war der höchste Punct auf welchen sich die Speculation nur immer schwingen ließe.« (Tennemann 1799:386)

Multiplicity and Oneness

It is obvious why both Schulze and Tennemann associated Fichte and Schelling with the Neoplatonics: their "intuitive vision" (intellektuelle Anschauung) resembled the Neoplatonic summit of ecstatic vision all too much. Tennemann even used the same term: "Even Plotinus, who sought the absolute via thinking, held that the absolute shows itself immediately to the soul through intuitive vision [intellektuelle Anschauung]."[178] All Neoplatonics sought "the being that is the ground of all being ... a being whose existence does not presuppose anything but is presupposed by all that is."[179] This could not possibly be anything composite; hence they "sought the absolute oneness in all that is composite, namely, that which is to things what the unit of one is to all numbers."[180]

Recent research on Platonism has identified such aspects of Neoplatonism as central elements of Plato's "unwritten teaching." Though research on Neoplatonism was in Tennemann's time still in its beginning stages, Plotinus was already studied by Goethe, translated by Creuzer, and quoted by Schelling. Tennemann analyzed, among other things, the differences between Plotinus and Proclus and came to the conclusion that Plotinus was content "to posit this Oneness as the first principle," whereas Proclus also wrote about "multiplicity and the connection between oneness and multiplicity."[181] Precisely this connection, so central for Schelling's thought, formed a major concern of Neoplatonism.

---

[178] »selbst Plotin, welcher das Absolute durch das Denken suchte, nahm doch an, daß das Absolute unmittelbar durch eine intellectuelle Anschauung sich der Seele darstelle.« (Tennemann 1799:387)

[179] »dasjenige Wesen, dessen Seyn der Grund alles Seyns ist ... ein Wesen, welches zu seinem Seyn nichts anderes voraussetzt, aber von allem, was ist, vorausgesetzt wird.« (Tennemann 1799:387–8)

[180] »nichts Zusammengesetztes seyn; man suchte also die absolute Einheit zu allem Zusammengesetzten, welches sich zu den Dingen verhielt, wie die Einheit zu allen möglichen Zahlen.« (Tennemann 1799:388)

[181] »diese Einheit als Urprincip aufzustellen«; »Mannigfaltigkeit und Verbindung der Einheit mit der Mannigfaltigkeit.« (Tennemann 1799:388)

Tennemann wrote: "What preoccupied them most was the attempt to deduce all things from absolute oneness and unitary original being."[182]

This was also the central theme of Schelling's book *Philosophie und Religion*. Like some Neoplatonics, he held that the absolute objectified itself in different levels. The first step consists in the "self-objectification of the absolute within itself."[183] However, "the absolute would not really become an object if it did not transmit the power to convert its ideal nature and to objectify it in particular forms. This second production is that of the ideas."[184] The third step of this "continuing subject-objectification" (Subject-Objectivirung) results in "the entire absolute world with all its gradations of beings" that in reality constitute "nothing that is truly diverse."[185] Schelling's three-step scheme as well as his view of All-Oneness is congruent with the dominant view of Neoplatonism. We will see that in the course of 1814 Schopenhauer developed a similar vision of objectifications of the One on different levels, where Platonic ideas also formed an intermediary between oneness and multiplicity.

All systems that postulate fundamental oneness in the manner of the Neoplatonics and Schelling need to offer an explanation for the emergence of the many from the one. Schelling classified such attempts into three categories. The most frequently used and also oldest method is that of *emanation*. According to Schelling the emanation theory holds that "emissions from the divinity lose their divine perfection by degrees in proportion to their distance from the original source, and are in the

---

[182] »Am meisten beschäftigte die Köpfe der Versuch, aus dem absolut Einen und einfachen Urwesen alle Dinge abzuleiten.« (Tennemann 1799: 389)

[183] »Selbstobjectivirung des Absoluten ... in sich selbst« (Schelling 1804:29).

[184] Das »Absolute würde in dem Realen nicht wahrhaft objectiv, theilte es ihm nicht die Macht mit, gleich ihm seine Idealität umzuwandeln und sie in besonderen Formen zu objectiviren. Dieses zweyte Produciren ist das der Ideen« (Schelling 1804:29).

[185] »fortgesetzte Subject-Objectivirung«; »die ganze absolute Welt, mit allen Abstufungen der Wesen« enthält »nichts wahrhaft Besonderes« (Schelling 1804:30).

end transformed into the opposite (matter, privation)."[186] Schelling regarded this as a mistaken explanation; but at least it did not slander God by portraying him as the creator of evil. Schelling noted that this wrong notion underlies the emanation theory of some Platonics.

The second method to let the Many emerge from the One is, according to Schelling, *dualism*—for instance that of the ancient Persian religion which features two original beings fighting each other. In Schelling's eyes this approach necessarily "turned God into the author of evil" (Urheber des Bösen) and was therefore so false a notion that he immediately dismissed it (p. 34).

The third and, in Schelling's eyes, solely correct explanation of the link between oneness and multiplicity is that of a *fall*. It rejects a gradual transition "from the absolute to the real" and instead holds that there was "a total break ... by a leap."[187] According to Schelling, "the absolute is the only reality" and "finite things, by contrast, are not real;" thus he held that this leap from the reality of all-oneness to the illusion of multiplicity can only be interpreted as "a *fall* from the absolute."[188] Schelling emphasized that this doctrine, which he called "as clear and simple as it is sublime," is "also the genuinely platonic one" because Plato had the soul drop from its original beatitude "by a fall from the original image" (Urbild) whereby it was "born into the temporal universe."[189] In his view it was Plato's "practical teaching that the soul, the fallen divine element in man, must be purified and as much as possible freed from

---

[186] »Ausflüsse der Gottheit, in allmäliger Abstufung und Entfernung von der Urquelle, die göttliche Vollkommenheit verlieren und so zuletzt in das Entgegengesetzte (die Materie, die Privation) übergehen« (Schelling 1804:30–1).

[187] »vom Absoluten zum Wirklichen« »ein vollkommnes Abbrechen ... durch einen Sprung« (Schelling 1804: 34).

[188] »Das Absolute ist das einzige Reale, die endlichen Dinge dagegen sind nicht real«, und der Sprung von dieser Realität der Einheit in die Illusion der Vielheit kann nur »in einem *Abfall* von dem Absoluten liegen« (Schelling 1804:35).

[189] »durch den Abfall vom Urbild«; »in das zeitliche Universum gebohren werden« (Schelling 1804:35).

its link and communion with the body in order to regain the absolute and the vision of the original image (Urbild) through mortification of sensuality."[190]

For Schelling, asceticism thus has a platonic basis. The unfolding by stages of the one into the many featuring Platonic ideas as intermediary, the illusory multiplicity of the phenomenal world following the fall, and of course the return to oneness through asceticism and ecstatic vision are all elements that link the Neoplatonics and their heirs among the Christian mystics to thinkers of all-oneness like Giordano Bruno and German idealists including Schelling. We will soon see that both Prince Dara Shukoh (1615–1659), the translator of the *Oupnek'hat*, and its reader Schopenhauer also form part of this extremely widespread neoplatonic tradition whose two major branches extended from the Mediterranean sea north- and westward to Christian Europe and eastward via the heartland of Islam to Persia and India. Though the terminology differs—Dara' calls his all-oneness "Allah" or "Brahman" and Schopenhauer "Wille," and their fall into illusory multiplicity *maya* and *principium individuationis*—the main elements of this tradition (including the possibility of salvation through a kind of awakening to all-oneness and the shedding of individuality with its illusion of multiplicity) are present. And was not exactly this also the essence of Zacharias Werner's injunction to "become again nothing and everything" and of the core teaching of his brotherhood: "All is you / When you are everything rather than something"?[191]

Schelling's "fall" led from the "realm of reality" (Reich der Realität) to the "realm of nihility" (Reich des Nichts) and from the true world

---

[190] Plato's »practische Lehre, welche darin bestand, daß die Seele, das gefallene Göttliche im Menschen, so viel wie möglich von der Beziehung und Gemeinschaft des Leibes abgezogen und gereiniget werden müsse, um so, indem sie dem Sinnenleben abstere, das Absolute wieder zu gewinnen und der Anschauung des Urbildes wieder theilhaftig zu werden« (Schelling 1804:36).

[191] »auf dass du werdest wieder Nichts und Alles« (Werner 1823:2.265) und seiner Erkenntnis: »Alles bist du selber, / Wenn du Alles bist, nicht Etwas« (Schelling 1804:271).

to a mere "mirage" (Scheinbild) because in fallen man "the nihility (Nichts) of sensual things gets produced."[192] The result of this process is the mirage of a universe perceived by the senses and an "illusory life."[193] With regard to the reason for this "fall," Schelling had recourse not only to Plato and Böhme but also to Fichte.

> Fichte says: I-ness is only *its own act*, its own activity, and apart from this activity it is *nothing* ... This *nihility* of I-ness taken as the principle of the world is a pure expression of the age-old doctrine of genuine philosophy.[194]

The fall, which produces the mirage of a universe perceived by the senses and characterized by multiplicity, is the fall into I-ness (Ichheit); and the relinquishing of such I-ness—or, as Zacharias Werner put it inspired by Madame Guyon, its "crucifixion" and "putrefaction"—is the home-coming to Oneness. In Schelling's words:

> Only by the casting off of selfhood and the return to ideal Oneness is it once more capable of seeing the divine, and producing what is absolute.[195]

This is the "old, sacred teaching" which—according to Schelling—cuts in one fell swoop through all the millennia-old doubts of philosophers and had found expression in Plato's myth of the souls forced to "descend from the spiritual world into the world of senses where they, as

---

[192] »Fall« oder »Abfall« vom »Reiche der Realität« ins »Reich des Nichts« (Schelling 1804:42); »durch und für sich selbst das Nichts der sinnlichen Dinge producirt« (Schelling 1804:38).

[193] »Scheinleben« (Schelling 1804:40).

[194] »Fichte sagt: die Ichheit ist nur *ihre eigene That,* ihr eignes Handeln, sie ist *nichts* abgesehen von diesem Handeln ... Wie rein spricht sich die uralte Lehre der ächten Philosophie in diesem zum Princp der Welt gemachten *Nichts* der Ichheit aus« (Schelling 1804:43).

[195] »Nur durch die Ablegung der Selbstheit und die Rückkehr in ihre ideale Einheit, gelangt sie wieder dazu, Göttliches anzuschauen, und Absolutes zu produciren« (Schelling 1804: 44).

CHAPTER FIVE

punishment for their selfhood," are imprisoned in a body and must strive to regain the lost Oneness.[196]

Schelling summarized his view in three points:
1. His philosophy of nature "expresses in the clearest fashion the unreality of the entire phenomenal world"
2. it teaches a strict separation between the "world as it appears" and the "world as it really is"
3. it "consistently holds and explains that *I-ness* (Ichheit) is the actual point of separation and transition between particular forms and Oneness, and [that *I-ness* is] the real principle of finiteness."[197]

In his *Inquiries on Freedom* of 1809, which Schopenhauer also studied in the winter of 1811/12, Schelling criticized Spinoza's teaching of All-Oneness on account of its "abstract conception of the essence of the world." In addition, he felt that the entire system lacked life and treated even "will as a thing"[198]—a critique that Schopenhauer also adopted. In Schelling's view, Spinoza had created "a one-sidedly realistic system" whose basic conception was in need of being modified and completed. This was the task Schelling set for himself in his treatise about freedom. However, as Schopenhauer immediately noticed, Schelling's

---

[196] »alte, heilige Lehre«; »daß die Seelen aus der Intellectualwelt in die Sinnenwelt herabsteigen, wo sie zur Strafe ihrer Selbstheit und einer diesem Leben (der Idee, nicht der Zeit nach) vorhergegangenen Schuld an den Leib, wie an einen Kerker sich gefesselt finden« und zurückstreben müssen zur verlorenen Einheit (Schelling 1804:49).

[197] 1. »die absolute Nicht-Realität der gesammten Erscheinung«; 2. »erscheinende Welt« und »schlechthin-reale Welt«; 3. »die *Ichheit* als der eigentliche Absonderungs- und Uebergangspunct der besondern Formen aus der Einheit, als das wahre Princip der Endlichkeit aufgestellt und von ihr dargethan« (Schelling 1804: 52–3).
The similarity of Schelling's three main doctrines to Schopenhauer's later philosopy (in particular, the first and second book of his major work) is evident. Under the influence of the *Oupnek'hat* and the *Asiatick Researches*, the third point was to issue in a particularly interesting equation: *principium individuationis* = *Maya* (see Chapter 9).

[198] »abstrakter Begriff der Weltwesen«; »Wille als eine Sache« (Schelling 1809:417–8).

Multiplicity and Oneness

answer was built on his adoption and reformulation of Jacob Böhme's teachings. This inspiration is particularly conspicuous at the end of Schelling's critique of Spinoza which ends with a thunderclap:

> In the ultimate instance there is no other being than willing. Willing is Ur-being, and to it alone all its predicates apply: groundlessness, eternity, timelessness, self-affirmation. Philosophy as a whole seeks but to find this highest expression.[199]

This is precisely the apex, Schelling argued, that modern philosophy was able to reach thanks to idealism. The similarity of the basic direction and layout of Schelling's Böhme-inspired standpoint and that of Schopenhauer was already mentioned several times. This similarity might be due to the direct or indirect influence on Schopenhauer of mysticism (particularly Böhme) and Platonism / Neoplatonism. However, the philosophies of Spinoza, Giordano Bruno, Kant and Fichte were certainly also important factors. Like the Neoplatonics, Schelling was concerned with the movement from Oneness to Multiplicity and described this based on Böhme as a "primordial and basic willing" (Ur- und Grundwollen); and Schelling's view of the birth of everything from the One has, exactly as in Böhme's *Mysterium magnum*, its ultimate ground in a "longing felt by the eternal One to give birth to itself."[200] This longing is "not the One itself, but it is equally eternal":

> It [this longing] wants to give birth to God, in other words to the unfathomable Oneness; but in this respect there is no Oneness in itself. Therefore, taken by itself, it is also will.[201]

---

[199] »Es giebt in der letzten und höchsten Instanz gar kein andres Seyn als Wollen. Wollen ist Urseyn und auf dieses allein passen alle Prädikate desselben: Grundlosigkeit, Ewigkeit, Unabhängigkeit von der Zeit, Selbstbejahung. Die ganze Philosophie strebt nur dahin, diesen höchsten Ausdruck zu finden.«(Schelling 1809:419)

[200] »Sehnsucht, die das ewige Eine empfindet, sich selbst zu gebähren« (Schelling 1809:431).

[201] »Sie will Gott, d.h. die unergründliche Einheit gebähren, aber insofern ist in ihr selbst nicht die Einheit. Sie ist daher für sich betrachtet auch Wille.« (Schelling 1809:431-2)

Schelling described this primordial longing—whose islamic-Indian form we will encounter in the next chapters—as one that, "as the ground still obscure, represents the first stirring of divine existence" and takes form within God as "an inner reflexive representation" shown by God to himself.[202] In the rhapsodical style of Jacob Böhme, and inspired by St. John's *logos* doctrine, Schelling proclaims that this first reflection is "the *word* of that longing" and "the eternal spirit that feels the word in itself" and has "a boundless longing, driven by the love that he himself is."[203] Schelling regarded this longing—the "primordial and fundamental willing" (Ur- und Grundwollen; p. 468)—as the ultimate ground of the One's unfolding to multiplicity.

> The first beginning of creation is the longing of the One to give birth to itself, or the will of the ground. The second is the will of love, whereby the word is emitted into nature and God renders himself for the first time personal. The will of the ground can therefore not be free in the sense in which the will of love is free.[204]

The third, then, is the unfolding or objectification of the One which, according to Schelling, takes place in different levels or degrees.

> With each degree of the division of forces a new being is generated from nature ... until, in the supreme division of forces, the innermost center unfolds.[205]

---

[202] Ur-Sehnsucht »welche als der noch dunkle Grund die erste Regung göttlichen Daseyns ist«; »eine innre reflexive Vorstellung« (Schelling 1809:433–4).

[203] »das *Wort* jener Sehnsucht« und »der ewige Geist, der das Wort in sich und zugleich die unendliche Sehnsucht empfindet, von der Liebe bewogen, die er selbst ist« (Schelling 1809:434).

[204] »Der erste Anfang zur Schöpfung ist die Sehnsucht des Einen, sich selbst zu gebähren, oder der Wille des Grundes. Der zweite ist der Wille der Liebe, wodurch das Wort in die Natur ausgesprochen wird, und durch den Gott sich erst persönlich macht. Der Wille des Grundes kann daher nicht frey seyn in dem Sinne, in welchem es der Wille der Liebe ist« (Schelling 1809:482).

[205] »bei jedem Grade der Scheidung der Kräfte ein neues Wesen aus der Na-

The "fall"—which Schelling regarded as the only correct explanation for the emergence of the Many from the One—ultimately has its root also in a "will to revelation" full of longing.[206] Such revelation of the One requires "selfhood and opposition,"[207] which explains why "the will of the ground, already in the initial act of creation, also kindles the own-will of the creature." When "the spirit becomes the will of love, it thus finds something opposed to it in which it can realize itself."[208]

Like Böhme, Schelling located the origin of evil in the birth of own-will: "Man has thus from eternity grasped himself in selfhood (Eigenheit) and egotism (Selbstsucht)."[209] This is the original sin that separates man from God: "The principle, inasfar as it stems from the ground and is obscure, is the own-will of the creature;" and this own-will "is pure addiction or desire, that is, blind will."[210] Evil springs from this "sinister or selfish principle" (p. 450). But simultaneously there is also a longing for the opposite pole: the return of "me and mine" to the "one-and-all." This corresponds exactly to the teaching of young Schopenhauer's friend and mentor Zacharias Werner who was an admirer of both Böhme and Schelling.

---

tur entsteht ... bis in der höchsten Scheidung der Kräfte das allerinnerste Centrum aufgeht« (p. 430). In his 1810 private lectures in Stuttgart, Schelling was to propose the following tripartite scheme for the transition from Oneness to multiplicity: 1. emanation; 2. fall; 3. a modified emanation doctrine modeled after Böhme, which Schelling conceived as "creation" (Schöpfung): the "overcoming of divine egotism through divine love" (»Überwindung des göttlichen Egoismus durch die göttliche Liebe«) (Beierwaltes 2004:127).

[206] »Willen zur Offenbarung« (Schelling 1809:454).

[207] »die Eigenheit und den Gegensatz« (Schelling 1809:454).

[208] »der Wille des Grundes gleich in der ersten Schöpfung den Eigenwillen der Kreatur mit erregt, damit, wenn nun der Geist als der Wille der Liebe aufgeht, dieser ein Widerstrebendes finde, darin er sich verwirklichen könne« (Schelling 1809:455).

[209] »so hat der Mensch sich von Ewigkeit in der Eigenheit und Selbstsucht ergriffen« (Schelling 1809:471).

[210] »Das Prinzip, sofern es aus dem Grunde stammt, und dunkel ist, ist der Eigenwille der Kreatur« welcher »bloße Sucht oder Begierde, d.h. blinder Wille ist« (Schelling 1809:430).

CHAPTER FIVE

We have seen that already around the end of 1811 Schopenhauer knew Böhme's *Mysterium magnum* so well that he immediately detected its influence in Schelling's *Inquiries on Human Freedom*. Böhme describes the One as follows:

> It is distinct from creature as an eternal nothing; it has neither ground nor beginning nor abode, and possesses nothing but itself: it is the will of the Ungrund, in himself but One, and needs neither space nor time.[211]

For Böhme this longing of the One to reveal itself also forms the original fount of creation:

> We recognize that God in his own essence is no being but only a groundless eternal will, a force or impulsion toward being. Everything lies in this will, and though it is itself everything, it is only One. Yet it desires to reveal itself and to enter into a spiritual being; and this happens through the fire of loving desire, in the power of light.[212]

The engine of creation is this divine longing for self-revelation:

> Look, the desire of the eternal word that is God is the beginning of eternal nature and the embodying of the eternal Nothing into Something; it is the origin of all beings.[213]

---

[211] »das Eine gegen der Kreatur, als ein ewig Nichts; er hat weder Grund, Anfang noch Stätte; und besitzet nichts, als nur sich selber: er ist der Wille des Ungrundes, er ist in sich selber nur eines: er bedarf keinen Raum noch Zeit« (Böhme 1843:5.7).

[212] »Wir erkennen, daß Gott in seinem eigenen Wesen kein Wesen ist, sondern nur bloß die Kraft oder der Verstand zum Wesen als ein ungründlicher ewiger Wille, in dem alles liegt, und der selber Alles ist, und doch nur Eines ist, und sich aber begehret zu offenbaren, und in ein geistlich Wesen einzuführen, welches durch Feuer in der Liebebegierde, in Kraft des Lichts geschieht« (Böhme 1843:5.26).

[213] »Siehe, die Begierde des ewigen Worts, welches Gott ist, ist der Anfang der ewigen Natur, und ist die Fassung des ewigen Nichts in Etwas; sie ist die Ursache aller Wesen« (Böhme 1843:5.28).

Multiplicity and Oneness

Other writings by Böhme contain similar statements. For example, the first chapter of his treatise *On Election by Grace* is entitled "Von dem einigen Willen Gottes, und von Einführung seines Wesens seiner Offenbarung. Was der einige Gott sei" (Of the singular will of God and of the introduction to the essence of his revelation. What the one God is). It contains explanations such as:

> In the non-natural, non-creaturelike godhead there is nothing but a singular will which is also called the One God. In itself it no longer wants anything except to find and grasp itself, to step out of itself, and in doing so to enter into contemplation.[214]

Such words of Böhme inspired not only Schelling but also contemporaries like Friedrich Schlegel, Novalis, Zacharias Werner, K. C. F. Krause, Franz Baader, and Schopenhauer.

At the end of his essay *On the Basis of Morality* (1841) Schopenhauer adduced a rationale for his doctrine of the oneness of everything: Kant's doctrine of the ideality of space and time that he called Kant's "triumph" because he regarded it as one of the "very few metaphysical doctrines that can be regarded as truly proven."[215] Only what is in space and time can be manifold; and since the "thing in itself" is not in space and time it cannot involve multiplicity.

> Consequently, in all the numberless appearances of this sensual world there can only be One; and only the One and identical being can manifest itself in all of them.[216]

---

[214] »Denn in der unnatürlichen, unkreatürlichen Gottheit ist nichts mehr als ein einiger Wille, welcher auch der Einige Gott heißt, der will auch in sich selber nichts mehr, als nur sich selber finden und fassen, und aus sich selber ausgehen, und sich mit dem Ausgehen in eine Beschaulichkeit einführen« (Böhme 1843:4.469).

[215] ... eine der »höchst wenigen metaphysischen Lehren, die man als wirklich bewiesen« betrachten kann (SW4, §22:268; Z6:308).

[216] »folglich kann dasselbe in den zahllosen Erscheinungen dieser Sinnenwelt doch nur Eines seyn, und nur das Eine und identische Wesen sich in diesen allen manifestiren« (SW4, §22:268; Z6:308).

CHAPTER FIVE

According to Schopenhauer this doctrine is far older than Kant:

> First of all it constitutes the principal and fundamental doctrine of the world's oldest book, the sacred *Vedas*, whose dogmatic part, or rather the esoteric teaching, we possess in the *Upanishads*. There we find that great doctrine on almost every page. It is unflaggingly repeated in countless formulations and expounded by means of various metaphors and similes.[217]

Schopenhauer also found this doctrine in Pythagoras and the Eleatic school, Neoplatonics like Plotinus, Scotus Eriugena, the mysticism of the Sufis, Giordano Bruno, Christian mystics, etc., and of course in Spinoza. In the long line of predecessors Schopenhauer also mentions Schelling, though with a measure of disdain:

> Finally, in our days, after *Kant* had destroyed the old dogmatism and the world was stunned by the smoldering wreckage, that same notion [of all-oneness] was resuscitated through the eclectic philosophy of *Schelling* who amalgamated the teachings of Plotinus, Spinoza, Kant, and Jacob Böhme with the results of modern natural science and quickly assembled them into a whole in order to satisfy the urgent need of his contemporaries. Subsequently he produced variations of it, and the notion became generally accepted by German scholars to the point of becoming prevalent even among the merely well educated.[218]

---

[217] »Denn zuvörderst ist sie die Haupt- und Grundlehre des ältesten Buches der Welt, der heiligen *Veden*, deren dogmatischer Theil, oder vielmehr die esoterische Lehre, uns in den *Upanischaden* vorliegt. Daselbst finden wir fast auf jeder Seite jene große Lehre: sie wird unermüdlich, in zahllosen Wendungen wiederholt und durch mannigfache Bilder und Gleichnisse erläutert« (SW4, §22:268; Z6:308–9).

[218] »In unsern Tagen endlich, nachdem *Kant* den alten Dogmatismus vernichtet hatte und die Welt erschrocken vor den rauchenden Trümmern stand, wurde jene Erkenntniß wieder auferweckt durch die eklektische Philosophie *Schellings*, der, die Lehren des Plotinos, Spinoza's, Kants und Jakob Böhmes mit den Ergebnissen der neuen Naturwissenschaft amalgamirend, schleunig ein Ganzes zusammensetzte, dem dringenden Bedürfniß seiner Zeitgenos-

Multiplicity and Oneness

Though Schopenhauer later (as in the just cited passage of 1841) was fond of criticizing Schelling, it is abundantly clear that in his youth he was very much indebted to this "amalgamation."

At what point did India enter into the picture? In spite of some remarks about India's ancient culture in the lectures of his Goettingen professors Heeren and Schulze (1811), in 1813 Schopenhauer probably knew hardly anything about Indian monism and even less about Sufism. His independent interest in the Orient dates from December of 1813 when he borrowed the *Asiatisches Magazin* from Weimar's ducal library, and the most influential event was without any doubt his encounter with his favorite book in the spring of 1814: the *Oupnek'hat that* by his account contains on almost every page the teaching that multiplicity and distinctions pertain only to appearance and that "One and the same being" manifests itself in everything. From the he *Oupnek'hat* he learned that the ancient Indians even had a specific term for this illusion of multiplicity: *Maya*. But before turning to Weimar and Dresden where Schopenhauer in 1814 encountered this key idea we need to explore the exotic realms where his favorite book was born.

---

sen einstweilen zu genügen, und es dann mit Variationen abspielte; in Folge wovon jene Erkenntniß unter den Gelehrten Deutschlands zu durchgängiger Geltung gelangt, ja, selbst unter den bloß Gebildeten fast allgemein verbreitet ist.« (SW4, §22:269; Z6:309–10)

6. Ishq and Fanā

The eighteenth century was the age of the first universal histories of philosophy. This was in part due to Thomas Stanley's *History of Philosophy* whose Asia section—first published in 1662—argued for an Asian origin of Greek philosophy (1701:1). At that time, few people on the continent could read English; but the Latin translation of Stanley's section on Asia by Jean le Clerc, published in Amsterdam in 1690, received considerable attention not least because of the title le Clerc gave to it: instead of Stanley's *The History of the Chaldaick Philosophy* (1662), le Clerc's translation was entitled *Historia philosophiae orientalis* (History of Oriental Philosophy).[219] But Brucker's *Historia critica philosophiae* (Critical History of Philosophy, 1741–4), which contained detailed accounts of what was then known about of the philosophies and religions of Asia, had the deepest impact.[220] The first volume of the

---

[219] See Urs App, *The Cult of Emptiness*, pp. 194–8.
[220] Brucker's first volume describes post-diluvial oriental philosophy under the headers Hebrews (1.69–102), Chaldeans (102–42), Persians (143–89),

famous *Encyclopédie*, the banner of French enlightenment, contained a much noted article by Denis Diderot about Asian philosophy that shows the profound influence of Brucker.[221]

In 1757, Adrien-François Pluquet (1716–1790) summarized some of the available information about the doctrine of all-oneness. He called this doctrine "fatalisme" and included in it "all systems which posit a single substance of the world" (1757:2.i) and which assert "that everything necessarily exists" while ascribing "all of nature to a force without freedom" (1757:1.1). For Pluquet, this so-called "oriental system" issued in the philosophy of Spinoza to whose presentation he devoted an entire volume. Had Pluquet written a century later, he probably would have added one more volume about Schopenhauer whose metaphysics of will corresponded rather closely to Pluquet's definition of "fatalism." Pluquet believed that this teaching, whose presence he detected in East and West, had its roots in ancient India. Though their evaluation differed, similar beliefs about Indian influence were held by Anquetil-Duperron, Friedrich Majer, Friedrich Schlegel, Schopenhauer, and many others.[222]

In 1804, when Friedrich Schlegel returned to Germany after a brief period of Sanskrit studies in Paris and held a series of lectures in Hei-

---

Indians (190–212), Arabs, and Phoenicians (213 ff.). The second part of volume 4 (1744) contains much about India (pp. 826–45), China (pp. 846–906) and Japan (pp. 907–19) as well as a general introduction to "oriental philosophy" (pp. 804–826) with excerpts of the reports by Chardin and Bernier (see here below). Brucker's numerous corrections and additions in volume 6 (1767) demonstrate the quick growth of European knowledge about Asia in this period. Schopenhauer owned the six-volume edition of Brucker's *Historia critica philosophiae* which he cited in later works; but these volumes seem to have been lost and it is unknown when Schopenhauer had purchased them (HN5:21–2).

[221] This article is entitled »Asiatiques, philosophie«. Diderot relied mostly on the second edition of Bayle's *Dictionnaire historique et critique* (1702) and on Brucker's *Historia critica philosophiae* (1741–4). See chapter 4 of App 2010c.

[222] The background and early history of such beliefs is discussed at length in App 2010c and App 2012.

Ishq and Fanā

delberg for a circle of friends (1804–6), he called this system "speculative mysticism" (Schlegel 1836:1.209). Like Pluquet he regarded it as the world's oldest philosophical system, thought that it had spread in all directions from India, and detected its subsequent impact on Egyptians, Persians, and even on Jews such as Philo and Josephus (pp. 204–5). According to Schlegel, this system was "adopted in the school of Pythagoras" and also influenced Plato's teaching. It finally received "its best elaboration and perfection with the philosophers of Alexandria and the Neoplatonics" (p. 205). This philosophy of Indian origin, so Schlegel asserted, had also enthralled the gnostics and some famous early Christians such as Origen and Clement of Alexandria, and it consisted of the following main doctrines: (1) the origin of all things from God through emanation; (2) spiritual vision [übersinnliche Anschauung] or revelation; (3) transmigration of souls or metempsychosis; (4) pessimism or the view of the world as a great evil; and (5) reunification of individual beings with the divinity as the supreme goal (pp. 207–8). Denouncing this extremely ancient and widespread doctrine as a "misunderstanding of revelation," Schlegel wished to "correct" it with the help of the Bible and Böhme—a process that was accompanied by his conversion to the catholic faith.

One product of this process was Schlegel's book about *The Language and Wisdom of India* of 1808 which immediately became a *cause célèbre* in Germany and provoked Schelling into publishing a rebuke in his treatise on freedom.[223] The well-known literary critic, novelist (*Lucinde*), and German pioneer of Sanskrit studies asserted that long before philosophy's arrival in Greece there existed philosophical systems in India of which the above-mentioned oriental system of emanation is singled out as the most ancient. Schlegel insisted that this system must not be confounded with pantheism (for example the kind ascribed to Spinoza) since pantheism is fundamentally optimistic: "Pantheism

---

[223] Schlegel's book figures among Schopenhauer's first library borrowings in Dresden, just prior to the works of Hemsterhuis (July 1814) and four months after his encounter with the Latin Upanishads (*Oupnek'hat*).

teaches that all is good because all is one, and that any semblance of injustice or evil is nothing but empty illusion."[224] By contrast, the system of emanation regards "all being as unfortunate [unseelig] and the world as rotten and evil at its core" (Schlegel 1808:98). This "oldest known thought system of the human mind" exerted "an incalculable influence on the entire subsequent development and history."[225] According to Schlegel it forms the root not only of pessimism but also of polytheism (pp. 123, 159), fatalism (p. 114), oriental materialism (p. 117), and the worship of forces of nature (p. 119); and furthermore it is said to have formed the foundation for the transmigration doctrine popular among Pythagoreans, followers of Plato, Egyptians, and even Celtic druids (pp. 111–2).

Thus even the purportedly pure source of all philosophy in Greece appeared to be a derivative of an oriental system forming the common root of countless eastern and western branches. They include China's *Book of Changes* (*Yijing*; p. 143), Buddhism (p. 147) and the "pantheistic" Vedanta doctrine (pp. 147–8), but also speculative systems of modern "sophists" [Vernünftler] such as Schelling who boast of "having made the great discovery ... that all is one," regard all knowledge of other peoples as "no more than error, illusion and imbecility," and think that "all change and all life is only empty semblance."[226]

Schlegel drew information about this ancient Indian emanation system mainly from sources that were frequently cited throughout the 18th century, for example Diderot's article on *Philosophie asiatique* in

---

[224] »Der Pantheismus lehrt, daß alles gut sey, denn alles sey nur eines, und jeder Anschein von dem, was wir Unrecht oder Schlecht nennen, nur eine leere Täuschung« (Schlegel 1808:97).

[225] Diese »älteste Denkart des menschlichen Geistes, die wir historisch kennen« hat auf »die ganze nachfolgende Entwickelung und Geschichte einen unübersehlichen Einfluß gehabt« (Schlegel 1808:99).

[226] »Vernünftler« wie Schelling, welche »diese große Entdeckung gemacht ... daß Alles Eins sei« und sich einbilden, alles was andere wissen und glauben sei »nur Irrthum, Täuschung und Verstandesschwäche, so wie alle Veränderung und alles Leben ein leerer Schein« (Schlegel 1808:142).

Ishq and Fanā

the first volume of the *Encyclopédie* (1751) and Pluquet's work on fatalism (1757). Other major sources for this vision of an "oriental system" were culled from the late seventeenth-century reports by François Bernier and Jean Chardin[227] and a letter by the Jesuit missionary Jean François Pons (1688–1752) of 1740.[228]

Father Pons explained that the Brahmins of the Vedanta school regard all that is perceived as a "constant illusion" and think that the "*Maya* of I-ness" is the reason for this mistake (Pluquet 1757:1.216). According to Pons, "this *Maya* or principle of illusion lets us perceive things outside of ourselves and is not opposed to egotism," and the eclipse of this illusion is attained when one is able to say: "I am the supreme Being" (p. 217).[229] Pons also reported that there are Indians who posit a world soul and regard the "I" as illusory; for them "all souls are ... but modifications or aspects of the world soul united with matter and thus can be perceived even though they exist neither in themselves

---

[227] Bernier's first report on this was published in the *Suite des Mémoires du sieur Bernier sur l'empire du Grand Mogol* (Paris: Barbin 1671). See App 2012:161–186 for more information about this report and its impact in Europe. Chardin's account was published as late as 1711. Brucker published extensive quotes from both of these reports at the beginning of his chapter *De philosophia exotica* in the second part of volume 4 of his history of philosophy (Brucker 1744:807–10).

[228] In *Lettres édifiantes et curieuses, écrites des missions étrangères,* edited by C. Le Gobien. Paris: G. Merigot: 1781 (vol. 14, pp. 65–90).

[229] In his letter Pons explains: "La sagesse consiste donc à se délivrer du *Mâyâ* par une application constante à soi-même, on se persuadant qu'on est l'Être suprême, éternel, & infini, sans laisser interrompre son attention à cette prétendue vérité par les atteintes du *Mâyâ*. La clef de la délivrance de l'âme est dans ces paroles, que ces faux sages doivent se répéter sans cesse avec un orgueil plus outré que celui de Lucifer. Je suis l'Être suprême, *Aham ava param Brahma*." ("Wisdom thus consists in freeing oneself from Maya through constant work on oneself while persuading oneself that one is the supreme Being, eternal and infinite, and in preventing one's concentration on this pretended truth from being interrupted by the effects of *Maya*. The key to the salvation of the soul is contained in the words that these false sages must ceaselessly repeat with a measure of pride that surpasses that of Lucifer: I am the supreme Being, *Aham ava param Brahma*." (Pons 1781:86–7)

nor in matter" (p. 219). From this perspective, Pons explained, the "I" is not real and does not exist (p. 220). In this letter which for the first time explained Indian philosophical systems to European readers, Father Pons portrayed the goal of all Indian philosophers as supreme wisdom (suprême sagesse) consisting in *union* and stated:

> This union begins with meditation and the contemplation of the supreme Being and ends with a kind of identity wherein all feeling and all will has vanished. The processes of metempsychosis remain until that happens.[230]

In his multi-volume travel account one of the rare early experts on Persia, Jean Chardin (1643–1713) who had stayed twice for longer periods in Persia and India, wrote in a chapter dedicated to philosophy that in the Orient there is a fully developed philosophy which follows the Greek pattern (Chardin 1811:4.445–7). This "great and universal philosophy of the Indians and all idolaters of the Orient," Chardin asserted, originated with Pythagoras and is also taught by Muslims, "in particular by those called Sufis."[231] The Sufis believe in a great world soul, and their main teachers say of themselves: "I am what is, i.e., the true Being; whatever you are perceiving is like a dress covering the eternal and infinite essence that one calls God."[232] It is for this reason, Chardin explained, that conservative Muslims are accusing them of atheism and circulate a couplet called "the secret of the Sufis":

---

[230] "cette union, dis-je, commence par la méditation & la contemplation de l'Être suprême, & se termine à une espece d'identité, où il n'y a plus de sentiment ni de volonté. Jusques-là les travaux des Métempsicoses durent toujours." (Pons 1781:83)

[231] "La philosophie d'Epicurus et de Démocrite n'est point connue en Perse, mais bien celle de Pythagore, qui est la grande et universelle philosophie des Indiens et de tous les peuples idolâtres de l'Orient. Cette philosophie est enseignée entre les Mahométans, et sur-tout entre les Persans, par une cabale de gens, particulièrement qu'on appelle *soufys*." (Chardin 1811:4.449)

[232] "*hackmenem*, je suis ce qui est, c'est-à-dire l'*Être véritable; ce que vous voyez est comme un habit qui couvre l'Essence éternelle, infinie, que l'on appelle Dieu.*" (Chardin 1811:4.455)

Ishq and Fanā

There is a single Essence, but a thousand forms and figures.
No form of a separate thing has the slightest consistency or reality.[233]

Chardin regarded this as an expression of the Sufi doctrine that all seemingly separate beings are in reality but different forms through which a single, unchanging divine essence manifests (p. 456). The Sufis seek to realize this all-oneness by putting themselves by various means into a state of ecstasy and "unite with God" (pp. 458–9). Chardin thought it very likely that this "mystical theology of the Sufis" had spread via North Africa also to Spain and Western Europe (p. 464).

The second early Persia expert, François Bernier (1625–1688), was already famous before he set foot on Asian soil because of his multivolume presentation of the philosophy of his teacher Gassendi.[234] As an employee of a rich Indian, Bernier had for six years translated the writings of Gassendi and Descartes into Persian and explained them to his master (Bernier 1699:2.134). Bernier informed his readers about a doctrine of emanation of Indian origin that is professed by Sufis as well as learned Persians. They believe that God drew from his own substance not only all souls but also everything material and corporeal in the universe. Bernier explained that they have no conception of a creation from nothing and instead believe in an emanation from God. For this they use the metaphor of a spider that spins its web out of itself and can at any time pull it back in again.[235] For them, creation is therefore "nothing other than a drawing out or an extension that God makes of

---

[233] "*Yek Vojoud amed vely souret asar / Kosrot souret ne dared ahtebar.* C'est-à-dire: Il y a une seule Essence, mais il y a mille formes ou figures. / La forme d'aucune chose n'a point de consistance ou de réalité." (Chardin 1811:4.455–56)

[234] Bernier's *Abrégé de la philosophie de Gassendi* first appeared in 1674 (Paris: Langlois), followed by reprints and new editions in 1675 and 1678 (eight volumes). The second, revised edition in seven volumes was published in 1684 (new edition Paris: Fayard 1992).

[235] For a description of this emanation theory and its interesting history in Europe, starting with Athanasius Kircher's *China illustrata* (Kircher 1667:156), see App 2012:11–128, 161–172, and the graph on p. 173.

his own essence."[236] For this reason "there is nothing real and substantial in all that we believe to see, hear, smell, taste, and touch: this entire world is but a kind of dream and a pure illusion because all multiplicity and diversity of perceived things is in reality a sole unity, namely, God himself."[237] The manifold things are like different numbers multiplying the single One. God could therefore be compared to light, which has the same nature in the entire universe even though it can appear in a hundred different ways depending on the object it illumines.[238]

Bernier, who at the time of his letter was not yet aware of Spinoza, regarded such teachings as totally absurd, criticized them in schoolmasterish manner, and later connected them with the quietism of Western mystics such as Molinos and Madame Guyon (Bernier 1688). In order to vitiate doubts about his reliability due to his lack of familiarity with Sanskrit, he declared that his main informant was one of India's most celebrated scholars whom Bernier's employer had called at Bernier's suggestion. Bernier spent more than three years in the company of this great Indian scholar and reported (1699:2.133) that this man had been a member of the court of crown prince Dara Shukoh (1615–1659), the son of the fifth Mughal emperor Shah Jahan (1592–1666).

---

[236] "La création donc, disent ces Docteurs imaginaires, n'est autre chose qu'une extraction & extension que Dieu fait de sa propre substance, de ces rets qu'il tire comme de ses entrailles, de même que la destruction n'est autre chose qu'une reprise qu'il fait de cette divine substance, de ces divins rets dans luy-même" (Bernier 1699:2.164).

[237] "Il n'est donc rien, disent-ils, de réel & d'effectif de tout ce que nous croyons voir, ouir ou flairer, goûter ou toucher; tout ce Monde n'est qu'une espece de songe & une pure illusion, entant que toute cette multiplicité & diversité de chose qui nous apparoissent, ne sont qu'une seule, unique & même chose, qui est Dieu même; comme tous ces nombres divers que nous avons, de dix, de vingt, de cent, de mille, & ainsi des autres, ne sont enfin qu'une même unité répetée plusieurs fois" (Bernier 1699:2.165).

[238] "Ou bien ils vous diront qu'il en est de Dieu comme de la Lumiere, qui est la même par tout l'Univers, & qui ne laisse pas de paroître de cent façons differentes des objets où elle tombe, ou selon les diverses couleurs & figures des verres par où elle passe." (Bernier 1699:2.165)

Ishq and Fanā

This crown prince plays a central role in our book. He was the eldest son of Emperor Shah Jahan and his wife Mumtaz Mahal (1593–1631) whose mausoleum is the famous Taj Mahal in Agra. Bernier had made the acquaintance of Prince Dara when, shortly after his arrival in India, he provided medical treatment to one of Dara's wives and was asked to serve the prince. But at the time of this encounter Prince Dara was about to lose the dynastic succession struggles to his younger brother Aurangzeb and was trying to escape his pursuers accompanied by a force that had shrunk to barely five hundred cavalrymen. Bernier thus met Dara in the period between the Upanishad translation (1656) and his execution on the order of his brother Aurangzeb (1659).

Crown prince Dara and his team translating the Upanishads in 1656

The main pretext for Aurangzeb's fratricide was that his brother Dara, the designated heir to the Mughal throne, had propagated a heretical conception of divine all-oneness (*Tauḥīd*) in some of his writings including the Persian translation of fifty Upanishads entitled *Sirr-i akbar* (The Great Secret). This was the work whose Latin translation Anquetil-Duperron published in 1801–2 under the title *Oupnek'hat*: Schopenhauer's favorite book.

Bernier's "famous Indian scholar"—the *pandit* who had told him about the doctrine of all-oneness held by Sufis and Indians—had been a member of Prince Dara's Upanishad translation team, and what he explained to Bernier was entirely congruent with the thought of his murdered former master. In the preface to the Upanishad translation Prince Dara wrote of himself in the modest third person: "Since a desire had arisen to encounter the savants of all religious communities and to hear their lofty words about *Tauḥīd*, and since he had [already] perused many books about Sufism and written tractates [about it], his thirst for *Tauḥīd*, which is an infinite sea, kept increasing" (Göbel-Gross 1962:14).

Having intensively studied the Koran and also "the Torah, the Evangile, the Psalms, and other scriptures," Dara found that all these sacred texts contain a "compressed and allegorical" description of all-oneness. At last, so he explained, he had immersed himself in India's most ancient sacred scriptures, the Vedas, and had found that their quintessence— the Upanishads—contain "all secrets of askesis and of the meditation methods of *Tauḥīd*" (pp. 15–6). Dara's preface continued:

> And because at present the city of Benares, the center of learning of this [Indian] people, was governed by this seeker of truth [Dara], he convoked the most learned *pandits* and *sannyasis* of the time who know the Veda and the Upanishads. In the year 1067 (1656–57 A.D.) he himself translated, without any worldly motivations, the quintessence of *Tauḥīd* represented by the Upanishads: the secrets to be safeguarded, and the final goal of all efforts by the saints.[239]

---

[239] Göbel-Gross 1962:15–16.

Ishq and Fanā

Since his youth Prince Dara had been in search of this all-oneness. He had, under the guidance of Sufi masters and with the help of various techniques of meditation and breath control, attempted to understand it not just intellectually but to realize it existentially. At age forty he had already authored six works. Like the *Compass of Truth* (*Risala-i-Haq Numa*) which he had written when he was thirty-two years old, they all treated of Sufi masters and their teachings (Hasrat 1982:9–10). Comparable to Schopenhauer's descriptions of saints in the fourth book of his main work, they exhibit the basic bearing of the author's compass. Everything turns around the overcoming of illusory multiplicity and the awakening to all-oneness. Such overcoming can, so Dara asserted, only be realized through the extirpation of the basic illusion of selfhood that the Sufis call *fanā*: Self-abolition (Schimmel 1992:42). This is the only way for human beings to realize that all is one. Bernier's informant compared individuals to glass phials full of water floating in the sea. Only their breakup reveals that their entire content is nothing other than that of the sea. Anything perceived through the senses is "but a kind of dream and a pure illusion because the entire multiplicity and variety of the phenomenal world is a single, unique, and identical thing, namely, God" (Bernier 1696:2.165–6). This reflects Prince Dara's view. The prince's compass needle thus pointed toward Self-abolition, the death of the I, or *fanā* since the goal—the realization of all-oneness—could only be reached in that way.

In the fourth decade of his life Prince Dara, who was a member of the Qadiriyya order of Sufism, studied with increasing fervor texts about the unity of being (*Wahdat al-Wujud*; Rizvi 1983:2.134 ff.). Such Sufi teachings have a long and complex history that cannot be unfurled here; suffice it to say that pre-islamic movements like gnosticism, Christianity, and especially Neoplatonism played an important role. Texts by neoplatonic philosophers such as Plotinus and Proclus had been disseminated in various Arabic translations and had a decisive influence on Arabic, Jewish, and Persian philosophy. Of particular importance was the so-called *Theology of Aristotle* (which in reality is a paraphrase

CHAPTER SIX

of Plotinus's fourth, fifth, and sixth *Ennead*) and also the *Liber de causis* containing excerpts from Proclus's theology (Zimmermann 1986; Hyman 1992). The influence of Christian mysticism colored by Neoplatonism is also evident. The key figure linking the Mediterranean area with India was the Spanish mystic Ibn Arabi (1165–1240), the grandfather of Sufism, whose writings Dara had studied (Rizvi 1983:2.112). Ibn Arabi's numerous treatises circle around the absolute One and its relation to the multiplicity of the phenomenal world. The perfect man "annihilates his essence [*zat*] in the Essence of the Absolute" and "annihilates his actions in the actions of the Absolute;" thus "in his fully illumined consciousness there is no longer any trace of his old personal ego. Indeed, he is the Perfect Man" (p. 49). Rather than some sort of mystical union, this kind of annihilation consists in an awakening to all-oneness. Dara described it in the words of his first Sufi master Mian Mir:

> In the beginning of his sufic journey, the neophyte is a drop of water in the ocean, who feels he has been transformed into a pearl. When he is perfect and attains *fanā*, he loses his identity as a pearl and returns to his early state as a drop of water annihilating himself into the ocean (Being). (Rizvi 1983:2.111)

This annihilation or dissolution of self is final and is likened to the melting of a lump of ice in the sea:

> There is no way melted ice (as an entity) can be reassembled. The final state of sufi perfection is like this; there is a situation in which the sufi's individual existence is effaced and he is nothing but Ocean." (pp. 111–12)

Prince Dara and his Sufi masters aimed at existentially realizing and concretely living this all-oneness. In the words of a Sufi master's words quoted by Dara: "By uttering the formulae of God's Unity, thou canst not become a monotheist—the tongue cannot taste sugar by only professing its name" (Hasrat 1982:109). The prince's *Compass of Truth* indicated the path from the world of common waking consciousness via meditative practices to such "tasting" of all-oneness.

Ishq and Fanā

In his preface to the translation of Upanishads the prince also wrote that the master Mulla Shah Badakhshi, the successor of Mian Mir, "encouraged him to study non-islamic texts," whereupon he immersed himself in the Old and New Testaments and finally turned his attention to the sacred scriptures of India (Göbel-Gross 1962:18). Mulla Shah distinguished three kinds of faith: first the common faith in God, the prophet, angels, revealed books, a life after death, and heaven and hell; second the obedience to divine inspirations; and third the highest form of faith in which "the veil of ego is lifted and the mind is illumined with the light of Divine manifestations" (Hasrat 1982:89). In the course of years the prince increasingly surrounded himself with people of various faiths who seemed to have lifted this "veil of the ego." In his company there was for example an Armenian Jew by the name of Sarmad who not only was familiar with different religions and languages but also enjoyed great renown as a mystic poet. This ascet was, among other things, known for never wearing a thread even in presence of the emperor. In a profound poem addressed to the Mughal emperor the mystic Sarmad justified his nakedness as follows:

> He who made thee rule this universe,
> Has endowed us with the cause of all distraught.
> Those with deformity, He has covered with dress;
> To the immaculate He gave the robe of nudity. (p. 102)

Crown prince Dara called this man in a letter his "guide and teacher" and openly shared his mystical perspective transcending particular religions. The poems quoted or written by Dara keep returning to stock metaphors: drops of water and waves as symbols of the illusion of individuality and multiplicity, and the ocean as the emblem of all-oneness and selflessness. The prince wrote for instance:

> Whatever thou beholdest except Him, is the object of thy fancy;
> Things other than He have their existence like a mirage.
> The existence of God is like a boundless ocean—
> Men are like forms and waves in its water. (p. 139)

CHAPTER SIX

As soon as the I and the shackles of egotism are broken, man "tastes" unity: "Thou art Muhammad and God too" (p. 143). When all traces of duality have vanished, not even the assertion of God's unity remains:

> When thou sayest: (God is) One, duality is clearly established:
> The Unity of God goes off the point when thou proclaimest it.
> (p. 147)

Likewise there can be no search for God or a mystical union with him:

> O, thou, who seekest God everywhere,
> Thou verily art the God and not separate from Him.
> Already in the midst of a boundless ocean,
> Thy quest resembles the search of a drop for the ocean. (p. 148)

Time and again, Dara evokes the oneness of all:

> The Unity does not become manifold through numerousness:
> As the waves do not cause the ocean to be split up into parts
> (p. 150).

Dara's understanding of awakening to all-oneness (*Tauḥīd*) forms the heart of his doctrine. He declared:

> I tell thee the secret of *Tauḥīd*, if thou wert to understand it aright,
> Nowhere exists anything but God,
> All you see or know other than Him
> Is separate in name, but in essence one with God. (p. 152).

For Dara this was the only correct and orthodox conception of *Tauḥīd*; but his preface to the Upanishad translation shows that he was criticized by conventional representatives of Islam. He took them to task, calling them know-nothings and brigands: "On the other hand there are the know-nothings of the present time who pretend to be learned and become brigands on the highway of God by falling into empty discussions, pestering, and charges of heresy addressed to the [true] knowers of God and *Muwaḥḥid*, as they oppose all expressions of *Tauḥīd*, which are quite evidently present both in the venerable Koran and in certified prophetical traditions" (Göbel-Gross 1962:15).

Ishq and Fanā

As a *Muwaḥḥid* or confessor of divine all-oneness, Dara's search for the confirmation of his views in the sacred scriptures of other religions increasingly focused on Indian texts because the extremely ancient Indian religion appeared to support his conception of all-oneness. In the preface of the Upanishad translation he wrote of himself:

> He asked himself why in India discussions of *Tauḥīd* are so frequently met with and why the ancient priests and mystics not only feel no resistance toward *Tauḥīd* but also do not scold the *Muwaḥḥid*, and why on the contrary this forms the foundation of their faith. (p. 15)

Already Dara's *Compass of Truth* shows clear signs of his familiarity with Indian Yoga practices and with Persian translations of Indian scriptures. In his fortieth year the prince went on to produce a work that for the first time thematized the parallels between Sufism and Indian religion and thus rang in the last phase of his work: the *Confluence of Oceans* (*Majma-ul-Bahrain*). In this book Dara attempted to open a breach in the artificial dam separating the "oceans" of Indian religion and Islam by exposing their fundamental unity.

In the introduction to the *Confluence of Oceans* Dara states that there are only terminological differences between Sufism and Indian monotheism. He adduces numerous corresponding terms, but in our context one equivalence is of particular importance: *ishq* = *maya*. Already in Neoplatonism the question was central why the One produced the Many; it was a core question of Plotinus, for example in the fifth *Ennead* (V 1.6). Emanation furnished an answer and provided, in form of the doctrine of hypostases, the possibility to account for evil by the growing distance from the One and the absolute Good (Hyman 1992:115–6). For Sufism the thought of Ibn Arabi proved decisive. Building on Neoplatonism and its Islamic adaptations, it promoted a view of creation that also exerted profound influence on Prince Dara. This doctrine of divine manifestation in creation was rooted in a famous phrase from the prophetical tradition in which God says:

CHAPTER SIX

> I was a hidden treasure, and I desired [*aḥbabtu*, 'loved'] to be known. Accordingly I created the creatures and thereby made Myself known to them. And they did come to know Me.[240]

According to Ibn Arabi, the origin of multiplicity in creation lies in the desire of the One to be known; and this One, manifesting itself as world, knows itself in the mirror of its creatures. Henri Corbin translated in this vein:

> I was a hidden treasure and longed to be known. Then I created creatures in order to become in them the object of my own knowledge. (Corbin 1969:114)

Readers who replace Ibn Arabi's "God" by Schopenhauer's "will" might already at this point notice a striking similarity to Schopenhauer's "single thought" as formulated in note #662: "The world is the self-cognizance of the will."[241] Ibn Arabi saw the world as the self-revelation of the absolute (Corbin 1969:118) springing from a primordial desire that he often called "love":

> The most fundamental and first movement was the move of the world from non-existence (i.e., the archetypical state), in which it rested, to the state of existence. ... And this movement of the generation of the world is the movement of love. This clearly appears in the statement of the apostle (who reproduces God's own words): "I was a hidden treasure and I *loved* to be known." Without this love the world would never have appeared in this concrete existence. In this sense the movement of the world toward existence is a movement of the love which created it. (p. 136–7)

In this manner the absolute appears "to itself in the forms of the world" (p. 137). According to Ibn Arabi, God willed to see himself in the mirror of the world, and this is why the macrocosm or "Great Man" reveals the secret (*sirr*) of the absolute (p. 220). But the universe is a

---

[240] Izutsu 1984:136. This *hadith* figures prominently in Sufi literature; in the following several different sources and translations will be cited.

[241] »Die Welt ist die Selbsterkenntnis des Willens« (HN1:462).

Ishq and Fanā

hazy, unpolished mirror; and for Ibn Arabi it was precisely because of this that the creation of man was necessary: "God's second creation, in order to mirror himself in him, was man"—the microcosm or "Small Man." The creation of man thus constituted nothing other than "the polishing of the mirror of the universe." (p. 221)

In Ibn Arabi's writings, which were influenced by Neoplatonism, the absolute seeks to manifest itself through archetypes and via them in concrete things; but the human being sees everything only as a representation (Vorstellung) and "shadow" of the absolute. This is why Ibn Arabi taught:

> If what I just explained to you is true, then the world is an illusion which has no real existence in itself. And that is exactly what is called representation (imagination). In other words, the world appears as if it were something independent and autonomous outside of the absolute. (p. 93)

Ordinarily one sees only this "shadow world;" but a perfect man whose "I" has completely vanished (*fanā*) and who has attained the "continuity after self-annihilation" (*baqā*) possesses the perfect view in which the One is revealed as the Many and the Many as the One (p. 94). According to Ibn-Arabi, only such a man is a perfectly polished mirror of the absolute, and only this constitutes the complete "unveiling" through which everything finally can appear as it is in itself:

> When a person has [in mystical self-annihilation] entirely vanished and has lost its name and personal identity so totally that no trace of egoity and particularity remains: then it becomes possible to attain insight in reality through reality inasmuch as he himself is reality. (p. 181–2).

On this background one can understand why Prince Dara rendered, both in the *Confluence of Oceans* and in his Upanishad translation, the Indian term *maya* by the word *ishq* (love). Usually *maya* signifies "cosmic illusion" or the force that projects the illusion of a world of multiplicity. In the developed Vedanta system *maya* is not an act of love but rather something akin to original sin that can only be expunged by awakening to non-duality. But Dara interpreted this concept on the basis of Ibn Arabi's doctrine of creation and adduced as "proof" of the identity of *ishq* and *maya* the phrase from the *Hadith* tradition that was already quoted several times: "I was a hidden treasure, then I desired to be known; so, I brought the creation into existence" (Mahfuz-ul-Haq 1990:39). For Dara creation is an act of desire and love (*ishq*) by the absolute, and simultaneously a veiling (*maya*) of the absolute through the illusion of diversity and multiplicity. Creation simultaneously reveals and hides; as long as there is an "I" that is looking at "the world," the One remains hidden in the Many. Prince Dara thus portrays the treasure, which was revealed through love, as a treasure hidden underneath the veil of *maya*:

> Thus, know and be mindful (of the fact) that before its creation, this world of ours was concealed in His Self, and now His Holy Self is concealed in the world. (p. 43)

The absolute can only be revealed through "the annihilation and disappearance of all particularities" whereby one can know "everything in this world as One." Only thus can the One be seen in the Many:

> He is manifest in all; and everything has emanated from Him. He is the first and the last and nothing exists, except Him. (p. 37)

The "annihilation and disappearance of all particularities" signifies the end of transmigration or metempsychosis whose meaning in Indian thought Prince Dara had sought to grasp. In a documented meeting of the year 1653 he questioned the Sikh guru Baba Lal (1561–1641) about this: "In the Persian books it is said that the mystic (*narad*) is without birth." Baba Lal replied:

> This is how it is expressed in the books. In reality these mystics have no longer any existence whatsoever. Concerned that an existence might put them back into the shackles of diversity, they eradicated it completely and freed themselves from it; which is why they absolutely have no rebirth. (Huart 1926:326–7)

Ishq and Fanā

Asked by the prince about the relationship between the Persian and Indian view of this, Baba Lal stressed that both come to the same thing:

> The authors of Persian books were mostly people who had attained perfection; therefore they had purified their hearts of carnal desire and had annihilated themselves before they died. With regard to someone who has reached this perfection, the word "birth" is not adequate, regardless of whether it is taken in the Persian or Indian sense, because such a person has reached a state without equal from which there is no return into existence. The Indians call this state *mukti*. (p. 327)

In his *Confluence of Oceans* Prince Dara wrote two years later: "*Mukt* [deliverance] means the annihilation and disappearance of determinations" and declared that *jiwan mukt* or "salvation in life" signifies seeing and recognizing the oneness of everything in this world (Mahfuz-ul-Haq 1990:67–8).[242]

When in the last phase of his life Prince Dara was not satisfied with older Persian translations of Indian texts he simply ordered the making of new ones. This happened in the year 1655 with the *Yoga vasishta*, a famous text of Indian idealism. In 1656 he also wished to have a better Persian translation of the *Bhagavat Gita*—the text that, as we will see below, first put Schopenhauer into contact with the Indian doctrine of all-oneness[243]—and in the same year Dara's Upanishad translation was made. It was not only Dara's last work but also by far the most voluminous and, by general acclaim, the greatest. In his preface the prince wrote about the end of a long search:

> And in this quintessence of the ancient book [of the Vedas] he [Prince Dara] found the solution to all the difficulties and sublime problems he had thought about and that he had sought without success. It is without any doubt the first of the heavenly

---

[242] For an excellent recent study and Italian translation of this text see D'Onofrio & Speziale 2011. On related broader issues see Ernst 2005.

[243] For a detailed account of Schopenhauer's earliest independent encounter with Indian thought see App 2006c:59–75.

books and the source for the realization of *Tauḥīd*—a book that is congruent with the Koran or rather is its commentary! (Göbel-Gross 1962:17)

Prince Dara regarded the Upanishads as the most ancient divine revelation and concluded his preface with the words:

> Blessed is he who, having discarded the prejudices of base egotism, with total devotion to God reads and understands this translation entitled *Sirr-i akbar*, and regards it as a communication of divine utterances while discarding all bias! He will be immortal, without anxiety and distress, free and eternal! (pp. 17–18)

The extent of the prince's own contribution to this translation is not entirely clear. It is true that in his preface he states without any ambivalence that he himself produced the translation with the help of excellent scholars. Nevertheless, some modern specialists doubt that he was equipped with the necessary indological expertise. It appears likely that members of the translation team contributed various interpretations and prepared a draft translation that was subsequently discussed with the prince who then redacted it. In his preface the prince offered the following information about his motivation, interest in languages, and content of the translation:

> Since this seeker of truth was interested in the foundation of the oneness of being rather than the Arabic, Syriac, Hebrew, and Sanskrit languages, he wanted to translate these Upanishads—a treasure trove of *Tauḥīd* known to few experts even among the [Indian] people— word for word into Persian without any omissions and additions, without prejudices, and with a complete explanation. (p. 16).

What neither Anquetil nor Schopenhauer realized is that the expressions "without any omissions and additions" and "word for word" only apply to the Upanishad translation itself and that Dara did not present his book as a pure translation project. On the contrary: his preface clearly states that it also includes "a complete explanation." The

Ishq and Fanā

case studies by Göbel-Gross (1962) and Piantelli (1986) have shown that part of these explanations must have stemmed from the learned experts who consulted various Upanishad commentaries and often relied on Shankara. At times such commentaries were integrated into the translated Upanishadic text. In addition, the text contains many explanations that appear to stem from the pen of the prince. For example, when a section of the Sanskrit Upanishad text only uses the word *maya*, Dara's Persian translation consistently has "Maya, that is, love" (Piantelli 1986:177)—which expresses precisely the identification of love (*ishq*) with *maya* that Dara had already propagated in his *Confluence of the Oceans*.

An example for the kind of "complete explanation" mentioned in Dara's preface is found at the beginning of the *Eischavasieh* (Isha) Upanishad. Paul Deussen's translation (1921:523–8), which follows the Sanskrit text, contains no explanation of the title of this Upanishad. But in the Latin *Oupnek'hat*, which closely follows Dara's Persian text, the text begins with an explanation of the elements of the Upanishad's title *Eischavasieh*:

Eisch, cum significatione, dominus omnis (rei) est; et *vas*, cum significatione, opertum: id est, omnis mundus in domino mundi absconditus et coopertus est. (OUP1:395)	*Eisch* signifies: he is the lord of all (things); and *vas* means what is hidden; i.e., in the lord of the world the entire world is hidden and veiled.

This is, as we have already learned, a central theme of the prince since divine all-oneness was his foremost concern. The aim—expressed in Dara's preface—to support exactly this doctrine against the "ignorant" and the "brigands" of his Islamist opposition, and his will to achieve this by means of a faithful translation of the world's most ancient sacred scripture, help explain the tendency and volume of commentary that is evident here and in other places mentioned below. Probably because he found this explanation so important and thought that it formed part of

CHAPTER SIX

the original Sanskrit Upanishad text, Anquetil had this explanation set in larger type. As his double lines in the margins underneath the title show, Schopenhauer also regarded this as important. This is only one of many instances where both the translator Anquetil and the reader Schopenhauer exhibited interest in commentary that appeared to be part of Upanishadic text but in fact stemmed from Prince Dara's pen.

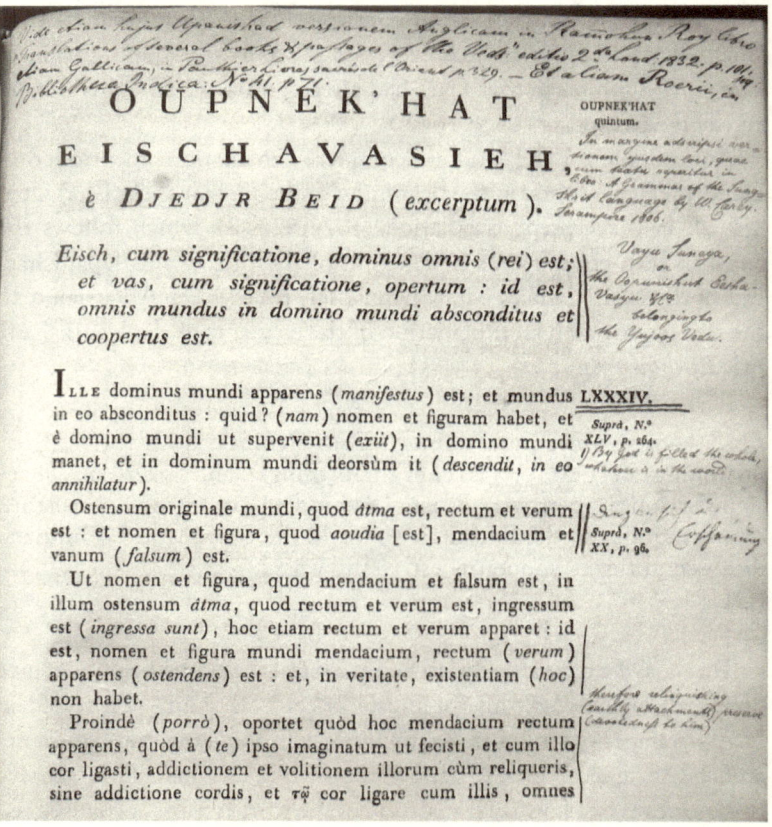

Oupnek'hat vol. 1, p. 395; with Schopenhauer's handwritten notes

Ishq and Fanā

In Deussen's translation this Upanishad begins with a Sanskrit verse that he rendered as a simple injunction: "Immerse this universe in God / Along with everything living in this world!" However, in the *Oupnek'hat* (vol. 1, p. 395) one finds at the beginning some detailed explanations that once again appear to be from Dara's pen:

ILLE dominus mundi apparens (*manifestus*) est; et mundus in eo absconditus: quid? (*nam*) nomen et figuram habet, et è domino mundi ut supervenit (*exiit*), in domino mundi manet, et in dominum mundi deorsùm it (*descendit, in eo annihilatur*). (OUP1:395)	That lord of the world is apparent (*manifest*); and the world is hidden in him. How so? (*Because*) it has name and form, and since it emanated from the lord of the world, remains in the lord of the world, and returns into him (*descends, is annihilated in him*).

This is followed by Dara's explanation of this commentary in which the manifold names and forms of the phenomenal world—wherein all-oneness is hidden—are illusion and deceit. Dara furnishes Indian terms both for this illusion (*aoudia*, Skt. *avidya* = ignorance, deceit) and for the absolute (*atma*). Schopenhauer again emphasized this explanation by double lines in the margin:

Ostensum originale mundi, quod *âtma* est, rectum et verum est: et nomen et figura, quod *aoudia* [est], mendacium et vanum (*falsum*) est. (OUP1:395)	What is originally revealed of the world, which is *âtma*, is what is correct and true, while name and form are *aoudia*: mendacious and vain (false).

Schopenhauer regarded this, as his pencil note below the middle of the right margin shows, as an ancient Indian conception of the distinction between the "thing in itself and the phenomenon" (Ding an sich u. Erscheinung).

CHAPTER SIX

Dara's commentary continues with his interpretation of that "deceit." It involves name and form, that is, the diversity and multiplicity of the phenomenal world which appears to be real yet is but illusion—an illusion that in the following is also called *maya*.

Ut nomen et figura, quod mendacium et falsum est, in illum ostensum *âtma*, quod rectum et verum est, ingressum est (*ingressa sunt*), hoc etiam rectum et verum apparet: id est, nomen et figura mundi mendacium, rectum (*verum*) apparens (*ostendens*) est: et, in veritate, existentiam (hoc) non habet. (OUP1:395)	Once name-and-form, which is mendacious and false, has found its way into that revealed *âtma*, which is right and true, then it also appears as right and true; that is, though name-and-form of the world is illusory, it still appears to be right (*true*) and real (*obvious*); yet in truth (*this*) has no existence.

In this manner the Sanskrit words at the beginning of this Upanishad, translated by Deussen in five words ("Immerse this universe in God"), were turned into a small treatise of deep interest to Schopenhauer. The second part of this short verse, rendered by Deussen as "[immerse in God] everything that lives on earth," appears in the *Oupnek'hat* as an explanation about the return of the many to oneness:

Proindè (*porrò*), oportet quòd hoc mendacium rectum apparens, quòd à (*te*) ipso imaginatum ut fecisti, et cum illo cor ligasti, addictionem et volitionem illorum cùm relinqueris, sine addictione cordis, et τῷ cor ligare cum illis, omnes actiones, et omnes voluptates, et omnes gustus, quae vis (*volueris*), fac (*exequaris*), et in corde addictionem et desiderium horum non habens sis (*fias*). (OUP1:395)	It is therefore necessary that you abandon your addiction and your desire of this illusion which appears as truth—an illusion that you have imagined and to which you have bound your heart—and that you free yourself without attachment of heart from all actions, all lusts, and all pleasures that you want (*wanted*), thus ridding yourself of the addiction in your heart and of any desire for all of this.

Ishq and Fanā

Whereas the extent of Prince Dara's knowledge of Sanskrit is subject to debate, this brief example already shows that the prince may not have exaggerated much when he called this rendering of the Upanishads his own. Göbel-Gross noticed that Dara frequently omitted passages dealing with religious ritual; but it seems to me that the additions and commentaries characteristic both of Dara's Persian *Sirr-i akbar* and its Latin translation would form an even worthier subject of study.

Schopenhauer's favorite book thus appears to be an extraordinary melting pot of Oriental and Occidental philosophies and religions. It contains fifty texts of Indian origin that were redacted, collected, and transmitted in the course of many centuries as "Upanishads." But it also contains interpretations based on Shankara and other Indian philosophers, some of which belong to the Vedanta school and also reflect influences by the idealism of the Mahayana Buddhist Yogacara school. The concept of *maya*, as used by Shankara, is a good example of such influence on early Vedanta since it embraces both a "favorable *maya*"— the creative power of God, especially Vishnu—and an "unfavorable *maya*" that had its roots in the illusionism of Mahayana Buddhism (Hacker 1950:269). Thus Prince Dara's interpretation of *maya* is not just linked to the Islamic esoteric doctrine of all-oneness but also to the Vedantic thought of Shankara and the illusionist monism of Brahmins which both show traces of Buddhist influence. Apart from studying Sufi literature and practicing with Sufi masters Dara also consulted Indian *pandits* and spiritual masters of various schools, for example Baba Lal of the Kabir tradition (Huart 1926). Furthermore he was familiar with classical Indian religious literature and seems to have appreciated the monotheist Siddha literature of South India and Kashmir, a body of texts that also greatly impressed Christian missionaries such as Roberto de Nobili and Bartholomäus Ziegenbalg.[244] Moreover, Dara's philosophy shows the influence of Persian thinkers such as Suhrawardi who in turn were inspired by Neoplatonism and ancient Persian reli-

---

[244] See chapter 2 of App, *The Birth of Orientalism*, in particular pp. 94–106.

gion (Walbridge 2000).[245] Various Sufi movements—among them especially the religious orders that emerged from the thirteenth century including Prince Dara's Qaddiriyya order—were not only inspired by Neoplatonism and Christian models but also absorbed Buddhist practices and ideas from Afghanistan, Kashmir, Tibet, and Central Asia. Sufism therefore formed not only a bridge between Europe, the Arab world, Persia, and India, but it was a formidable amalgam of ideas and practices from many ages and from regions between Spain, Central Asia, and South Asia.

Prince Dara himself was also a kind of melting pot: a north Indian prince of Persian mother tongue with Mongolian ancestors who had for many years studied Islamic mysticism and Indian religion. Apart from Arab, Persian, and Sufi literature he had read Old Testament scriptures, New Testament gospels, and Indian philosophical literature while seeking advice from Sufi masters and a variety of ascets. The thought of this prince is thus the result of a remarkable confluence of philosophies and religions since antiquity; and his last work and testament, the *Sirr-i akbar*, is the fruit of a long and complex process.

Fortunately the prince's ultimate work not only survived his execution in 1659 but also made its way to Europe when in 1775 the French commercial representative Le Gentil sent a copy of the Persian manuscript from the North Indian town of Oudh (Awadh) to his old friend Anquetil in Paris. This set the stage for additional chapters of a fascinating philosophical and religious East-West interaction.

---

[245] Conversely, though the question of influence is still disputed, the fathers of Neoplatonism (Ammonius Saccas and his disciple Plotinus) expressed strong interest in Indian thought.

7. Amor and Unification

After having in December of 1775 received the manuscript of Dara's Persian Upanishad translation, the *Sirr-i Akbar*, Abraham Hyacinthe Anquetil-Duperron (1731–1805) immediately began to translate it into French. Already the work's preface seemed to indicate that he had reached the goal of a long search. It stated unequivocally that the Upanishads represent the essence of the four Vedas that God had revealed to the first of all prophets: Adam![246] From his youth the Frenchman had been searching for traces of God's original revelation to mankind. From the mid-17th century Spinoza, Isaac La Peyrère and other authors had expressed doubts about the authenticity of the Old Testament's creation story as contained in the Pentateuch that was ascribed to Moses. If the Pentateuch had been written by Moses, how come it contained a passage about Moses's death? Just when young An-

---

[246] In a second manuscript that Anquetil later obtained and deposed at the Royal library in Paris he found the variant "Brahma, i.e. Adam." (OUP1:4)

quetil was studying theology, Jean Astruc published a book about the sources of Moses (1753) that attempted to apply a measure of textual criticism. A manuscript by Anquetil that forms part of his manuscript remains (Bibliothèque Nationale Paris, NAF 8858) reflects similar preoccupations. It is entitled *Le Parfait Théologien* (The Perfect Theologian) but Anquetil later rayed out the word "Parfait." In this manuscript the student discusses his doubts regarding the Old Testament and argues that a perfect theologian must not only know the Bible and its entire cultural and linguistic background but also be familiar with rivaling revelations of other peoples that are also ascribed to God. Such ancient revelations seemed without exception to come from Asia.

As early as the mid-16th century, Guillaume Postel (1510–1581) had speculated that antediluvian texts could have found their way to India where they had been safeguarded by the Brahmans whom he regarded as descendants of Abraham (Postel 1553:72). Postel referred in particular to the legendary *Book of Enoch* that is ascribed to the eponymous seventh-generation patriarch after Adam who, according to traditional chronology, had known Adam for no less than 308 years and had ascended to heaven 669 years before the great deluge (Boulduc 1630:148–9). In the 17th century the candidates for oldest book of the world were joined by the Chinese *Book of Changes* (*Yijing*),[247] but in the 18th century interest focused increasingly on the sacred scriptures of ancient India. The first descriptions of the Vedas by missionaries had reached Europe around the beginning of the 17th century, and subsequently various European books disseminated the glad tidings that the first of these Vedas treats of the creator God, first matter, angels, their fall, and so on.[248] In the early 18th century, Bartholomäus Ziegenbalg's sensational missionary reports from South India reinforced the impression that pure monotheism had reigned in ancient India.[249] From the mid-18th century Voltaire's *Essai sur les moeurs* and other books trum-

---

[247] See App, *The Birth of Orientalism* (2010c: 266–290).

[248] Baldaeus 1732:891; Caland 1918; App 2010c, chapter 6.

[249] App 2010c, chapter 2.

Amor and Unification

peted with increasing fervor that human civilisation had begun in India and even that the Jews had copied their creation story from the Indians.[250] Thus it is no cause for surprise that the main motive of Anquetil's famous journey to India (1755–1761) was the study of the Sanskrit language and the purchase of Veda manuscripts.[251] He intended to identify the basis of "the religious institutions of all of Asia" and was convinced that it could be found in the Indian Vedas (Anquetil 1762:418). He achieved neither of these objectives and instead studied Zoroastrian texts from Surat (India) whose translation he published in 1771 under the title of *Zend Avesta*. This multi-volume work (which also contained a verbose account of Anquetil's journey to India) was immediately denounced by the famous orientalist William Jones (1746–1794). In an anonymous pamphlet written in impeccable French, Jones criticized Anquetil's endeavor as a worthless waste of time on forged texts (Jones 1771; App 2009). But Anquetil's *Zend Avesta* also disappointed readers such as Voltaire who had hoped to lay hands on a better and more ancient Old Testament from Persia.

Just when Anquetil and his work were severely criticized as inauthentic he obtained the Persian manuscript of Prince Dara's Upanishads. It must have seemed like a gift from heaven: the essence of the four Vedas presented not in Sanskrit (which he did not know) but in a language he felt able to handle: Persian. He immediately decided to translate it into French and first announced this endeavor to the public in his 1778 work *Législation orientale*. Dara's work that "hitherto has not been mentioned by any traveller" is said to contain "in 51 sections the complete system of Indian theology that boils down to the unity of the first Being whose perfections and personified operations carry the names of the principal Indian deities, and the reunion of the whole of nature with this first Agent."[252]

---

[250] App 2010c, chapter 1 (in particular pp. 28–76) and note 26, p. 494.

[251] App 2010c, chapter 7 (in particular pp. 403–7).

[252] "Cet ouvrage est l'extrait des quatre Védes. Il présente en 51 Sections le système complet de la Théologie Indienne, dont le résultat est l'unité du

It seems that Anquetil had from the outset some mistaken notions about Prince Dara. The extant manuscript of Anquetil's French translation shows that in 1787 he did not yet understand Dara's assertion in the *Sirr-i akbar*'s preface that the prince himself had produced the translation. In Anquetil's announcement of 1778, the translation from Sanskrit to Persian is still attributed to the Indian savants convened by Dara. Anquetil explained that Dara had "publicly manifested his indifference towards the Islamic faith" and had ordered in 1656 in Delhi that "the Sanskrit work *Oupnekat*, i.e. *Word that must not be enunciated* (secret that must not be revealed), be translated by Brahmans of Benares."[253] Anquetil appears to have been ignorant not only of the prince's Sufi background but also of the fact that Dara's critique of conventional Islam did not constitute a fight against Islam but rather a battle for his view that the only correct interpretation of monotheism is all-oneness. The passage of Dara's *Sirr-i akbar* preface where the prince asserts having "read many books about Sufism and written tractates about it" (Göbel-Gross 1962:14)—a passage correctly translated by Anquetil's critic Alexander Hamilton[254]—was translated by Anquetil as follows: "A great number of books about mystical theology were brought in (his) presence, and also books composed (by him)."[255]

Though Anquetil had of course been familiar with Bernier's and Chardin's writings on the subject and had later received information

---

premier Etre, ses perfections & ses opérations personnifiés sont le nom des principales Divinités Indiennes; & la réunion de la nature entiere à ce premier Agent" (Anquetil 1778:21). The announcement of the future publication of this French translation is found on the same page and on pp. 244–5.

[253] Bibliothèque Nationale, Nouvelles Acquisitions Françaises 8857, Fonds Anquetil-Duperron, p. 21. Anquetil's spelling of the book's title later changed.

[254] "...had perused various treatises of the Sufi philosophers, and even composed some himself" (Hamilton 1803:417).

[255] "un grand nombre de livres de Theologie mystique eurent été apportés en (sa) présence, et des ouvrages composés (par lui)" (Anquetil 1787a:2). Anquetil's Latin translation differs but also makes no mention of Sufism: »et plurimos libros mysticos cum conspectu (*in conspectum suum*) attulisset, et resalha (*scripta breviora*) composita fecisset« (OUP1:2).

about Sufism from his young friend Sylvestre de Sacy, he never wavered in his conviction that the *Sirr-i akbar*'s text of the Upanishads represents (apart from a few strewn-in Islamic concepts) the pure ancient wisdom of India and the record of God's primal revelation transmitted throughout Asia and beyond. In the preface of his Latin translation Anquetil expressed his conviction in the following manner:

> I examined the books of Solomon, the ancient Chinese *Kims* [classics], the sacred *Beids* [Vedas] of the Indians and the *Zend-avesta* of the Persians and found therein transmitted—clearly and pellucidly as it behooves the fount of truth—the identical doctrine of a creator of the universe and of a unique spiritual principle.[256] (OUP1:viij).

In a handwritten note (NAF 8857: 230a) that he glued into the manuscript of his French translation of the *Sirr-i akbar*, Anquetil draws an even wider circle that includes the Neoplatonics.

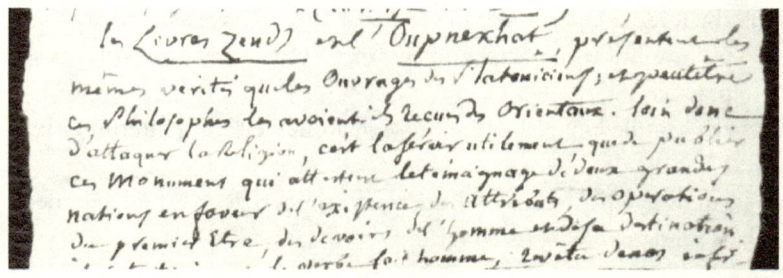

Note in Anquetil's French translation of the *Sirr-i akbar* (NAF 8857, p. 230a)

> The [Zoroastrian] *Zend books* and the *Oupnekhat* present the same truths as the works of the Platonics; possibly these philosophers have adopted them from the Orient. Far from attacking the

---

[256] "Libros Salomonis, antiquos Sinarum *Kims*, sacros Indorum *Beids*, Persarum *Zend-avesta* perlegas, idem dogma, unicum Universitatis parentem, unicum principium spirituale invenies, in illis clarè et pellucidè, uti veritatis fonti convenit, traditum." (OUP1:viij)

[Christian] religion, the publication of these sources is a useful service to her as it furnishes the testimony of two great nations in favor of the existence, attributes and actions of the supreme Being as well as the duties and destiny of man.[257]

Since his youth Anquetil had been on a mission to locate traces of God's original revelation and of mankind's original religion; and now he was convinced of having laid hands on its purest and most ancient relic: the essence of the Vedas in form of a literal Persian translation.

Today we know that the Upanishads stem from diverse ages and religious backgrounds and that there exist many different collections which sometimes contain not merely fifty (as in the *Sirr-i akbar / Oupnek'hat*) but over one hundred Upanishads. Nietzsche's friend, the indologist Paul Deussen, classified such texts roughly in four categories:

1. the oldest Upanishads, mostly redacted in ancient Sanskrit prose, that often interpret sacrifices in a philosophical manner
2. the middle Upanishads in verse that already have a primarily philosophical character and are freer from association with ritual practice
3. the middle Upanishads in prose that often cite and interpret older Upanishads
4. younger Upanishads of more recent times that are often regarded as fundamental texts by various sects.

The oldest Upanishads (No. 1) stem mostly from the pre-Buddhist era, i.e., from the seventh and sixth centuries before the common era. The middle verse Upanishads (No. 2) are mostly from the last four centuries before the common era and often show a strong theistic tendency. Both the older and the more recent Upanishads are valuable sources for tracing the transition from ancient vedic ritualism to new religious forms, institutions, and philosophical conceptions.

---

[257] For my transcription of the original French text see Appendix 1, p. 286.

However, such information only became available after Anquetil's death, and neither he nor Prince Dara were aware of it. Both regarded this collection of fifty Upanishads as excerpts from the ancient Veda and as a record of India's oldest theology. Anquetil first presented this theology to European readers in a work on geography published in 1787. Probably because he wanted to convince the public of India's ancient monotheistic orthodoxy he chose to first translate and publish four Upanishads that we today regard as relatively late theistic texts.[258]

The first Upanishad published in Europe is Anquetil's French rendering of the Narayana Upanishad which describes the god Vishnu alias Narayana as the origin of everything. Deussen later translated the first phrase of this Upanishad as follows from Sanskrit: "Om! It so happened that Purusha Nârâyaṇa desired to create the creatures" (Deussen 1921:747). In Anquetil's French translation it begins in the typical style of Prince Dara, and there is little doubt that Dara's comment was a major reason for Anquetil's choice:

> Naraïn, i.e. the Being that is in the soul of everything that is alive, and the soul of all that is alive is in him; this Being that is one had this desire: I want, having become many, make myself appear (externally); that is, to come from unity to multiplicity.[259]

Anquetil urged the readers of his translations to study the letter of the Jesuit Pons and the Sufi sections of Bernier (Anquetil 1787b:297); but he also emphasized that his Upanishad translations should speak for themselves. He was of course not aware that the cited beginning of the seventh Upanishad is not an ancient Indian text but rather an introduction by Prince Dara from 1656. Anquetil explained his understanding of ancient Indian theology in a long note that is typical of

---

[258] The translated Upanishads are listed in note 372 (p. 209) below.

[259] "Naraïn, c'est à dire l'Être qui est dans l'ame de tout ce qui est animé, & l'ame de tout ce qui est animé est en lui; cet Etre, étant un, eut ce desir: je veux, étant devenu beaucoup, me faire paroître moi-même (au dehors): c'est à dire de l'unité venir à la multiplicité" (Anquetil 1787b:297–8). Schopenhauer highlighted this passage in the corresponding Latin version (OUP2:1).

CHAPTER SEVEN

his view of the Upanishads and shows how faithfully he had adopted Dara's interpretation.[260] Anquetil explains the term *maya* as follows:

> I compared what is stated about *Māyā* in the *Oupnekhats*, 6, 8, 13, 26, 41, & 50. This principle is the primordial love [amour original], the *Desire of Brahm*, of *Atma*, distinguished and as separated from *Knowledge*. Mixed with this *Source of light*, with Knowledge, it has given birth to all that exists; that is, it *continually has let and still lets appear* all beings separately; which, from that moment onward, are but *appearances*. Man believes them to be existing substances: this is the ignorance springing from *Māyā*. In reality there is but one single and same substance which, by virtue of *Māyā*, shows itself perpetually in the multitude of forms that constitutes the actual universe.[261]

As we saw in the previous chapter, this reflects Prince Dara's Sufi interpretation of maya: maya as God's primordial longing and love that sets the entire creation process in motion. Everything is in God and God is in everything; but this all-oneness is hidden by the veil of maya which creates the semblance of multiplicity. Anquetil thus sees maya not only as the creative drive of God but also that of man:

> *Māyā* exists, in particular beings—that is to say in [the realm of] these *appearances, forms*—[it appeas as] the desire of creation, the love, liking, taste for particular beings, as [it is] in *Brahm*. The

---

[260] Anquetil mentioned this French version in the notes to the Latin *Oupnek'hat* studied by Schopenhauer. There is no evidence that Schopenhauer read this French translation of four Upanishads. However, the notes and explanations of the Latin *Oupnek'hat* take the same line.

[261] "J'ai comparé ce qui est dit du *Maïa*, dans les *Oupnekhats*, 6, 8, 13, 26, 41, & 50. Ce Principe est l'*amour original*, le *Désir* de *Brahm*, d'*Atma*, distingué & comme séparé de la *Connoissance*. Mêlé avec cette *Source de lumiere*, avec la Connoissance, il a donné naissance à tout ce qui existe; c'est à dire qu'il *a fait, & fait continuellement paroître* séparément tous les êtres, qui dès lors ne sont que des *apparences*. L'homme croit que ce sont des substances existantes: voilà l'ignorance qui vient du *Maïa*. Réellement, il n'y a qu'une seule & même substance, qui, par le *Maïa*, se montre perpétuellement sous cette multitude de formes qui constituent l'univers actuel." (Anquetil 1787b:305)

error of man consists in believing—because he begets, produces, and sees production, birth, and beginning—that in nature there is something more than *Brahm* and different from *Brahm*. With his eyes he sees but *forms*; and by virtue of *Māyā* he takes them to be separate *substances*. He ought to see in everything the *universal* substance, the *unique and true substance*. Yet he names only particular beings, or rather *appearances, without reality*. That is the man who, when seeing a rope on the floor, mistakes it for a snake, and seeing a snake mistakes it for a rope.[262]

In summary, Ibn Arabi's concept of the creator's longing (*ishq*) had married neoplatonic emanation to the Old Testament's and Islam's conception of creation; and Prince Dara linked the result—divine love as the fundamental creative drive from the One to the many—with the Indian concept of maya as explained by Shankara and other representatives of Vedanta. In this way Dara's formula of love = maya formed a bridge between Neoplatonism, mystical Islam, and Upanishadic thought in Vedantic perspective. The allegory of snake and rope is standard in Indian philosophy and plays an important role in Buddhist idealism (Yogācāra) as well as Vedanta. In classic Vedanta, maya is not regarded as "primeval love" (amour original) or Ur-longing but rather as a kind of original mistake or sin. But Dara had found an interesting solution by linking the love of the creator with the illusory multiplicity perceived by his creatures. Anquetil saw this as "the *error* that in this

---

[262] "Le *Maïa* est, dans les êtres particuliers; c'est à dire dans ces *apparences*, ces *formes*, le désir de la production, l'amour, le penchant, le gout pour ces êtres particuliers, comme dans *Brahm*. L'erreur de l'Homme est de croire, parce qu'il engendre, qu'il produit, qu'il voit produire, naître, commencer; son erreur est de croire qu'il y a dans la Nature quelque chose de plus que *Brahm*, de different de *Brahm*. Il ne voit de ses yeux que des *formes*; & par le *Maïa* il les prend pour des *substances* à part; il devroit voir en tout la substance *universelle, unique, la vraie substance*; & il ne nomme que des existences particulieres, ou plutôt des *apparences, sans réalité*. C'est l'Homme qui voyant à terre une Corde, la prend pour une Couleuvre, appercevant une Couleuvre pense que c'est une Corde." (Anquetil 1787b:305–6)

base and impermanent world, by shackling man to creatures, *detains him in the fetters of sin.*"²⁶³

Prince Dara identified the self-annihilation of Sufism (*fanā*) and the realization of divine all-oneness (*Tauḥīd*) with the lifting of the veil of maya and the Upanishadic deliverance through realization of all-oneness. His translator Anquetil understood this as follows:

> *Deliverance, supreme happiness* in the present lifetime consists in stripping oneself through *Knowledge*, through *Realization*, from the impressions that external objects make on us: *keeping one's senses captive and, knowing that this is all there is, seeing but a single and identical Being in everything* and unifying with this Being in thought as in reality, substantially, one differs from it only in appearance.²⁶⁴

According to Anquetil, the four Vedas were only revealed to man in order to indicate the path toward this goal (Anquetil 1787b:306). These sacred texts and their quintessence, the Upanishads, furnish the compass for this journey. At the end of his brief presentation of the "system," Anquetil defines the goal succinctly:

> Someone who has truly realized *Atma* and *Brahm* in himself and knows that his own being is in itself but an appearance, a form, one of the shapes of Atma: this man is no longer in need of external aid, he himself is *Atma*.²⁶⁵

---

²⁶³ "Telle est l'*erreur*, qui, dans ce bas Monde, ce Monde passager, attachant l'Homme aux créatures, le *retient dans les liens du péché*" (Anquetil 1787b:306).

²⁶⁴ "La *délivrance*, le *souverain bonheur*, dès cette vie, consiste à se dépouiller par la *Science*, par la *Connoissance*, des impressions que les objets extérieurs font sur nous; *à se tenir les sens captifs, ne voyant en tout, sachant qu'il n'y a en tout ce qui existe, qu'un seul & même Etre*, auquel on se réunit en pensée, comme réellement, substantiellement, on n'en diffère que par l'apparence" (Anquetil 1787b:306).

²⁶⁵ "Mais celui qui est parvenu à connoitre en lui-même ce que cest que l'*Atma*, que *Brahm*; & que son propre être, à lui, n'est qu'une apparence, une form, une des figures de l'*Atma*: cet homme n'a plus besoin de secours étrangers; il est lui même l'*Atma*" (Anquetil 1787b:306).

Amor and Unification

We will now turn to the reception of Anquetil's literary output. When he published his annotated French translation of four carefully chosen Upanishads he had certainly hoped for a positive echo. But he had a threefold handicap. First, this translation appeared in the second volume of an expensive work on the geography and history of India; second, it was published in French in Berlin; and third, this happened precisely in the year when the Prussian army invaded the Netherlands and when the troubles leading to the French revolution amplified. But there was an additional reason that Anquetil mentioned in an appendix at the very end of the work: in the year 1785 the first translation of a Sanskrit text into a European language had been published. The English translation by Charles Wilkins of the *Bhagavad Gita* rang in a new age in which Europeans could gradually gather information about ancient India not from Persian sources or hearsay but rather from translations of original Sanskrit texts. The foundation of the Asiatick Society of Bengal in the year 1784 by Anquetil's harsh critic William Jones and Wilkin's *Bhagavad Gita* rendering (1785) were only the first steps. They were followed by the publication of the first volumes of the *Asiatick Researches* (from 1788) which soon made their way to France and triggered an orientalist revolution whose first phase came to a close in 1815 with the establishment on the European continent of the first academic chairs for Indology and Sinology in Paris.[266]

On March 18 of 1787, Anquetil wrapped up his French translation of the fifty Upanishads of Dara's *Sirr-i akbar*, and on August 16 of the same year he finished his revision of the manuscript (Anquetil 1787b:862–3). During the troubles of the French revolution he went on to translate the entire text anew into Latin because of he felt that Latin word order and grammar are more appropriate for a literal translation from Persian. His view of the Upanishads as a "secret to be safeguarded" (*secretum tegendum*) may also have played a role; he may have

---

[266] For more information about this revolution and the role of British indologists see App 2010c, Marchand 2009, and the still valuable book by Raymond Schwab on what he called the Oriental Renaissance (1950/1984).

seen this as a work not for the masses but for a select readership capable of appreciating its doctrine. Anquetil's preface to the Latin translation is dated September 30, 1797 (OUP1:cx). But this Latin version, published in two volumes in 1801 and 1802, contains not only Anquetil's new translation that in many ways differs from his initial French rendering. In addition it features an incredible number of notes and explanatory essays whose total volume exceeds the translation part (see Appendix 1 below). In his preface (OUP1:cviij) Anquetil states that this work represents the original form of the famous *doctrina orientalis* that from the second half of the 17th century had so much occupied European authors such as Bernier, Burnet, Brucker, Mosheim, Diderot and Pluquet. This "Oriental doctrine" was regarded not only as the basis or kernel of Oriental religions but also as the root of such diverse movements as gnosticism, Neoplatonism, Kabbalah, Sufism and also the systems of Indian philosophy discussed by Father Pons.[267]

In the *Dissertatio* at the beginning of his first *Oupnek'hat* volume, Anquetil filled close to one hundred pages with his presentation of major Upanishadic doctrines and of parallels of the *doctrina orientalis* in European theology and philosophy. He specifically treated four themes: 1. God; 2. emanation and creation; 3. the suprasensory world; and 4. the relationship of macrocosm and microcosm. The dominance of Neoplatonic influences in these discussions is striking. Regarding God, pages upon pages are filled with citations from Bishop Synesius and the neoplatonic-Christian mystic Pseudo-Dionysius, and regarding emanation Pseudo-Dionysius is joined by Origen as well as Thomas Burnet's views about the Kabbalah, the Cambridge Platonist Ralph Cudworth, and the historian Isaac de Beausobre who in his history of Manicheism had proposed a defense of emanationism that Anquetil appeared to accept: as long as emanation is conceived in a manner that does not smudge the sharp dividing line between creator and crea-

---

[267] For a description of the invention of this *doctrina orientalis* and its impact in Europe before Anquetil's time see App, *The Cult of Emptiness. The European Discovery of Buddhism and the Invention of Oriental Philosophy* (2012).

Amor and Unification

ture, it is acceptable and evades the danger of falling into Spinozism (OUP1:xlviij-xlix).

Readers of Anquetil's two large *Oupnek'hat* volumes were impressed by his presentation of the tenets of the *doctrina orientalis* but not necessarily convinced by his arguments regarding its compatibility with Christian orthodoxy. The French senator Lanjuinais, who already in 1803 published an extensive overview of the complex content of Anquetil's *Oupnek'hat* tomes,[268] saw in its *doctrina orientalis* "a true mishmash of Spinozism or pantheism, theosophism or illuminism, and even of an idealism in the style of Berkeley."[269] He judged the *Oupnek'hat's* pantheism to be "clearly delineated," its union with God "an illuminism of the highest degree," and the happy state without thinking and without good and evil "a very dangerous quietism." On the other hand he regarded the idealism of the *Oupnek'hat*, in which "our world is but a simple appearance" and "but a series of modifications of our spirit," as "a more refined spiritualism than the Berkeley's."[270] Lanjuinais accepted that this system represents "the primeval traditions of mankind" that had been transmitted "with some additions and changes" thanks to Anquetil. He suspected that such additions existed in the *Oupnek'hat's* portrayal of quietism which according to him had degenerated into "the most pernicious excesses" and even exceeded the quietism of Madame Guyon and of the Sufis (Lanjuinais 1823:3.82). Nevertheless, Lanjuinais thought the *Oupnek'hat* is worthy of great attention because its philosophical system is 1. more than 4,000 years

---

[268] Senator Lanjuinais's review that was originally published in the *Magasin Encylopédique* of 1803 was reprinted in 1823 in two volumes of the *Journal Asiatique* with minor cuts: vol. 2 (pp. 213-236; 265-282; 344-365) and vol. 3 (pp. 15-34; 71-91). Schopenhauer mentioned this review several times and referred in various handwritten remarks in his personal *Oupnek'hat copy* to the senator's translations from Anquetil's Latin to French. Lanjuinais was so interested that he studied some Sanskrit.

[269] "Ce système est un vrai mélange de Spinosisme ou de panthéisme, de *théosophisme* ou d'*illuminisme*, de quiétisme, et même d'idéalisme à la manière de Berkeley" (Lanjuinais 1823:2.226).

[270] Lanjuinais, *ibid*.

old; and 2. extremely widespread since it reigns from Persia, India and Tibet to China, Japan and Siberia (pp. 85–6). Among other things it is said to form "the basis of the religion of the Brahmans and that of the disciples of the Buddha." In short, this "indianisme" is said to prevail in almost all of Asia, to be more sublime than the conceptions of the Greeks and Romans, and more radical in its idealism than Collier and Berkeley (p. 86). Lanjuinais saw the goal of this most ancient oriental doctrine in the realization of all-oneness through "the abnegation of oneself and one's individual existence in a kind of philosophical or religious death consisting in feeling and seeing oneself exclusively in the immense Ocean of the unique spiritual Being."[271]

Due in part to its complex Latin style interspersed with Greek particles and countless transliterated Persian terms, the *Oupnek'hat* was often called difficult or even illegible. Max Müller wrote for instance that it is "so utterly unintelligible that it required the lynxlike perspicacity of an intrepid philosopher, such as Schopenhauer, to discover a thread through such a labyrinth."[272] Senator Lanjuinais also deplored this fatal flaw. Yet his very detailed review featuring his translation into French of a great many passages and paragraphs shows that Schopenhauer was not the only reader capable of appreciating Anquetil's work. Lanjuinais learned, like Schopenhauer a few years later, how man can arrive at the goal of "philosophical or religious death" and thereby at the existential realization of all-oneness. In a paragraph entitled "Theory of unification" (Théorie de l'unification) the senator cites numerous passages from the *Oupnek'hat* about the path toward this unification. For example:

> When the heart has renounced all desires and actions, it thereby joins its principle which is the universal soul; when it joins its principle it has no more will whatsoever, other than that of the

---

[271] ""faisant abnégation de soi-même et de sa propre existence individuelle, par une sorte de mort philosophique et religieuse, qui consiste à ne vouloir plus se sentir et se voir que dans l'immense Océan de l'Être unique et spirituel" (Lanjuinais 1823.2:87).

[272] Max Müller 1962: lviii-liv.

Amor and Unification

veritable Being. Man must purify his heart with great care; when he has purified his heart (*of all desire*) then he has attained victory over the world.[273]

Another doctrine the *Oupnek'hat* explained and documented in Lanjuinais French translations is of the kind that must have impressed Schopenhauer who read this in the Latin original:

> The impure heart is that which has will; the pure heart is that which has absolutely none [...] (*In this state*) one desires nothing because all desires are fulfilled, for one is full of the being which is everything, and since in truth one possesses everything. (*This is what true life consists in*); so to desire is to die, and to not desire anything is to live.[274]

Lanjuinais could have translated many more passages to this effect since this constitutes a major theme of Dara's Upanishads: *fanā* or, as Lanjuinais correctly understood, "a kind of philosophical or religious death" in which the veil of maya of the individual soul (*djiw ātma*), caught up as it is in self-centered illusion, is suddenly lifted, thereby revealing that the individual soul is nothing other than the universal soul (*pram ātma*). As Lanjuinais realized, "will" (Fr. *volonté*, Lat. *volitio*) or "willing" (Fr. *vouloir*, Lat. *volle*) and the liberation from it are central themes of the *Oupnek'hat*. Just after the *Oupnek'hat* passage cited and translated in Lanjuinais's review, a student of the *Oupnek'hat* such as Schopenhauer could read:

---

[273] "lorsque le coeur a renoncé aux désirs et aux actions, par là même il va à son principe qui est l'âme universelle; lorsqu'il va à son principe, il n'a aucune volonté que celle de l'être véritable. L'homme doit purifier son coeur avec un grand soin; lorsqu'il a purifié son coeur (*de tout désir*), il a vaincu le monde" (Lanjuinais 1823.2.281; the words in parentheses and italics in Lanjuinais's text mark his own addition to Anquetil's text).

[274] "Le coeur impur est celui qui a des volontés; le coeur pur est celui qui n'en a conservé aucune. [...] (*Dans cet état*), on ne désire rien, parce que tous les désirs sont accomplis, parce qu'on est plein de l'être qui est tout, parce que, dans la vérité, on possède tout" (Lanjuinais 1823.2:282; the words in parentheses and italics in Lanjuinais's text mark his own addition to Anquetil's text).

Oupnek'hat vol 1, p. 358; markings by Schopenhauer who frequently underlined the word "volitio" (will) and its declinations and wrote in the margin.

Quemadmodùm cum collectione (*junctione*) lampadis (*vasis*) et olei, et funiculi igniarii, lampas lumen manet; tempore quo oleum è medio exivit, haec utensilia collecta *Brahm* comedit: ipso hoc modo, volitio, quae com loco (*vice*) olei lampadis corporis est, et cum causâ (*operâ*) hujus volitionis, corpus et mundus, *djiw âtma* et *pram âtma* separata apparent: tempore quo haec volitio è medio ivit, corpus et mundus, et *djiw âtma* et *pram âtma* unum fiunt; differentia, quam in mundo parvo et mundo magno dat (*producit*), è latere fit (*removetur*) (OUP1:358)

Just as, through the combination (*junction*) of a lamp (*vessel*) with oil and a wick, a lamp emits light and, after the oil runs dry, *Brahm* consumes all of this: in the same way through the extinction of will—the oil in the lamp of the body through which body and world, *djiw âtma* and *pram âtma*, appear to be distinct— [through the extinction of will] body and world, *djiw âtma* and *pram âtma*, become one; and the difference, which [will] gives (*produces*) in the microcosm and macrocosm, disappears (*is removed*).

Amor and Unification

Schopenhauer's copious markup of this passage of the *Oupnek'hat* shows, as does his handwritten remark in the margin,[275] that he read such explanations about will (*volitio*) and *liberatio* from it with much attention.

It has been suggested that these two volumes of the *Oupnek'hat* were barely noticed or soon forgotten and that they exerted little influence apart from their impact on Schopenhauer. That is not the case. Interest in France was stoked by Lanjuinais's extensive review (1803) which was reprinted in France's first Orientalist journal (1823); and in Germany the *Oupnek'hat* quickly became required reading for a public interested in remote antiquity and intrigued by questions of origins. For Johann Gottfried Herder, an avid reader of earlier works by Anquetil, the publication probably arrived too late since he died in 1803. But for disciples of Herder such as Friedrich Majer and admirers such as Arnold Kanne and Joseph Görres, the *Oupnek'hat* was a long-awaited ray of light illuminating the obscure beginnings of mankind: a text that appeared to be far older than Herder's "oldest document"[276] (the Old Testament) and was moreover linked to Kashmir, the very region that Herder and others had suspected of being the cradle of mankind.

Furthermore, the *Oupnek'hat* was published in a period of heightened interest in India that was fueled not only by eminent writers such as Voltaire[277] and Herder but also by romantics such as Friedrich Schlegel, author of a seminal book on India,[278] and Joseph Görres. In his *On*

---

[275] Schopenhauer's handwritten comment in the margin reads: »Unterschied des Makrokosmos u. Mikrokosmos aufgehoben« (Difference between macrocosm and microcosm abolished).

[276] "Älteste Urkunde des Menschengeschlechts" (Oldest Document of Mankind) is the title of a book by Herder (Riga: Johann Friedrich Hartknoch, 1774) inspired by Herder's study of Anquetil's *Zend Avesta* (1771).

[277] See chapter 1 (pp. 15–76) of App, *The Birth of Orientalism* where Voltaire's interest in India and his major influence on the European perception of India are discussed.

[278] Friedrich Schlegel, *Über die Sprache und Weisheit der Indier*. Heidelberg: Mohr und Zimmer, 1808.

the *Language and Wisdom of the Indians* (1808), Schlegel presented his view of mankind's earliest monotheistic religion and the historical sequence of its degeneration into the doctrines of emanation, dualism, and pantheism. Basing his argument on evidence from the *Oupnek'hat*, Joseph Görres (1776–1848) criticized Schlegel's scenario in the *Heidelberger Jahrbücher* of 1811:

> There is no religion where pantheism and the doctrine of emanation were regarded as opposites; the idea of omnipresence already demolishes such a notion. On the contrary: emanation, dualism and the other forms were universally acknowledged as implied in original pantheism. The predicament of existence has its origin in the fact that by its particularity it excludes the universality that would bring it in tune with the divine idea; the inner drive toward lost bliss and holiness constitues the striving for such universality.[279]

Already in his review of the *Oupnek'hat* in the *Jahrbücher* of 1809 Görres had praised Prince Dara's "doctrine of unification" and the age-old "extract from the sacred Vedams" prepared by "the Munis of the earliest times," and rejected as unjustified "the accusation of President Jones" that the translator had adulterated the Vedic text through "arbitrarily inserted glosses" (Görres 1811:311). Görres asserted having found no more than three or four passages where "Indian Devetas had been translated into Islamic angels," and he declared that all Islamic elements in the *Oupnek'hat* can immediately be identified as glosses (p. 312). Görres's comparison of two translations of the Iśa-Upanishad—that by Jones from Sanskrit and that by Anquetil from Persian—led to

---

[279] »Der Pantheismus und die Emanationslehre sind in keiner Religion als Gegensätze betrachtet worden, schon die Idee der Allgegenwart vernichtet eine solche Entgegensetzung. Man hat vielmehr die Emanation, den Dualism und die andern Formen als inbegriffen im ursprünglichen Pantheism allerwärts anerkannt. Die Unseligkeit des Daseyns ist daher gekommen, daß es durch seine Besonderheit ausschließt von sich die Allgemeinheit, die es zur göttlichen Idee ergänzen würde; das Streben nach dieser Allgemeinheit ist der innere Trieb zur verlornen Seligkeit und Heiligkeit« (Görres 1935:5.308).

the following conclusion: "We can thus with certainty conclude that in this work [the *Oupnek'hat*] we have, due to the scrupulous faithfulness of both translators, a trustworthy rendering of the Sanskrit original into Europe's language of the learned."[280] With regard to the age of the *Oupnek'hat* Görres wrote: "This much is certain: the work always and everywhere presents itself as a pure extract of the Vedam. Based on another tradition and on the comparison of all other probabilities, it is more than probable that it can be dated to 4900 years before the present time."[281] Görres concluded:

> In the Upnek'hat we indeed possess the system of the ancient Vedams on which the entire Asian myth is based. In it alone can we grasp this common mother system, which makes this book immeasurably important for the religious and philosophical history of the Orient until such time as the Vedas themselves, from which it originated, become accessible.[282]

For his *History of Myth of the Asiatic World* (*Mythengeschichte der asiatischen Welt*, 1810) Anquetil's *Oupnek'hat* thus became the fixed reference point and the "foundation of the entire superstructure": "I have presented the system of the Veda based on this book, and those who have tested their patience on it know what difficulties this involved."[283]

---

[280] »Wir können also mit Gewißheit uns versichert halten, daß wir in diesem Werke bey der gewissenhaften Treue beyder Uebersetzer eine zuverlässige Uebertragung des samscritischen Originals in das europäische gelehrte Idiom besitzen« (Görres 1811:312).

[281] »So viel ist gewiß, daß das Werk sich immer und überall als reinen Auszug des Vedams gibt deren Ursprung eine andere, alle Probabilitäten verglichen, mehr als wahrscheinliche Tradition 4900 Jahre hinter die gegenwärtige Zeit versetzt« (Görres 1811:314)

[282] »daß wir im Upnek'hat wirklich das System der alten Vedams besitzen, daß auf ihm die ganze asiatische Mythe ruht, und in diesem gemeinsamen Muttersystem allein begriffen werden kann, daß das Buch selbst also für die religiöse und philosophische Geschichte des Orients von unendlicher Wichtigkeit ist, so lange bis uns die Vedams selbst, von denen es ausgegangen, aufgeschlossen sind« (Görres 1811:325).

[283] »festen Punkt« ... »Untersuchungen zum Grund gelegt, als Basis auf die

CHAPTER SEVEN

In the year 1810—four years before Schopenhauer began to study it—Anquetil's *Oupnek'hat* thus became Görres's "Urmythe," i.e. the foundational doctrine of all great religions of antiquity. As Görres showed on a map especially commissioned for his *History of Myth of the Asiatic World*, this earliest revelation or "Urmythe" radiated from its cradle in Kashmir in all four directions where it formed the four "Ancient Laws" ("Alte Gesetze" of South, East, North, West) which in turn became the basis of the world's great religions such as Judaism in the West, and in Asia (which alone is shown below) Brahmanism, Buddhism, Confucianism, Daoism, Shintoism, Zoroastrianism, and Shamanism.

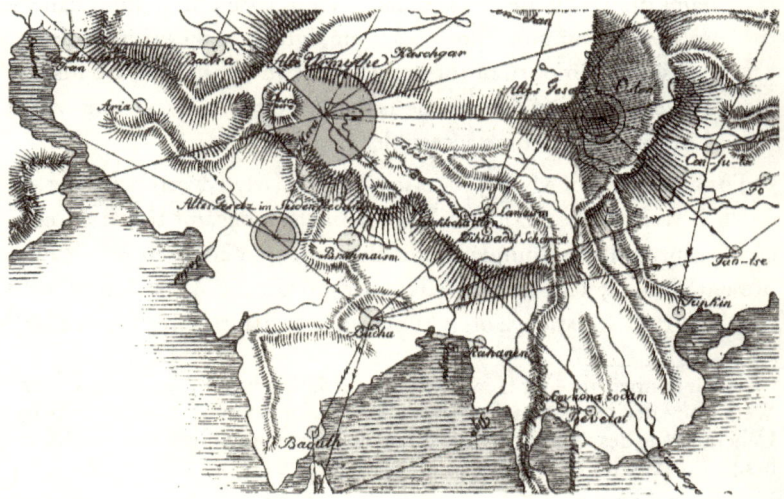

Part of Asia in the mythological map of the ancient world (*Mythentafel der alten Welt*, Görres 1810). The larger dark grey circle indicates the "Urmyth" in the Kashmir region; the smaller grey circles in India and China the "Ancient Laws" of South and East from which Brahmanism, Buddhism, Confucianism, Daoism, and Shintoism were born.

das ganze Gewölbe des Baues ursprünglich gegründet ist« ... »Ich habe das System der Veda's aus diesem Buch dargestellt, unter welchen Schwierigkeiten, wird der beurtheilen, der schon einmal seine Geduld an diesem Werk geprüft« (Görres 1811:6).

Amor and Unification

Dara's formula of love = maya also found its way into Görres's universal history of religion. According to him, the Vedas understood creation in a more profound and lofty manner because of their conception of maya. According to them, the godhead had spread this veil in an affect of creation "in which love is at work, and in love beauty and semblance and illusion."[284] Görres saw in this doctrine the ancestor of the "eros of the Greeks and Phoenicians" which was regarded as the "root of the world."[285]

But Görres and Schopenhauer were far from the only Germans who, in spite of all the difficulties this involved, decided to engage in the arduous study of the *Oupnek'hat*. Though it tends to be ignored even in recent studies on orientalism,[286] this work formed for example the basis of the theories of Georg Friedrich Creuzer, the author of the famous multi-volume *Symbolism and Mythology of the Ancient Peoples* (*Sym-*

---

[284] I spare the reader a full translation of Görres's stylistic excesses, but here is his romantic rambling in the original German: »Tiefer [als die chinesische Lehre] haben die Veda's die Schwierigkeit gefaßt, und feiner, und in höherer Anschauung durch die *Maia* sie gelöst. Als einen Schleier hat die Gottheit diese Maia nach eigenem Wohlgefallen um sich her gebreitet, mit einem süßen Liebesrausche hat sie sich umwebt, mit lieblichem Taumel und freudigem Selbstvergessen hat sie sich umfangen, denn es ist der Affect des Schaffens, der in dieser Maia wirkt, im Affecte aber ist die Liebe, der Liebe aber Schönheit und Schein und Täuschung sonder Schmerz und Reue, Scherz und Spiel ist alles Bilden im Affecte, bedeutend nur im Kunstgebilde, das sich damit gestaltet« (Görres 1811:290).

[285] In dieser Lehre ist »Liebe, der Eros der Griechen und Phönizier« nichts anderes als »die Wurzel der Welt«, denn in ihr hat sich »Gott in ein Liebendes geschieden und ein Geliebtes, aus der Liebe ist die Frucht hervorgegangen, über allen aber ist das erste Sein, das selbst jene Liebe in sich aufgenommen und die Spaltung, und in ihm ist allein der wesenhafte Urbestand der Dinge, die Liebe aber hat in bloßem Schein ein Conterfay gewebt; und ein erfreulich Bild es vor das Wesen hingesetzt«. (Görres 1811:291)

[286] Examples are the recent 600-page study by Andrea Polaschegg on German orientalism at the beginning of the 19th century (2005) that contains not a single mention of the *Oupnek'hat*, and Suzanne L. Marchand's otherwise rich *German Orientalism in the Age of Empire* (Cambridge: Cambridge University Press, 2009) that mentions it once on p. 300, stating merely that Schopenhauer "as early as the 1810s, read Anquetil's *Oupnekhat*."

bolik und Mythologie der alten Völker, [1]1819–1821). Creuzer wrote in 1819:

> But if we compare the content of these Upnekhata, through which the most ancient Indian sources have been transmitted to us, with what the English researchers have so far published from the Vedas, we can indeed say: the Vedas contain the world's most ancient religious system, and there could hardly be another people possessing older religious documents.[287]

According to Creuzer, the Greeks had borrowed "the entire inventory of their mythological faith and knowledge from the Orient" (Creuzer 1818:93), and he was convinced that Indian Ur-monotheism, as documented in the Vedas, represents the proper ur-tradition of mankind.[288] This is how it came about that Dara's formula of love=maya helped Creuzer to explain the myths of Hesiod and the ancient Greeks:

> In the Vedas there emerges, among the first actions of the eternal, the drive to create. It is called *Maya*, i.e., *illusion, speciousness*, because everything that emerges from the essence of the eternal into reality is vain, illusion and *speciousness* if compared to the eternal. The daughter of this Maya is *Cama*, love. Cama is the emotion of creation, and in emotion there is love. Maya is the mother of the world; but what she gave birth to is born in mere illusion. This world is an illusory appearance; but the fact that this is so is the effect of *love*.[289]

---

[287] »Vergleichen wir aber das, was diese Upnekhata, wodurch uns also die ältesten Indischen Quellen vermittelt worden sind, enthält, mit dem, was uns die Englischen Forscher bis jetzt aus den Veda's gegeben haben, so können wir wohl sagen: es ist in den Veda's das älteste Religionssystem auf Erden enthalten, und es möchte nicht leicht ein Volk seyn, das ältere Religionsurkunden aufzuweisen hätte« (Creuzer 1819:1.551).

[288] »Urtradition des Menschengeschlechtes« (Creuzer 1818:100–1).

[289] »In den Veda's tritt unter den ersten Actionen des Ewigen hervor der Schöpfungstrieb. Er heißt *Maja*, d.h. *Täuschung, Schein*, weil alles, was aus dem Wesen des Ewigen in die Wirklichkeit tritt, eitel, Täuschung und *Schein* ist, nämlich mit dem Ewigen verglichen. Dieser Maja Tochter ist *Cama*,

Amor and Unification

According to Creuzer this elucidates the true meaning of "*deception* and *love* and *strife*" in Hesiod's text, and of "longing, craving, and obsession" in the Samothracian doctrine.[290]

Arnold Kanne's *Chronus* of 1813 also relied on the *Oupnek'hat* and Dara's conception of maya. Kanne defined it as "Maya, God's eternal love, also the quality of Brahm's desire which is called his eternal, divine will."[291] Indeed, at the very beginning of his introductory list of Sanskrit terms that precedes the Upanishad translations, Prince Dara had equated the Indian sacred word OUM with Allah, and Anquetil had rendered this equation by "OUM = Deus." Kanne adopted Dara's vision and concluded that Maya is nothing other than God's divine will that becomes manifest in the world "*as* his will" and constitutes "God's desire to go out of himself, i.e. God's longing and love for the world and for creatures." Through Maya "Oum is spread out to the particular life" since it is "God's longing to posit creatures and being outside of himself in order to love them."[292] This "downward migration" corresponds to a "return and upward migration to the supreme and original life": "all selfhood having died off in the spirit, there are not spirits but rather One Spirit": "the All without any something."[293]

---

die Liebe. Jene ist der Affect des Schaffens, und im Affect ist Liebe. Diese ist die Weltmutter; aber was sie gebohren, ist im blosen Schein gebohren. Ein Scheinbild ist diese Welt, aber daß sie ist, ist der *Liebe* Werk« (Creuzer 1818:169).

[290] »*Täuschung* und *Liebe* und *Streit*« in der hesiodischen Urkunde und »Sehnen, Schmachten und Sucht« in der Samothrakischen Lehre (Creuzer 1818:169–70).

[291] »Maja, die ewige Liebe Gottes, auch die Qualität von Brams Verlangen, sein ewiges, göttliches Wollen, genannt« (Kanne 1813:75).

[292] »sein göttliches Wollen selbst«; »*als* sein Wille«; »das Verlangen Gottes, aus sich hervorzugehen, d.i. Gottes Sehnsucht und Liebe zur Welt und Creatur« (Kanne 1813:76). Durch Maya ist »das Oum zum Leben des Besondern ausgebreitet«, denn sie ist »die Sehnsucht Gottes, Creatur und Wesen außer sich zu stellen, um sie zu lieben« (pp. 79–80).

[293] »Herabwanderung«; »Rück- und Hinaufwanderung in das höchste und ursprüngliche Leben«; »aller Selbstheit ist der Geist hier abgestorben, hier

Regarding the goal of this return Kanne once again refers to the *Oupnek'hat*:

> *Laout* or *Lahut* is in the Oupnekhat the final divine world in which there is no one who says 'I'—the great demersion wherein man is conscious of being pure joy: where he is freed from the Maya of the three other worlds, where there is tranquillity, no world, and no duality.[294]

Dara's and Anquetil's work also indicated to Kanne the method leading to this state:

> Discarding thoughts and willing, contemplating only Brahm. He must attract and arrest all will on the outside and inside, except for God; since only a heart without any willing is pure. In this manner he is liberated from everything particular, from multiplicity and from duality forming its ground, and therewith from time, finitude, and death.[295]

According to Kanne this constitutes the "Oumadketet" of Anquetil's *Oupnek'hat*: "*Being-Knowing*: the supreme state where all consciousness as partial I-ness has ceased and all dualism of seeing and being is overcome."[296]

---

sind nicht Geister, sondern nur Ein Geist«; »das All ohne Etwas« (Kanne 1813:84).

[294] »*Laout*, oder *Lahut*, ist den Oupnekhat die letzte göttliche Welt, in welcher keiner ist, der *Ich* sagt, — die große Demersion, wo der Mensch sich reine Freude weiß; wo er frei wird von der Maja der drei andern Welten, wo Ruhe, keine Welt und keine Zweiheit ist« (Kanne 1813:84).

[295] »Gedanken und Wollen ablegen, Brahm allein betrachten. Allen Willen außen und innen muß er in sich ziehen und fesseln, außer den nach Gott; denn rein ist das Herz, in dem kein Wollen ist. So dann wird er von allem Partialen, von der Vielheit und, woraus diese entsprang, von der Zweiheit befreit, mithin von der Zeit, Endlichkeit und Tode« (Kanne 1813:95–6).

[296] »das *Seyn-Wissen*, — der höchste Zustand, in welchem, weil alle Intelligenz als partiale Ichheit aufgehört hat, aller Dualismus des Schauens und Seyns aufgehoben ist« (Kanne 1813:96).

Amor and Unification

We will soon see that Schopenhauer understood the *Oupnek'hat* in a very similar way. This can also be said of Adolph Wagner, the composer Richard Wagner's favorite uncle who authored an "overview of the mythical system" as an appendix to his friend Kanne's work. Apart from extensive quotes from Jacob Böhme about the "will of the Ungrund [non-ground]" and about that which is "all in all" even though it appears to the "self-hood of one's own willing" as "a Nothing" (Kanne 1813:573), Adolph Wagner's survey also contains much evidence of his intensive study of the *Oupnek'hat*. From Böhme's "sacred Ur-ground" of God's unity, Wagner saw creation arise due to the holy "urge of love and the drive (Maya) to manifest himself and to become conscious, to grasp himself."[297] Whereas in unity there is no time and space, "all creation begins with free dividing and separating—as the purest and most pervasive forms of knowing, time and space, already demonstrate." (p. 575)

Wagner wrote this in 1813, the very year when his nephew Richard was born. As described in our next chapter, it was just one year later in 1814 that Schopenhauer began to study the *Oupnek'hat* and arrived at a similar understanding. Wagner wrote about the "Will of the un-ground" (Willen des Ungrundes) in Böhme's sense but also of the *principium individuationis* that creates the illusion of distance and sequence, i.e. space and time, even though what is "separated" cannot be anything other than "the One" (das Eine; p. 575). But how can a self liberate itself and become non-selfhood or, as Wagner put it, "a Nothing and thus the eternally tranquil spirit, the silent God (*Abakt* of the Oupnekhat)"? One year prior to Schopenhauer's encounter with the *Oupnek'hat*, Adolph Wagner (who like young Schopenhauer admired Jakob Böhme and read Kant, Giordano Bruno and Spinoza) drew a conclusion that—provided that one leaves God out of the equation—

---

[297] Böhmes »heiliger Urgrund«—der »heilig stille Abgrund« der Einheit Gottes—aus der »das schaffende Wort« aufsteigt durch den heiligen »Liebesdrang und Zug (Maïa), sich selbst zu offenbaren und bewußt zu werden, sich zu fassen« (A. Wagner in Kanne 1813:575).

comes surprisingly close to the final passage of Schopenhauer's *The World as Will and Representation* and cites the *Oupnek'hat*:

> As one's self-creating and one's willing ceases, the divine creating and willing arise: and what is without will is identical with Nothingness, which is the nature of us all; and this non-ground is God himself. As the Oupnekhat [says]: A pure heart is without will.[298]

"A pure heart is without will"—could this not almost serve as the motto of Schopenhauer's soteriology to whose formation we will now return?

---

[298] »Ists nun, daß das eigen selber-Bilden und Wollen stille steht, so geht das göttliche Bilden und Wollen auf: dann was willenlos ist, das ist mit dem Nichts Ein Ding und ist unser aller Natur, welcher Ungrund ist Gott selber. Und die Oupnekh.: ein reines Herz ist willenlos« (A. Wagner in Kanne 1813:581).

8. Delusion and Awakening

Schopenhauer returned to Weimar in the winter 1813-14 and remained there for six months. J. W. Goethe, who had read his doctoral dissertation with much interest, described him after a meeting as "a remarkable and interesting man" who "with a certain acute-minded obstinacy" is throwing a joker card into the game of modern philosophy (Steiger 1988:5.756). Goethe invited him to study together the phenomenon of colors, and for this purpose they met seven times and usually spent the entire evening together during which they certainly also discussed philosophy.[299] Before the turn of the century Goethe had promoted the nomination of young Schelling as professor of philosophy at the University of Jena and was thus very familiar with Schelling's philosophy of nature that Schopenhauer had so intensively studied. Apart from his favorite philosopher Spinoza, Goethe highly

---

[299] On 29 November 1813 Schopenhauer for the first time spent an evening with Goethe, and their last study meeting took place on 3 April 1814. For all dates and additional information see App 2006c:46 ff.

esteemed Giordano Bruno and knew his "Of Cause, Principle and the One" through extensive excerpts contained in Jacobi's letters to Mendelssohn (1789).[300] Major themes of Jacobi's letters were "the power of the world-soul that manifests itself as the general form of the universe" (Jacobi 1789:263–4) and the idea that "*as regards substance, all is one*" (p. 288). According to Giordano Bruno this world-soul is all in all, and recognizing this all-oneness is "the aim of all philosophy and investigation of nature" (p. 292). Bruno regarded the universe as a single organism that ceaselessly changes yet essentially always remains the same:

> What first was a seed becomes grass, then a shoot, then bread – chyle – animal semen – embryo – man – corpse; then again earth, stone or another material, and so on. Here we thus recognize something that transforms itself into all these things but remains in itself always one and the same.[301]

This constitutes "in the same manner the whole and every individual thing, all and one; therefore [it has] limit yet no limit, form yet no form, matter yet not matter, soul yet no soul."[302] Jacobi remarked that this exactly matches the kind of conception found in Spinoza (p. 297). One of Goethe's poems stemming from the year prior to his study meetings with Schopenhauer reflects a world view that would have met the approval both of Giordano Bruno and Prince Dara:

> What God would it be who only pushes from outside
> Letting the universe whirl round his finger!

---

[300] Later on, Goethe received an Italian edition of Giordano Bruno's works prepared by Richard Wagner's uncle Adolph who in our previous chapter was mentioned as one of the ardent readers of Anquetil's *Oupnek'hat*.

[301] »Was erst Samen war, wird Gras, hierauf Aehre, alsdenn Brodt – Nahrungssaft – Blut – thierischer Samen – ein Embrio – Mensch – Leichnam; denn wieder Erde, Stein, oder andre Masse, und so fort. Hier erkennen wir also Etwas, welches sich in alle diese Dinge verwandelt, und an sich immer eins und dasselbe bleibt« (Jacobi 1789:280–1).

[302] Es ist »auf gleiche Weise das Gesammte und ein Jedes, Alles und Eins; also Grenze und dennoch keine Grenze; Form und dennoch keine Form; Materie und dennoch keine Materie; Seele und dennoch keine Seele« (pp. 295–6).

> It behooves Him to move the world from the inside
> Tending nature in Himself, Himself in nature
> So that what lives and thrives in Him and exists
> Never lacks His power nor His spirit.[303]

Some of Schopenhauer's book borrowings during his Weimar months and the first months in Dresden may have been inspired by Goethe. They include, apart from Jacobi's letters and the works by Hemsterhuis and Bruno[304] cited by Jacobi, several books by Lorenz Oken and Henrich Steffens, authors esteemed by Goethe because they described the world as a holistic organism.[305]

It is well known that Goethe had a deep interest in the Orient (Polaschegg 2005, Mommsen 2014). The libraries of Weimar and Jena that he for some time supervised contained, partly also because of the bibliophilia of the polyglot Christian Wilhelm Büttner (1716–1801), a fair amount of Orient-related works. After Büttner's death it fell to Goethe to manage the cataloguing of Büttner's enormous library. For the Chinese books he was assisted by Julius Klaproth (1783–1835), the son of Schopenhauer's chemistry professor in Berlin, Martin Heinrich Klaproth.[306] Though the linguistically gifted Julius was then not even 20 years old, he used his brief stay in Weimar to find a publisher for a journal he founded, the *Asiatisches Magazin*. This monthly jour-

---

[303] »Was wär' ein Gott, der nur von außen stieße, / Im Kreis das All am Finger laufen ließe! / Ihm ziemt's, die Welt im Innern zu bewegen, / Natur in Sich, Sich in Natur zu hegen, / So daß, was in Ihm lebt und webt und ist, / Nie Seine Kraft, nie Seinen Geist vermißt.« Cited by Werner Beierwaltes in his introduction to Bruno (1993:xxxviii).

[304] On July 21 of 1814, Schopenhauer borrowed the *Oeuvres philosophiques* of Hemsterhuis and on July 27 Giordano Bruno's *De Triplici minimo et mensura*.

[305] On January 16 of 1814 Schopenhauer borrowed Oken's *Über Licht und Wärme* as well as his *Abriss der Naturphilosophie*; on February 9 of 1814 Steffens's *Beyträge zur innern Naturgeschichte der Erde*; and on April 30 of 1814 three books by Oken that include *Über das Universum als Fortsetzung des Sinnensystems*.

[306] For a description of Klaproth's activities in Weimar see the detailed study by Martin Gimm (1995) and the book on Klaproth by Walravens (1999).

nal appeared only for two years (1802 and 1803), and the majority of contributions were by editor Klaproth and by an indophile disciple of Herder, Friedrich Majer who from 1796 had held private lectures in Göttingen about the land of his dreams (Majer 1818:v) before moving to Weimar.

In late autumn of 1813 both Klaproth and Majer were staying in Weimar. It is likely that one of them informed Schopenhauer about the *Asiatisches Magazin*; at any rate Schopenhauer borrowed its two volumes from the Weimar ducal library on December 4, 1813. Though he usually restituted books expeditiously, he kept these volumes for almost four months. The *Asiatisches Magazin* was Schopenhauer's first Asia-related book borrowing; the second was the *Oupnek'hat*, and the third Colonel Polier's *Mythologie des Indous* (both checked out on March 26, 1814). Schopenhauer's "introduction to Indian antiquity" by courtesy of Friedrich Majer falls into this period. In a letter Schopenhauer later portrayed his encounters with Goethe and Majer as the most memorable events of his Weimar days:

> In 1813 I prepared myself for the doctoral degree in Berlin; but displaced because of the war I spent the fall in Thuringia. Unable to return [to Berlin] I was forced to get the doctorate in Jena with my tractate about the principle of sufficient reason. Thereafter I spent the winter in Weimar where I enjoyed contact with Goethe that became as close as 39 years of age difference permitted and had a beneficial effect on me. At the same time the orientalist Friedrich Majer introduced me without solicitation to Indian antiquity, which influenced me significantly.[307]

---

[307] »1813 bereitete ich mich zur Promotion in Berlin vor, wurde aber durch den Krieg verdrängt, befand mich im Herbst in Thüringen, konnte nicht zurück und sah mich genöthigt mit meiner Abhandlung über den Satz vom Grunde in Jena zu promoviren. Darauf brachte ich den Winter in Weimar zu, wo ich Göthe's nähern Umgang genoß, der so vertraut wurde, wie es ein Altersunterschied von 39 Jahren irgend zuließ, und wohlthätig auf mich gewirkt hat. Zugleich führte, unaufgefordert, der Orientalist Friedrich Majer mich in das Indische Alterthum ein, welches von wesentlichem Einfluß auf mich gewesen ist.« (Briefe 261)

Delusion and Awakening

It remains unclear what exactly Majer's "introduction to Indian antiquity" involved and what attracted Schopenhauer's interest in the *Asiatisches Magazin*. Its volumes contained, among other things, an article about Chinese Buddhism that Klaproth had for the most part translated from Joseph de Guignes's French and that included Klaproth's German rendering of the earliest published translation into a European language of a Buddhist sutra.[308] Among Majer's contributions we note voluminous ruminations about the incarnations of Vishnu[309] and his German rendering of much of Charles Wilkins's pioneering English *Bhagavad Gita* translation.[310] Majer's introduction to the latter contained a remark that can hardly have escaped Schopenhauer's attention:

> No attentive reader will overlook that these ideas and dreams—at least four thousand years old and born from a most peculiar combination of curious tales and impressions with the most abstract speculations of Oriental wisdom—show a wonderful connection with the thoughts and beliefs of a Plato, Spinoza, or Jacob Böhme about the most interesting topics, even though they stem from totally different times and countries and are expressed and expounded in different forms.[311]

---

[308] Without explicitly mentioning this, Klaproth simply translated Joseph de Guignes's pioneering French translation of the Chinese *Forty-two Sections Sutra*; see App 1998a. For more background, an appraisal of de Guignes's translation, and a stemma of the Chinese Zen version used by de Guignes see App 2010c:223–231.

[309] *Das Asiatische Magazin* vol 1, pp. 116–138, 221–244, 395–405; vol. 2, p. 11-70.

[310] *Das Asiatische Magazin* vol 1, pp. 406–453; vol. 2, pp. 105–135, 229–255, 273–293 and 454–490.

[311] »Keinem aufmerksamen Leser wird es entgehen, wie diese wenigstens viertausend Jahre alten Ideen und Träume der aus einer höchsteigenthümlichen Verbindung seltsamer Fabeln und Einbildungen, und der abstractesten Speculation bestehenden Weisheit des fernen Orients—in einem wunderbaren Zusammenhange mit dem stehen, was in ganz andern Zeiten und Himmelsstrichen ein Plato, Spinoza oder Jacob Böhm über die interessantesten

CHAPTER EIGHT

A number of loose sheets in Schopenhauer's Manuscript Remains contain notes about the *Bhagavad Gita* which he probably jotted down in late 1813 or early 1814 (App 2006c:59–75). Though his earliest encounter with Indian thought appears to have taken place through the *Bhagavad Gita*, we are here focusing on the better documented and deeper influence of the *Oupnek'hat* on the genesis of Schopenhauer's metaphysics of will. Was it Majer's "introduction to Indian antiquity" that led him to borrow this two-volume work on March 26 of 1814?

In the previous chapter we encountered four Germans who invested much time and effort in the study of the *Oupnek'hat*. Friedrich Majer, Schopenhauer's "teacher about India" (Merkel 1945/48), was also full of praise for the "praiseworthy Indiafarer" Anquetil and the *Oupnek'hat* which "contains, as it were, the marrow of the four parts of the Veda." Majer was convinced that the "tireless sovereign" Dara had studied Sanskrit and translated "all sections of the said work into Persian." He had done so "with the help and advice of learned Brahmans from Benares" and taken care to translate the Sanskrit text "word for word, without any abbreviation or addition, and without any prejudice or partiality."[312] Anquetil's Latin rendering, too, is said to have been prepared "with the greatest scrupulousness and precision while consulting several Indian dictionaries," and the Frenchman is credited with having translated Dara's Persian text "word for word into Latin while maintaining the Persian construction."[313] In Majer's opinion the Latin version is "rather barbaric and almost throughout humpy and

---

Gegenstände des Nachdenkens glaubten und dachten, wenn auch in andern Formen sagten und vortrugen« (Majer 1802:406–7).

[312] »lobwürdiger Indienschiffer«; »gleichsam das Mark der vier Theile des Veda enthalte«; »der unermüdete Fürst«; »alle Abschnitte des genannten Werks in das Persische«; »Er vollführte es mit Beirath und Zuziehung gelehrter Brahmanen aus Benares und zwar auf das treueste, von Wort zu Wort, ohne Abkürzung oder Zusatz, ohne vorgefaßte Meinung oder Gunst« (Majer 1818:7–8).

[313] »mit der größten Aengstlichkeit und Genauigkeit und mit Zuziehung mehrerer indischer Wörterbücher«; »von Wort zu Wort und mit Beibehaltung der persischen Construction, ins Lateinische« (Majer 1818:9).

clumsy," which is why its study must be called "not just unappealing and not easy" but even "repulsive and difficult." But it is "not so totally incomprehensible" as critics have claimed, and Majer maintains that the assiduous reader of the *Oupnek'hat* will be "richly rewarded for his steadfastness and perseverance."[314] In spite of its stylistic shortcomings, this Latin work is said to represent "a rich collection of genuine Veda-Upanishads" and to merit the first place among "all the works of importance for the study of India's religious history and antiquity" until such time as the Sanskrit originals themselves will become available.[315]

Majer's book *Brahma oder die Religion der Indier als Brahmaismus* (Brahma or the religion of the Indians as Brahmaism), which was published in 1818 (i.e., four years after his conversations with Schopenhauer), presents his view of Indian antiquity in general and the *Oupnek'hat* in particular. Schopenhauer's sole markup in his copy of Majer's book concerns precisely a passage about the significance of Maya. Based on Anquetil's translation and commentary, Majer had faithfully adopted Dara's equation of love=maya and understood Maya as "eternal divine willing" (das ewige göttliche Wollen)—a willing that ends with insight (Erkenntnis). The beginning of Majer's chapter on the Vedic view of the origin of all things reads as follows:

> *Brahm*, the pure being, is without end; name-and-form of the world is also without end, but only *Brahm* is truly existing and not name-and-form. The reason of their ostensible existence lies in *Maya* (*Mascha*). It gives lust to all living beings and represents

---

[314] »nicht wenig barbarisch ausgefallen und fast durchgehends holprig und stolprig«, weswegen man deren Studium »nicht etwa nur nicht anziehend und nicht leicht« nennen müsse, sondern »sogar abstoßend und schwer«. »Demungeachtet ist sie aber nicht so gar unverständlich, wie man. behauptet hat, ja man findet sich im Gegentheil für die zur Durchlesung derselben erforderliche Standhaftigkeit und Ausdauer sehr reichlich belohnt« (Majer 1818:10).

[315] »eine reiche Sammlung ächter Veda-Upanischaden«, welcher »unter allen für die indische Religionsgeschichte und Alterthumskunde wichtigen Werken« so lange der erste Platz gebühre, bis die Sanskrit-Originale selbst erhältlich sind (Majer 1818:13).

Brahm's characteristic of desire, the eternal divine willing. It is also called eternal love because love has no beginning but has an end when insight arrives. (*Jajusch-Veda* and *Athar-Veda*).[316]

> **Dritter Abschnitt.**
> **Vom Ursprung der Dinge.**
>
> I.
>
> **Nach den Vedas.**
>
> Brahm, das reine Wesen, ist ohne Ende; auch Name und Gestalt der Welt ist ohne Ende, aber nur Brahm ist wahrhaft bestehend, nicht Name, nicht Gestalt. Der Grund ihres scheinbaren Daseyns liegt in Maja (Mascha). Allem Lebendigen Luft gebend, ist sie die Eigenschaft des Verlangens von Brahm, das ewige göttliche Wollen. Ewige Liebe auch heißt sie, weil die Liebe keinen Anfang hat, wohl aber ein Ende, wenn kommt die Erkenntniß. (Jajusch- und Athar-Veda.)

Friedrich Majer's *Brahma* (1818:36) with Schopenhauer's markup

---

[316] »*Brahm*, das reine Wesen, ist ohne Ende; auch Name und Gestalt der Welt ist ohne Ende, aber nur *Brahm* ist wahrhaft bestehend, nicht Name, nicht Gestalt. Der Grund ihres scheinbaren Daseyns liegt in *Maja* (*Mascha*). Allem Lebendigen Lust gebend, ist sie die Eigenschaft des Verlangens von *Brahm*, das ewige göttliche Wollen. Ewige Liebe auch heißt sie, weil die Liebe keinen Anfang hat, wohl aber ein Ende, wenn kommt die Erkenntniß. (*Jajusch-* und *Athar-Veda*)« (Majer 1818:36)

It appears that Dara's interpretation fell on fertile ground in early 19th-century Germany where the writings of Jakob Böhme, Madame Guyon, Plotinus, and Schelling were ardently studied and discussed.

Majer's hymns of praise for the *Oupnek'hat* make it likely that it was he who in early 1814 recommended its study to the young doctor of philosophy. At any rate, on March 26 of 1814 Schopenhauer went to the ducal library in Weimar and borrowed Anquetil's two large volumes along with Colonel Polier's *Mythologie des Indous*. He returned both books on May 18 of 1814 prior to his departure for Dresden. Two weeks later, on June 8, the *Oupnek'hat* is listed as Schopenhauer's first book borrowing from the Dresden library[317] and we can assume that around the return date (July 21) Schopenhauer had purchased his copy that has fortunately been preserved with all of his markup.

We can thus divide Schopenhauer's study of the *Oupnek'hat* in the year 1814 into three phases: 1. the last seven weeks in Weimar (end of March to mid-May); 2. six weeks in Dresden (June to July); and 3. the period after the reception of his own copy when he began to mark it up.[318] Traces of each of these phases are found in Schopenhauer's notebooks to which we will now turn in order to arrive at a first appraisal of the role of Schopenhauer's favorite book in the genesis of his philosophical system. This period (the last months in Weimar and the first six months in Dresden) saw the core of Schopenhauer's system emerge. Rudolf Malter was right in observing that the year 1814 forms a "decisive break" leading "from the first groping trials to the fully formed system of *The World as Will and Representation*" (Malter 1988:4). In spite of numerous studies about this crucial period, however, the nature of this "decisive break" has remained hazy, as has the question of *Oupnek'hat* influence.[319] Surprisingly, even the few authors who men-

---

[317] See Jochen Stollberg's list of Schopenhauer's book borrowings from the Dresden library (apps.webable.de/cms/fileadmin/doc/Dresdner_Liste02.pdf).

[318] Without any foundation, several French authors claim that Schopenhauer had encountered the *Oupnek'hat* already in 1811 (Droit 1989:203; Kapani 1996:46; Lenoir 1999:119).

[319] Of many pertinent examples I will here only mention two. For Thomas

tion the *Oupnek'hat* as an influence in this crucial period seem (with the notable exception of Piantelli) to have never actually studied this work and keep citing modern Upanishad translations from Sanskrit that did not exist in Schopenhauer's time.[320]

Prior to our excursion into the history of Schopenhauer's favorite book and the description of its very particular character we have seen that in his doctoral dissertation Schopenhauer performed, as it were, a structural analysis of ordinary empirical consciousness. As a diagnosis of suffering this was still wanting since precisely the question of its ultimate origin had to remain unaddressed. The limits of reason as demonstrated by Kant prevented the discussion of metaphysical issues, and Böhme's/Schelling's "Ur-Sehnsucht" (primordial longing) or "Ur- und Grundwollen" (Ur-willing, fundamental willing) went beyond the scope of rational analysis. But suffering and the moments of release from it, which Schopenhauer had long known from personal experience and had sought to philosophically comprehend as "empirical" and

---

Bohinc (1989:215 ff.) Schopenhauer's discovery of will was a flash of insight without any discernible foundation, and Rüdiger Safranski explicitly denies any influence of the *Oupnek'hat* on the formation of Schopenhauer's system: "In the years when his philosophical system took form, Arthur Schopenhauer did not get more [from the Upanishads] than confirmations." (»Mehr als solche Bestätigungen [in den Upanischaden, dass er auf dem richtigen Weg sei] hat sich Arthur Schopenhauer in den Jahren der Herausbildung seines philosophischen Systems nicht geholt« [Safranski 1987:305]). For some other opinions and scenarios see Appendix 2 here below.

[320] The book by Werner Scholz with the promising title *Arthur Schopenhauer— ein Philosoph zwischen westlicher und östlicher Tradition* (Arthur Schopenhauer: A Philosopher between Western and Eastern Tradition) excels in this respect; its bibliography (1996: 241-252) does not list a single work that Schopenhauer read about Eastern thought, not even the *Oupnek'hat*. But the most extreme example may be Icilio Vecchiotti's 600-page book about Indian influences on the formation of Schopenhauer's philosophical system (1969) which contains no reference at all to the *Oupnek'hat* and Anquetil-Duperron. The books by Douglas Berger (2000, 2004) apportion a central role to the concept of Maya yet develop this argument without any reference to the content of the *Oupnek'hat* and thus fail to grasp its true significance in the genesis of Schopenhauer's system.

Delusion and Awakening

"better" consciousness, had to have a foundation. His structural analysis of empirical consciousness moved for the most part along the trajectory blazed by Kant's transcendental philosophy, but we have seen that at several decisive junctures in his dissertation a deeper dimension peeked through—a dimension that according to Schopenhauer would let his dissertation appear like a dream. What he sought was a comprehension of suffering that not only probes its ultimate ground but also explains the possibility of a temporal or permanent release from it. I argue that Schopenhauer found the key to his metaphysics of will in Anquetil's Latin rendering of Prince Dara's *Oupnek'hat*, and in this and the following chapters I will explain how this came about.

In January of 1814, roughly two months prior to the encounter with his favorite book, Schopenhauer described three diagnoses that had hitherto been offered for what he called the "main problem of philosophy" (Hauptproblem der Philosophie):

1) We spirits who have no rest (κατάπαυσις, Hebrews iv, 1) can also never find rest (Spinoza, Schelling in the World Soul and the Ideas on Natural Philosophy) —

2) We spirits who have no rest have only *lost* it and can find it again (all systems of emanation; Schelling in Philosophy and Religion) —

3) We spirits who have no rest have never yet had it, have come into existence, and will attain it (all theories of creation, rational theism, Schelling on Human Freedom).[321]

---

[321] 1) Wir Geister die keine Ruhe (κατάπαυσις, Hebräer iv, 1) haben, können auch eben nimmermehr Ruhe finden (Spinoza, Schelling in der Weltseele und den Ideen zur Naturphilosophie) —

2) Wir Geister die keine Ruhe haben, haben sie nur *verloren*, können sie wiederfinden (Alle Emanationssysteme; Schelling in Philosophie und Religion) —

3) Wir Geister die keine Ruhe haben, haben sie noch nie gehabt, sind geworden, werden zu ihr gelangen (Alle Schöpfungstheorien, rationaler Theismus, Schelling über die menschliche Freiheit). (HN1 #126)

CHAPTER EIGHT

All three diagnoses concern suffering (here in the aspect of restlessness or unease) and deliverance from it. The fact that Schelling represents all three approaches highlights once more the similar basic thrust of Schelling's and Schopenhauer's fundamental query. These two readers and admirers of Böhme were also in fundamental agreement regarding the "source of all true happiness" and the "secure solace built not on loose sand but rather on firm and solid ground": "better consciousness," which signifies "complete perdition, death, and destruction for our empirical consciousness." In order to be true to that better consciousness "we must renounce empirical consciousness" and "wrest ourselves free from it;" and such liberation can only be achieved through "death of the ego" in the sense of Jacob Böhme and Madame Guyon.[322] With regard to "sinfulness" and "the fundamental error of *attempting to measure eternity through time,*" too, Schelling would have agreed with his younger contemporary Schopenhauer since both were attracted by a better consciousness that can only "be grasped at one stroke by stepping from time into eternity and from empirical into better consciousness."[323]

But at that time Schopenhauer's diagnosis of the "fundamental error" (Grundirrtum) did not truly explain man's desire to extend the existence of the individual (greed, avarice, hatred) or the species (sexual drive) and simply associated them with the essence of life: "Life is to desire temporal existence and to continue desiring it."[324] The question about the origin of such willing was at this point still unanswered. The

---

[322] »Quelle aller wahren Seeligkeit« und des »sicheren und nicht auf losem Sande sondern unerschütterlichem Boden gebauten Trostes«—des besseren Bewußtseins, welches »für unser empirisches Bewußtseyn gänzlicher Untergang, Tod und Vernichtung« bedeutet; »um jenem bessern Bewußtseyn treu zu seyn« muss man »diesem empirischen entsagen« und sich »von ihm losreißen«, was nichts anderes bedeutet als »Selbsttödtung« (#128).

[323] »Sündhaftigkeit«; »Grundirrthum, *die Ewigkeit durch die Zeit ausmessen zu wollen*«; »mit Einem Schlage ergriffen werden kann, durch das Uebertreten aus der Zeit in die Ewigkeit, aus dem empirischen ins bessre Bewußtseyn« (#143).

[324] »Gier, Habsucht, Feindseligkeit«; »Geschlechtstrieb«; »Zeitliches Daseyn wollen und immerfort wollen ist Leben« (#143).

polarity of suffering and release from suffering also found expression in Christian terminology. Schopenhauer wrote that "Adam's fall," which is an expression of "the finite, animal, and sinful nature," has its opposing pole in Jesus's "expiatory death" which stands for "the eternal supernatural side, freedom, the deliverance of man."[325] The original sin is said to consist in nothing other than "life itself," whereas "the desire of bliss" is "the opposite of the desire of life" (#146).[326] Shortly before Schopenhauer's encounter with the *Oupnek'hat*, the twin poles of his compass stood for will-to-live and the liberation from it. However, at this stage the self-mangling blind will—in our metaphor, the fundamental bipolar magnetic force behind the bearing of the compass—was not yet in the cross-hairs of Schopenhauer's thinking as his "better consciousness" was still paired with a "better will." However, he sketched the goal and the path as follows:

> All of us must aspire to the light, to virtue, to the holy spirit, to the *better consciousness*: this is the unison, the eternal key-tone of creation. Only there are two ways. Either there arises from within, freely and of itself, the better will and we voluntarily abandon the will-to-live, gladly repudiate the world, destroy with our own strength the illusion, overcome as free heroes, and are saved. Or else we follow the darkness, the grim urge of the will-to-live, sink ever deeper into vice and sin, into death and vanity until the wrath of life gradually turns against itself and we become aware of the path we had chosen and the kind of world we had wanted—until through our torment, dismay and agony we come to our senses, take stock of ourselves, and better knowledge is born out of pain.[327]

---

[325] »Adams Sündenfall«, der »die endliche, thierische, sündige Natur des Menschen ausspricht«; »Jesu Opfertod«, welcher »die ewige übernatürliche Seite, die Freiheit, die Erlösung des Menschen« bezeugt (#145).

[326] Die Erbsünde bestehe aus nichts anderem als dem »Leben selbst«; wohingegen »Seeligkeit-wollen das Gegentheil von Leben-wollen« sei (#146).

[327] »Zum Lichte, zur Tugend, zum heiligen Geiste, zum *bessern Bewußtseyn*—müssen wir Alle: das ist der Einklang, der ewige Grundton der Schöpfung. Nur sind der Wege zwei. Entweder von Innen erhebt sich frei und von

CHAPTER EIGHT

Schopenhauer was inexorably approaching what was to become the core of his philosophical system. He asked himself, among other things, how the coincidence of will and knowledge in an "I" (which in the dissertation he called "the miracle κατ' ἐξοχήν [par excellence]") could be rationally explained. Does madness consist in the will's loss of control over cognition (#148)? Does man's faculty to know constitute merely the emergence into visibility of his intelligible character, and is it but the mirror of what man "wills to be, has willed, hence wills, and therefore is"?[328] Can human beings perceive mere images in a mirror or shadows on a wall, as Plato argued in the allegory of the cave?

We do not know things-in-themselves, said Kant; that is to say, what is known is for that very reason representation. But that which represents cannot be representation, and therefore it also cannot be known. Things-in-themselves that exist *without being represented* and that therefore are something different from representations: to *imagine* such things is the greatest possible contradiction.[329]

---

selbst der bessre Wille, freiwillig lassen wir vom Lebenwollen, stoßen gern die Welt von uns, zerstöhren aus eigner Kraft die Täuschung, überwinden als freie Helden und sind erlöst. Oder wir folgen der Finsterniß, dem grimmigen Drange des Lebenwollens, gehn tiefer und tiefer in Laster und Sünde in Tod und Nichtigkeit—bis nach und nach der Grimm des Lebens sich gegen sich selbst kehrt, wir inne werden welches der Weg sei den wir gewählt, welche Welt es sey die wir gewollt, bis durch Quaal, Entsetzen und Grausen wir zu uns kommen, in uns gehn und aus dem Schmerz bessre Erkenntnis geboren wird.« (#158)

[328] Ist das Erkennen des Menschen »das Sichtbarwerden des *intelligiblen Karakters*«: der Spiegel dessen, was der Mensch »seyn will, gewollt hat, also will und darum ist« (#159).

[329] »Wir erkennen keine Dinge an sich, sagte Kant: d.h. was erkannt wird ist eben darum Vorstellung: was aber vorstellt kann nicht Vorstellung seyn, also auch nicht erkannt werden. Dinge an sich, die da wären *ohne vorgestellt zu werden,* die folglich etwas andres als Vorstellungen wären—solche Dinge uns *vorzustellen* ist der größtmögliche Widerspruch« (#171).

Delusion and Awakening

Access via the subject also seemed blocked because "whoever tries to *explain himself* is obliged to posit himself (the subject) both as *ground* and *consequence*" and is thereby turning himself into a representation:

> Whatever can merely be known and can consequently be explained is for that very reason simply representation. It is utter nonsense to want to explain and to know oneself! Attempting to make oneself into a representation and being left with nothing that can actually have these avowed (connected) representations: is this not like letting the earth be carried by Atlas, Atlas by the elephant, the elephant by a turtle, and the turtle by nothing?[330]

In the spring of 1814 Schopenhauer wrote of a "delusion" (Täuschung, #158) and of the "veil of nature" in which only for a genius there is a small opening: "a small superhuman morsel in man."[331] Shortly after such reflections we find the first unmistakable evidence of *Oupnek'hat* influence: in note #189 the "veil" (Schleier) becomes an "illusion" (Wahn) whose expression is life itself. In Chapter 6 we already mentioned a passage that Schopenhauer highlighted in the *Oupnek'hat* where Dara wrote of a deceit or delusion (*mendacium*):

> Though name-and-form of the world are illusory, they still appear to be right (*true*) and real (*obvious*); yet in truth (*this*) has no existence.[332]

In the *Oupnek'hat* this delusion is called *maïa*. The most important passage—cited by Schopenhauer not only in a crucial early note (#213)

---

[330] »wer *sich selbst erklären* will, der muß sich selbst, (das Subjekt) als *Grund* und *Folge* setzen «; »Was immer nur erkannt und folglich erklärt werden kann ist ja eben deshalb nur Vorstellung. Welcher Unsinn sich selbst erklären, sich selbst erkennen zu wollen! sich selbst zur Vorstellung machen zu wollen und dann nichts übrig zu lassen das eben alle diese erklärten (verbundenen) Vorstellungen hat! Ist das nicht die Erde vom Atlas, den Atlas vom Elephanten, diesen von einer Schildkröte und diese von Nichts tragen lassen?« (#171)

[331] »Schleier der Natur«; »ein übermenschliches Stückchen im Menschen« (#176).

[332] "nomen et figura mundi mendacium, rectum (*verum*) apparens (*ostendens*) est: et, in veritate, existentiam (*hoc*) non habet." (OUP1:395)

CHAPTER EIGHT

and in various later writings but also presented as the motto for the fourth book of *The World as Will and Representation*—stems from the *Atma*-Upanishad: "Tempore quo cognitio simul advenit, amor è medio supersurrexit" (Just when insight arrives, desire leaves the scene). This phrase must be read in context (*Oupnek'hat* vol. 2, p. 395–6):

Et *maïa*, quòd amor aeternus est, ex illo dicunt, quòd amor initium non habet, et fines habet: quid? (*nam*) tempore quo cognitio simul advenit, amor è medio supersurrexit (surgit).	And *Maya*, which is eternal desire, is so called because desire has no beginning but has an end. How so? (Because) just when insight arrives, desire leaves the scene (gets up).
Et è τῷ *maïa*, rectum (*verum*) mendacium apparet; et mendacium, rectum (*verum*): quemadmodùm, funis, quòd mendacium (*falsum*) est, coluber apparet; et coluber, quòd rectum (*verum*) est, funis apparet.	And because of *Maya* the right (true) appears as lie, and what is lie as right (true); just as a cord falsely appears to be a snake, and what really (truly) is a snake appears as a cord.
Et *maïa*, quòd non rectum (*non verum*) potest dixit (*possunt dicere*), et non mendacium (*non falsum*): quid?	And *Maya* can both be called what is incorrect (untrue) and and not a lie (not false). How come?
(*nam*) ostensum sine est (*sine existentiâ*) mundum est (*existentem*) ostendit; et est (*existentem*) existentiam universalem non est (*non existentem*) ostendit. Tò non est, existit; et τὸ existit, non est, ostendit: ens verum, quòd apparens est, non ostendit; et mundum, quòd existens non est, ostendit. (OUP2: 215–216)	(Because) [Maya] lets the world, which is unreal (without existence), appear as real; and conversely it lets that which exists in everything appear as unreal (without existence). What does not exist shows itself as existing and what exists as non-existing; true being which is apparent does not manifest, but the world which does not exist manifests.

Delusion and Awakening

This commentary to the Atma-Upanishad reflects an aspect of Prince Dara's view of Maya. In the *Oupnek'hat* Maya has a double meaning. On one hand Dara takes it as *ishq*, the longing of the still hidden divinity to manifest in creation as an act of *love*. On the other hand Maya has, as here, the Vedantic connotation of *illusion* or *delusion*: the *veil of Maya* that hides all-oneness and conjures up an illusory world of multiplicity. This double meaning has caused headaches for a number of commentators and translators: should one render Anquetil's "amor" as "love" or as "desire"? The translators of the new Cambridge edition of Schopenhauer's works were right to choose "desire" but translated the motto at the beginning of the fourth book of *The World as Will and Representation* in a manner that goes against both the cited *Oupnek'hat* context and Schopenhauer's reading of it:

> *Tempore quo cognitio simul advenit, amor è medio supersurrexit* ['When knowledge asserted itself, thence arose desire'].[333]

Indeed, Schopenhauer chose this phrase (which I translate "Just when insight arrives, desire leaves the scene") as motto of the crucial fourth book of his major work precisely because it treats of the *end* of beginningless desire rather than its rise. Dara's explanation in his list of Sanskrit terms reflects both aspects of Maya, God's creative will and illusion:

---

[333] Arthur Schopenhauer, *The World as Will and Representation*, vol. 1. Translated by J. Norman, A. Welchman and C. Janaway. Edited by C. Janaway. Cambridge: Cambridge University Press, 2010, p. 297. This translation is followed by the remark: "*Oupnek'hat* is a Latin version of the *Upanishads* (1801). The passage corresponds to *Ātma Upanishad*, 3, though as Deussen points out, no equivalent words are found there." Payne (1969: 269) translates: "The moment knowledge appeared on the scene, thence arose desire." However, in his translation of the Manuscript Remains (vol. 1, p. 130) Payne offers an entirely different and more appropriate translation: "The moment knowledge appeared on the scene, thence abated desire."

> *II, 32, 520* *Anahed*: vox universalis (*principalis*, *absoluta*). *Oum.*
> *I, 321* *Maïa*: voluntas æterna; quod causa ostensi sine fuit (*existentiâ*) est. *II, p. 17.*
> *Prahrat*: justa temperatio trium (3) qualitatum (*tres qualitates simul, equâ lance, in homine existentes*).
> *Petr loh*: mundus spirituum (*animarum*) patrum.

Oupnek'hat vol. 1, p. 10, with Schopenhauer's handwriting in ink and pencil

Anquetil's rendering (OUP1.10) reads: "*Maïa*: eternal will; the ground of appearance of what is without reality (existence)." Schopenhauer initially followed Dara's and Anquetil's interpretation of Maya as "will" and illusion, though he saw this with the eyes of a convinced atheist.[334] His atheistic reading is clearly apparent in his copy of the *Oupnek'hat* where he consistently rayed out words such as "Deus" (God) and "creator." One of many examples is found at the beginning of Dara's list of Sanskrit terms that immediately follows the Prince's introduction:

> (*Explicatio præcipuorum verborum samskreticorum, quæ in* OUPNEK'HAT *adhibentur.*)
>
> O U M : ~~Deus~~ ¹. *Brahm, Omitto, p. 15, not 2.* II.
> et *Pranou* etiam nomen ipsum hoc est, id est, obsignata (*clausa, finita*) faciens secreta. *II, p. 20. 16.*
> *Brahm*: ~~creator.~~

Oupnek'hat vol. 1, p. 7: Beginning of Prince Dara's explanation of Sanskrit terms with Schopenhauer's markup and the crossed-out *Deus* and *creator*

---

[334] Already in the year 1812 an acquaintance reported: "We spoke of young Schopenhauer who the previous day wanted to learnedly prove that there is no God" (»Wir sprachen vom jungen Schopenhauer, der Tags zuvor gelehrt beweisen wollte, es gäbe keinen Gott« (Gespräche 24).

Delusion and Awakening

Here the sacred Indian word OUM is defined as "Allah" which Anquetil translated as "Deus" (God). But Schopenhauer vigorously crossed out this word and replaced it by "Brahm. Omitto."[335] He also refused to regard "Brahm" as creator, which is why he also doubly crossed out the word "creator." For Schopenhauer Brahm meant—in accordance with the text but stripped of any divine dimension—the creative force that in the *Oupnek'hat* is constantly associated with terms such as "maïa," "amor," "desiderium" (desire), and "voluntas" (will). But the *Oupnek'hat* also frequently mentions, as in the motto used by Schopenhauer, that there is the possibility of an end of Maya, desire or will with the arrival of insight (*cognitio*). Dara's comments take every opportunity to comment on an all-oneness that both reveals and hides itself in the multiplicity of the world. This all-oneness, and thus the true nature of everything, is only realized when man attains liberation from any and all will and desire through insight.

A passage in the *Oupnek'hat* that Schopenhauer heavily underlined and that he appears to have regarded as very important discusses liberation from will in the following terms:

> Quisquis unificationem et cognitionem acquisivit, *maht* et liberatus (*beatus*) est.
> Et cum verificatione (*certitudine*), hoc omne, expositio statuum personæ est, quæ cum volitione capta est (*quæ τοῖς velle detinetur*).
> Post ab hoc, persona quæ à volitione et desiderio immunis facta, status ejus scito.
> Et illa persona, quæ volitionem non habet, *aham* est, id est, sine volitione.
> Et causa τȣ sine volitione, illud (*est*), quòd desiderium è corde ejus deletum redditum.

Oupnek'hat vol 1, p. 255 with Schopenhauer's markup

---

[335] For the significance and background of "Omitto" (Ch. *A-mi-tuo*, Jap. *Amida*) see App 2006d, 2007, and 2010a.

CHAPTER EIGHT

> Whoever has attained unification and insight is *makt* and liberated (*happy*). And with certitude all [that was said above] is related to the explanation of the states of a person caught in will (*ensnared in willing*). Now you must know about the state of a person that has become free of will and desire. Such a person devoid of will is *akam*, which means without will. And the reason of being without will is that desire has been expunged from his heart. (OUP1:255)

It was mentioned above that in note #189 of the philosophical notebook used by Schopenhauer in spring of 1814 we find the first unmistakable traces of *Oupnek'hat* influence. Already three notes later (#192), the "wiser Indians" and their philosophical method of setting out from the subject are mentioned in a way that betrays Schopenhauer's intensive study of Anquetil's translation. Shortly before, in note #188 he had described the "sinful tendency" ensconced in the human body and written of the body of Jesus who could therefore only have had a phantom body ("Scheinleib"). In the subsequent note #189 this sinful tendency is suddenly called illusion (Wahn) and discussed in terms that betray the influence of the *Oupnek'hat* and echo Prince Dara's and Anquetil's explanations about Maya:

> For insofar as he is alive and is a human being, man is doomed not only to *sin* and *death* but also to *illusion*, and this *illusion* is as real as life, as real as the world of senses itself; indeed he is identical with these (the Maya of the Indians). On it are based all our aspirations and cravings which are again but the expression of life, just as life is but the expression of illusion: insofar as we live, want to live, are human beings, the illusion is truth; only in reference to the better consciousness it is illusion. If quietude, bliss and peace are to be found then illusion must be abandoned, and if this is to be abandoned, then life must be given up.[336]

---

[336] »Denn sofern als er lebt, sofern als er Mensch ist, ist er nicht bloß der *Sünde* und dem *Tode* anheim gefallen, sondern auch dem *Wahn*, und dieser *Wahn* ist so real als das Leben, als die Sinnenwelt selbst, ja er ist mit diesen Eines (das Maja der Indier): auf ihn gründen sich alle unsre Wünsche und Suchten, die wieder nur der Ausdruck des Lebens sind wie das Leben nur der Ausdruck

Delusion and Awakening

All life and will-to-live, and thus also all ordinary human existence, is said to necessarily entail illusion "since just as with life the illusion is ineluctably given, so too is life with the illusion." Not even death brings an end to this illusion because "whoever persists in willing life will live even though this body dies."[337] This conception of illusion (Wahn) substantially broadened Schopenhauer's view of empirical consciousness, affecting also its opposite pole that Schopenhauer called "divine peace" and "appearance of *better consciousness.*" Reaching this goal requires "that man, this frail, finite and trivial being, be something quite different, no longer a human being at all."[338] Now not only consciousness was involved but human existence in its most basic dimension: man's will to live and his body that in itself is nothing but a manifestation of illusion (#189).

Paul Deussen explained that the fundamental thought of the Upanishads consists in the identity of Brahman and Atman. He calls *Brahman* "the force we see incorporated in all beings, the force that creates all worlds, sustains, preserves, and eventually reabsorbs them." This eternal force is said to be "identical with *Atman*, with what we find after subtracting everything external to be our innermost and true being,

---

des Wahns ist: sofern wir leben, leben wollen, Menschen sind, ist der Wahn Wahrheit, nur in Bezug auf das bessre Bewußtseyn ist er Wahn. Soll Ruhe, Seeligkeit, Friede gefunden werden, so muß der Wahn aufgegeben werden, und soll dieser, so muß das Leben aufgegeben werden.« (#189)

Even in recent publications this note #189 (HN1, p. 104) is often identified as the earliest to include the word Maya. But what in Hübscher's edition appears in parentheses ("das Maja der Indier) is in the manuscript clearly a later addition that Schopenhauer wrote in darker ink in the margin. However, the content of this paragraph leaves no doubt that it was inspired by the *Oupnek'hat.*

[337] »denn wie mit dem Leben unausbleiblich der Wahn gesetzt ist, so ist auch mit dem Wahn das Leben gesetzt«; »wer beharrt auf dem Lebenwollen, wird leben, wenn auch dieser Leib stirbt« (# 189).

[338] »Hervortreten des *bessern Bewußtseyns*«; »daß der Mensch, dies hinfällige, endliche, nichtige Wesen, etwas ganz andres sey, gar nicht mehr Mensch« (#189).

as our proper self, as the soul in us."³³⁹ Therefore the core doctrines of the Upanishads are according to Deussen *tat tvam asi*, "this thou art," and *aham brahma asmi*, "I am Brahman;" and this unity of Brahman and Atman also constitutes the fundamental dogma of Vedanta.³⁴⁰ In the first Upanishad of the *Oupnek'hat* where the "great word" *tatoumes* (*tat tvam asi*) is explained, the human body is called *Brahmpour* (city of Brahm; OUP1:79). It is portrayed as the residence of immortal Atma because the embodied Atma or *djiw âtma* allows recognizing Brahm in one's own body (OUP1:93–5). It is precisely in the veil of one's own body that the eternal will is said to be hidden (p. 154); and true self-knowledge consists in the insight "that I myself am all these creatures as a whole, that apart from me there is no other being, and that I have created all" (OUP1:122).

> *maschghouli* perseverantiam ostendat, quòd, hæ omnes creaturæ in totum ego sum, et, præter à me, aliud (*ens*) non est, et omnia ego creata feci: tùm is etiam, post à τῷ deserere corpus, *Haranguerbehah* efficitur.

Oupnek'hat vol. 1, p. 122 with Schopenhauer's underlining & lines in margin

This universal being "appears bound" in man's will where it manifests as "the fetter of 'I' and 'mine.'"³⁴¹ As we have seen in the passage that Schopenhauer first cited in the spring of 1814 (#213) and later used as motto for the fourth book of *The World as Will and Representation*,³⁴²

---

³³⁹ »die Kraft, welche in allen Wesen verkörpert vor uns steht, welche alle Welten schafft, trägt, erhält und wieder in sich zurücknimmt«; »identisch mit dem *Âtman*, mit demjenigen, was wir, nach Abzug alles Äußerlichen, als unser innerstes und wahres Wesen, als unser eigentliches Selbst, als die Seele in uns finden« (Deussen 1922:1/2.36–7).

³⁴⁰ Deussen 1922:1/2.37.

³⁴¹ "Ex hac volitione, hoc (*ens*) universale ligatum apparet ... et in vinculum tē 'ego' et tē 'a me' ingreditur" (OUP1:306).

³⁴² The phrase "Tempore quo cognitio simul advenit, amor e medio

Delusion and Awakening

the *Oupnek'hat* associates liberation from this fetter with *cognitio*: the realization by virtue of which any and all desire (and thus also Schopenhauer's will-to-live) is extinguished.

From April of 1814, the two poles of the *Oupnek'hat*, amor/will and cognitio/insight increasingly put their stamp on Schopenhauer's reasoning. At one pole we find Brahm/Maya, the timeless will and source of illusory multiplicity; and on the other pure insight and the end of all willing. In Schopenhauer's earliest notes that clearly show *Oupnek'hat* influence (spring of 1814, notes #189–193) we can already see traces of what Hans Zint with reference to note #213 has called the "base frame" (Grundgerüst) of Schopenhauer's metaphysics: the change from a psychological *two-fold nature of consciousness* to a metaphysical *two-fold nature of will* (Zint 1921:43). In the course of this process, the "empirical consciousness" of Schopenhauer's earlier writings is transformed into the "affirmation of will," and the "better consciousness" into the "negation" or overcoming of will. Soon after the beginning of Schopenhauer's study of the *Oupnek'hat* this process is apparent. The body (corporeal man) that in note #189 was called the manifestation of illusion is just two notes later defined as "nothing but the will that has become visible," and the true timeless being (Kant's intelligible character) is called "the will" whose mirror is life:

> The body (corporeal man) is *nothing but the will that has become visible*. The form of all object is time. The will itself, the intelligible character, remains unchanging and is not in time, otherwise it itself would merely be visibility, not that which has become visible. Therefore man does not change; he neither becomes better nor worse in life. Rather, man's life is only the development in time—as it were the unfolding—of the will. In the succession of

---

supersurrexit" (Just when insight arrives, desire leaves the scene; OUP2:216) was first cited by Schopenhauer in his notebook in the spring of 1814, soon after the beginning of his study of the *Oupnek'hat* (#213, HN1:120); for its use as motto in the first edition of his major work see Schopenhauer 1819:385. See also p. 202 below.

life man knows his will as in a mirror, and conscience is the shock resulting from this realization.[343]

In the next paragraph Schopenhauer sings the praise of "the wiser Indians" who set out "from the *subject*, from Atma, Djiw-Atma." Instead of merely linking representations in the manner of the Europeans, the wiser Indians start out from the fact *that* the subject has representations, that is, from the illusory world of Maya. Unlike the European dogmatists who posit a God who fashions the world and who "use the principle of sufficient reason as mortar to pile stone upon stone" and hence remain "unable to ever find the foundation on which the building is to rest," the Indians use introspection and attempt to understand the world by starting with the subject:

> Only from within can it come. The essential is not what objects present themselves to man but rather how he regards them and how he is determined by them.[344]

Indeed, true knowledge that "forever, per se and by nature is *incomprehensible*" is characterized by the fact "that the principle of sufficient reason cannot be applied to it at all" since this principle does not precede such knowledge but rather "is first given with it and in consequence of it."[345]

---

[343] »*Der Leib*, (der körperliche Mensch) ist *nichts als der sichtbar gewordne Wille*. Die Form alles Objekts ist die Zeit. Der Wille selbst, der intelligible Karakter, steht fest, ist nicht in der Zeit, sonst wäre er selbst nur Sichtbarkeit, nicht das sichtbar Gewordne. Daher ändert der Mensch sich nicht, wird nicht besser noch schlechter im Leben. Sondern das Leben des Menschen ist nur die Entwickelung in der Zeit, gleichsam die Auseinandersetzung, des Willens. Der Mensch erkennt in der Succession des Lebens, wie in einem Spiegel seinen Willen: der Schreck über diese Erkenntniß ist das Gewissen.« (#191)

[344] »Nur von innen kann es kommen. Nicht welche Objekte sich ihm präsentieren ist das Wesentliche, sondern wie er sie ansieht und wie er sich nach ihnen bestimmt« (#192).

[345] Die wahre Erkenntnis, welche »für immer, schlechthin, wesentlich, *unbegreiflich* ist« zeichne sich gerade dadurch aus, »daß der Satz vom Grund auf sie gar nicht anzuwenden ist, als welcher ihr nicht vorhergeht, sondern erst mit ihr und in Folge derselben gegeben ist« (#193).

Delusion and Awakening

At the end of the first phase of Schopenhauer's study of the *Oupnek'hat* that lasted from the end of March to mid-April of 1814, a new vision of the body already stood like a pillar on the newly cast foundation of "will." The body was now, based on the *Oupnek'hat* model of Maya=will/illusion, conceived as the visible appearance of illusion (#189) and as nothing other than "the visibility of the will" (#191). As in the Upanishadic teacher's *tatoumes* (tat tvam asi, "thou art that") where everything from the seeing man's eye to the infinite universe is said to be a manifestation of the one Brahman, life as a whole now appeared to Schopenhauer as a manifestation of one will that through man's insight can become transparent to itself and recognized as the true essence of the world (#191). The *Oupnek'hat* played a crucial role in the germinating stage of Schopenhauer's metaphysics of will, and our next chapter will continue tracing this influence.

9. Willing and Contemplation

The second phase of Schopenhauer's *Oupnek'hat* study began after his arrival in Dresden (May 24, 1814). On June 6 he checked out the two volumes from the Royal library and kept them for six weeks. The only other borrowed book during this period was *Kritik der theoretischen Philosophie* (Critique of Theoretical Philosophy) by Schulze, his former philosophy professor in Göttingen. After settling down in Dresden Schopenhauer repeatedly reflected on the difference between empirical and better consciousness. Empirical consciousness shows itself to be "incapable of any consolation" and characterizes the mind of philistines who are "unable to get clear of themselves" and whose vision is clouded by egoism and subjectivity.[346] By contrast, the creative genius must be capable of being objective since "all art should be only the revelation of the world in its innermost essence."[347] But what is this

---

[346] »keines Trostes fähig« (#202); »nicht von sich loskommen« (#206).

[347] »alle Kunst soll nur seyn die Offenbarung der Welt in ihrem innersten Wesen« (#206).

CHAPTER NINE

innermost essence? Schopenhauer's search for the fundamental essence of everything—and therewith for the ground of all suffering and evil as well as the possibility of "bliss" (Seeligkeit)—was now rapidly closing in on the goal. In the previous year he had still singled out "subjective reflection" as the "fundamental error"[348] and subsequently the search for eternity in time (#143), life (#143), and the will-to-live (#158, 191). In the early summer of 1814 it was again the will-to-live and man's clutching to temporal existence. But for the philosopher who "has found and described the [Platonic] idea of all that *is* and lives," the only outcome can be "*not willing to be.*"[349] Schopenhauer elaborated:

> For then it will have become evident how the idea of *being* in time is the idea of a wretched state; how being in time, the world, is the realm of chance, error and wickedness; how the body is the visible will that always wills and can never be satisfied; how life is a constantly inhibited dying, an eternal struggle with death certain to end in defeat; how suffering mankind and the suffering animal world are the idea of life in time; how *willing-to-live* is true damnation, and virtue and vice are only the weakest and strongest degrees of willing-to-live.[350]

From "willing-to-live" conceived as true damnation there was but a small step to "willing" in general that soon afterwards is portrayed as the "fundamental error":

---

[348] »subjektive Betrachtung«; »Grundirrthum« (#86).

[349] »die Idee alles dessen was *ist* und lebt gefunden und dargestellt haben wird«; »*Nichtseynwollen*« (#210).

[350] »Denn es wird sich gezeigt haben, wie die Idee des *Seyns* in der Zeit, die Idee eines unseligen Zustandes ist, wie das Seyn in der Zeit, die Welt, das Reich des Zufalls, des Irrthums und der Bosheit ist; wie der Leib der sichtbare Wille ist, der immer will und nie zufrieden seyn kann; wie das Leben ein stets gehemmtes Sterben, ein ewiger Kampf mit dem Tode, der endlich siegen muß, ist; wie die leidende Menschheit und die leidende Thierheit, die Idee des Lebens in der Zeit ist; wie das *Lebenwollen* die wahre Verdammniß ist, und Tugend und Laster nur der schwächste und stärkste Grad des Lebenwollens« (#210).

Willing and Contemplation

> That we are *willing* at all constitutes our calamity: it does not matter at all what it is that we will. But willing (the fundamental error) can never be satisfied, which is why we never cease to will and life is continual misery, for it is nothing but the manifestation of willing, the objectified willing.[351]

Now it is no longer just the body that is objectified will but life and even the world as a whole. Willing itself is now called the fundamental error and the world its manifestation or phenomenal apparition. In the long note #213 of early summer 1814 the basis of Schopenhauer's metaphysics of will is established; willing is now identified as the origin of evil and the world "which actually are one and the same."[352] Will, whose objectification or manifestation is the world, is portrayed as the ground of suffering, and empirical consciousness as inseparably and essentially bound to it. Better consciousness, by contrast, "does not form part of the world but stands opposed to it, does *not* will it."[353]

In note #213 the two poles of Schopenhauer's compass are for the first time wholly defined on the basis of will, that is, as *affirmation of will* (empirical consciousness that obeys will) and *negation of will* (better consciousness that does *not* will). In the equation will = ground of suffering = essence of the world, Schopenhauer's search for the most fundamental basis of suffering attained its philosophical anchor point. The same can be said of the opposite pole that is now for the first time defined as "better consciousness" rooted in the cessation of willing. It is significant that all of this takes place in note #213 where Schopenhauer for the first time quotes a dogma of the *Oupnek'hat*:

---

[351] »Daß wir überhaupt *wollen* ist unser Unglück: auf das was wir wollen kommt es gar nicht an. Aber das Wollen (der Grundirrthum) kann nie befriedigt werden; daher hören wir nie auf zu wollen und das Leben ist ein dauernder Jammer: denn es ist eben nur die Erscheinung des Wollens, das objektivirte Wollen.« (#213)

[352] »Ursprung des Uebels und der Welt (die eigentlich eins sind)« (#213).

[353] »Das bessre Bewußtseyn gehört ja eben nicht zur Welt, sondern steht ihr entgegen, will sie *nicht*« (#213).

CHAPTER NINE

That we *will* at all is our calamity; it does not matter in the least *what* we are willing. But willing (the fundamental error) can never be satisfied, which is why we never cease to will and why life is a continual state of misery; for it is nothing but the phenomenal appearance of willing, objectified willing. We constantly imagine that the desired object can put an end to our willing, though only we ourselves can achieve that end precisely by ceasing to will. This (the liberation from willing) occurs through better knowledge. Thus *Oupnekhat*, Vol. II, p. 216 says: "*tempore quo cognitio simul advenit amor e medio supersurrexit*" [Just when insight arrives, desire leaves the scene]; here by *amor* is meant *Maya* which is nothing other than that willing, the love (for the object) whose objectification or manifestation is the world. As the fundamental error it [*amor/maya*] is at the same time, as it were, the origin of evil and of the world (which actually are one and the same).[354]

Here we see how deeply Dara's and Anquetil's interpretation of *Maya* is connected with Schopenhauer's conception of *will*. As we have seen, the *Oupnek'hat* defines Maya as the *voluntas aeterna* or eternal will[355] which desires (*amor*) its manifestation as world. This corresponds to Schopenhauer's interpretation of Maya as "willing, the love (for the object) whose objectification or manifestation is the world" (#213)—a

---

[354] »Daß wir überhaupt *wollen* ist unser Unglück: auf das *was* wir wollen kommt es gar nicht an. Aber das Wollen (der Grundirrthum) kann nie befriedigt werden; daher hören wir nie auf zu wollen und das Leben ist ein dauernder Jammer: denn es ist eben nur die Erscheinung des Wollens, das objektivirte Wollen. Wir wähnen beständig das gewollte Objekt könne unserm Wollen ein Ende machen, da vielmehr nur wir selbst es können indem wir eben zu Wollen aufhören: dies, (die Befreiung vom Wollen) geschieht durch die bessre Erkenntniß: daher sagt *Oupnekhat* Vol: II, p 216, »*tempore quo cognitio simul advenit amor e medio supersurrexit*«; unter *amor* wird hier *Maja* verstanden, welche eben das Wollen, die Liebe (zum Objekt) ist, deren Objektivirung oder Erscheinung die Welt ist, und die als der Grundirrthum, zugleich gleichsam der Ursprung des Uebels und der Welt (die eigentlich Eins sind) ist.« (#213)

[355] "*Maïa: voluntas aeterna; quod causa ostensi sine fuit (existentiâ) est*" (OUP1:10; see here above p. 190).

phrasing that already evokes the title of his major work, *The World as Will and Representation*. Significantly, this first quotation[356] by Schopenhauer of the *Oupnek'hat* concerns the liberation from willing. One can therefore state that precisely in note #213, where he first adduces a dogma of the *Oupnek'hat* and offers his own interpretation of Maya, the philosopher's system found its earliest valid expression.

This fruit of Dara's and Anquetil's interpretation of the Upanishads has hitherto remained almost as hidden as Allah's treasure. For instance, the eminent Schopenhauer expert Hübscher (1973:50) claimed that the philosopher's encounter with the Upanishads had taken place "only late." The philosopher is also said to have exaggerated the *Oupnek'hat*'s influence since in the best case it had "encouraged rather than influenced him" (Schirmacher 1985:15) or occurred at a time when "no philosophically sufficient reflection was yet present" (Kamata 1988:254). Rüdiger Safranski (1987:305) stated that Schopenhauer adduced "Indian philosophemes only as illustration," and Brian Magee denied all oriental influence and squarely contradicted Schopenhauer's own appraisal of such influence in the genesis of his system:

> Working entirely within the central tradition of Western philosophy—before all else continuing and completing, as he believed, the work of Kant—he arrived at positions which *he then almost immediately discovered* were similar to some of the doctrines central to Hinduism and Buddhism" (Magee 1997:15; emphasis by Magee).[357]

A connected line of argument holds that the Upanishads were for Schopenhauer "not so much a source of inspiration or revelation" but rather a "mirror and medium of self-presentation."[358] But even authors who

---

[356] See note 336, p. 192 above.

[357] Most recently, Stephen Cross expressed a similar view: "To him [Schopenhauer] the *Oupnek'hat* came not so much as a revelation of ideas that were new as an almost miraculous confirmation, from a remote time and place, to his own insights" (Cross 2013:26). See also our Appendix 2.

[358] »nicht so sehr eine Quelle der Inspiration oder Offenbarung«; »Spiegel

accepted Schopenhauer's claims of Upanishadic influence invariably used modern Upanishad translations and failed to take Schopenhauer's source, the *Oupnek'hat*, into consideration. For example, Urs Walter Meyer asserted that Schopenhauer "in using the concept of mâyâ" was wrong to refer to the *Oupnek'hat* and "mistakenly took mâyâ to mean the world as illusion,"[359] and Douglas Berger (2000, 2004) based his argument about Indian influence on Schopenhauer upon a Vedantic conception of Maya rather than that of the *Oupnek'hat*.[360]

Behind the lifted veil of Schopenhauer's Maya we find the exact opposite of such views, namely:

1. Schopenhauer encountered his favorite book exactly at the right time, that is, just when the core of his philosophical system was taking shape.
2. The *Oupnek'hat* played a crucial role in the genesis of his system; this centrally concerned not the theory of knowing, as Berger argues, but rather the formation of Schopenhauer's central conception of will, its affirmation, and its negation.
3. What influenced Schopenhauer was not some modern theory or Upanishad translation from the Sanskrit but rather Prince Dara's creative renderings and interpretations as presented and explained by Anquetil in his annotated Latin translation.
4. Schopenhauer's understanding of the concept of Maya in the *Oupnek'hat* was relatively faithful to Anquetil's text but atheistic.
5. The Upanishads were for Schopenhauer, as they had been for Kanne and Görres a few years earlier, not a medium for self-presentation but rather a source of great interest that inspired key ideas of their

---

und ein Medium der Selbstdarstellung« (Halbfass 1987:59).

[359] »mit der Verwendung des Begriffs der mâyâ zu Unrecht auf das Oupnek'hat« berufe; »fälschlicherweise unter mâyâ die Welt als Illusion« verstanden (Meyer 1994:122).

[360] Though he did not discuss this in terms of system genesis, only Piantelli (1986:203–4) has hitherto seen a direct connection between the Maya of the *Oupnek'hat* and Schopenhauer's conception of will.

respective systems but required intensive study and effort (as is evident in Schopenhauer's case from his notes, his handwritten index to the *Oupnek'hat*, and the profusion of remarks and underlinings in its text and margins).

6. A decisive factor of the *Oupnek'hat*'s influence on Schopenhauer was the Sufism of Prince Dara that (unbeknownst to both Anquetil and his readers) transpired from his translations. As will be shown, the *Oupnek'hat*'s emphasis on overcoming of self (*fanā*) and of will (*nolitio*) was particularly inspirational for Schopenhauer's conception of the negation or abolition of will.

7. A factor that was hitherto also overlooked pertains to the neoplatonic influences at work both in the Orient (Prince Dara) and the West (Böhme, Anquetil, Schelling).

Based on all this we can already at this juncture conclude that there was ample reason for Schopenhauer to list, as early as 1816, the Upanishads as the first of three major influences on the formation of his philosophical system (#623), and that choosing this work as his favorite book and calling it "the consolation of his life and death" was not a regrettable mistake or exaggeration but rather a reflection of his genuine appreciation of its influence on him.

On the backdrop of the *Oupnek'hat*'s doctrine about the ceasing of will with the arrival of insight, Schopenhauer attached new labels to the poles of his compass though its fundamental bearing did not change.

> As *subject of willing* I am an exceedingly miserable being, and all our suffering consists in willing. Willing, wishing, striving and aspiring are definitely finiteness, definitely death and distress.[361]

At the opposite pole of the compass we find the *Oupnek'hat*'s pure knowledge or insight (*cognitio*) associated with the overcoming of will that now takes the place of "better consciousness":

---

[361] »Als *Subjekt des Wollens* bin ich ein höchst elendes Wesen und all unser Leiden besteht im Wollen. Das Wollen, Wünschen, Streben, Trachten, ist durchaus Endlichkeit, durchaus Tod und Quaal« (#220).

On the other hand, as soon as I am wholly and entirely the *subject of knowing*—that is, with pure absorption in knowing—I am blissfully happy, perfectly contented, and nothing can assail me. Whatever the object that I contemplate, I am that object. If I see a mountain with blue sky behind it and the sun's rays on its summit, then I am nothing but this mountain, this sky, these rays of the sun ... But woe unto me if the slightest willing joins this, if the least aim gets to the forefront: then I plunge at once down from my exalted position and am no longer the infinite subject of knowing but the miserable and suffering subject of willing.[362]

For the first time Schopenhauer is now associating the possibility of deliverance with the self-overcoming of will: "The will can want to abolish its concrete phenomenal appearance, whereby it overcomes itself; and this is the *freedom*, the possibility of deliverance."[363] Even though total lack of willing is impossible as long as the body is alive, this is what asceticism aims at. Genuine deliverance can only be achieved by wresting oneself free from will:

> Willing is always that which robs us of the bliss of contemplation; it is the perpetual disturbance of this bliss which never lets the majority of human beings reach this state, which deprives them of all peace of mind, which chases them around like haunted spirits. And what is all this willing for? Whither can it lead? What can it give us that can replace the stolen bliss of contemplation? Call out

---

[362] »Sobald ich hingegen ganz und gar *Subjekt des Erkennens* bin, d.h. rein im Erkennen aufgehe bin ich seelig, allgenugsam, mich kann nichts anfechten. Welchen Gegenstand ich betrachte, der bin ich. Sehe ich den Berg, mit blauem Himmel dahinter und Sonnenstrahlen auf dem Gipfel, so bin ich nichts als dieser Berg, dieser Himmel, diese Strahlen ... Aber wehe mir wenn sich das mindeste Wollen hinzugesellt, der mindeste Zweck sich mir vorsetzt; alsbald stürz ich herab von meiner Höhe, bin nicht mehr das unendliche Subjekt des Erkennens, sondern das dürftige leidende Subjekt des Wollens.« (#220)

[363] »Der Wille kann seine konkrete Erscheinung aufheben wollen, wodurch er sich selbst aufhebt, und dies ist die *Freiheit*, die Möglichkeit der Erlösung« (#220).

to yourself at every moment *'sapere aude!'* [dare to know], wrest yourself free from the shackle of aims, and be the pure subject of knowing.[364]

In the kind of pure and aimless contemplation described in so many passages of the *Oupnek'hat*, man becomes an immaculate subject of knowing, leaves all willing behind, and enjoys—as Schopenhauer puts it—"a holiday from the penal servitude of willing."[365] Schopenhauer calls the object of such will-free contemplation, i.e. knowing liberated from the principle of sufficient reason and its subject-object matrix, "platonic idea." He thus describes what happens in the "bliss of contemplation" as "the realization of the true nature of the world, that is, the idea."[366] This constitutes the foundation of a system of *aesthetics* based on willing and not-willing. Soon Schopenhauer also linked Plato's doctrine of eternal forms, the doctrine of ideas, to Kant's *things-in-themselves* (#228). In this period he stated that his "new doctrine" consists in the teaching that "the body is will which has become objectified."[367] What he, at the beginning of his *Oupnek'hat* study, had called "the method of the Indians"—namely, the setting out from the subject—was now fully adopted as his own method which is said to permit "seizing the entire problem of empirical consciousness, as it were, by the topknot."[368]

---

[364] »Wollen ist allemal was uns die Seeligkeit des Anschauens raubt, was die immerwährende Stöhrung derselben ist, was die meisten Menschen nie zu dieser Seeligkeit kommen läßt, ihnen alle Ruhe nimmt, sie wie gequälte Geister umhertreibt. Und was soll all das Wollen! Wohin kann es leiten? Was kann es geben, das die geraubte Seeligkeit des Anschauens ersetzte? ›Sapere aude!‹ ruf dir in jedem Moment zu, und reiß dich los von der Kette der Zwekke und sei das reine Subjekt des Erkennens.« (#220)

[365] »einen Sabbath der Zuchthausarbeit des Wollens« (#221).

[366] »Wonne der Kontemplation«; »die Erkenntniß des wahren Wesens der Welt, d.i. der Idee« (#221).

[367] »neue Lehre«; dass »der Leib der Objekt gewordne Wille ist« (#232).

[368] »Methode der Indier« (#192); »das ganze Problem des empirischen Bewußtseyns [...] gleichsam beim Schopf« zu fassen (#234).

CHAPTER NINE

Schopenhauer penned such remarks toward the end of his second phase of *Oupnek'hat* study while reading—possibly inspired by his conversations with Goethe in spring of 1814—Jacobi's letters about Spinoza and Giordano Bruno.[369] In his summary of Bruno's doctrine, Jacobi explained that everything is filled with a force that forms the "omni-present inside" and "is in ceaseless operation in everything." Though this force transforms itself into all things, it is said to remain "in itself always the same." He called the recognition of this "soul of the world"—the "one-and-all"—the goal of philosophy.[370] In a brief remark on Bruno's philosophy, Schopenhauer criticizes the Italian author's use of the word "God" for the "inner driving force (the *Maya* of the *Vedas*)" (HN1 #234). This comment confirms that at this crucial juncture Schopenhauer interpreted Maya exactly along the line of the *Oupnek'hat*'s word list as *voluntas aeterna* (eternal will), though he firmly resisted all forms of theistic interpretation.

Pradjapat petierunt , quòd, LXIV.

:o alio τȣ̃ *Beid* etiam memo-
quod] producens omne est, à
xequi facit; et τὸν *bhout âtma*
'rt). Proindè, operans, *bhout*

Oupnek'hat vol 1, p. 307; with Schopenhauer's remark on will in the margin

---

[369] When he restituted the *Oupnek'hat* to the Royal library in Dresden on 21 July 1814, Schopenhauer borrowed Friedrich Schlegel's *Die Sprache und Weisheit der Indier* (1808) and the philosophical works of Hemsterhuis. One week later (27 July) he borrowed Jacobi's *Ueber die Lehre des Spinoza in Briefen an den Herrn Moses Mendelssohn* (²1789) and Giordano Bruno's *De triplici minimo et mensura*. The remark about Bruno is based on the first appendix of Jacobi's Spinoza letters (second edition, 1789).

[370] Das »inwendige Allgegenwärtige«; »unaufhörlich und in Allem wirket« (Jacobi 1789:264–5); »an sich immer eins und dasselbe« (p. 281); »Seele der Welt«; »Eins-und-Alles« (pp. 292–5).

This is why Schopenhauer stated in the margin of the first volume of his *Oupnek'hat* copy that "the essence of will is baseness and vileness," adding that "the form of its appearance [is] individuality and multiplicity."[371]

As he studied the *Oupnek'hat* its theistic tendency irritated him. Indian divinities such as Brahma, Shiva and Vishnu could well be interpreted as aspects of the will (creation, preservation, and destruction). But the *Oupnek'hat* also contained very theistic Upanishads that Anquetil particularly liked,[372] and Prince Dara had written in his preface that the *Oupnek'hat* can be regarded a sort of commentary to the Koran. After the reception of his own copy in the summer of 1814, Schopenhauer began to systematically strike out the word *Deus* in his newly acquired sacred scripture. Whereas Prince Dara's *Allah* had been much appreciated by Anquetil who translated the word as *Deus*, Schopenhauer showed an allergic reaction. For example, in the passage where the *Oupnek'hat* recommends to the penitent (*saniasi*) to expunge all willing from his heart and exhorts him to read the Veda "seeking God with ardent desire" (OUP2:244), Schopenhauer struck out this last exhortation and drowned Anquetil's word *Deum*—the accusative case of *Deus* (God)—in thick black ink. By contrast he wholeheartedly approved and underlined the *Oupnek'hat*'s strict admonitions regarding the elimination of all willing from one's heart that is said to constitute the only means of becoming a true penitent.

---

[371] »Das Wesen des Willens ist Schnödigkeit und Bosheit, die Form seiner Erscheinung Individualität u. Vielheit« (OUP1:307).

[372] These include the four Upanishads that Anquetil chose for translation and publication in French in order to give European readers a first impression of the content of Indian Upanishads: Upanishad no. 7 (*Naraïn*; 1787b:297–301), no. 8 (*Tadiv*; 1787b:301–308), no. 9 (*Athrbsar*; 1787b:308–322), and no. 19 (*Schat Roudri*; 1787b:323–344). Anquetil's translation was first published in French (1787) and four years later in German (1791). Anquetil's French translation of the other 46 Upanishads was not published and exists only in manuscript form because he judged that Latin was more appropriate for a literal translation of the Persian text (see Appendix 1 below).

> Tempore quo hac u...
> Et quodcunque tempus [quo] (*librum*) *Beid* legerit, et
> statim [quòd] petitum divinum simul provenire facit (D...
> *ardenter quærit*), et volitiones super cor ejus frigidum fit,
> *saniasi* fiat.
> Et si plura ex operibus fecerit, et plura non fecerit; ipsâ
> hac horâ quòd volitiones è corde ejus è latere (*semotæ*) fiunt,
> *saniasi* est.

Oupnek'hat vol. 2, p. 244 with Schopenhauer's markup

Schopenhauer regarded such traces of theism as additions by translators or copyists. But when he saw that the three ancient sacred Vedas were associated with three *Fereschteh* (angels) called Brahma, Beschn (Vishnu) and Mehisch (Shiva) and related them to the archangels Gabriel, Michael and Raphael, Schopenhauer first expressed his disapproval by wavy lines and then simply struck these names out, explaining in the margin: "Gabriel, Michael & Raphael: this consequently is an Islamic addition."[373]

> Et quique tres (3) (*libri*) *Beid*; quòd, *Rak Beid*, et *Djedjr
> Beid*, et *Sam Beid*, sit: et quique tres *Fereschteh*; quòd, *Brahma*,
> et *Beschn*, et *Mehisch* sit; id est, *Djibril, et Mikaïl, et Esraphil*: Gabriel, Michael
> et quique tres (3) ignes; quòd, ignis apparens, et ignis solis; & Raphaël: est
> et ignis naturalis (*corporum*) sit: et quæque tres (3) qualitates, *Suprà, T. 1,* [illeg. addi-
> quòd; *satouguen*, et *temouguen*, et *radjouguen* sit: in illis *N.° LIV,* tamentum
> tribus litteris (*hoc*) est. *p. 274.* Muhamedanicum.

Oupnek'hat vol. 2, p. 201 with Schopenhauer's markup and explanation

Anquetil explains in a note that Brahma (the creator), Beschn (Vishnu; the preserver) and Mehisch (Shiva; the destroyer) are "three characteristics, three faculties of Brahm that are also contained in the supreme and incommunicable name of *prana* (*Oum*).[374] This reflects the identi-

---

[373] "Gabriel, Michaël & Raphaël: est igitur additamentum Muhammedanicum" (OUP2:201).
[374] "*Brahma*, creator; *Beschn*, servator; *Mehisch*, destructor; tres qualitates,

fication, common with Christian India missionaries, of Brahm (Brahman) or Parabrahma with the Christian creator God, and of the three supreme Indian deities (Brahma, Vishnu and Shiva) with aspects of his omnipotence.³⁷⁵ By contrast, for Schopenhauer Brahm / Parabrahma / Oum signified nothing other than eternal will (Anquetil's *voluntas aeterna* but without God): will that blindly and constantly creates, preserves and destroys all phenomena. In countless passages of the *Oupnek'hat* we find the doctrine that the multiplicity of the phenomenal world is nothing other than universal Atma (OUP1:260) which is identical to *djiw âtma*, that is, Atma bound to a body which is but "a form of will" (p. 254). The cosmic will that conjures up the entire world of multiplicity is said to constitute the singular essence of everything. Thus questioners in the dialogues of the *Oupnek'hat* constantly hear from their teachers: You yourself are nothing other than what is the essence of everything. The sun, the earth, your breath, your eye: everything is "your Atma which is the Atma of all things."³⁷⁶ This essence of everything, inside and outside, forms the central subject of the Upanishads,³⁷⁷ and the *Oupnek'hat*'s methodology of insight is reflected in Schopenhauer's remark that one must not strive to understand oneself through the world but rather to understand the world through oneself. Already in the earliest note that explicitly mentions Indian doctrines (#192), Schopenhauer called it "the method of the

---

tres facultates tē *Brahm*, quo cum, in supremo et incommunicabili nomine *pranou* (*Oum*) continentur" (OUP2:210).

³⁷⁵ See App 2010c:44–45, 80–100.

³⁷⁶ "Ipse hic *atmaï* tuus, *âtmaï* omnium existentium rerum est" (OUP1:191).

³⁷⁷ A modern Upanishad translator explains: "The terminal point of such a spiritual experience is the realisation of the unity of the individual self, *âtman*, with the supreme Self, *parâtman* or *brahman*. The *brahman* is the changeless essence which upholds the universe and also indwells the human spirit. This identification of the *brahman* (supreme Self) with *âtman* (individual self) is a basic premise of the Upanishads, and the ways through which this unity can be realised, the central concern of its teaching." (*Upanishads*, tr. by Suren Navlakha. Ware: Wordsworth, 2000: XI–XII).

Indians" (die Methode der Indier) to start from the subject in order to gain insight into the essence of the universe as a whole.

In the second Upanishad of the *Oupnek'hat* this doctrine is expressed with great clarity:

> *Kandherp* said: Whoever knows this link that is firmly tying together everything and the essence found inside: he knows *Brahm*, knows the worlds, knows the *fereschtehha* [angels], knows the books of the Veda, knows the *korbanha* [sacrifices], knows the elements, knows himself, knows everything.[378]

To all questions that follow concerning the essence of the earth, the sun, all creatures, the body, the eye etc. the teacher's response is always the same: "Ipsum illud (*ens*) est *atmaï* tuus; in omni re est; et sine cessatione est" ("That being is your Atma; it is in all beings; and it is without cessation" OUP1:124). The sequence of beings that are mentioned ends with the human body which embodies this unperishable essence of everything and performs its actions. The questioner in this second Upanishad only turns silent after the following lesson about cognition highlighted by Schopenhauer with three lines in the margin:

> It is invisible yet sees everything; inaudible yet hears everything; unknowable yet knows everything; incomprehensible yet comprehends everything: Apart from it no being exists that is seeing, knowing, hearing and comprehending. Your *Atma* is in all beings; and it is without cessation; and whatever is outside of it is subject to corruption (perishing).[379]

---

[378] "*Kandherp* dixit: quisquis hunc funem, quòd omne com eo (*per eum*) firmiter constrictum est, et illus (*ens*), quod in interioribus est, scit; is est sciens Brahm, et cognoscens mundos, et cognoscens *fereschtehha*, et cognoscens (*libros*) *Beidha*, et cogniscens *korbanha* (*sacrificia*), et cognoscens elementa, et cognoscens seipsum, et cognoscens omne." (OUP1:196; emphases in italics by Anquetil, underlining in pencil in Schopenhauer's copy).

[379] "Id videndum non est; omnia videt: et id audiendum non est; omnia audit: sciendum non est; omnia scit: et intelligendum non est; omnia intelligit: praeter id, videns et sciens, et audiens, et intelligens, (*ens aliud*) non est. Atmaï tuus in omni (*re*) est; et sine cessatione est; et praeter id quidquid est, corruptionis (*tē perire*) capax est." (OUP1:201–2; italics by Anquetil).

On this backdrop it becomes easier to understand why Schopenhauer wrote that Giordano Bruno's "inner driving force"—the essence of everything that Bruno chose to call "God"—corresponds to the "*Maya* of the *Vedas*" (#234). If Schopenhauer, following the *Oupnek'hat*'s definition, understood Maya as eternal will (*voluntas aeterna*) that also assumes the form of the human body, one would expect that such embodiment would come to encompass everything, just like the *Oupnek'hat*'s Atma. This is precisely what occurred in the summer of 1814 during Schopenhauer's second *Oupnek'hat* study phase when he wrote in his notebook:

> Every immediate object of knowledge is also the object of a will, indeed only the material phenomenal appearance of a will. It thus seems that no object could exist unless it is the expression of a will. Is consequently the whole globe also such an expression?[380]

In the same note Schopenhauer also addresses a topic that was to play an important role in his metaphysics of will: polarity. Electrical and magnetic polarity as well as attraction and repulsion in general were, among others, also thematized by Kant, Schelling and Goethe; but Schopenhauer sought to anchor polarity in the will. Already in note #242 we can observe the outline of his new philosophy of nature: "*Man's body and the animal's are nothing but their will in manifestation*, their will that has become object in space."[381] But plants, too, are embodied will:

> Like man and the animal, the plant must be the phenomenal manifestation of a will, an embodied will; for all growth, vegetation and reproduction can only be conceived as the manifestation of a will. ... Its life in time, as well, is only a single act, namely its

---

[380] »Jedes unmittelbare Objekt des Erkennens, ist auch Objekt eines Willens, ja nur die Materiale Erscheinung eines Willens. Es scheint also als könnte kein Objekt seyn, wenn es nicht der Ausdruck eines Willens ist. Ist denn auch der ganze Erdkörper ein solcher?« (HN1 #240)

[381] »*Der Leib des Menschen und des Thieres ist nichts als sein Wille in der Erscheinung*, sein im Raum Objekt gewordner Wille.« (HN1 #240)

embodiment and development; its will reveals itself only as an existence: without any knowledge in the proper sense it also cannot perceive any motives and *act* accordingly. Its form exhausts the entire content of its will.[382]

This first draft of a philosophy of nature based on will also encompasses anorganic matter:

> Finally, mineralogy reveals to us more and more that all rock is crystal and that everything that is noncrystalline consists merely of shattered crystal, of fragments. Crystallization itself is evidently a striving, a polarization, and every self-driven striving or tendency is a will. Therefore the stone must also be regarded as expression of a will.[383]

In this important note, Schopenhauer thus arrives at a conclusion that matches the doctrine of the *Oupnek'hat* provided that one understands, as he did, 'Brahm' as will. It constitutes, as it were, Schopenhauer's doctrine of creation and theodicy:

> Overall we see that everything that exists is only phenomenal manifestation of *will*, embodied *will*. But we know that all our suffering only arises from will, that only in will we are wretched, whereas in pure knowing we are happy since we are freed from will. — The will therefore is *the origin of evil* and also of *affliction*

---

[382] »Die Pflanze muß, wie Mensch und Thier, Erscheinung eines Willens, ein verkörperter Wille, seyn; denn alles Wachsen, Vegetiren, Reproduciren ist nur als Erscheinung eines Willens denkbar. ... Ihr Leben in der Zeit ist gleichfalls nur ein einziger Akt, nämlich ihre Verkörperung und Entwickelung, ihr Wille offenbart sich nur als ein Daseyn: ohne eigentliche Erkenntniß kann sie auch keine Motive erkennen und sonach *handeln*. Ihre Gestalt erschöpft den ganzen Inhalt ihres Willens.« (HN1 #242)

[383] »Die Mineralogie endlich offenbart mehr und mehr daß alles Gestein Krystall ist und alles unkrystallinische bloß zerstöhrtes Krystall, Trümmer. Die Krystallisation selbst ist sichtlich ein Streben, eine Polarisation, und jedes eigne Streben ist ein Wille. Auch der Stein also ist anzusehn als Ausdruck eines Willens.« (HN1 #242)

that exists only for its manifestation, namely the body; and the will is also the *origin of the world*.[384]

Already in note #213, will had been singled out as the source of all evil and of the world, and "knowledge" hailed as liberation from willing; and Schopenhauer supported his argument with a first quote from the *Oupnek'hat*. But now he came to concretely identify our entire "vain and sad world, bereft of satisfaction" and all evil as a manifestation of will (#246). Schopenhauer's *ethics*, too, were now being developed from the vantage point of will. Man regards as "good" what serves his will: "thus we say good weather, good food, good roads, good weapons: that is, everything as we *want* it and by our nature must want it; as they suit our will."[385]

In the fall of 1814 Schopenhauer for the first time redacted a comprehensive formulation of his system. A phrase from note #274 could serve as its motto and almost reads like a Schopenhauerian variation on his favorite quote from the *Oupnek'hat* about the end of willing at the arrival of knowledge: "When *willing* we are *wretched* and when *knowing* we are *happy*."[386] In this note Schopenhauer first thematizes the polarity or "inner diremption" (innere Entzweiung) of will and presents a

---

[384] »Ueberhaupt aber sehn wir daß Alles was ist nur Erscheinung von *Willen* ist, verkörperter *Wille*. Wir wissen aber daß alle unsre Quaal nur aus dem Willen kommt, wir nur in ihm unseelig, dagegen im reinen Erkennen, als von ihm befreit, seelig sind.—Der Wille ist also der *Ursprung des Bösen* und auch des *Uebels* das nur für seine Erscheinung, den Leib, da ist: und der Wille ist auch der *Ursprung der Welt*« (HN1 #242). In this context Schopenhauer also refers to note #220 where he stated: "As *subject of willing* I am an exceedingly wretched being, and all our suffering consists in willing. Willing, wishing, striving, aiming are necessarily finitude, necessarily death and agony." (»Als *Subjekt des Wollens* bin ich ein höchst elendes Wesen und all unser Leiden besteht im Wollen. Das Wollen, Wünschen, Streben, Trachten, ist durchaus Endlichkeit, durchaus Tod und Quaal«).

[385] »so sagen wir gutes Wetter, gutes Essen, gute Wege, gute Waffen: d.h. alles wie wir sie *wollen* und unsrer Natur nach wollen müssen; wie sie unserm Willen gemäß sind.« (HN1 #248)

[386] »als *wollend unseelig*, als *erkennend seelig*« (HN1 #274).

summary of his will-based diagnosis of suffering and doctrine of deliverance:

> The purpose of life (here I use an expression that is only allegorically true) is knowledge of the will. Life is the mirror of the will whose true nature, consisting in inner dissension, becomes in [this mirror] an object; through such knowledge the will can turn about and salvation is possible. Were we merely willing and not knowing, we should be doomed to eternal damnation. Life is therefore a blessing only in so far as we are *knowing*; because inasfar as we are *willing* it is agony. *Knowing* is the promise of deliverance, the true gospel; whereas *willing* is properly hell.[387]

In this way the miracle *par excellence* of which Schopenhauer wrote in his dissertation—that we as willing subjects are simultaneously knowing subjects—now appears as a ray of hope that shines only on the human being equipped with rationality. This "true gospel" is said to call out to us: "But you willing one (i.e., you wretched one) are also a knowing one, and this shall deliver you from willing."[388] At the pole of Schopenhauers compass facing us, the word "willing" now rules, and the opposite extremity of the compass needle points toward "the true gospel": pure, will-less knowing. In note #277 Schopenhauer describes the loneliness one experiences on a high mountain peak, and in the subsequent note he specifies the kind of thoughts that occupied his mind in the clarity of high altitude:

---

[387] »Der Zweck des Lebens (ich brauche hier einen nur gleichnißweise wahren Ausdruck) ist die Erkenntniß des Willens. Das Leben ist der Spiegel des Willens, dessen in innrer Entzweiung bestehendes Wesen darin Objekt wird, durch welche Erkenntniß der Wille sich wenden kann und Erlösung möglich ist. Wären wir bloß wollend und nicht erkennend, so wären wir ewiger Verdammniß Preiß gegeben. Das Leben ist daher nur in sofern eine Wohlthat als wir *erkennend* sind: denn sofern wir *wollend* sind ist es eine Quaal: das *Erkennen* ist die Verheißung der Erlösung, ist das wahre Evangelium: das *Wollen* dagegen ist die Hölle selbst.« (HN1 #274)

[388] »Du Wollender, (d.i. Unseeliger) bist aber auch Erkennender, und dies wird dich vom Wollen erlösen« (HN1 #274).

Willing and Contemplation

The world as thing-in-itself is a great will that does not know what it wants; for it does not *know* but merely *wills* just because it is a will and nothing else. The *world as representation* is the knowledge of itself that is imparted to this will, by virtue of which it knows what it wills. — If this knowledge is realized it destroys the will which then no longer wills, because what it wills contradicts itself and it now knows what it wills. Here, too, the identity of the subject of knowing with the subject of willing appears as a miracle. For can the will ever *know*? Can the *will* do anything other than *to will*? On the other hand, can knowledge guide the *will*—the very will that precisely is what *guides*, what *creates the world*?[389]

Schopenhauer continues: "Since I myself am that identity, I can say with equal truth: the world is my representation, and: the world is nothing but will."[390]

As is evident from the last-cited remark, in the fall of 1814 Schopenhauer was already seeing the twin peaks of his major work jutting out from the cloud cover of ordinary philosophy: the world that on one hand is nothing but *will* and on the other hand nothing but *representation*. The *Oupnek'hat*'s keys of Maya and *fanā* had helped open the gates to this system, and Schopenhauer now regarded it as his philosophical task to demonstrate "the identity of what seems to be different"[391] using

---

[389] »*Die Welt als Ding an sich* ist ein großer Wille, der nicht weiß was er will; denn er *weiß* nicht sondern *will* bloß, eben weil er ein Wille ist und nichts Andres. Die *Welt als Erscheinung* ist die Erkenntniß seiner Selbst die diesem Willen beigebracht wird: in der er erkennt was er will.—Sofern diese Erkenntniß zu Stande kommt vernichtet sie ihn, er will dann nicht mehr, weil was er will sich widerspricht und er nun weiß was er will. Die Identität des Subjekts des Erkennens mit dem des Wollens, erscheint auch hier als Wunder. Denn kann der Wille je *erkennen*? kann der *Wille* etwas andres als *Wollen*? Kann andrerseits die Erkenntniß den *Willen* lenken, ihn der eben nur das *Lenkende*, das *Weltschaffende* ist?« (HN1 #278)

[390] »Da ich selbst jene Identität bin, kann ich mit gleicher Wahrheit sagen: die Welt ist meine Vorstellung: und die Welt ist lauter Wille.« (HN1 #278)

[391] »Identität des verschieden Scheinenden« (HN1 #280).

CHAPTER NINE

a method that shows striking resemblance to the "method of the Indians" of note #192 and of Prince Dara in the *Oupnek'hat*:

> And so I will attempt to show everywhere that what seems to be different when considered from several points of view is in reality one. ... Thus, if only we should gain the right point of view, the entire world should gradually appear as one, and this one only as the visibility of the will; what is neither will nor world must be kept apart. — That demonstration of the identity of the seemingly different should replace the derivation of one different thing from another based on the principle of sufficient reason.[392]

Prepared by his study of Schelling and several Christian mystics, Schopenhauer learned in the *Oupnek'hat* about the identity of the seemingly different on a breathtaking universal scale. The Upanishads ceaselessly hammer in the point that what Maya lets appear in countless different forms is in reality nothing other than the one and only Brahm "which appears in everything and is manifest (visible) in everything."[393] Schopenhauer identified will (the *voluntas* of the *Oupnek'hat*) with Kant's "things-in-themselves" that consequently had to appear, as documented in note #278, in the singular: "*The world as thing-in-itself* is a great will that does not know what it wants."

---

[392] »Und so will ich suchen überall zu zeigen, daß Eins ist was von verschiedenen Standpunkten betrachtet als Verschiedenes erscheint ... So soll nach und nach die ganze Welt, wenn man nur den rechten Standpunkt gewinnt als Eines erscheinen, und dieses Eine nur als die Sichtbarkeit des Willens: getrennt davon gehalten soll werden, was nicht Welt noch Wille ist. — Jene Nachweisung der Identität des verschieden Scheinenden, soll an die Stelle treten der Ableitung des Verschiedenen auseinander als Folge aus dem Grunde« (HN1 #280).

At the end of 1816, when all essential parts of Schopenhauer's system were complete, he called this methodology "my revolutionary principle" (»Das ist mein revolutionaires Princip« [#621]).

[393] "Et hic *âtmaï* memoratus *Brahm* est, qui in omni apparens est, et in omni manifestus (*visibilis*)" (OUP1:201). This is but one of countless examples in the two *Oupnek'hat* volumes.

BREHDARANG. 181

Illo tempore, cum figurâ volantis (*volatilis*), id est, corpus | OUPNEK'HAT
subtile (*leve*) cùm sumpsisset, in omnia corpora intravit. Et | IL
(*illud ens*) porsch dicunt.

Et hoc corpus adhuc ipse ille *porsch* est.

Porsch, ex illo (*indè*) dicunt, quòd *por*, in vocabulariis,
mansio (*sedes*) est; et *s* (*sin*), illud quod intrà mansionem
sedet, et in eâ occupationem (*operationem*) facit.

Et ille *porsch* in omni (*re*) plenus est (*omnia implet*), et
ullus locus ab eo vacuus non est.

Proindè in creaturis, cum investigare (*inquirendo*) non
potestas invenit (*non possunt invenire*) aliquid quod, in exteriori et intùs ejus, *âtma* non sit.

Et *schehed* (*testis*, *testimonium*) hæc scientia est; quòd cum
certâ scientiâ scis, quòd ipse ille *âtma*, cum his figuris egressus, et ipsum hoc est figuræ ejus in apparentiâ (*hæ figuræ
formam τȣ âtma apparentem constituunt*).

Et ille *pormesir*, causâ τȣ *maïa*, cum figuris plurimis et
sine numero apparet : et cum unâquâque ex his figuris sensus
plurimos, ut, decem, centum, et mille, et alios (*etc.*) ad
suum finem perductos habet (*illorum objectum adimplet*).

Certum (*est*) quòd hi sensus, adhuc is est : et quidquid
super eum, hoc et illud, addictum potestas facit (*quidquid ei
possunt attribuere*), illud *Brahm* est.

Et porrò, qui, antè eum aliquis non fuit, et post eum
aliquis non est futurus, intrà et extrà impedimentum et velamen non est; et ab eo aliquid extrà non est.

Et hic *âtmaï* memoratus *Brahm* est, qui in omni apparens
est, et in omni magnifestus (*visibilis*). | *Infrà*, N.°
XLIII.

Hoc *anbhou* edocendum est.

Oupnek'hat vol. 1, p. 201 with Schopenhauer's markup

10. Veil of Maya and Wisdom of the Veda

Subsequent to the discovery of the system kernel during the first phase of *Oupnek'hat* study[394] and its first consequences (the above-mentioned foundations for his philosophy of nature, ethics, and aesthetics) there began a phase in which Schopenhauer elaborated his core insights, sought to clarify his young metaphysics of will to himself, and relate it to the systems of the greatest minds of his discipline. The last mentioned of these endeavors is apparent in his book borrowing record: in July of 1814 he studied works of Spinoza and Giordano Bruno,[395] in September of Böhme, and in October of Kant (numerous works of whom he had already acquired). Between October of 1814 and May of 1815 he ploughed through the multi-volume histories of philosophy published by Tennemann, Tiedemann, and Buhle. This study phase is marked by a variety of attempts to marry Plato's "idea" and Kant's

---

[394] From the end of March to end of July 1814, copies borrowed from the Weimar and Dresden libraries; notes from around #188 to #230.
[395] Notes from #232.

"thing-in-itself" with his "will." Such attempts have been portrayed as the birth of Schopenhauer's metaphysics of will, for example by Rudolf Malter who saw the decisive step in note #305 where Schopenhauer proclaimed the identity of the *Platonic idea*, Kant's *thing-in-itself*, and *will* (Malter 1988:26). But Schopenhauer's reflections must be regarded not as dogmatic pronouncements but rather as trial balloons. Schopenhauer sought "to show everywhere that what appears as different from various standpoints is [in reality] One,"[396] and he had a scheme in mind that juxtaposed the universal and the particular. The Platonic idea and Kant's Thing-in-itself were already in the first column of "Universal" when Schopenhauer attributed to them freedom from time and space and therewith freedom "from multiplicity, change, beginning and end."[397] Such attempts at linkage to his new metaphysics of will resulted in several new interpretations of such terms. This activity did not cease even with the publication of *The World as Will and Representation* and has understandably confused many commentators about the formative stage of Schopenhauer's metaphysics when this tendency was particularly pronounced.

The column of "Universal" in Schopenhauer's scheme was based on will, which is why Schopenhauer could assert that "the world as thing-in-itself is a great will."[398] The column of "Particular," on the other hand, had to contain everything labeled as "objectity" of the will. In note #286, where Schopenhauer first used this term, we also find the last occurrence of "better consciousness" (»besseres Bewußtsein«): everything now revolved around will and its affirmation/dominance or negation/overcoming. The column entitled "Particular" refers to the realm of affirmation of will. By contrast, the negation of will and of its manifold objectifications—for example that of the body in asceticism—are from this point onward associated with the column entitled

---

[396] »überall zu zeigen, daß Eins ist was von verschiedenen Standpunkten betrachtet als Verschiedenes erscheint« (#280).
[397] »von Vielheit, Wechsel, Anfang und Ende« (#250).
[398] »*Die Welt als Ding an sich* ist ein großer Wille« (#278).

"Universal." Schopenhauer's *philosophy of law* grew on the same soil of affirmation and negation of will: "Injustice is thus the act of will denying another's body, that is of the will, for the purpose of the stronger affirmation of one's own."[399] The principle of diversity—"that whereby things are *different*"—is "*time* and *space*."[400] But it was not easy to squeeze the world into a two-column scheme with the headers "Universal" and "Particular." In the saint, for example, the body as objectity of the will continues to live in spite of his abolition of will, and Plato's ideas also hovered somewhere between the universal and the particular. Schopenhauer was aware of such difficulties:

> After the elimination of the diversity of individuals, which consists solely in our perceiving them in time and space, there still is a diversity that is not to be found in them and which I would therefore like to call transcendental diversity: this is the diversity of the species itself that we can also call the diversity of the [Platonic] Ideas. All copper, albeit in innumerable fragments and individual things, still remains copper and exhibits accurately at all times the qualities of copper; and so also does all zinc remain zinc. But the fact that zinc is never copper represents quite a different kind of diversity which is not to be attributed to time and space.[401]

---

[399] »Unrecht ist also der Willensakt der Verneinung eines fremden Leibes d.i. Willens, zur stärkeren Bejahung des eigenen« (#286).

[400] »das, wodurch die Dinge *verschieden* sind«—ist »*Zeit* und *Raum*« (#287).

[401] »Nach Aufhebung der Diversität der Individuen, welche einzig darin liegt daß wir sie in Zeit und Raum anschauen, giebt es noch eine Diversität, die nicht darin liegt, und welche ich deshalb transcendentale Diversität nennen möchte: dies ist die Diversität der Species selbst, man kann auch sagen die Diversität der Ideen. Alles Kupfer, in unzähligen Stücken und Individuen, bleibt freilich Kupfer und zeigt pünktlich zu aller Zeit die Qualitäten des Kupfers; so alles Zink bleibt Zink: aber daß Zink nie Kupfer ist, das ist eine ganz andere Diversität und ist nicht der Zeit und dem Raum zuzuschreiben« (#287). For a discussion of problems involved in Schopenhauer's conception of Platonic ideas see Korfmacher 1994:84 f.

It is revealing that note #287 ends with the question: "Will I find the way out from this valley's depths?"[402] Friedrich Schiller's poem "Longing" to which Schopenhauer's verse alludes[403] calls for faith and courage and ends with "Only a miracle can carry you / to the beautiful wonderland."[404] The miracle did not yet happen in note #305; though he called the Platonic idea, Kant's thing-in-itself, and will "one," as Malter correctly observed (1988:26), Schopenhauer's remark in the margin rejects this equation: "This is incorrect: the adequate objectity of the will is the idea."[405] A further refinement is found in note #321:

> The ideas are not the wills but rather the way in which the wills become knowable, become knowledge — knowledge that makes salvation, i.e. the abolition of the wills possible. The ideas are therefore avenues of knowledge, and these avenues are the path to salvation. The wills are what ought to be known. The individuals are the manifestation of separate individual wills by means of many ideas.[406]

The emergence of multiplicity from oneness was thus not only a preoccupation of Prince Dara who found a solution in Maya, i.e. in the loving desire of Allah to reveal the hidden treasure of his all-oneness in the form of the universe. For Schopenhauer, however, this treasure had

---

[402] »Aus dieses Thales Gründen / Wird ich den Ausgang finden?« (#287)

[403] *Die Sehnsucht*. "Ach, aus dieses Thales Gründen, / Die der kalte Nebel drückt, / Könnt' ich den Ausgang finden, / Ach, wie fühlt ich mich beglückt!" (»Aus dieses Thales Gründen / Wird ich den Ausgang finden?« ("Ah! Out of the depths of this valley, / Weighed down by chilly fog, / Were I to find an exit, / How happy I would feel!").

[404] »Du mußt glauben, du mußt wagen, / Denn die Götter leihn kein Pfand; / Nur ein Wunder kann dich tragen / In das schöne Wunderland.« (#287)

[405] »Dies ist unrichtig: die adäquate Objektität des Willens ist die Idee« (#305).

[406] »Die Ideen sind nicht die Willen; sondern die Art wie die Willen erkennbar werden, Erkenntniß werden, durch welche Erkenntniß Erlösung d.i. Aufhebung der Willen möglich ist. Die Ideen sind also die Wege der Erkenntniß und diese der Weg des Heils. Die Willen sind das was erkannt werden soll. Die Individuen sind Erscheinung einzelner Willen mittelst vieler Ideen.« (#321)

Veil of Maya and Wisdom of the Veda

a negative connotation. In his view it was not a good creator God who desired to reveal himself but rather the ground of this entire world of suffering: eternal will (Anquetil's *voluntas aeterna*). Schopenhauer was convinced that Anquetil's translation was literal and trustworthy, and he could not know that Anquetil had attempted different renderings of Prince Dara's definition of Maya. In fact the unpublished manuscript of Anquetil's French *Oupnek'hat* translation contains an interesting correction.

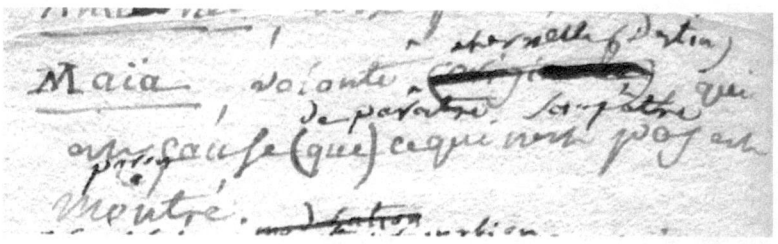

Maya in Anquetil's French *Oupnek'hat* manuscript (NAF 8857, p. 10)

First, Anquetil had translated Prince Dara's definition of Maya as a sentence: "*Maya*, (original) will, which is the cause (for) the manifestation of that which does not exist."[407] But in Anquetil's revision of 1787, written in darker ink, the word "originale" in parentheses was replaced by the word "éternelle" without parentheses: "*Maya*, eternal will (fate) which is the cause of appearing without being."[408] In Anquetil's Latin version, which is the sole published one, Maya appeared, as we have seen, as *voluntas aeterna* (eternal will). The definition in the Latin *Oupnek'hat* is no longer a complete phrase but seems, thanks to a semi-

---

[407] "*Maïa*, volonté (originale), qui est cause (que) ce qui n'est pas est montré." (Anquetil-Duperron, French *Oupnek'hat* translation manuscript, NAF 8857, p. 10).

[408] "*Maïa*, volonté eternelle (Destin) qui est cause de paraître sans être" (NAF 8857, p. 10).

colon, to be a concise definition of the term Maya with an appended explanation. Schopenhauer knew only this Latin version (OUP1:10) which seemed unambiguous:

> Maïa: voluntas aeterna; quod causa ostensi sine fuit (*existentiâ*) est"
>
> (*Maya*: eternal will; the cause of the manifestation of what is without reality [*existence*])

For the atheist Schopenhauer, this "eternal will" was the ground of all illusion and suffering and thus furnished the answer to the philosopher's initial question about the ground of empirical consciousness and the ultimate origin of suffering. Regarding Schopenhauer's second initial question about the path to better consciousness and deliverance from suffering, Prince Dara and Schopenhauer arrived at the same answer: will-free knowledge. In Schopenhauer's newly born metaphysics of will, deliverance is possible when "the will, after having recognized itself, turns and ends."[409] It needs to be stressed that the liberating knowledge in Schopenhauer's system is not empirical consciousness—i.e. "knowledge split into subject and object" and bound to will (#328)—but rather the will-free, contemplative insight of better consciousness. Empirical consciousness reigns, among other domains, in science which is "merely the application of the principle of sufficient reason" and therefore is "poor and necessitous."[410] True philosophy and art differ from this: philosophy consists in the conceptual analysis of the true nature of the world and art in its sensual representation (#328). Among the arts, music is seen as particularly excellent:

> *Music* is what all art aspires to be, namely a repetition of the world in a uniform homogeneous material, so much so that whoever would manage to fully explain music—in other words to repeat its nature in concepts—would thereby also conceptually explain

---

[409] »indem der Wille, nachdem er sich erkannt hat, sich wendet und endet« (#328).

[410] »nur Anwendung des Satzes vom Grunde«; »arm und dürftig« (#338).

and repeat the world, which is why a true explanation of music would at the same time be a true philosophy.[411]

Here we witness the emergence, in late autumn of 1814, of Schopenhauer's theory of art; and from the end of that year reflections about will-based epistemology, aesthetics, and ethics emerged in a form that was to permit their inclusion in his main work. Everything now bore the stamp of Schopenhauer's central idea of the will as fundamental essence of the world, of will as ground of all suffering, and of its abolition in will-free insight. He obviously wanted his metaphysics of will to lock into Kant's transcendental philosophy and later insisted in *The World as Will and Representation* that the study of Kant's philosophy is absolutely essential for the understanding of his own. As Weiner (2000) has somewhat too reductively shown, such remarks caused much confusion among his interpreters and led them to regard his philosophy as a "continuation" or "crowning" of Kant's philosophy. However, as soon as one relies on Schopenhauer's Manuscript Remains rather than his main work and even later writings, it becomes clear that his metaphysics of will was not mainly based on Kant. Indeed, he reproached Kant for having used "certain turns of phrase" as point of departure for his search for the innermost nature of the world instead of having, like Schopenhauer, used "the object of pure, will-free and reflexion-free contemplation" as avenue toward the understanding of this nature.[412]

The evidence presented in the present book indicates that in the genesis of his system, Schopenhauer's juxtaposition of egoism and selflessness along with his early experience of a "better consciousness" played central roles. He found that this "better consciousness" is explained and confirmed in writings of mystics and in the *Oupnek'hat*. Contrary

---

[411] »Die *Musik* ist so sehr was alle Kunst zu seyn strebt, nämlich Wiederholung der Welt in einem einartigen Stoff, daß wer die Musik völlig erklärt d.h. ihr Wesen in Begriffen wiederholt hätte, eben damit auch die Welt erklärt und in Begriffen wiederholt hätte, daher eine wahre Erklärung der Musik zugleich eine wahre Philosophie wäre.« (#349)

[412] »gewisse Wortfügungen«; »das Objekt der reinen, willensfreien und reflexionsfreien Anschauung« (#557).

CHAPTER TEN

to the arguments of Booms (2003) and Berger (2004), the analysis of Schopenhauer's early notes clearly shows that it was his metaphysics of will rather than his theory of cognition that forms the core of his philosophy. The "better consciousness" described by Schopenhauer does not concern knowledge based on the principle of sufficient reason as analyzed in his dissertation but rather Prince Dara's pure contemplative knowledge that puts an end to the illusion of Maya and all willing. Though in his major work the philosopher stressed the influence of Kant and Plato, the notes of 1814 documenting the genesis of the metaphysics of will show that these philosophies did not furnish the key to his system. Where in Kant or Plato would one find notions such as that knowledge based on the principle of sufficient reason is a servant of the will, and that knowledge of the Platonic idea, when it is perfect, abolishes the will (#369)? Far more than by the thought of Kant and Plato, Schopenhauer's metaphysics of will is colored by the *Oupnek'hat* and the Sufism of Dara whose understanding was of course facilitated by his study of the writings by Christian mystics and Schelling that also contain Neoplatonic elements.

The influence of the *Oupnek'hat* is not only evident in Schopenhauer's theory of knowledge and of art where Maya-illusionism and will-free knowledge of ideas play central roles, but of course also in his conception of a permanent abolition of suffering. What the *Oupnek'hat* teaches in this respect appears to lack any connection with Kant's transcendental philosophy. The pure contemplative insight of the *Oupnek'hat* through which beginningless desire finds an end closely corresponds to the "better consciousness" of Schopenhauer's early philosophy that had long defined the direction of Schopenhauer's thought. The >*volle*< (willing) and >*nolle*< (not-willing) of the *Oupnek'hat* inspired Schopenhauer's conception of the ultimate basis and aim of his metaphysics of will. Moreover, Schopenhauer learned in the work of Prince Dara about the "Indian method" that sets out from the subject and in which the body and introspection are central, and about the methodology of rising from "empirical" to "better" consciousness. Schopenhauer's remark in the margins of the second Upanishad (OUP1:129), where this methodology is explained, describes this way to salvation succinctly: "The individual purifies itself to [become] the pure subject of knowing."[413]

> :s (*coram illis*), hic *djiw âtma*
> *ia*] erat : post ab illo quòd τὸν
> *iw âtma* ipse ille *âtma* magnus
> aliquis tempore quo dixit : ego
> nedium) τᾶ procùl facere imagi-
> (*abire*) multitudinem (*entium*),
> ia [τᾶ *Brahm*], et forma omnis

Oupnek'hat vol. 1, p. 129 with Schopenhauer's emphasis and remark in margin

In the *Oupnek'hat* this purification is often associated with *maschgouli*, that is, with contemplation or meditation—a topic that had interested Schopenhauer from the earliest days of his philosophical studies (1810) to such an extent that he accused Kant of "not having known contemplation."[414] He found no such deficiency in the *Oupnek'hat*. On the contrary: this work advocates a way to deliverance that very much resembles Schopenhauer's: deliverance from willing through cessation of willing (*nolitio*) and will-less pure knowing. For Schopenhauer, a genius is "more than other people the *pure* subject of knowing" and thus appears "among the philistines like a saint among scoundrels."[415] Plato's doctrine of ideas was closer to the *Oupnek'hat* than Kant's transcendental philosophy because Schopenhauer held that it is the pure, will-less subject that intuits Platonic ideas (#374).

---

[413] "Das Individuum läutert sich zum reinen Subjekt des Erkennens."
[414] »die Kontemplation nicht gekannt« (HN1 #17).
[415] »mehr als andre Menschen das *reine* Subjekt des Erkennens«; »unter den Philistern was der Heilige unter Gaunern« (HN1 #369).

CHAPTER TEN

Schopenhauer's philosophy of nature and its basis—that man can get to know the nature of everything through insight (#621)—was also born in the wake of his *Oupnek'hat* study. Did Dara's work not ceaselessly preach that the innermost nature of man is nothing other than the nature of everything: thou art that (*tat tvam asi*)? This is of course one of the *Oupnek'hat's* core doctrines, and it fascinated Schopenhauer to such an extent that he not only heavily marked up its every occurrence in his copy but also kept quoting this *Mahāvākya* (great utterance) with awe throughout his career.[416] This fascination is reflected in a note about the "deciphering of the true *signature of all things*."[417]

> [In this deciphering of the true nature of things] the philosopher recognizes the manifold different degrees and modes of the manifestation of the will which in all beings is only one and the same, wills everywhere the same thing, and objectifies itself as life in so many different forms that are all adaptations to different outer conditions and resemble multiple variations on a theme. They all reveal the world as representation in all its [Platonic] ideas: the philosopher knows their innermost essence through the *Sopatkit tatoumis* that he repeats with each single one.[418]

---

[416] The argument by Kapani (1996, 2011:80 ff.) that Schopenhauer's understanding of *tat tvam asi* as "Dies bist du" is substantially different from Deussen's "Das bist du" seems to constitute hairsplitting to this native speaker. With respect to *tat tvam asi*, Kapani (2011:80) accuses Schopenhauer of "errors of interpretation caused by the well-known phenomenon of projection: one finds what one is looking for, one has texts say what one expects of them." Interestingly, Kapani cites the *Oupnek'hat* not once and does not even list it in the bibliography. Since her intention is mainly comparative (the study of similarities and differences between Schopenhauer and Indian thought) this is no cause for reproach; yet as soon as the philosopher's understanding, misunderstanding, or projection is in question one would expect the use of Schopenhauer's own sources—in this case mainly the *Oupnek'hat*—rather than modern studies and recent Upanishad translations from Sanskrit.

[417] »Entziffern der wahren *signatura rerum*« (#627). *Signatura rerum* (the signature or nature of all things) is an allusion to Jacob Böhme's book of this title.

[418] »[In diesem Entziffern] erkennt der Philosoph die mannigfaltigen Grade

The "Sopatkit tatoumis" refers to the ceaselessly repeated *Mahāvākya* (great utterance) of the *Oupnek'hat*: "O Sopatkit! *tatoumes* [tat twam asi]; that means, you are that Atma."[419] This is the core doctrine of the first Upanishad read by Schopenhauer in the sprint of 1814. After the purchase of his own copy he underlined every single instance of this phrase, highlighted it additionally with lines in the margins, and later added in some places also comments about other translations that he compared with the *Oupnek'hat* (OUP1:60–5).

Oupnek'hat vol. 1, p. 60 with Schopenhauer's remarks and lines

Schopenhauer's changing pronouncements about the connection of his philosophy with Kant show the necessity of great care when using later comments of Schopenhauer to explain earlier events. In the case of the *Oupnek'hat* we fortunately have not only Schopenhauer's notebooks at our disposal but also the two *Oupnek'hat* volumes acquired in

---

und Weisen der Manifestation des Willens, der in allen Wesen nur Einer und derselbe ist, überall dasselbe will, was eben als Leben sich objektivirt in so verschiedenen Gestalten, die alle Akkomodationen zu verschiedenen Bedingungen von Außen sind und vielen Variationen eines Themas gleichen. Sie alle offenbaren die Welt als Vorstellung in allen ihren Ideen: ihr innerstes Wesen erkennt der Philosoph durch das *Sopatkit tatoumis*, das er bei jeder wiederholt« (#627).

[419] »O Sopatkit! *tatoumes* [tat twam asi]; das heißt, du bist jenes Atma.«

the summer of 1814. In spite of dating issues that future scientific analysis might resolve, the philosopher's markup and remarks in the margins are a good indicator of his focus of interest. From the beginning of his study of the *Oupnek'hat* he was fascinated by its fundamental doctrine that multiplicity is only apparent and masks essential oneness. Decades later he put this as follows:

> This teaching that multiplicity is only apparent and that in all individuals of the world—innumerable as they may be, and presenting themselves simultaneously and successively—one and the same truly existing being manifests that is present and identical in all: this doctrine, I say, existed long before *Kant*; indeed one might want to say that it existed from remotest antiquity. For it is, first of all, the principal and fundamental doctrine of the world's oldest book, the sacred *Vedas*, whose dogmatic part, or rather esoteric teaching, we possess in the Upanishads. There we find this great doctrine on almost every page; it is unflaggingly repeated in countless formulations and expounded by means of many parables and similes.[420]

Implications of this doctrine of all-oneness also left their imprint on Schopenhauer's philosophy of nature that he further worked out in the spring of 1815.

> *Plants* and crystals are nothing but the phenomenon, the *objectity*, of the same *will* which also presses and urges in me and which manifests in the highest degree in my body and in my actions that are mediated by knowledge and motives. It is magical; that is to

---

[420] »Diese Lehre, daß alle Vielheit nur scheinbar sei, daß in allen Individuen dieser Welt, in so unendlicher Zahl sie auch, nach und neben einander, sich darstellen, doch nur Eines und dasselbe, in ihnen allen gegenwärtige und identische, wahrhaft seiende Wesen sich manifestire, diese Lehre ist freilich lange vor *Kant*, ja man möchte sagen von jeher dagewesen. Denn zuvörderst ist sie die Haupt- und Grundlehre des ältesten Buches der Welt, der heiligen Veden, deren dogmatischer Theil, oder vielmehr esoterische Lehre, uns in den Upanischaden vorliegt. Daselbst finden wir fast auf jeder Seite jene große Lehre: sie wird unermüdlich, in zahllosen Wendungen wiederholt und durch mannigfaltige Bilder und Gleichnisse erläutert.« (SW4, §22:268; Z6:308)

say, the number of its phenomenal manifestations makes no difference to it. What manifests of it in plant and crystal is so low a degree that it cannot be compared even remotely to the state in which sleep has extinguished my cognition and where only a dull obscure urge is left that keeps the heart, blood vessels and lungs in motion and maintains the vegetative activity of the body. This [obscure urge] and the growth of plants, the formation of crystals, and the life of all animals and human beings are manifestations of the One Will. The diversity of forms in space and their change and sequence in time: all of this is only phenomenon, that is to say it exists only for *knowledge*; it is in such forms that the will is *known*; but the will itself is not affected by that multiplicity."[421]

In the spring of 1815 Schopenhauer continued his search for corresponding ideas in the history of philosophy, and he continued to find correspondences to the central pair of concepts that ended up in the title of his major work: will and representation. He persisted for example in his study of Spinoza and initially attempted to identify Spinoza's *extensio* with will and Spinoza's *cogitatio* with representation (#428); but not long afterwards he reconsidered and wrote: "Also *natura naturans* is the *will*, and *natura naturata* the *representation*."[422] Kant's thought

---

[421] »Die *Pflanzen*, die *Krystalle*, sind nichts als Erscheinung, *Objektität* desselben *Willens* der auch in mir drängt und treibt und der im höchsten Grad in meinem Leib und in meinem durch Erkenntniß und Motive vermittelten Handeln sich offenbart. Er ist magisch, d.h. die Zahl seiner Erscheinungen ist für ihn ohne Bedeutung. Das was von ihm in Pflanze und Krystall sich offenbart ist ein so niedriger Grad, daß er noch bei weitem nicht dem Zustand zu vergleichen ist, wo der Schlaf mein Erkennen verlöscht hat und nur ein dumpfes dunkles Treiben übrig bleibt das Herz, Adern und Lunge in Bewegung hält und den Leib vegetiren läßt. Diese und das Wachsen der Pflanze, das Anschießen der Krystalle und das Leben aller Thiere und Menschen ist Erscheinung Eines Willens: die Verschiedenheit der Gestalten im Raum ihr Wechsel und Folge in der Zeit, dies alles ist nur Erscheinung, d.h. es ist nur für die *Erkenntniß*; in diesen Formen wird der Wille *erkannt*: den Willen selbst trifft jene Mannigfaltigkeit nicht« (HN1 #387).

[422] »Auch ist die *natura naturans* der Wille, und die N[*atura naturata*] die Vorstellung« (#491).

was of course also at issue. In a note stemming from the spring of 1816, Schopenhauer's identification of the thing-in-itself with the will became dogma:

> What are things in addition to being our representation? What are they independently of this [representation], what are they *in themselves*?—Precisely that which we know in ourselves as *will*. This is the kernel of all things, this is 'what holds together the world at its innermost core.'[423]

In a comment about this Schopenhauer once more referred to Spinoza: "Will is the *natura naturans*, representation the *natura naturata*."[424]

In 1815 he adopted from the scholastic philosophers the term "principium individuationis" (principle of individuation) to refer to the transition from oneness to multiplicity and linked this principle in two succinct phrases not only to his metaphysics of will but also to Kant's categories and Plato's ideas:

> The *principium individuationis*, a principal point of dispute of the Scholastics, is *space* and *time*. Through these the [Platonic] idea, i.e. the objectity of the will, is broken down into individual things.[425]

In tune with Anquetil's explanation of Maya, Schopenhauer states that due to this *principium individuationis* "what is one appears as separate and different."[426] Schopenhauer immediately linked this to his initial question about the origin of suffering and called the *principium individuationis* "the genuine theodicy" which explains "why in this world

---

[423] »Was die Dinge sind außerdem daß sie unsre Vorstellung sind? was sie unabhängig von dieser, was sie *an sich* sind? — Eben das was wir in uns als *Wille* erkennen. Das ist der Kern aller Dinge, dies ist es ›was die Welt im Innersten zusammenhält‹.« (#521) Schopenhauer here cites Goethe's *Faust*, Part I.

[424] »Der Wille ist die *natura naturans*, die Vorstellung ist *natura naturata*« (#521).

[425] »Das *principium individuationis*, ein Hauptstreitpunkt der Scholastiker, ist *Raum* und *Zeit*. Durch diese zerfällt die Idee d.h. die Objektität des Willens, in Einzeldinge.« (#433)

[426] »erscheint als getrennt und verschieden was Eins ist« (#503).

one person lives in joy and sensual pleasure while on his porch another person dies in agony of destitution and cold."[427] By contrast there exist no such differences for the pure subject of knowledge:

> As the pure *subject of knowing* we are all *one*; it is the *one* world-eye that looks out of the bodies of all animals, only here more and there less clouded by the will, with significant gradations; but apart from this with no other difference.[428]

This line of thought was elaborated in Schopenhauer's ethics of compassion that was also much influenced by his *Oupnek'hat* study. This influence is apparent, among other things, in the multitude of quotations and the philosopher's frequent use of the 'great word' of the Upanishads (*tat twam asi*, "this you are"). At the opposite pole we still find the impulse of self-preservation that necessarily implies self-centeredness: selfishness and the war of all against all (#538). Based on this, Schopenhauer's philosophy of law and politics turned around the question how and to what degree such selfishness needs to be restrained for the common good.

From November of 1815 Schopenhauer also sought to cover the Asian front and studied the renowned *Asiatick Researches* volume by volume. Around this time he first met K.F.C. Krause, another passionate student of the *Oupnek'hat* whose connection with Schopenhauer was not only due to the vicinity of their living quarters but also their common interest in Indian thought. From late 1815, Krause was also often found studying near the Dresden library's India-related book case, and it is likely that these two men discussed various topics. At that point in time Schopenhauer's metaphysics of will was already fully formed. However, it is possible that Schopenhauer, who from September 1815

---

[427] »*die ächte Theodicäe*«; »warum in dieser Welt hier einer in Freuden und Wollüsten lebt und vor seiner Thüre ein Andrer vor Mangel und Kälte quaalvoll stirbt« (#503).

[428] »Als reines *Subjekt des Erkennens* sind wir alle *Eines*: es ist das *eine* Weltauge, was aus allen thierischen Leibern blickt, nur hier mehr dort weniger getrübt durch den Willen, mit großen Abstufungen; außer diesem aber mit keinem andern Unterschiede« (#520).

CHAPTER TEN

consulted Asia-related materials of the library, followed Krause's advice in focusing on the *Asiatick Researches* that he had first heard mentioned by Professor Heeren, his ethnology professor at Göttingen University. Be this as it may, between November of 1815 and May of 1816 Schopenhauer worked his way through the first ten volumes of the *Asiatick Researches* and found them to be so rich in information about Asian religions and philosophies that he filled an entire notebook with observations and excerpts.[429] Already in the first volume he found important explanations by an Englishman about the term Maya and copied part of these in his notebook:

> *Máyá*: the word is explained by some Hindoo Scholars 'the first Inclination of the Godhead to diversify himself by creating worlds.' She is feigned to be the mother of universal nature & of all the inferior Gods; as a Cashmirian informed me, when I asked him, why *Cama* or *Love* was represented as her son: but the word *Maya* or *delusion* has a more subtle & recondite sense in the *Vedanta* philosophy, where it signifies the system of *perceptions*.[430]

Schopenhauer also took notes about the Vedas (pp. 24–6) and Upanishads (pp. 15–6, 24–32), for example to the effect that the Upanishads are regarded as a manual of the Vedas (p. 15) and are older than 3000 years (p. 16).[431] He also showed interest in Indian philosophical systems such as Vedanta (pp. 15–18), philosophers such as Shankara (pp.16–18) and Buddha (pp. 18, 20–1), and of course also concepts such as "Brahm." The fifth volume contained a prayer that Schopenhauer highlighted and excerpted with its commentary. This commentary to the chief prayer *Gayatry* seemed to confirm Schopenhauer's view:

---

[429] See the transcription and translation of all of Schopenhauer's manuscript notes related to the *Asiatick Researches* in App 1998b. Emphases by Schopenhauer.

[430] App 1998b:15. Schopenhauer wrote this excerpt in English. Emphases by Schopenhauer.

[431] Most voluminous are Schopenhauer's notes about Colebrooke's long article in *Asiatick Researches* vol. 8 (App 1998b:24–32).

Veil of Maya and Wisdom of the Veda

> We meditate on the adorable light of the resplendent generator which governs our intellects; which is water, lustre, savour, immortal faculty of thought, Brahme, earth, sky, & heaven.
>
> Commentary to it, or reflections with which the text should be inaudibly recited:
>
> On that effulgent power, which is *Brahme himself,* & is called the light of the radiant sun, do I meditate; governed by the mysterious light which resides *within me,* for the purpose of thought; that very light is the earth, the subtle ether & all which exists within the created sphere; it is the threefold world containing all which is fixed or moveable; *it exists internally in my heart, externally in the orb of the Sun, being one & the same with that effulgent power. I myself am an irradiated manifestation of the supreme Brahme.*[432]

In volume 6 of the *Asiatick Researches* he found much interesting information about Asian religions and learned, among other things, about the Nirvana (Pali: *Nibbana,* earlier *Nieban*) of the Buddhists. He made the following excerpt in his notebook:

> When a person is no longer subject to any of the following miseries, namely, *to weight, old age, disease, & death,* then he is said to have obtained *Nieban.* No thing, no place, can give us an adequate idea of *Nieban*: we can only say, that to be free from the 4 above mentioned miseries, & to obtain salvation, is *Nieban.* In the same manner, as when any person labouring under a severe disease, *recovers* by the assistance of medicine, we say he has obtained health: but if any person whishes to know the manner, or cause of his thus obtaining health, it can only be answer'd, that to be restored to health signifies no more, than to be recover'd from disease. In the same manner only can we speak of Nieban: & after this manner Godama taught.[433]

---

[432] App 1998b:19. Schopenhauer wrote this excerpt in English. Emphases by Schopenhauer.

[433] App 1998b:21. Schopenhauer wrote this excerpt in English. Emphases by Schopenhauer.

CHAPTER TEN

This is one of the passages that so impressed Schopenhauer that he decided to cite in *The World as Will and Representation*. Now he had found an additional label for the salvation pole of his compass: Nieban or Nirvana.[434] But of most interest in the present context are Schopenhauer's notes about Colebrooke's long essay on the Vedas in volume 8 of the *Asiatick Researches*. The philosopher's notes in German accompanying his English excerpts from Colebrooke show that in the spring of 1816 he now saw his own system, developed since 1814, confirmed by Indian doctrines: "Dependency of the object from the subject,"[435] "the macrocosm demands the microcosm,"[436] "dependency of the subject from the object,"[437] "Only for the subject of knowing the world exists,"[438] "the best cannot be taught,"[439] "the idea appears manifoldly in the individuals,"[440] "mythical exposition of my doctrine that the tormentor and the tormented are different in manifestation through the principium individuationis only, but in themselves One."[441]

A note about Colebrooke's article is especially worthy of note. Schopenhauer summarized the Englishman's argument as follows:

> Out of the 2d Taittiryaca Upanishad. YajurVeda.
>
> That, whence all beings are produced: that, by which they live, when born: that, towards which they tend; & that, into which they pass; do thou seek, for that is Brahme.[442]

---

[434] For an overview of the development of Schopenhauer's view of Nirvana see App 2010b.

[435] »Abhängigkeit des Objekts vom Subjekt« (App 1998b:27).

[436] »Der Makrokosmos fordert den Mikrokosmos« (p. 28).

[437] »Abhängigkeit des Subjekts vom Objekt« (p. 28).

[438] »Nur für das Subjekt des Erkennens ist die Welt« (p. 29).

[439] »Das Beste lässt sich nicht lehren« (p. 32).

[440] »Die Idee erscheint vielfach in den Individuen« (p. 32).

[441] »Mythische Darstellung meiner Lehre, daß der Peiniger u. der Gepeinigte nur in der Erscheinung, durch das princ. individuationis, verschieden sind, an sich aber Eins« (p. 33).

[442] App 1998b:31. Emphases by Schopenhauer.

Veil of Maya and Wisdom of the Veda

In the margin Schopenhauer commented: "The will-to-live is the source and essence of things."[443] This confirms that in 1816 he regarded terms such as "Brahm" and "Parabrahma" as "will" or "will-to-live," and his statement in 1833 about the choice of the word "will" rings true:

> I have named the *thing-in-itself*, the inner essence of the world, after that of it which we are *most intimately familiar* with: *will*. Admittedly this is a term chosen subjectively, that is with regard to the *subject of knowing*; but this regard is essential since we are communicating *knowledge*. Therefore it is infinitely better than having named it *Brahm, Brahma*, world soul, or something of the kind.[444]

In many passages of the *Oupnek'hat* everything that exists (including man) is called a manifestation of Brahm; and if one consistently replaces this word by "will" it becomes even clearer why Schopenhauer named this work as a main influence on the genesis of his system.

Through his diligent study of the *Asiatick Researches* Schopenhauer gained between late 1815 and mid-1816 a first overview about ancient Indian literature and several Asian religions. Now he felt able to write with a measure of confidence about themes such as Buddhism, transmigration, and their connection with his metaphysics of will. But he also noted that William Jones, Colebrooke, and other famous British pioneers of Indian studies used the term Maya in a sense that substantially differed from what he had gathered from Anquetil. Though they explained it as "the first Inclination of the Godhead to diversify himself by creating worlds,"[445] there was no mention of an "eternal will." Later on, as he got hold of new Upanishad translations from Sanskrit, he kept

---

[443] »Der Wille zum Leben ist die Quelle und das Wesen der Dinge« (p. 31).

[444] »Ich habe das *Ding an sich*, das innre Wesen der Welt, benannt nach dem aus ihr, was uns am *genausten bekannt* ist: *Wille*. Freilich ist dies ein subjektiv, nämlich aus Rücksicht auf das *Subjekt des Erkennens* gewählter Ausdruck: aber diese Rücksicht ist, da wir *Erkenntniß* mittheilen, wesentlich. Also ist es unendlich besser, als hätt' ich es genannt etwa *Brahm*, oder *Brahma*, oder Weltseele oder was sonst« (HN4a:143, No. 148).

[445] App 1998b:15.

searching without success for this eternal will. His disappointment found expression in numerous remarks that he wrote in the margins of his *Oupnek'hat* copy next to long excerpts from such more recent translations. These remarks show that in his opinion Dara and Anquetil had a far better understanding of Upanishadic doctrine, that the *Oupnek'hat* was based on better Sanskrit sources, that translators such as Rammohun Roy were Indian apostates infected by Jewish monotheism, and so on. But in 1816 Schopenhauer was not yet in a position to compare since Colebrooke furnished only a very limited number of excerpts from the Upanishads.

Still, it appears that these studies caused a shift in his conception of Maya. Prior to his study of the *Asiatick Researches* he had regarded Maya as "the inner driving force" of the universe that corresponded to Giordano Bruno's "God" (#234), and in the fall of 1815 he still saw Maya as *eros* or creative principle of the universe:

> The world is the objectity of the will (to live). The will's most powerful phenomenon is the *sexual drive*, which is the ερως [eros] of the ancients. Therefore the poets and philosophers of antiquity, Hesiod, and even Parmenides very meaningfully said that ερως is first, the principle of the world, that which creates; the *Maya* of the Indians means the same thing.[446]

After reading in the above-mentioned explanation of Maya in the *Asiatick Researches*, and after having found similar comments in Anquetil's notes and explanatory essays of the *Oupnek'hat*, Schopenhauer scribbled a correction in the margin next to the note that was just quoted: "P.S. Not exactly: *Maya* is rather the objectity of the will, is Kant's phenomenon, knowledge according to the principle of sufficient

---

[446] »Die Welt ist die Objektität des Willens (zum Leben). Des Willens stärkste Erscheinung ist der *Geschlechtstrieb*: dieser ist der ερως der Alten: die alten Dichter und Philosophen, Hesiod und selbst Parmenides, sagten daher sehr bedeutungsvoll, der ερως sei das Erste, das Princip der Welt, das Schaffende: dasselbe bedeutet die *Maja* der Indier« (#461).

Veil of Maya and Wisdom of the Veda

reason."[447] Through this correction Maya, "the principle of the world, that which creates" was transformed into the phenomenal manifestation of the creative principle. This shift from his earlier *will*-centered interpretation of Maya to a *representation*-based one is comparable to the metamorphoses of the "Platonic idea" and the Kantian "thing-in-itself" that were noted above.[448] But Schopenhauer's major work, *The World as Will and Representation*, was not yet written and what we today read in his Manuscript Remains are merely working notes. However, precisely for this reason they are also a fascinating source for the study of the genesis of his philosophical system.

The revised interpretation of Maya was prominently introduced in note #564 where it appeared linked to Plato and Kant:

> The "Maya" of the Vedas, Plato's "aei gignomenon men, on de oudepote" [what eternally becomes but never is], Kant's "phenomenon" are one and the same thing: this world in which we are living, we ourselves in so far as we belong to it. This has not yet been recognized.[449]

This new conception of Maya underlies a note that Schopenhauer (probably after the redaction of the quoted note #564, i.e. around mid-1816) added in the margin of note #359:

> One must therefore distinguish between 1) the will-to-live itself; 2) the perfect objectity of it which are the ideas; 3) the manifestation of these ideas in the form whose expression is the principle

---

[447] »NB nicht ganz: die *Maja* ist vielmehr die Objektität des Willens, ist Kants *Erscheinung*, die Erkenntniß nach dem Satz vom Grund« (#461).

[448] Berger (2000, 2004) did not notice this evolution and argued that Schopenhauer's interpretation of Maya was from the outset a vedantic-illusionistic one; hence Berger's overall argument about a "falsification theory" as the principal Upanishadic influence on Schopenhauer.

[449] »Die ›*Maja*‹ der Vedas, das ›aei gignomenon men, on de oudepote‹ [das ewig Werdende, aber nie Seiende] des Platon, die ›Erscheinung‹ des Kant sind Eins und dasselbe, sind diese Welt in der wir leben, sind wir selbst, sofern wir ihr angehören. Das hat man noch nicht erkannt« (#564).

of sufficient reason, i.e., the real world, Kant's phenomenon, the Maya of the Indians.[450]

In this manner the Indian Maya became for Schopenhauer the *Principium individuationis* whose overcoming signifies salvation.

> For man who practises works of love the veil of Maya has dropped from the eyes, and the illusion of the *principium individuationis* has left him. He recognizes himself in every being, even in the sufferer [...] To be cured of this delusion and phantasmagoria of Maya and to practise works of love are one and the same thing. Whoever has arrived at this makes all the suffering he sees his own [...] All of this reduces in him the will-to-live, until it is completely extinguished and salvation is achieved.[451]

The double nature of Dara's Maya, which married the desire of creation (*ishq*) and manifestation of the All-One as world with the shrouding of the One in the Many, received an equally striking form in the thought of atheistic Schopenhauer: the will's conflict with itself. Schopenhauer explained this as follows: blinded by the veil of Maya— the *principium individuationis*—the author of someone else's suffering

---

[450] »Man hat also zu unterscheiden 1) den Willen zum Leben selbst. 2) Die vollkommne Objektität desselben welche die Ideen sind. 3) Die Erscheinung dieser Ideen in der Form deren Ausdruck der Satz vom Grund ist, d.i. die wirkliche Welt, Kants Erscheinung, der Indier *Maja*.« (#359, note in margin). This notion corresponds to note #577 (see below) and was in all likelihood not added before mid-1816. John Atwell thought that it stems from 1814 and marks the completion of Schopenhauer's system: "Therewith we have the philosophical system that Schopenhauer was never substantially to alter" (Atwell 1995:78). Moreover, note #321 which according to Atwell has the same content (p. 201), does not mention Maya and forms part of an earlier evolutionary stage of Schopenhauer's system.

[451] »Der die Werke der Liebe übt, dem ist der Schleier der Maja von den Augen gefallen, und die Täuschung des *principii individuationis* hat ihn verlassen. Er erkennt sich in jedem Wesen, und auch in dem Leidenden [...] von diesem Wahn und Blendwerk der Maja geheilt seyn und Werke der Liebe üben, ist Eins: wer dahin gelangt ist, macht jedes Leiden das er sieht zu seinem eigenen [...] dies Alles dämpft den Willen zum Leben in ihm, bis dieser ganz verlischt und die Erlösung für ihn da ist.« (#626)

Veil of Maya and Wisdom of the Veda

appears to be different from the sufferer; but *in themselves* they both are nothing but "the One will-to-live." This is why fundamentally "the sufferer and the one who causes suffering are one.[452] But how can this One, the will, both benefit and harm itself? Through the bedazzlement of Maya!

> Thus dazzled and deluded by Maya, the will-to-live falls into conflict with itself, since, by seeking enhanced well-being in one of its manifestations, it causes great suffering in others precisely through this seeking—yet it is also will itself that must endure it.[453]

In note #577 stemming from mid-1816, Maya appears in the abovementioned two-column table as the opposite of the "wisdom of the Vedas." Schopenhauer introduces this table with the explanation that "the opposition of the universal and the particular" is evident everywhere, and that the "universal" indicates the right path whereas the "particular" represents the wrong one.[454] This table presents, as it were, the map and compass for Schopenhauer's major work where the terms in the two columns stand for the two poles. In its metaphysics section we find the three items—"the Upanishads, Plato, and Kant"— that Schopenhauer soon afterwards (note #623) identified as the three main influences on the genesis of his system. One interesting aspect of this table is that its metaphysics row does not feature Schopenhauer's most important term: the will. But based on the analysis of his notes and handwritten remarks in his *Oupnek'hat* it should by now be clear what influence the "wisdom of the Vedas" had on him: it was the trigger for his conception of will including its affirmation and negation that in this table also represent the "right" and "wrong" paths in the fields of aesthetics and ethics. Here is the table of Schopenhauer's note #577:

---

[452] »der Eine Wille zum Leben«; »der Leidende und der das Leid verhängt, [sind] nur Einer« (#600).

[453] »Daß also, durch die Blendung der *Maja*, der Wille zum Leben mit sich selbst in Widerstreit geräth, indem er in der einen seiner Erscheinungen gesteigertes Wohlseyn suchend eben dadurch in der andern großes Leiden hervorbringt, welches doch auch nur er selbst dulden muß« (#600).

[454] »Weisheit der Vedas«; »der Gegensatz zwischen dem Allgemeinen und dem Einzelnen« (#577).

	ALLGEMEINES	EINZELNES
METAPHYSIK	Platonische Idee	Das Werdende, nie Seiende.
	Kants Ding an sich	Erscheinung.
	Weisheit der Vedas	Maja.
AESTHETIK	Reines Subjekt des Erkennens, mit Ruhe und Seeligkeit	Dem Willen fröhnendes Erkennen mit Angst und Sorge.
	Heiterkeit der Kunst	Erbärmlichkeit der Wirklichkeit.
	Platonische Idee als Objekt der Kunst	Einzelnes Ding als Objekt des Willens
MORAL	Aus Erkenntniß des Wesens der Welt entsprungene Abwendung des Willens vom Leben zeigt sich als Resignation, Tugend, Weltüberwindung, Asketik, wahre Gelassenheit, Willenslosigkeit	Heftiger Wille zum Leben überhaupt, aber Krieg mit der einzelnen Erscheinung, Leidenschaft, Geiz, Zorn, Neid, stets wachsender Durst, Laster, Bosheit, Selbstmord, nach schwerem Kampf; als völlige Erscheinung der Entzweiung des Willens zum Leben mit sich selbst.
	Liebe	Egoismus.
	Tödtung des Willens	Tödtung des Leibes.
	Theorie	Empirie.

Schopenhauer's system table (note #577; German original)

Veil of Maya and Wisdom of the Veda

	Universal	**Particular**
Meta-physik	Platonic Idea	That which becomes, never is.
	Kant's thing-in-itself	Phenomenon.
	Wisdom of the Vedas	Maya.
Aesthe-tik	Pure subject of knowing, with tranquility and bliss	Knowledge slaving for the will, with anxiety and anguish.
	Exhilaration of art	Wretchedness of reality.
	Platonic Idea as the object of art	Particular thing as the object of the will
Moral	The turning away of the will from life due to the realization of the world's true nature, manifesting as resignation, virtue, overcoming of the world, asceticism, true detached serenity, will-lessness	Intense will-to-live in general, but war with its particular manifestation, passion, avarice, anger, envy, constantly increasing thirst, vice, malice, suicide after a severe struggle; as a complete manifestation of the diremption of the will-to-live with itself.
	Love	Egotism.
	Mortification of the will	Mortification of the body.
	Theory	Empiricism.

Schopenhauer's system table (note #577; English translation)

Whereas Kant's philosophy prepared the ground for Schopenhauer's theory of knowledge in the first book of *The World as Will and Representation*, Plato's allegory of the cave and doctrine of ideas fecundated (in tandem with Kant and romantic notions of art and genius) his theory of aesthetics in the third book. But the work of Prince Dara that treated of beginningless desire, its manifestation as world, and its overcoming through pure insight was the muse not only of Schopenhauer's theory of will as the nature of the world in the second book but also of its temporary abolition in the third and the permanent abolition in the fourth book (for which it appropriately also furnished to motto). Thus Schopenhauer's positioning of the *Oupnek'hat* as the first of three major influences on the genesis of his philosophy, followed by Plato and Kant, appears justified. Granted that his study of Schelling, Fichte, Spinoza, Giordano Bruno and various European mystics also played important roles, Schopenhauer's "confession" of late 1816 identifies only three major influences:

> By the way, I confess that I do not believe my doctrine could ever have formed before the Upanishads, Plato and Kant cast their rays simultaneously into a man's mind. Admittedly (as Diderot says) many pillars were standing there and the sun illuminated all of them—yet only Memnon's pillar chimed.[455]

---

[455] Ich gestehe übrigens, daß ich nicht glaube, daß meine Lehre je hätte entstehn können ehe die Upanischaden, Plato und Kant ihre Strahlen zugleich in eines Menschen Geist werfen konnten. Aber freilich standen (wie Diderot sagt) viele Säulen da und die Sonne schien auf alle: doch nur Memnons Säule klang. (#623)

11. Affirmation and Abolition of Will

In spite of slight oscillations, a compass always maintains the same fundamental bearing. The same can be said of Schopenhauer's longing for salvation. Already when he began studying philosophy in early 1811 he was, according to Wieland's niece, "devoted with heart and mind to a philosophy ... that is exceedingly austere; any and all inclinations, desires, and passions must be suppressed and subdued" (Gespräche 23). Early descriptions of "better consciousness" characterize the target direction as virtue, asceticism, breaking away from the world (#79), liberation from temporal consciousness (#86), saintliness, love, humaneness (#87), freedom, purity (#120), voluntary abandonment of life (#157), etc. Not only Schopenhauer's early philosophy focuses on the theme of salvation (de Cian 2002) but also his metaphysics of will: it presents Schopenhauer's answer to his initial questions about the origin of suffering and the possibility of its eradication. As with a compass, the general direction was set from the beginning: "Toward light, to *virtue*, to the holy spirit—we all must go: that is the unison, the eternal keynote of creation." (#158)

At the beginning of 1814 it was already clear to Schopenhauer that there are basically two paths toward this light. In rare cases there arises, without any external stimulus, the spontaneous urge to voluntarily let go of the will-to-live, to repudiate the world, and to destroy illusion (Täuschung). The second path consists in the birth of better knowledge out of pain and the crushing feeling of sin and life's vanity (#158). We noted that such early views were in the course of 1814 gradually deepened and systematized, and that Prince Dara's ideal of the death of ego (*fanā*) and of the end of desire through realization (*cognitio*) played a decisive role in this process. The table of note #577 (here above, pp. 245–245) summarizes the result. At its heart is the teaching of salvation that in the morality section of the table is characterized as follows: "The turning away of the will from life due to the realization of the world's true nature, manifesting as resignation, virtue, overcoming of the world, asceticism, true detached serenity, will-lessness."[456]

The table of note #577 also contains, somehow out of category, old acquaintances such as love and egotism. But it was another pair of opposing concepts that gave occasion to Schopenhauer's construction of this table: the "killing of the will" in the column of the "correct path," and the "killing of the body" belonging to the "incorrect path." Schopenhauer's related note begins as follows:

> *Suicide* is the master-stroke of *Maya*; we abolish the apparition [Erscheinung] and do not see that the thing-in-itself remains unchanged—just as the rainbow stands firm, however rapidly the raindrops fall, each of which becomes its support for a moment. Only the abolition of the will-to-live in general can save us. The diremption with any one of its apparitions leaves the will itself un-

---

[456] »Aus der Erkentniß des Wesens der Welt entsprungene Abwendung des Willens vom Leben zeigt sich als Resignation, Tugend, Weltüberwindung, Asketik, wahre Gelassenheit, Willenslosigkeit« (#577).

moved and unshaken; and so the abolition of that particular appearance leaves the will's manifestation in general unchanged.[457]

Schopenhauer's "asceticism" and his "letting go of the will-to-live" are thus not at all an invitation to suicide. Rather they point to another kind of death: the death of ego and thus of egotism with which Schopenhauer became familiar, if not earlier, through the works of Zacharias Werner and his talks with him in 1808. After that encounter he had deepened his understanding through the reading of mystics which—just as was the case with Görres, Kanne, and Adolph Wagner—greatly facilitated his comprehension of Prince Dara's *Oupnek'hat*. Already at the beginning of 1814 Schopenhauer wrote: "Only he is truly happy who *within life, does not want life.*"[458] After his encounter with the *Oupnek'hat*'s true realization through which beginningless desire finds an end, he described man's most blissful state as the one in which "having disengaged from willing, one has become the *pure subject of knowing.*"[459] Unlike Hegel who portrayed and dismissed this "oriental" state as stupid apathy and torpor (App 2008a:36), Schopenhauer realized that what is involved here is nothing other than the "turning" of the will: "The saint is thus someone who ceases to be an apparition of the will-to-live; in him the will has turned."[460]

---

[457] »Der *Selbstmord* ist das Meisterstück der *Maja*: Wir heben die Erscheinung auf und sehn nicht daß das Ding an sich unverändert dasteht: wie der Regenbogen feststeht so schnell auch Tropfen auf Tropfen fällt und sein Träger wird auf einen Augenblick. Nur die Aufhebung des Willens zum Leben im Allgemeinen kann uns erlösen: die Entzweiung mit irgend einer seiner Erscheinungen läßt ihn selbst unerschüttert stehn, und so läßt das Aufheben jener Erscheinung das Erscheinen des Willens im Allgemeinen unverändert.« (#577)

[458] »Der allein ist wahrhaft glücklich, der, *im Leben, nicht das Leben* will« (#184).

[459] »wo er vom Wollen losgerissen, *reines Subjekt des Erkennens* geworden ist« (#257).

[460] »Der Heilige nämlich ist ein Mensch der da aufhört eine Erscheinung des Willens zum Leben zu seyn, in ihm hat der Wille sich gewendet.« (#363)

CHAPTER ELEVEN

When Schopenhauer wrote of "negation of life" and of "realization" (Erkenntnis) he did not mean physical death or knowledge in the usual sense but rather the overcoming of willing through pure *cognitio* as described in the *Oupnek'hat*. This corresponded to the victory of "better consciousness" that Schopenhauer had alluded to when in spring of 1813 he wrote of his ardent hope that better consciousness would eventually become his only one:

> The better consciousness in me lifts me into a world where there is no longer personality and causality nor subject-and-object. My hope and faith is that this better (suprasensory and extratemporal) consciousness will become my only one, and for that reason I hope that it is no God.[461]

Three years later he identified this goal as the opposite of the affirmation of will and of egotism:

> Egoism is so much the form in which the will-to-live appears that where egotism has ceased, this will also no longer exists, but rather salvation through the victory of realization.[462]

---

[461] »Das bessre Bewusstseyn in mir erhebt mich in eine Welt wo es weder Persönlichkeit und Kausalität noch Subjekt und Objekt mehr giebt. Meine Hoffnung und mein Glaube ist daß dieses bessre (übersinnliche ausserzeitliche) Bewusstseyn mein einziges werden wird: darum hoffe ich es ist kein Gott.« (#81)

[462] »Der Egoismus ist so sehr die Form der Erscheinung des Willens zum Leben, daß wo der Egoismus aufgehört hat auch dieser Wille nicht mehr ist, sondern Erlösung durch den Sieg der Erkenntniß.« (#638)

Paragraph 70 of Schopenhauer's *World as Will and Representation*, where Schopenhauer writes about the total change of man's fundamental character, deals precisely with this "better," "changed," "will-less" knowledge. This "changed mode of perception" (»veränderte Erkenntnisweise«) is nothing other than the "appeasement of willing" (»Quietiv des Wollens«). Hence Weiner is wrong in asserting that "Erkenntnis" (in the sense of the first book of Schopenhauer's main work) forms the "goal of the entire argument" (»Zielpunkt der ganzen Argumentation«) (Weiner 2000:74). Moreover, one cannot speak of an »Autarkie des Erkennens« (Malter 1982:52) or of its "primary function" (»Primärfunktion« des Erkennens »vor dem Wollen«) (Malter 1991:53).

Affirmation and Abolition of Will

In the table of note #577 egotism is opposed to love. For Schopenhauer, love in *this* sense (which differs from Anquetil's *amor*) is also an expression of the abolition of will and must be identical to compassion:

> In love one gives up the will-to-live, for one see the sufferings of others and alleviates them like one's own, which entails an aggravation of those [sufferings] that are actually ours.[463]

"All genuine *love* is compassion," he wrote, "and all love that is not compassion is selfishness."[464] Such compassion—that is, genuine selfless love—arises from seeing through the veil of Maya.

> This attitude springs from seeing through the *principium individuationis*; one who has done this recognizes the suffering of everyone else and of the entire world as his own. He is therefore extremely helpful and good, and for this very reason he does not need personally to experience suffering, for he appropriates the pain of the whole world.[465]

Schopenhauer saw this teaching reflected not only in the explanations by Christian saints and mystics about pure love, true ease, the death of own-will, the total oblivion of one's own person, etc., but also "in the doctrines of the Hindus as they appear in the Vedas, Puranas, myths, legends, sayings, etc. (Oupnek'hat, the life of Fo [Buddha] in the *Asiatisches Magazin*, Bhagavat Gita, the Laws of Menu, the *Asiatic researches*, Polier's *Mythology* vol. 2, ch. 13" and elsewhere.[466]

---

[463] »In der Liebe giebt man also den Willen zum Leben auf, indem man fremde Leiden sieht und sie gleich den eignen mildert, mit Vermehrung der wirklich eignen.« (#470)

[464] »alle ächte *Liebe* [ist] Mitleid«; »jede Liebe die kein Mitleid ist, ist Selbstsucht« (#584).

[465] »Diese Gesinnung entspringt aus dem Durchschauen des *principii individuationis*: der es hat, erkennt das Leiden aller Andern und der ganzen Welt für sein eignes: daher ist er höchst hülfreich und gut und eben daher auch braucht er nicht selbst das Leiden zu erfahren, da er sich den Schmerz der ganzen Welt zueignet« (#591).

[466] »in den Lehren der Hindus, wie sie gegeben sind in den Vedas, Puranas, Mythen, Legenden, Sprüchen u.s.w. (Oupnek'hat, Leben des Foe [Buddha]

CHAPTER ELEVEN

In the second half of 1816 Schopenhauer sought and found additional support in Asian sources. His subsequent readings in 1817 of mystics such as Fénelon, Swedenborg, Madame Guyon and Pseudo-Tauler reinforced the conviction that Asian and European mystics are confirming his metaphysics of will.[467] In May of 1817 he once again read Madame Guyon's autobiography and reflected upon the difference between philosophers who intellectually understand the abolition of will and mystics who realize it existentially:

> What is meant by *giving up the will-to-live* is taught by me in the dry terms of philosophy. The actualization of this teaching can be learnt from the description of *sanyassis* and saints in India, and from the biographies of holy souls among Christians, of which there are several compilations. Particularly detailed and exhaustive regarding this subject is the autobiography of *Madame de Guyon*. Every noble-minded person who gets acquainted with this truly saintly woman will disregard the deep superstition in which her mind was caught up and see it as an accidental admixture.[468]

Toward the end of 1815 Schopenhauer had already referred to Madame Guyon's three-volume autobiography as an example of the turn-

---

im *Asiatischen Magazin*, Baguatgeeta, Geseze Menu's, *asiatic researches*, Poliers *mythologie* ...« (#666).

[467] Schopenhauer's later explanations about Vedanta and Sufism, along with his handwritten marginalia in extant books, show that he never abandoned this conviction. He did not know that Prince Dara had been a Sufi and could not know the level of his contribution to the translation, but he did not overlook the similarity of their teachings.

[468] »Was es heißt den *Willen zum Leben aufgeben* wird von mir trocken philosophisch gelehrt: die Ausführung dieser Lehre kann man lernen aus der Beschreibung der *Saniassi* und Heiligen in Indien, und aus den Biographien Heiliger Seelen unter den Christen, von denen es mehrere Sammlungen giebt: besonders ausführlich und den Gegenstand erschöpfend ist die Selbstbiographie der *Mad: de Guyon*: jeder Edelgesinnte wird indem er diese wahrhaft heilige Frau kennen lernt, den tiefen Aberglauben in dem ihre Vernunft befangen war, übersehn, als eine zufällige Beimischung.« (#676)

Affirmation and Abolition of Will

ing of the will (#496). However, he quite possibly had learned of her at a much earlier stage, namely, during his conversations with Zacharias Werner as a twenty-year old man (1808). In the writings of Madame Guyon, who had gone through so much suffering, he found the clearest expression of the "killing of will" that in the table of note #577 stands opposed to the "killing of body."[469] Guyon described the abandonment of will as a death *during* life or a "first death." Schopenhauer quoted the phrase in the second volume of her autobiography which states that for those who have died this first death, there is no longer night and no longer fear of death "because death has overcome death, and he who dies the first death must no longer taste the second."[470]

This "first death" is the whole point of Schopenhauers doctrine of salvation, and it corresponds to the death of self (*fanā*) of Prince Dara. Both issue in a permanent state of selflessness for which the Prince used the Sufi term *baqā*. It signifies not only the extinction of will but also that of knowledge bound by subject-and-object (Schopenhauer's "empirical consciousness") and corresponds to the "better consciousness" of the young thinker: the freedom from all "I" and "mine." Not self-tormentation in order to reach a better state in the yonder after death, but rather this total and radical letting go during life is the meaning of the "asceticism" that was so much emphasized by Schopenhauer. Its goal is the birth of what the *Oupnek'hat* describes as genuine *cognitio*: the realization through which all desire gets extinguished. As Schopenhauer perfectly knew from his own experience as well as his reading as a young man of Tieck and Wackenroder, man can in the ecstasy of artistic experience and especially through music penetrate into a sphere of subject-and-objectless awareness where all willing is extinct. But such moments of ecstasy are by no means total and permanent self-abandonment in the sense of Madame Guyon but rather a temporary forgetting. Thus he observed:

---

[469] »Tödtung des Willens« vs. »Tödtung des Leibes« (#577).
[470] »weil der Tod den Tod besiegt hat und weil derjenige, der den ersten Tod erlitt, den zweiten nicht mehr schmecken muss« (#676).

If while contemplating, i.e. aesthetic observation of an object, only a *pure subject of knowing* remains and will is forgotten, that blissful state is soon enough disturbed by a slight twinge, which as a matter of fact is a gentle but troublesome reminder of personhood, i.e., of the will.[471]

For Schopenhauer, will is not extinct as long as there is a return to "I" and "mine." Only with genuine, pure love in the sense of Madame Guyon—the love that in note #577 stands opposed to "egotism" and corresponds to the "killing of will"—is the ultimate goal reached:

> It is this abandonment which I call the *turning of the will*; in this alone is to be seen the freedom of the will. Solely through this [turning] does there appear an actual alteration of the intelligible character: man has become a totally different being and that wicked will, in which his entire nature previously consisted, is now wholly foreign to him. He no longer wills at all what he willed throughout this entire life; actually he no longer wills life, although originally he is nothing but the phenomenon of the will-to-live.[472]

It is significant that the core of this conception of the abolition of will first appeared in one of the notes that Schopenhauer wrote immediately after his encounter with the *Oupnek'hat* in the spring of 1814. In it he wrote of the delusion—the Maya of the Indians—which is as real as life, and he already had a clear notion of the difference between

---

[471] »Wenn man bei Kontemplation, d.i. ästhetischer Anschauung eines Objekts, nur noch *reines Subjekt des Erkennens* ist und den Willen vergessen hat: so mischt sich in diese Seeligkeit doch bald ein leiser Schmerz, der eigentlich eine leise aber stöhrende Erinnerung an die Persönlichkeit, d.i. an den Willen ist.« (#408)

[472] »Dieses Aufgeben ist es, was ich die *Wendung des Willens* nenne. In ihr allein zeigt sich die Freiheit des Willens. Durch sie allein zeigt sich eine wirkliche Änderung des intelligiblen Karakters, der Mensch ist ein ganz andrer geworden, und jener böse Wille in dem vorher sein ganzes Wesen bestand ist ihm jetzt völlig fremd.« (#496)

Affirmation and Abolition of Will

a death that only dissolves the appearance of the mirage (the body) and a death that he calls "sanctification" (Heiligung):

> If peace, beatitude and bliss are to be found, then the illusion must be abandoned, and if this is to be abandoned, then life must be given up. This is the serious step, the problem that is insoluble in life and is to be solved only with the help of death—which in itself dissolves not the illusion but only the appearance thereof, namely, the body; this is sanctification.[473]

In the course of 1814, as Schopenhauer's metaphysics of will developed, this "sanctification" was of course adapted to the new context. In a note of early 1815, which may be considered the earliest draft of the final paragraph of Schopenhauers major work, Schopenhauer wrote that the saint is "an apparition of a will that is *not* concerned with life, in other words, [a will that] has turned"[474] and even used the term "sacred will":

> Now, as this sacred will is free from life and its horrors, it is an agreeable phenomenon to the knowing subject (in other words to all men and women, the person of the saint included). — Here, however, we can express ourselves only negatively just because the tools of philosophy, namely concepts, are representations and therefore conditioned by life and belonging to it. And so, for our point of view, the turning of the will, holiness, salvation, bliss are indeed—a transition into nothingness. But to this must be added that the concept of the concept of nothingness expresses a mere relation, is a mere boundary-stone.[475]

---

[473] »Soll Ruhe, Seeligkeit, Friede gefunden werden, so muß der Wahn aufgegeben werden, und soll dieser, so muß das Leben aufgegeben werden. Das ist der schwere Schritt, die im Leben unauflösliche und nur durch Hülfe des Todes,—der an sich nicht den Wahn sondern nur die Erscheinung desselben, den Leib auflöst,—aufzulösende Aufgabe; die Heiligung« (#189).

[474] »Erscheinung eines Willens der *nicht* auf das Leben geht, d.h. der sich gewendet hat« (#389).

[475] »Da nun dieser heilige Wille vom Leben und dessen Schrecknissen frei ist, so ist er dem Erkennenden Subjekt (d.h. allen Menschen, die Person des

CHAPTER ELEVEN

As Schopenhauer had already emphasized in his early criticisms of Schelling and Fichte before the birth of his metaphysics of will, a philosopher must not transgress this boundary-stone because he is obliged to operate with concepts. The theoretical understanding of what lies beyond this boundary-stone must be strictly distinguished from its actual and living realization. Even though Madame Guyon had given up any and all willing, Schopenhauer judged that her mind had remained caught in "profound superstition" (tiefer Aberglaube, #676). A philosopher, by contrast, may arrive at a perfect theoretical understanding of the abolition of will yet remain completely entangled in will.

> The consciousness *in concreto* of the emptiness and unreality of the *principium individuationis*—the awareness of the ideality of space and time, in so far as it is permanent, serious, and profound and therefore determines conduct—constitutes holiness. The same consciousness, insofar as is translated into abstract terms and formulated in clear conceptual terms, gives us genuine philosophy. The true philosopher is therefore the theoretical savior.[476]

These statements and the term "theoretical savior" confirm Schopenhauer's claim of a theory of the origin of suffering and of salvation. These were precisely the questions that had motivated the young man to study philosophy. And now he was convinced to have reached the goal: the riddle of the world had been solved. In the year 1817 he couched

---

Heiligen mit eingeschlossen) eine erfreuliche Erscheinung.— Freilich können wir uns hier *nur negativ ausdrücken*, eben weil der Stoff in dem die Philosophie arbeitet, nämlich Begriffe, Vorstellungen, und also durch das Leben bedingt, sind, und diesem angehören. Daher ist für unsern Standpunkt allerdings das Wenden des Willens, die Heiligkeit das Heil, die Seligkeit,—ein Uebergang ins *Nichts*. Hier aber schließt sich die Betrachtung an daß der Begriff *Nichts* eine bloße Relation ausdrückt, ein bloßer Grenzstein ist.« (#389)

[476] »Das Bewußtseyn *in concreto* von der Nichtigkeit des *principii individuationis*, d.i. von der Idealität des Raums und der Zeit giebt, sofern es permanent, ernst und tief ist und daher das Handeln bestimmt,—Heiligkeit. Dasselbe Bewußtseyn—wenn es in die Abstraktion übertragen und zur Deutlichkeit des Begriffs gebracht ist, giebt die wahre Philosophie. Der wahre Philosoph ist daher der theoretische Heiland.« (#470)

Affirmation and Abolition of Will

this philosophical solution in a single sentence: "My entire philosophy can be summarized in a single expression: the world is the will's cognition of itself."[477] In earlier notes, Schopenhauer had already spelled out in more detail the diagnosis and therapy condensed in this brief formula. In the middle of 1815 he wrote for instance: "What was and what is? *The will* whose mirror is life, and the *will-free pure subject of knowing* which contemplates that will in this mirror, and in doing so attains salvation."[478] What Rudolf Malter, citing Schopenhauer, has called the philosopher's "single thought" ("The world is the self-recognition of the will"[479]) is here formulated in a way that encompasses the dimension of the extinction of suffering through *knowledge that is free of will*. The self-recognition of the will in the mirror of human consciousness is only the starting point, that is, the point where awareness of suffering arises in the mind of a self-conscious being. This experience of suffering marked the starting point of Schopenhauer's thinking that found expression in his remark to Wieland that "life is a miserable affair."[480] But Schopenhauer did not leave it at that: he immediately added that he intended to devote his life to "thinking about this."

The result of such thought found expression in a two-page note of early 1816 which for the first time comprehensively discussed the notion of the primacy of will. The first part of this note represents, as it were, Schopenhauer's cosmogony in which he explains how will could arrive at its self-recognition as "world":

> The will acts blindly, that is to say without knowledge, for as long as it can, namely in the inorganic and vegetative realms, indeed up to the generation and development of every animal [...]. At this

---

[477] »Meine ganze Ph[ilosophie] läßt sich zusammenfassen in dem einen Ausdruck: die Welt ist die Selbsterkenntniß des Willens.« (HN1:462, #662)

[478] »Was war, was ist? *Der Wille*, dessen Spiegel das Leben ist, und das *willensreine Subjekt des Erkennens*, das jenen Willen, zu seinem Heil, in diesem Spiegel schaut.« (#468)

[479] Malter 1988:14. For Schopenhauer's note see note 477 here above.

[480] »Das Leben ist eine mißliche Sache« Gespräche 22.

stage the will engendered knowledge, represented by the brain or large ganglion. This happened, like the production of all other organs, as a μηχανη [device] for the preservation of the individual and for the propagation of the species. Now with this device the entire *world as representation* arises at one stroke. Before, the will had proceeded in the dark but with supreme steadiness (because it alone operated without the interference of a different nature, i.e. of understanding [Erkenntniß]). But now it kindles for itself a light as the ultimate means of eliminating the disadvantage afflicting [man,] its most advanced manifestation—a disadvantage that arose from the very concourse and mutual conflict of its appearances.[481]

Understanding and the human mind thus appear as a secondary phenomenon in this atheist cosmogony of Schopenhauer which posits blind will rather than an omniscient creator God. This notion of the primacy of will was to become a beacon for Nietzsche, Bergson, Freud and many others and proves, as already Richard Wagner remarked, to be remarkably compatible with Darwin's theory of evolution.[482] Thus the primacy of will was established and understanding [Erkenntnis] was reduced to the status of an epiphenomenon—a recent light that the will had lit to serve its purposes.

---

[481] »*Der Wille* wirkt blind d.h. ohne Erkenntniß, so lange er kann, nämlich in der unorganischen und vegetativen Welt, ja bis zur Hervorbringung und Ausbildung jedes Thiers [...]. So brachte auf dieser Stufe der Wille die Erkenntniß, im Gehirn oder großen Ganglion repräsentirt hervor, eben wie jedes andre Organ, als eine μηχανη [Hilfsmittel] zur Erhaltung des Individuums und Fortpflanzung des Geschlechts. Mit dieser μηχανη steht aber auf ein Mal die ganze *Welt als Vorstellung* da. Bis hieher war der Wille im Dunkeln, und höchst sicher, gegangen (weil er allein wirkte, ohne Stöhrung einer andern Natur, d.i. der Erkenntniß): jetzt zündet er sich ein Licht an, als das letzte Mittel was er ergreift um den Nachtheil, der aus dem Gedränge und Konflikt seiner Erscheinungen eben den vollendetsten erwächst, aufzuheben« (#532).

[482] Books such as *The Egoistic Gene* by Richard Dawkins might have brought even more satisfaction to Schopenhauer than the writings he adduced as confirmation of his view in *On Will in Nature*. For an appraisal of Schopenhauer's influence in various domains see Schubbe & Koßler (eds.) 2014.

Affirmation and Abolition of Will

Therefore out of the will itself and for its service knowledge appears; and in all animals and the great majority of human beings knowledge remains solely in the service of the will. Yet here it happens that, contrary to the intention of the will, its most powerful means works against it, for with the highest discreteness the will arrives at a knowledge of itself that can find expression in art and philosophy (in which the understanding that arose in order to serve the will *relinquishes* this service and acts *freely*) or lead to the abolition of will in virtue, asceticism, and in overcoming the world.[483]

In such notes of the first half of 1816 the future structure of Schopenhauer's main work is already evident: the will in nature which kindles a light for itself and forms the world as representation (books one and two of *The World as Will and Representation*); the temporary liberation of knowledge from the service of will in art and philosophy (book three); and the permanent overcoming of will (book four). What appears in the light of this self-servingly lit torch of knowledge is exactly what propelled Schopenhauer on his philosophical quest: the misery of life and suffering.

The wretchedness of life is already sufficiently clear from the simple consideration that, for the vast majority of human beings, life is nothing but a constant struggle for this existence itself, with the certainty of ultimately losing the fight. But when misery is reduced and a partial victory over it is gained, then a terrible

---

[483] »Aus dem Willen selbst also, und zu seinem Dienst geht die Erkenntniß hervor; auch bleibt sie einzig in seinem Dienst bei allen Thieren, bei den Menschen, dem größten Theil nach, auch; allein hier geschieht es, gegen die Absicht des Willens, daß sein stärkstes Mittel ihm entgegen wirkt, indem er hier bei der höchsten Besonnenheit zur Selbsterkenntniß kommt, die theils in Kunst und Philosophie (bei welchen die zum Dienst des Willens entstandene Erkenntniß, sich von diesem *losreißend, frei* wirkt) sich offenbart, teils die Aufhebung des Willens in Tugend, Asketik, Weltüberwindung, herbeiführt.« (#532)

emptiness and boredom at once appear, and the struggle against these is even more agonising.[484]

Schopenhauer's quest was ongoing even before he began to study philosophy, as his remark to Wieland about wanting to reflect upon life's misery proves. But it was in the spring of 1814 that he first identified its ground in terms of his metaphysics of will: "That we *will* at all is our misfortune; it does not matter the least *what* we are willing."[485] Two years later he saw the root of suffering in the fact that man himself is a manifestation of will and that

> [Man's] existence must consist in constant and restless willing and striving. If these are removed from him through satisfaction, then there arises that very emptiness by which he becomes a burden to himself. For the pleasure of the serene enjoyment of knowledge is granted only to exceedingly few, and even to these only for a short fraction of their time. Again, willing itself cannot but have deficiency and shortage, and thus suffering, as its basis. And so, from all points of view, life is essentially suffering.[486]

Schopenhauer did not believe in an otherworldly power or redeemer figure who could bring an end to suffering. He saw the sole possibility of salvation in the light that will had lit up for itself: knowledge.

---

[484] »*Der Jammer des Lebens* geht schon genugsam aus der einfachen Betrachtung hervor, daß das Leben der allermeisten Menschen nichts ist als ein beständiger Kampf um diese Existenz selbst, mit der Gewißheit ihn zuletzt zu verlieren. Ist nun aber die Noth weit zurückgedrängt und ihr ein Stück des Feldes abgewonnen, so tritt sogleich furchtbare Leere und Langeweile ein, gegen welche der Kampf fast noch quälender ist« (#571).

[485] »Daß wir überhaupt *wollen* ist unser Unglück: auf das *was* wir wollen kommt es gar nicht an.« (#213)

[486] » sein Daseyn daher in beständigem rastlosen Wollen und Streben bestehn muß; ist ihm dieses durch die Befriedigung entnommen, so entsteht eben jene Leere durch die er sich selbst zur Last ist. Denn die Freude des ruhigen Genusses der Erkenntniß ist nur höchst Wenigen und auch diesen nur auf einen kleinen Theil ihrer Zeit gegeben. Das Wollen selbst aber wiederum muß den Mangel, folglich das Leiden zur Unterlage haben. So ist von allen Seiten das Leben wesentlich ein Leiden.« (#571)

Affirmation and Abolition of Will

This state without any hope of salvation is merely the mirror of the *will's invincible nature*, and man is the manifestation of this will. A power outside of him cannot abolish or turn this will; this can be done solely through himself by means of knowledge. And there is no power able to liberate him from the possible torments of life, for this life is simply the manifestation of the will.[487]

It is for this reason that Schopenhauer's soteriology only allows for a radically immanent solution:

> If the will turns, then it is no longer to be seen in this mirror. In vain do we ask where it has now turned to, and we foolishly moan that it has become lost in *nothingness*. The human being whose will overcomes itself and turns cannot give any account of this to us and to his own mind; for what then lives, exists and thinks is still the will-to-live itself, and that which consists in the overcoming of this will cannot in any way be given to him and must for him be a nothing. Only the man who has realized it and has abolished his will, can know it—but only in so far as he existentially is it, in this act itself, not outside it, and still less for others.[488]

---

[487] »Diese Rettungslosigkeit ist eben nur der Spiegel der *Unbezwinglichkeit des Willens* dessen Erscheinung der Mensch ist. So wenig eine Macht außer ihm diesen Willen aufheben oder wenden kann, sondern dies einzig und allein nur durch ihn selbst, bei Vermittelung der Erkenntniß, geschehn kann; eben so wenig giebt es eine Macht die ihn von den möglichen Quaalen des Lebens befreien kann, da dies Leben eben nur die Erscheinung des Willens ist.« (#571)

[488] »Wendet sich der Wille, so ist er in diesem Spiegel nicht mehr zu sehn: wir fragen vergeblich wohin er sich jetzt wendet; wir schreien thörigt daß er ins *Nichts* verloren gehe. Der, dessen Wille sich aufhebt und wendet, kann uns und seiner eignen Reflexion keine Rechenschaft geben: denn was da lebt und ist und denkt, ist eben noch der Wille zum Leben selbst: und das was in der Aufhebung dieses Willens besteht, kann jenem auf keine Weise gegeben werden, muß ihm ein Nichts seyn: nur der welcher es ergriffen, welcher seinen Willen aufgehoben, erkennt es, aber auch nur sofern er es ist, in diesem Akt selbst, nicht außer dem, noch weniger für Andre.« (#571)

CHAPTER ELEVEN

The self-annihilation (*fanā*) of Prince Dara and the Vedantist awakening from the dream of Maya, of which Schopenhauer first learned from the *Oupnek'hat*, point in the same direction as the mystic writings of Jacob Böhme, Madame Guyon, and "Tauler": the pole of salvation that Schopenhauer named overcoming or annihilation of will. In the first note that shows unmistakable signs of *Oupnek'hat* influence, Schopenhauer still used the terminology of his youth:

> In order to share in the peace of God (that is, for the appearance of the *better consciousness*) it is necessary that man, this frail, finite and transitory being, be something quite different, no longer a human being at all, but become aware of himself as something quite different. For in so far as he is alive and is a human being, he is doomed not merely to *sin* and *death*, but also to *illusion*, and this *illusion* is as real as life, as real as the world of the senses itself; indeed it is identical with these (the Maya of the Indians).[489]

Toward the end of 1816, when this "appearance of the better consciousness" had long become "the turning of the will," Schopenhauer described in a note that he later used in the final passage of the last book of *The World as Will and Representation* the salvation pole of his compass:

> But if we now turn our glance from our own insufficiency and perplexity to those who have overcome the world and have totally given up the will-to-live—in other words to the saints who, after the will hardly exists any more, only await the dissolution of its manifestation, the body, and with this the complete extinction of the will—then we see in them, instead of the restless impulsion, the rapturous joy, and the violent suffering that make up the ac-

---

[489] »Um des *Frieden[s] Gottes* Theilhaftig zu werden (d. i. zum Hervortreten des *bessern Bewußtseyns*) ist erfordert, daß der Mensch, dies hinfällige, endliche, nichtige Wesen, etwas ganz andres sey, gar nicht mehr Mensch, sondern als etwas ganz andres sich bewußt werde. Denn sofern als er lebt, sofern als er Mensch ist, ist er nicht bloß der *Sünde* und dem *Tode* anheim gefallen, sondern auch dem *Wahn*, und dieser *Wahn* ist so real als das Leben, als die Sinnenwelt selbst, ja er ist mit diesen Eines (das Maja der Indier).« (#189)

Affirmation and Abolition of Will

tions of man who loves life, an unshakable calm and inner serenity: a state that we cannot consider without yearning and which we are bound to acknowledge as infinitely superior and as the only right thing, in face of which the nihility of everything else becomes apparent.[490]

This salvation pole of Schopenhauer remained stable like the magnetic field of our earth. It was not affected by the processes of development and change that are seen in Schopenhauer's interpretations and characterizations of his philosophy—processes that already began in 1817 and 1818 with the redaction of *The World as Will and Representation*. 154 years ago, when the 72-year-old Schopenhauer cast a glance at his gilded Buddha statue on the window sill and added a comment to the last word of his major work that equated *Nichts* with the supreme wisdom of the Buddhists *prajna paramita*, the needle of his compass still pointed straight at the "N" of Böhme's "nihilation," Prince Dara's non-willing, the Buddha's Nirvana, and of course the "N" that fills our heart with dread yet inexorably attracts us: *Nothingness*.

---

[490] »Wenden wir aber den Blick von unsrer eignen Dürftigkeit und Befangenheit auf diejenigen welche die Welt überwunden und den Willen zum Leben völlig aufgegeben haben, d.h. auf die Heiligen, die, nachdem der Wille fast nicht mehr da ist nur noch die Auflösung seiner Erscheinung, des Leibes, und mit ihm das gänzliche Absterben des Willens erwarten, so sehn wir in ihnen statt des unruhigen Dranges, der jubelnden Freude und des heftigen Leidens, daraus der Wandel des lebenslustigen Menschen besteht, eine unerschütterliche Ruhe und innige Heiterkeit, einen Zustand zu dem wir nicht ohne Sehnsucht blicken können und den wir als unendlich vorzüglich als das allein Rechte, dem gegenüber die Nichtigkeit alles andern klar wird, anerkennen müssen.« (#612)

Appendix 1

Schopenhauer's Favorite Book

Secretum Tegendum

Schopenhauer's favorite book was a Latin work entitled *Oupnek'hat, id est, secretum tegendum*. He called it "the most rewarding and uplifting reading in the world" and informed his readers that the *Oupnek'hat* "has been the solace of my life and will be the solace of my death."[1]

> How entirely does the Oupnekhat breathe throughout the holy spirit of the Vedas! How is every one who by a diligent study of its Persian Latin has become familiar with that incomparable book, stirred by that spirit to the very depth of his soul! How does every line display its firm, definite, and throughout harmonious meaning! From every sentence deep, original, and sublime thoughts arise, and the whole is pervaded by a high and holy and earnest spirit. Indian air surrounds us, and original thoughts of kindred spirits.[2]

---

[1] *Parerga and Paralipomena* §184; SW5.421; Z10.436.

[2] »Wie athmet doch der Oupnekhat durchweg den heiligen Geist der Veden! Wie wird doch Der, dem, durch fleißiges Lesen, das Persisch-Latein dieses unvergleichlichen Buches geläufig geworden, von jenem Geist im Innersten ergriffen! Wie ist doch jede Zeile so voll fester, bestimmter und durchgängig zusammenstimmender Bedeutung! Und aus jeder Seite treten uns tiefe, ursprüngliche, erhabene Gedanken entgegen, während ein hoher und heiliger Ernst über dem Ganzen schwebt. Alles athmet hier Indische Luft und ursprüngliches, naturverwandtes Daseyn.« *Parerga and Paralipomena* §184; SW5.421; Z10.437. English translation by Max Müller, *The Upanishads* (New York: Dover Publications, 1962), vol. 1: lxi.

Appendix 1

In spite of Schopenhauer's exuberant praise, this "incomparable book" remains a mystery—a *secretum tegendum* (secret to be safeguarded), as its translator Abraham-Hyacinthe Anquetil-Duperron (1731–1805) explained the word *Oupnek'hat* in the very title of the work. Before Upanishad translations from the Sanskrit became available, quite a number of people studied Anquetil's Latin rendering—and they did so in spite of its style described by Max Müller as "so utterly unintelligible that it required the lynxlike perspicacity of an intrepid philosopher, such as Schopenhauer, to discover a thread through such a labyrinth."[3]

While Anquetil's cryptic, rare, and expensive Latin *Oupnek'hat* was soon forgotten[4] and its Sanskrit-Persian-Latin "detour" replaced by direct translations from Sanskrit, the relationship between the Sanskrit Upanishads and their Persian translation (*Sirr-i akbar*) was sporadically studied.[5] Though Anquetil-Duperron's Latin translation (*Oupnek'hat*) was once more used by Paul Deussen for his pioneering German trans-

---

[3] Max Müller, ibid., pp. lviii-liv. For some of Schopenhauer's contemporaries who intensively studied the *Oupnek'hat* see pp. 163–172 here above.

[4] Almost equally forgotten was an attempt, inspired by the translator's admiration for Schopenhauer, to make the *Oupnek'hat* known to a wider public: Franz Mischel's *Das Oupnek'hat* (Dresden: C. Heinrich, 1882). Mischel decided to render only the translation part without Anquetil's notes and thus omitted more than half of the work.

[5] The first detailed study began to appear in Schopenhauer's lifetime in Albrecht Weber's *Indische Studien* (1850, 247–302, 380–456; 1853, 1–111, 170–236) and was completed some years thereafter (1865, 1–54). Twentieth-century studies include Tara Chand, "Dara Shikoh and the Upanishads." *Islamic Culture* 17, no. 1 (1943): 397–413; E. Göbel-Gross, *Sirr-i Akbar. Die persische Upaniṣadenübersetzung des Mogulprinzen Dārā Šukoh* (Marburg: Erich Mauersberger, 1962); Mark Dresden, "On the Genesis of Anquetil Duperron's Oupnek'hat," in: Ph. Gignoux & A. Tafazzoli, *Mémorial Jean de Menasce* (Louvain: Fondation Culturelle Iranienne, 1974), pp. 35–43; and Carl W. Ernst, "Muslim Studies in Hinduism? A Reconsideration of Arabic and Persian Translations from Indian Languages." *Iranian Studies* 36, (2003): 173–95. My thanks to Jochen Stollberg for sending me a copy of the thesis by Göbel-Gross.

lation of sixty Upanishads,[6] only intrepid admirers of Schopenhauer such as Richard Wagner still managed to get hold of a copy of Anquetil's work; but even they tended to shy away from its actual study.[7] The same can be said about Schopenhauer researchers. Authors of recent books and dissertations about oriental influences on Schopenhauer used almost without exception "more reliable" translations of the Upanishads from Sanskrit.[8] The neglect of Schopenhauer's favorite book by specialists was partly caused by Arthur Hübscher's systematic downplaying of the book's importance. Though he knew better, he claimed that its influence had begun "late" and that of Buddhism "even later,"[9] and in Hübscher's indispensable annotated bibliography of Schopenhauer's library the *Oupnek'hat* was described as follows:

> Ex libris in both volumes.— Numerous lines, translations of single words and passages, indications of sources and references, column titles and remarks in the margins (mostly ink, the majority from early period, after 1816, partly also from later times).[10]

---

[6] Paul Deussen, *Sechzig Upanishad's des Veda*. Leipzig: Brockhaus, 1897.

[7] Wagner ordered the *Oupnek'hat* on December 12 of 1873 in a letter to Judith Gautier: *Lettres à Judith Gautier*, edited by Léon Guichard. Paris: Gallimard, 1964, p. 55. But it was only in July and August of 1882, after the appearance of Mischel's German translation, that Wagner and his wife Cosima read a little and had some discussions about it; see Cosima Wagner, *Die Tagebücher*, vol. 2, München: R. Piper, 1977, pp. 977, 981, 986, 991.

[8] As mentioned above (p. 182, note 320), Werner Scholz (*Arthur Schopenhauer – ein Philosoph zwischen westlicher und östlicher Tradition*. Frankfurt / Bern: Peter Lang, 1996) does not even list the *Oupnek'hat* in its bibliography, and Icilio Vecchiotti never even mentions Anquetil-Duperron or the *Oupnek'hat* in his 600-page book about the genesis of Schopenhauer's doctrine and its relationship with Indian philosophy (*La dottrina di Schopenhauer. Le teorie schopenhaueriane considerate nella loro genesi e nei loro rapporti con la filosofia indiana*. Rome: Ubaldini, 1969). My thanks to Prof. Francesca Gambarotto for helping me to get hold of a copy of Vecchiotti's book.

[9] Arthur Hübscher, *Denker gegen den Strom. Schopenhauer: Gestern—Heute—Morgen*. Bonn: Bouvier Verlag Hermann Grundmann, 1973, p. 50.

[10] Arthur Schopenhauer, *Der handschriftliche Nachlaß*, ed. by Arthur Hübscher. München: Deutscher Taschenbuch Verlag, 1985, vol. 5, p. 338.

APPENDIX 1

Hübscher's brief description is followed by a total of three specific instances of Schopenhauer's handwriting in the *Oupnek'hat*. All stem from the first volume, and no handwriting in the second volume is mentioned:

Vol. I, 395. Schopenhauer [to the title "Oupnek'hat Eischavasieh, e Djedjr Beid"]: Vide etiam hujus Upanishad versionem Anglicam in Rammohun Roy libro "Translations of several books & passages of the Veds" editio 2da Lond: 1832 p. 101 seq: etiam Gallicam, in Pauthier Livres sacrés de l'Orient p. 329. — Et aliam Roerii, in Bibliotheca Indica: No. 41. p. 71. — Vol. I, S. 563, Schopenhauer [to the Valentinian fable of Bythus related by Irenaeus]: Ex hac fabula Jac: Böhm & deinde Schelling sua dogmata confecerunt. — On the cover sheets in the back of vol. I, tightly written index in Schopenhauer's hand.

The reader of these lines must assume that this reference to alternative translations, a remark about gnostic influence on Jacob Böhme and Schelling, and Schopenhauer's index are the only noteworthy traces in the *Oupnek'hat* of Schopenhauer's interest and that the rest only consists of some "lines, translations of single words and passages, indications of sources and references, column titles." This assumption was justified because in other cases (such as works by Kant in Schopenhauer's possession) Hübscher supplied very detailed lists of handwritten notes that sometimes fill six or more pages in small print. Other works in the Orientalia section, too, list many handwritten notes by Schopenhauer.[11]

Intrigued by those tantalizing "numerous lines," the "index in Schopenhauer's hand" and a strange contradiction in Hübscher's description[12] I wrote from Japan to the curator of the Schopenhauer Archive

---

[11] See for example Christian Lassen's *Gymnosophista sive Indicae Philosophiae Documenta* (no. 1130 of Hübscher's annotated bibliography; Handschriftlicher Nachlaß vol. 5, pp. 331–2) where Hübscher filled more than a page in small type with sixteen notes by Schopenhauer.

[12] Hübscher wrote in his annotated bibliography that Schopenhauer encoun-

and fixed a date for a visit during the summer of 1995. But when I explained my wish to see the *Oupnek'hat* after my arrival in Frankfurt, the curator refused to let me see it because "everything noteworthy is already documented in Hübscher's bibliography." The following year I was luckier with the new curator, Jochen Stollberg, and was astonished to find that on some pages of the *Oupnek'hat* there seemed to be more notes in Schopenhauer's hand than printed text! (see p. 5 above)

My notes from the 1996 visit list a total of 137 pages from vol. 1 and 174 pages from volume 2 as "worth taking photos of"—a category that at the time excluded pages where only a word or a few words were underlined. When including such pages, I found that about 840 pages, i.e., almost half of the two-volume *Oupnek'hat*, contained some trace of Schopenhauer's interest. When reporting some of my findings during lectures in 1997 at the Schopenhauer Society in Frankfurt,[13] the University of Zürich, and the University of California at Berkeley, I noted that henceforth studies about the genesis of Schopenhauer's philosophy would have to take Schopenhauer's favorite book into account. But almost twenty years later (and one hundred and fifty years after Schopenhauer's death) research about the one book that he prized above all others is still in its beginning stages.[14]

---

tered the *Oupnek'hat* in 1814 and "purchased it probably in the same year" (p. 339). At the same time, Hübscher categorically states that notes date from "after 1816" (p. 338). I asked myself: why would someone who has the habit of copiously marking up his books buy one in 1814 and refrain from writing anything in it during the most intensive phase of his encounter with it?

[13] Urs App, "Schopenhauers Begegnung mit dem Buddhismus." *Schopenhauer-Jahrbuch* 79 (1998a), pp. 39–42.

[14] Some other publications of mine communicate additional information. 1. "William Jones's Ancient Theology." *Sino-Platonic Papers* 191 (2009): 1–125 deals with one of Schopenhauer's must trusted orientalist sources. 2. "Schopenhauer and China: A Sino-Platonic Love Affair." *Sino-Platonic Papers* 200 (2010): 1–160 examines the roles of Buddhism and East Asia. 3. The chapter on Anquetil-Duperron in *The Birth of Orientalism*. Philadelphia: Pennsylvania University Press, 2010: 363–439 discusses Anquetil-Duperron's theological and philosophical background.

APPENDIX 1

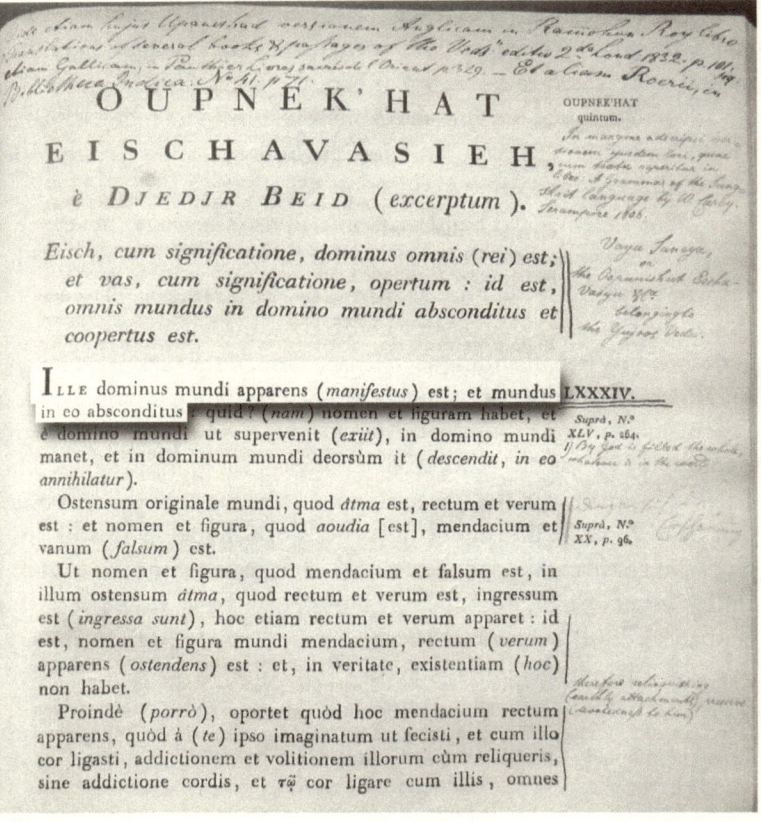

Different textual layers on p. 395 of *Oupnek'hat* vol. 1. The added highlight shows the minuscule amount of translated Upanishadic text on this page. Schopenhauer's notes and lines in the margins in various inks and pencil.

Secretum Legendum

In a Freudian slip, the "secret to be safeguarded" of Anquetil's title (*secretum tegendum*) has sometimes been misread *secretum legendum*, that is, "a secret one ought to read." 150 years after Schopenhauer's death the time has indeed come to begin with the study not of some modern translation of the Upanishads or even a virgin copy of Anquetil's *Oupnek'hat* but rather of the very work Schopenhauer regarded as the solace of his life and death: his Indian Bible that he "opened for prayers" before going to bed.[15] Its two volumes, chock-full with proofs of Schopenhauer's interest, are still almost totally unexplored. What I propose to do in this Appendix is to present this former "secret" like a newly discovered fossil. First I will cut a slice out of it to identify various layers; then I will summarily describe individual layers, their proportions, and age; and finally I will outline future tasks. This is a "physical" approach in the sense that it tries, as a first step, to measure the object and find out about its structure, provenance, and overall nature. For questions regarding the *Oupnek'hat*'s philosophical content, influence, etc. see the body of this book.

The "slice" or initial sample that will provide a first insight into our textual fossil is the first page mentioned by Hübscher in his *Oupnek'hat* description: page 395 of volume one. A glance at this sample on our p. 270 immediately shows that Hübscher omitted a few important facts about it. He quoted only the three and a half lines that Schopenhauer scribbled at the very top of the page. Perhaps most importantly, Hübscher did not mention the pencil note in the right margin around the

---

[15] Schopenhauer's friend Wilhelm Gwinner reported two years after Schopenhauer's death: "Before going to bed he not infrequently opened his Bible, the Oupnekhat, in order to perform his prayers. This book, he said, would also be his final solace in the hour of his death." Wilhelm Gwinner, *Arthur Schopenhauer aus persönlichem Umgange dargestellt. Ein Blick auf sein Leben, seinen Charakter und seine Lehre.* Leipzig: F. A. Brockhaus, 1862, p. 215.

Appendix 1

middle of the page that reads "Ding an sich u. Erscheinung" ("Thing-in-itself and appearance")— a remark that points to Schopenhauer's understanding of the corresponding paragraph or even the entire Upanishad and is thus of particular interest. But at this stage we only want to get an overview of our sample and identify its different layers. This most striking and youngest textual layer, Schopenhauer's handwriting, consists of four sub-layers:

(A) notes at the top of the page in deep black ink;
(B) notes in the margins in dark grey ink;
(C) one note in the margin and a line in pencil; and
(D) several underlinings in deep black ink.

The references in sub-layer A (Roy's translation was published in 1832, Pauthier's in 1840, and Röer's in 1853) indicate, since the same ink and pen appear to have been used, that they stem from the period between 1853 and Schopenhauer's death in 1860. Sub-layer B consists of Schopenhauer's quotations from William Carey's *A Grammar of the Sungskrit language* (Serampore 1806), a book that Schopenhauer possibly owned but that is not mentioned in Hübscher's annotated Orientalia bibliography. Sub-layer C, the above-mentioned remarks and line in pencil, possibly stems from the time when Schopenhauer's system was forming, that is, between 1814 and 1816. Sub-layer D, the deep black lines, appear to be written with a thicker (top three) and thinner (bottom two) ink pen and might stem from different periods.

The next major layer consists of Anquetil-Duperron's printed text. On page 455 of volume 2, Anquetil states that he finished this translation on October 9 of 1795, but he could have revised the text while writing notes to this Upanishad (vol. 1, pp. 633–5) between 1795 and 1801, the year the first volume was printed. The *terminus a quo* for this layer is the summer of 1787 when Anquetil finished revising his French translation and decided to publish the *Oupnek'hat* not in French but in Latin.[16]

---

[16] Anquetil's French translation is extant in the *Bibliothèque Nationale* in

As a basis for his initial French and the definitive Latin translations, Anquetil used a Persian manuscript which he had received in December of 1775 from his friend Le Gentil, the French envoy at Oudh.[17] Anquetil first announced his discovery in his book on Oriental legislation of 1778 where he wrote:

> Schahdjehan [Shah Jahan, 1592–1666], son of Djehanguir [Jahangir, 1569–1627] permits all religions as long as they serve the growth of his empire. Dara Shako [Mohammed Dārā Shikōh, 1615–1659], the eldest son of Shahdjehan, shows publicly his indifference for Islam. In Delhi in 1656, this prince has brahmins of Benares translate the *Oupnekat*, a Sanskrit work whose name signifies *The word that must not be enounced* (secret that must not be revealed). This work is the essence of the four Vedas. It presents in 51 sections the complete system of Indian theology of which the result is the unity of the first Being whose perfections and personified operations bear the name of the principal Indian divinities, and the reunion of the entire nature with this first Agent. I plan to publish as soon as possible the translation of this important work which I received in 1776 from North Bengal from Mr. Gentil, Chevalier of St. Louis and Captain of cavalry in the service of France. This work appears for the first time in Europe; no traveler has mentioned it until now.[18]

Paris, Western manuscript section, Nouvelles acquisitions françaises (Fonds Anquetil-Duperron) no. 8857. The date of completion is marked on page 862 (March 18, 1787), as is the date of completion of the revision (July 3, 1787).

[17] Anquetil later received from Bernier a second manuscript that he occasionally quotes in footnotes.

[18] "SCHAHDJEHAN, fils de Djehanguir, permet de même toutes les Religions, pourvu qu'elles aillent à l'accroissement de son Empire. Dara Schako, fils aîné de Schahdjehan, montre publiquement son indifférence pour le Mahométisme. Ce Prince fait traduire en Persan à Delhi en 1656, par des Brachmes de Benarès, l'OUPNEKAT, ouvrage Samskretam, dont le nom signifie, Parole qu'il ne faut pas dire (secret qu'il ne faut pas reveler). Cet ouvrage est l'extrait des quatre VÉDES. Il présente en 51 Sections le système complet de la Théologie Indienne, dont le résultat est l'unité du premier Etre, ses perfections & ses

Appendix 1

Anquetil assumed that the Persian layer of the *Oupnek'hat* represents a faithful, word-for-word translation of a Sanskrit text. But when comparing Anquetil's translation from Persian to Carey's translation from Sanskrit that he scribbled in the margins, Schopenhauer was unable to find corresponding passages for much of the text.[19] Indeed, on this entire page of "Upanishad translation," only the highlighted passage (see here above, p. 270) stems from the Sanskrit Upanishad as it appears in Patrick Olivelle's edition.[20] Most of page 395 of the *Oupnek'hat* represents a commentary layer consisting of explanations by Prince Dara, his religious instructors, and his Indian pandits. Some such explanations can be traced to specific Indian sources such as Shankara's Upanishad commentaries while others have more of a Sufi flavor.

The first survey of a single slice of our textual fossil already showed that scholars who think that they can use some modern translation or standard Sanskrit text to study the influence of the Upanishads on Schopenhauer (or compare Schopenhauer's philosophy with the "Indian" philosophy he knew) have a little problem. If so much of the text that Anquetil translated "word for word" and that Schopenhauer studied so intensively does not stem from the Upanishads but rather from commentators, then studies of reception must obviously rely on

---

opérations personnifiés sont le nom des principales Divinités Indiennes; & la réunion de la nature entiere à ce premier Agent. Je compte donner au premier jour la traduction de cet ouvrage important, que j'ai reçu du Nord du Bengale, en 1776, de M. Gentil Chevalier de St. Louis & Capitaine de Cavalerie au service de France. Cet ouvrage paroit pour la premiere fois en Europe; aucun Voyageur jusqu'ici n'en a fait mention." A.-H. Anquetil-Duperron, *Législation orientale*. Amsterdam: Marc Michel Rey, 1778, p. 21.

[19] Of the two handwritten sentences in the margins of p. 395 of volume 1 of the *Oupnek'hat* that Schopenhauer quotes from Carey ("By God is filled the whole, whatever is in the world," and "therefore relinquishing [earthly attachments] preserve [devotedness to him]") only the first has a true counterpart.

[20] There is no single standard version of Sanskrit Upanishads, and Olivelle's is not a critical edition. What is important to remember, however, is that modern translations as well as those consulted by Schopenhauer show many important differences with his reference text, the Latin *Oupnek'hat*.

the text Schopenhauer actually used and not some ideal, "unpolluted" source that was unknown to him. In other words, it is the *Oupnek'hat*— and not just any *Oupnek'hat*, but *Schopenhauer's annotated copy*— that must be read. Instead of a secret to be safeguarded (*secretum tegendum*), Schopenhauer's *Oupnek'hat* must become *legendum*: required reading. The study of Schopenhauer's markup shows that, on this page, he was most interested in commentary rather than Upanishad text. In one stroke, our sample thus puts in question most of what has been written about Schopenhauer and his reception of Indian philosophy and suggests that it would make sense to learn more about the book he so admired. For a start, let us look at the main layers of our fossil in some more detail.

1. From Sanskrit to Persian (1656–1657)

Crown prince Mohammed Dara Shikoh (1615–1659) was the eldest son of the Mughal emperor Shah Jahan (1592–1666) and of his favorite wife Mumtaz Mahal (1593–1631) whose mausoleum is the world-famous Taj Mahal in Agra. This monument's mixture of Persian and Indian elements echoes the crown prince's cultural and religious background. Since his youth Dara, whose mother tongue was Persian, had been interested in Sufism, and in his twenties he authored several books with biographies and teachings of Sufi masters.[21] But after meeting the famous *Muwaḥḥid* (unitarian) Mullā Shah, Dara's interest in other religions and their sacred scriptures grew by leaps and bounds. So did his entourage of experts of religions such as Judaism, Christianity, and Hinduism that also included Yoga adepts, Islamic mystics, and other holy men. For his study of the religions of India the prince consulted with some of the subcontinent's most famous scholars and had them translate important texts such as the *Bhagavad Gītā* and the

---

[21] Bikrama Jit Hasrat, *Dārā Shikūh: Life and Works*. Calcutta: Munshiram Manoharlal, ²1982.

Appendix 1

Yogavāsiṣṭha into Persian.²² In 1656 Prince Dara finished a book called *The Confluence of Oceans* that lays out what he regarded as the common core of Hindu and Sufi teaching.²³ In the same year the prince assembled in Benares a team of experts for the first ever translation of fifty Upanishads from Sanskrit into Persian.²⁴

The Upanishads stem from many different traditions and ages and diverse Sanskrit versions and manuscripts exist.²⁵ The two texts that our samples mainly stem from, the Isha and Mundaka Upanishads, represent the Yajurveda and Atharvaveda.

---

²² For these and similar translation projects bridging the Islamic and Indian spheres see Carl W. Ernst, "Muslim Studies in Hinduism? A Reconsideration of Arabic and Persian Translations from Indian Languages." *Iranian Studies* 36, (2003): 173–95. For an interesting 2-volume study of the *Yogavāsiṣṭha* see François Chenet, *Psychogenèse et cosmogonie selon le Yoga-vāsiṣṭha*. Paris: Collège de France / de Boccard, 1998.

²³ M. Mahfuz-ul-Haq, *Majima'-ul-Baḥrain or The Mingling of the Two Oceans, by Prince Muhammad Dârâ Shikûh*. Calcutta: Asiatic Society of Bengal, 1929. Reprint, Karachi: Royal Book Company, 1990. See also Daryush Shayegan, *Hindouisme et soufisme – Une lecture du confluent des deux océans: le Majma 'al-Bahrayn de Dârâ Shokûh*. Paris: Albin Michel, 1997; Lalita Sengupta, *Contribution of Darashiko to Hindu-Muslim Philosophy*. Kolkata: Sanskrit Pustak Bhandar, 2004; and D'Onofrio, Svevo, and Fabrizio Speziale. Muḥammad Dārā Šikōh: *La congiunzione dei due oceani* (Majmaʿ al-Baḥrayn). Milano: Adelphi, 2011.

²⁴ For detailed information about the genesis of this Persian Upanishad translation see Erhard Göbel-Gross, *Sirr-i Akbar. Die persische Upaniṣadenübersetzung des Mogulprinzen Dārā Šukoh* (Marburg: Erich Mauersberger, 1962, pp. 18–30; and Mark Dresden, "On the Genesis of Anquetil Duperron's Oupnek'hat," in: Ph. Gignoux & A. Tafazzoli, *Mémorial Jean de Menasce*. Louvain: Fondation Culturelle Iranienne, 1974, pp. 37–43. Useful background information is found in Saiyid Athar Abbas Rizvi, *Muslim Revivalist Movements in Northern India*. New Delhi: Munshiram Manoharlal, 1995, and in the volume by Svevo D'Onofrio and Fabrizio Speziale (2011).

²⁵ For a concise introduction to the background and history of Upanishadic literature see Patrick Olivelle, *The Early Upaniṣads*. New York / Oxford: Oxford University Press, 1998, pp. 3–27.

Schopenhauer's Favorite Book

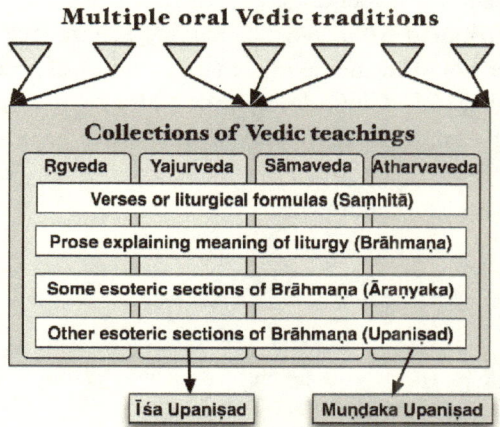

The exact working procedure of Prince Dara's six-month Upanishad translation venture that took place in Benares from 1656–7 is unknown, but it is likely that a team of experts first made a draft translation which was then edited and put into elegant Persian by crown prince Dara.[26] The beginning of the Isha Upanishad that was mentioned above suggests that a basic Persian translation of the Sanskrit Upanishad texts was discussed by experts, some of whose remarks were woven into the translation that was then redacted by Prince Dara who added further explanations that reflect his Sufi background and philosophy. Whatever the procedure might have been: its result, titled *Sirr-i akbar* (The Great Secret), was finished in 1657 and is the first ever translation of a collection of Upanishads into a non-Indic language.

As I observed with regard to the *Oupnek'hat*'s beginning of the Isha Upanishad, Dara's translation did not only include Upanishadic text but also various kinds of commentary. Usually such commentary is integrated in the text, which is why neither the translator Anquetil nor his reader Schopenhauer tended to notice its presence. But in some

---

[26] Göbel-Gross, *Sirr-i Akbar*, p. 29, calls this the "narrative" procedure.

Appendix 1

cases a commentator is mentioned. In the following example, a commentary is attributed to Shankara acharya ("Sankra tscharedj") and Schopenhauer noted in the margin that "the gloss of Shankara ends here" ("Soweit geht die Gloße des Sancara"). He also noticed a different kind of explanation that begins with "id est," which he underlined—a gloss whose presence is pointed out by Schopenhauer ("Gloße") but whose author remains unknown.

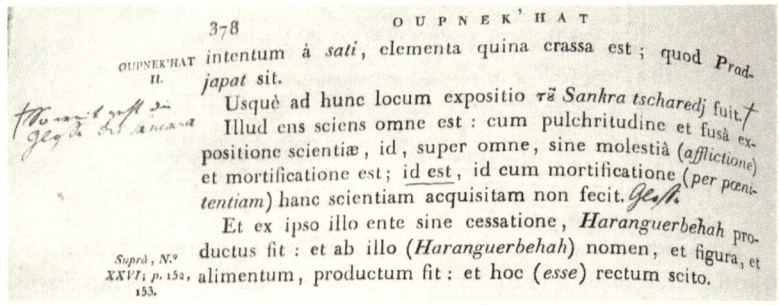

OUP1.378: Glosses identified by Schopenhauer

The *Oupnek'hat* also features numerous Islamic terms and names. Schopenhauer usually struck out what he identified as such or marked it by square brackets. In the case shown below, he did both and wrote in the margin "additamentum imprudentissimi librarii Islamitici" ("addition by the most imprudent Islamic copyist;" see also above, p. 210).[27]

OUP2.70: Islamic elements in the *Oupnek'hat* denounced by Schopenhauer

---

[27] Göbel-Gross, *Sirr-i Akbar*, contains a detailed analysis of such elements in the Praśna Upanishad.

Schopenhauer's Favorite Book

However, most commentaries and additions were integrated into the text and remained unnoticed. The following example of the Mundaka Upanishad shows how intricately intertwined Upanishadic text, commentary, and translator's explanations can sometimes be. The commentaries marked by "id est" can be easily detected; but how could Schopenhauer know that explanations following "quid?" are usually by Dara or the translation team? This example also shows another kind of explanation, namely, the italicized words in parentheses. These were used by Anquetil as a device to explain the literal translation from Persian that precedes such parentheses. At times they explain a technical term (*sak'hepat* is explained as "somni cum quiete"), and at other times they add precision, as in "fuit (*exivit*)" or "praestantia (*principalia*)." In the half page reproduced below, everything highlighted is commentary, whereas text without highlight also figures in present-day translations of the Sanskrit text of the Mundaka Upanishad such as Patrick Olivelle's.

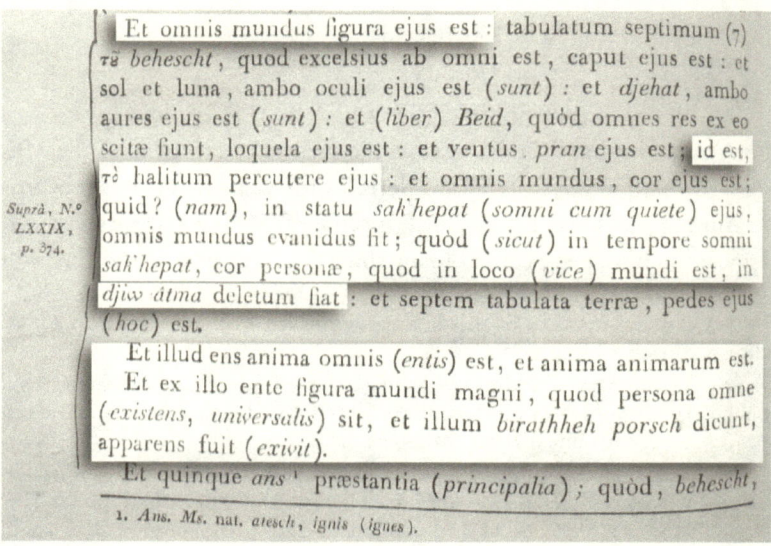

OUP1.382: Translated Mundaka text with integrated commentary

Appendix 1

The precise ratio of in-line commentary versus Upanishadic text is often, as here, guesswork because of our ignorance of the manuscript(s) used by Dara and his team. It also varies with each Upanishad and appears to reflect the interests of Prince Dara. Whereas philosophical passages (for example explanations about monism or maya) tend to include substantial amounts of commentary,[28] passages related to ritual are often abbreviated or entirely omitted. Using Olivelle's edition of the Mundaka Upanishad, it appears that about 18% of the corresponding *Oupnek'hat* text consists of commentary. Of course there is no single "canonical" text of the Upanishads; but researchers who use modern translations in order to study Schopenhauer's reception ought to be aware of the many omissions, additions, and variations that characterize the *Sirr-i akbar* and its Latin translation entitled *Oupnek'hat*.[29]

In 1657, Prince Dara and his team of experts completed the translation of fifty Upanishads into Persian and named it *Sirr-i akbar*: The Great Secret. It consisted of

(1) Prince Dara's preface;
(2) a list of translated Upanishads;
(3) a Sanskrit-Persian glossary;
(4) the Persian Upanishad translation with commentary.

Shortly thereafter, Prince Dara lost the succession struggles to the Mughal throne and was in 1659 murdered by the victor, his younger brother Aurangzeb (1618-1707). But Prince Dara's *Sirr-i akbar* survived and appears to have been copied many times.[30] In our next section we will

---

[28] An extreme example of this is the beginning of the Isha Upanishad, as shown above (vol. 1, p. 395).

[29] See the summary of findings regarding a single Upanishad in Göbel-Gross, op. cit., pp. 205–8. An annotated list of all translated Upanishads is found on pp. 39–56 of the same dissertation.

[30] For some references to information about extant Persian manuscripts see Dresden, "On the Genesis of Anquetil Duperron's Oupnek'hat," p. 37. The Persian text was first edited and printed in 1961: Muḥammad Riżā Jalālī Nā'īnī and Tārā Chand, *Upānishād / tarjumah-i Muḥammad Dārā Shikūh az matn-i Sānskrīt; bā muqaddimah u ḥavāshī u ta'līqāt u lughatnāmah u i'lām ba-sa'y u ihtimām-i Tārā Chand [va] Sayyid Muḥammad Riżā Jalālī Nā'īnī*.

Schopenhauer's Favorite Book

see that as many as nine or ten copies were brought to Europe and that two of these formed the basis of Anquetil's two-stage translation effort.

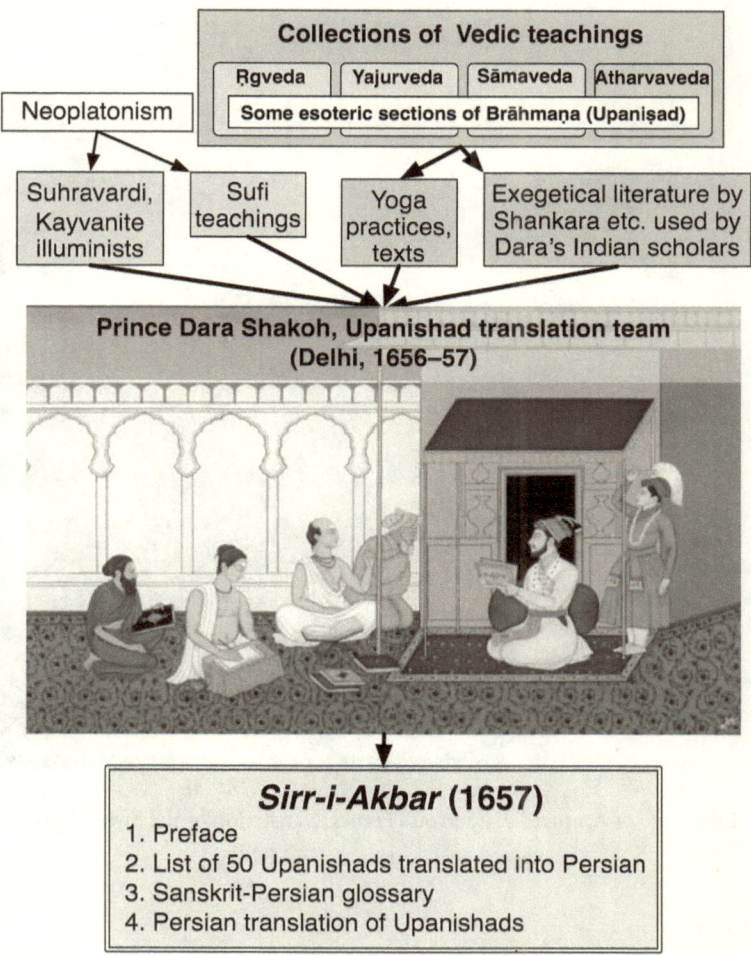

Appendix 1

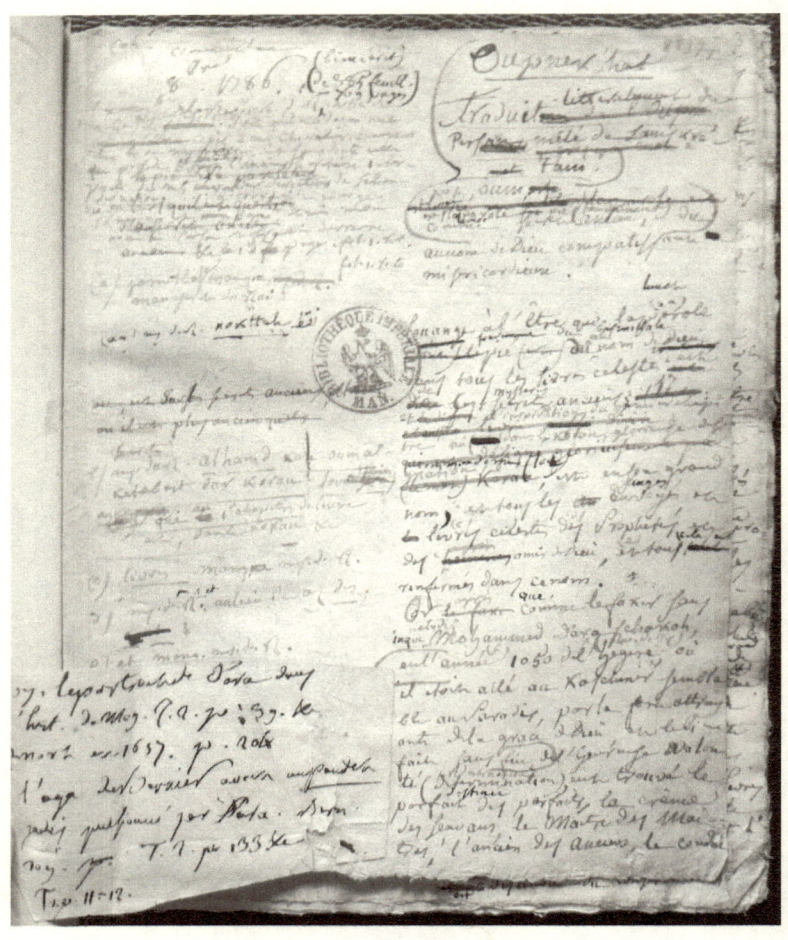

First page of Anquetil-Duperron's French translation of the *Sirr-i Akbar*
(Bibliothèque nationale, NAF 8857)

2. From Persian to French (1777–1787)

In December of 1775, Anquetil reveived from Le Gentil his first manuscript of Prince Dara's *Sirr-i akbar*.[31] The first part that he translated into French was Dara's preface. It contained the confirmation that the Upanishads represent the essence of the long-sought Vedas and are regarded as the world's most ancient record of divine revelation:[32]

Anquetil's draft French translation (NAF 8857)	English translation of Anquetil's French (App)	English translation by Hasrat from the Persian
Après la certitude de ces degrés (de cela), il a été scu que dans cette secte ancienne, avant tous les Livres celestes quatre Livres celestes qui (sont) le *Ragbeid* et le *Djedjèr Beid*, et le *Sam Beid*, et l'*Athrban Beid*, aux Prophetes de ce tems que le plus grand d'eux est *Brahma* qui est *Adam* choisi de Dieu, sur lequel soit le salut, avec tous les preceptes de conduite: et ce sens est paraissant de ces livres mêmes.	Due to the certitude of these degrees (of that), it was known that in this ancient sect, before all the heavenly books, four heavenly books which (are) the *Ragbeid*, and the *Djedjèr Beid*, and the *Sam Beid*, and the *Athrban Beid*, to the prophets of this time that the greatest of them is *Brahma* who is *Adam* chosen by God, may he be blessed, with all the precepts of conduct: and this meaning is apparent from these books themselves.	And after verifications of these circumstances, it appeared that among this most ancient people, of all their heavenly books, which are the *Ṛig Veda*, the *Yajur Veda*, the *Sama Veda*, and the *Atharva Veda*, together with a number of ordinances, descended upon the prophets of those times, the most ancient of whom was Brahman or Adam, on whom be the peace of God, this purport is manifest from these books.

---

[31] As mentioned above, Anquetil a few years later received a second Persian manuscript via Bernier.

[32] The French text of the following table stems from my transcription of the manuscript "Oupnek'hat, traduit littéralement du persan, mêlé du samskrétam." Bibliothèque Nationale, Nouvelles acquisitions françaises no. 8857, pp. 4–5. Hasrat's English translation is quoted from William Theodore de Bary, *Sources of Indian Tradition*. New York and London: Columbia Universiy Press, 1958, p. 440.

APPENDIX 1

Anquetil's draft French translation (NAF 8857)	English translation of Anquetil's French (App)	English translation by Hasrat from the Persian
Et l'essentiel (la partie la plus pure, la substance) de ces quatre livres, tous les secrets de conduite (religieuse) et la méditation sur l'unité pure y sont renfermés, et on le nomme Oupnek'hat.	And the essence (the purest part, the substance) of these four books, all the secrets of (religious) conduct and the meditation on the pure unity, are included in it, and one calls it Oupnek'hat.	And the *summum bonum* of these four books, which contain all the secrets of the Path and the contemplative exercises of pure monotheism, are called the *Upanekhats* [Upanishads].

Anquetil's draft translation of a section of Prince Dara's *Sirr-i Akbar* preface

This is a sample of Anquetil's overly literal translation style and quirky grammar that had already irked readers of his *Zend Avesta* translations published in 1771.[33] For nine years, from 1776 to 1787, Anquetil toiled with few reference materials to help him, and on March 18 of 1787 he finished his word-for-word translation of the entire *Sirr-i akbar* with a series of "OUM." On July 3 the revision was completed.[34] The result

[33] Abraham Hyacinthe Anquetil-Duperron, *Zend-Avesta, Ouvrage de Zoroastre*. Paris: Tilliard, 1771.

[34] "Oupnek'hat, traduit littéralement du persan, mêlé du samskrétam." Bibliothèque Nationale, Nouvelles acquisitions françaises no. 8857, p. 862. Apart from his two manuscripts of the *Sirr-i Akbar*, Anquetil communicated with Boughton-Rouse who also possessed two complete manuscripts. Taking into account that Halhed also had one complete and one incomplete copy, William Jones a complete one, Alexander Hamilton one, and Colebrooke two, we conclude that a total of at least ten manuscript copies made their way to Europe. The text can therefore hardly be called "rare." For Halhed see Rosane Rocher, "Nathaniel Brassey Halhed on the Upaniṣads (1787)." In *Annals of the Bhandarkar Oriental Research Institute, Diamond Jubilee Volume* (1977–78). Poona: Bhandarkar Oriental Research Institute, 1978, pp. 279–89. For Jones see *The Works of Sir William Jones*, edited by Anna Maria Jones. London: Robinson & Evans, 1799, vol. 6, p. 415. For Boughton-Rouse see Anquetil-Duperron, *Oupnek'hat* vol. 1, pp. vi–vii. For Colebrooke see Göbel-Gross, op. cit., p. 34. For Hamilton see his anonymous review: "Anquetil's Oupnek'hat." *The Edinburgh Review* 2, (1803), pp. 412–21 (here 415).

of this effort was a voluminous manuscript, today stored in the manuscript section of the Bibliothèque nationale in Paris. It is as difficult to decipher as it is interesting. It teems with corrections and notes made during translation, some of which Anquetil pasted onto its pages. Its study is of great help for explaining choices made by Anquetil in his later Latin translation and for understanding Anquetil's translation procedure and motivations. Furthermore, it aids our understanding of the translator's additions during the Latin translation (1787–1795) and annotation phases (1795–1801).

In this French translation one also finds several layers that are sometimes distinguishable by ink color (final revisions in darker ink) or placement. In some cases Anquetil pasted loose sheets or slips of paper with additional notes and reflections on the pages of his manuscript book. Some of these notes are helpful for the study of the translator's intentions, for example the following long remark on a piece of paper that Anquetil pasted onto page 230 of his manuscript.[35]

---

[35] For the background and significance of this note see App 2001 and chapter 7 of App 2010c.

APPENDIX 1

Les *Livres Zends* et l'*Oupnekhat* présentent les mêmes vérités que les ouvrages des Platoniciens; et peut-être ces philosophes les avaient-ils reçues des orientaux. Loin donc d'attaquer la religion, c'est la servir utilement que de publier ces monumens qui attestent le témoignage de deux grandes nations en faveur de l'existence, des attributs, des operations du premier Être, des devoirs de l'homme et de sa destination.	The [Zoroastrian] *Zend books* and the *Oupnekhat* present the same truths as the works of the Platonics; and possibly these philosophers have received them from the Orientals. Far from attacking the [Christian] religion, the publication of these sources is a useful service to her as it furnishes the testimony of two great nations in favor of the existence, attributes, and operations of the first Being, and of the duties and destiny of man.

In 1787, after completion of his French translation, Anquetil published under the title "Fond de la Théologie Indienne, tiré des *Beids*" (Basis of the Indian theology, taken from the Vedas) his French translation of four relatively short Upanishads in a geographical work.[36] He asked the geographers to pardon the interruption of the description of the course of the Ganges "as a favor to the Brahmins of Benares" of Dara's team who translated this Indian theology "word for word—these are the terms of the preface of the *Oupnekhat*—from Sanskrit into Persian."[37] This first ever publication of some Upanishads into a European language evoked a limited echo in France, but three years later a German translation of these four Upanishads was already published in Switzerland.[38]

---

[36] See the list in note 372, p. 209 above.

[37] Anquetil-Duperron, Abraham Hyacinthe. "Des Recherches historiques & géographiques sur l'Inde, & la Description du Cours du Gange & du Gagra, avec une très grande Carte." In *Description historique et géographique de "Inde,* ed by *Jean Bernoulli*. Berlin: Pierre Bourdeaux, 1787, pp. 297–344. The request for the reader's indulgence is on page 344 where Anquetil returns to the description of the Ganges.

[38] Anquetil-Duperron, Abraham Hyacinthe. "Vier Upnekhat, aus dem Samskrutamischen Buche die Upnekhat." In *Sammlung asiatischer Original-Schriften. Indische Schriften*, 269–315. Zürich: Ziegler und Söhne, 1791.

Frustrated by his inability to forge a rigidly literal French translation while maintaining an acceptable degree of intelligibility, Anquetil in 1787 decided to translate the entire Persian *Sirr-i akbar* into Latin.

3. FROM PERSIAN AND FRENCH TO LATIN (1787–1795)

The decision to publish the *Oupnek'hat* in Latin translation was severely criticized by the vast majority of readers because they rightly felt that Latin was in many respects less adequate than French or other modern European languages. However, the preparation of his draft French translation of four Upanishads for publication had convinced Anquetil that French was a poor choice for the world's oldest record of divine revelation. But the many Greek particles in Anquetil's *Oupnek'hat* and the tuned-up Latin grammar show that Latin was also a problematic choice. Anquetil decided to use whenever possible Sanskrit or Persian technical terms, thus forcing his readers to constantly refer to the included glossary. A slice of the first page of Anquetil's glossary will now serve as one more window into the innards of our textual fossil.

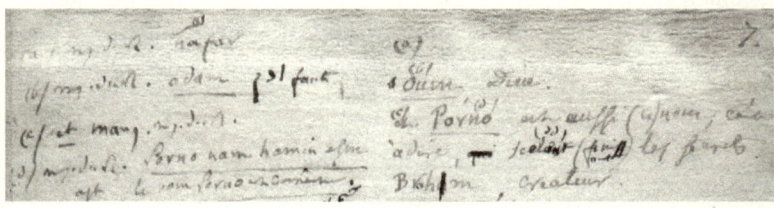

French *Oupnek'hat* draft translation, Bibliothèque nationale NAF 8857, p. 7

(a) *Oum*, Dieu
et *Porno* est aussi (ce) nom, c'est à dire, scelant (finissant) les secrets.
Brahm, createur

(a) *Oum*, God
and *Porno* is also (this) name, i.e., sealing (finishing) the secrets
Brahm, creator

APPENDIX 1

In Anquetil's published Latin version graced with Schopenhauer's notes, these lines appear as follows (*Oupnek'hat* vol. 1, p. 7):

(*Explicatio præcipuorum verborum samskreticorum, quæ in* OUPNEK'HAT *adhibentur.*)

O U M : ~~Deus~~ [1]. *Brahm, Omitto, p. 15, not 2.*
et *Pranou* etiam nomen ipsum hoc est, id est, obsignata (*clausa, finita*) faciens secreta. *II, p. 20. 1 § 2.*
Brahm : ~~creator.~~

— — — — — — —

1. De Guignes, *Mém. de l'Acad. des Insc. et bell. lett.* T. 26, p. 776, n. (h).

At one glance we can here observe five different strata: (1) the Sanskrit OUM that Dara translated as (2) "Allah" and that Anquetil rendered as (3) "Deus" (God). This definition is supported by (4) a footnote reference to an article of Joseph de Guignes about Buddhism.[39] Schopenhauer, the reader of this entry in the *Oupnek'hat*'s Sanskrit glossary, (5) crossed out "Deus" and redefined OUM as "Brahm" and "Omitto." He found his definition supported by Anquetil's second note on page 15, which he cross-referenced,[40] and fended off the pos-

---

[39] Joseph de Guignes, "Recherches sur les Philosophes appelés Samanéens." *Mémoires de Littérature tirés des Registres des l'Académie Royale des Inscriptions & Belles Lettres* vol. 26 Paris: Imprimerie royale, 1759, pp. 770–804; here referred to is note h on p. 776 which furnishes (wrong) information about Omitto (Amitabha Buddha). For the background of this definition see Urs App, "How Amida got into the Upanishads: An Orientalist's Nightmare." In *Essays on East Asian Religion and Culture*, ed. by Christian Wittern and Lishan Shi. Kyoto: Editorial Committee for the Festschrift in Honour of Nishiwaki Tsuneki, 2007, pp. 11–33, and chapters 6 & 7 here above.

[40] Anquetil's note explains the OUM at the beginning of the first Upanishad as Omitto (Amitabha Buddha, Japanese: Amida, Chinese: Amituo). See preceding note.

sibility of defining Brahm as creator God by striking out the definition of Brahm as "creator." This thin slice of our textual fossil thus shows

(1) the Sanskrit layer;
(2) Prince Dara's interpretation / translation layer;
(3) Anquetil's Latin translation layer;
(4) Anquetil's Orientalist annotation layer; and
(5) Schopenhauer's markup layer.

This tiny sample shows clearly how indispensable Schopenhauer's marked-up copy of the *Oupnek'hat* is for the understanding of his reception of Indian thought. No amount of study of Sanskrit texts, of Indian philosophy, of modern Upanishad translations, or even of an unmarked copy of the *Oupnek'hat* could produce the kind of insight into Schopenhauer's reception that can be drawn from this one line with its crossed out "God," his preferred definitions, and his cross-references. But there is an additional compelling reason for Schopenhauer researchers to use and study the *Oupnek'hat* rather than modern Upanishad translations: less than half of the text in Anquetil-Duperron's two *Oupnek'hat* volumes actually consists of Upanishad translation. Taking into account that (based on the Mundaka ratio) about one-sixth of the translation consists of extraneous commentary, we can surmise that only approximately forty percent of Anquetil's *Oupnek'hat* represent Upanishad translation. And these forty percent have been indelibly colored by Anquetil's approach and understanding that found expression in his voluminous notes, commentary, and explanatory essays. Instead of being viewed as unnecessary baggage unrelated to the translation, or even as a hindrance to its understanding, this larger half of the *Oupnek'hat* is just as much in need of study.

Appendix 1

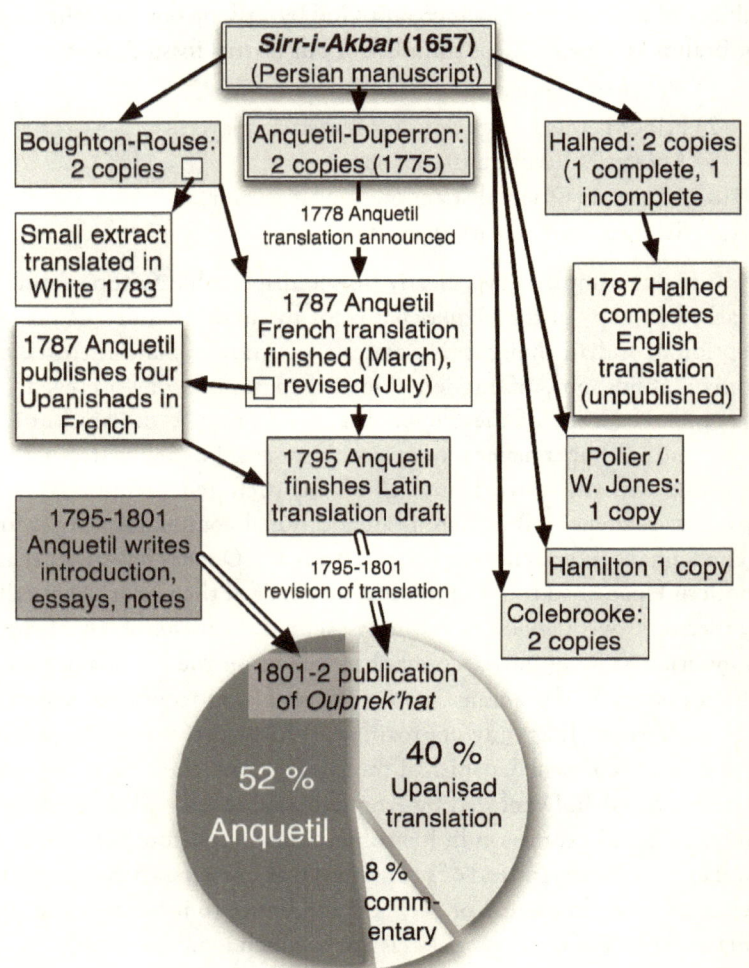

Sirr-i Akbar manuscripts in Europe; Anquetil's French and Latin translations; translation to commentary ratio in Anquetil's Latin *Oupnek'hat* (Urs App)

4. Anquetil's Essays and Annotation (1795–1801)

We now turn to the fourth layer, a glimpse of whose importance we already caught in Schopenhauer's reference to "Omitto": Anquetil's annotation and essays. At least in terms of volume, they are more important than the translation. According to Anquetil's note at the end of the *Oupnek'hat* translation part, he finished the draft of his Latin translation on October 9 of 1795, that is, after about eight years of labor during the turmoil of the French revolution. Rudiments of annotation—for the most part directly related to the text—are already found in the left column of Anquetil's manuscript French translation; but for the Latin translation we have no manuscript and cannot be sure when Anquetil wrote his notes. However, we can assume that the vast majority of non-translation material stems from the last years of the eighteenth century, i.e. from the period between the autumn of 1795 and the year 1800 when the extremely complicated process of bringing the huge, multilingual work to press had already begun.

The two volumes of Anquetil's printed *Oupnek'hat*, the first of which appeared in 1801 and the second in 1802, add up to almost 1800 pages. The second volume is slightly larger. If Anquetil had put all his notes and essays in one volume they would fill the entire second volume while the first would be filled with translation. But Anquetil chose a different architecture for his work. The 872-page first volume shows the following content distribution:

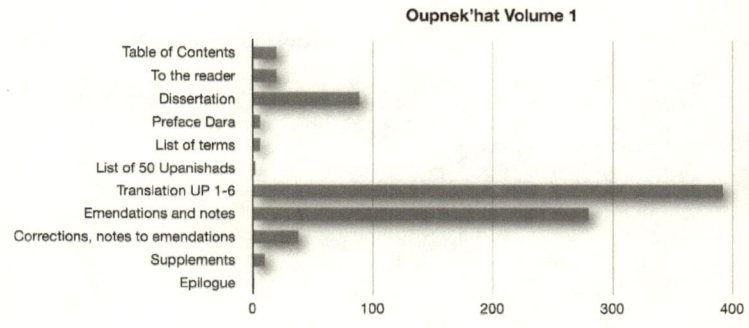

Appendix 1

Some of these sections merit particular attention. Anquetil's extensive *Table of Contents* is useful because it not only lists individual parts of the translated six Upanishads and of Anquetil's essays but also provides a very brief summary of their content. The table thus presents in a nutshell what Anquetil found noteworthy in each Upanishad subsection and each section of his introduction and notes (which sometimes fill several pages and are essays rather than notes). This table of contents informs us, for example, that the objective of the long introductory *Dissertatio* is to present occidental vestiges of the "Oriental system"— i.e., what Anquetil in the wake of Mosheim and Brucker held to be the world's oldest religion and philosophy (pp. 4–5; separate page numbering). We have already noted the importance of the glossary of Sanskrit terms, which is indispensable for understanding Anquetil's translation and overall approach as well as for the underlying vision of Prince Dara and his team. This glossary highlights the gulf separating ordinary translations of the Upanishads from this particular interpretative rendering. Anquetil's emendations, notes, and supplements (which surpass the volume of translated text) treat of so many topics that they cannot be listed here. In the table of contents, Anquetil mentions a total of 148 different themes that range from his reflections on emanation, Brahma, and maya to discussions of quietism, Rosicrucianism, cartography, and Kant's philosophy.

The second volume of the *Oupnek'hat*, published in 1802, has the following main sections:

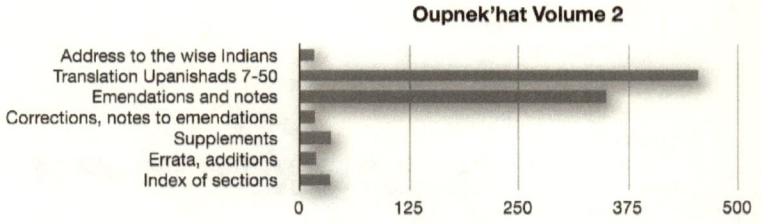

I will now briefly analyze two samples. The first stems from the Athrb sar (Atharvaśira) Upanishad.[41] All that Göbel-Gross has to say about this text is that it "forms part of the Atharvaveda" and was "completely translated" by Dara's team. But we now know that the Latin *Oupnek'hat* consists of far more than just translation from the Persian *Sirr-i akbar* and that the Persian and Sanskrit texts represent only two layers of the Latin *Oupnek'hat*. Here we are interested in Anquetil's annotation. In the case of this Upanishad I found that Anquetil's translation and his notes to the translation are dwarfed by the amount of his commentary that sometimes only tangentially relates to the Upanishads.

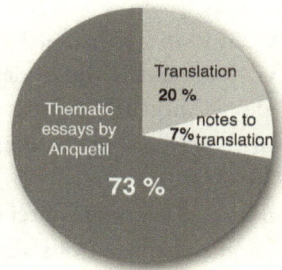

Ratio of translated Athrb sar Upanishad text to Anquetil annotation

Anquetil's translation of the Athrb sar Upanishad, inclusive of footnotes, occupies 15 pages of the *Oupnek'hat*, and Anquetil's endnotes keyed to the translation by page and line amount to 5 ½ pages. But between these clearly translation-related notes, Anquetil inserted no less than 53 pages of essays on various subjects: the colonial policy by the British and French, theism and atheism, a huge essay of 45 pages on the origin of evil (vol. 2, pp. 471–515), and four pages of reflections on the limits of reason and on faith. Anquetil's discussion of theodicy in

---

[41] In Anquetil's *Oupnek'hat* the *Athrb sar* is the ninth Upanishad.

APPENDIX 1

his notes to the Athrb sar Upanishad is thus three times as long as the entire translated Upanishad text!

In terms of the ratio of Anquetil's essays vs. translation and translation-related notes, the Athrb sar is an extreme case; but the content of the annotation of other Upanishads is not less colorful. For example, Anquetil's 13th Upanishad (the "Sataster" or Śvetāśvatara Upanishad; vol. 2, pp. 547–568) has only slightly more annotation than translation text (39 pages versus 34), but Anquetil's notes veer once more from ancient India to post-revolution France. He explains not only Brahm and Maya (pp. 548–551), the Sanskrit alphabet (551–2), his publication plans of dictionaries and grammars (553–4), and monism (555–7), but also discusses the imitation of Christ according to Thomas of Kempis (561), the fourteenth-century mysticism of Jean Gerson (562–3), the platonism in Cudworth and Plotinus (565–8), emanation (569, 584–5), and meditation (583–4). After this, the reader is hardly surprised to find, smack in the middle of Anquetil's commentary to the Athrb sar Upanishad, ten pages on the reform of the French education system after the revolution (571–581)!

Anquetil's annotation layer also features literature references, cross-references in notes or margins, explanations about textual variants of the two used manuscripts, explanations of words and terms in the footnotes, etc. In sum, this layer is not only dominant in terms of physical volume but also crucial for the reader's comprehension of the translation. Though the translation strives to convey the impression of an extremely literal and faithful translation of an ancient text, the annotation inserts it into the eighteenth-century theological and philosophical discussion and relates it to the thought of eminent Europeans like Plotinus, Malebranche, Bayle, Leibniz, and in an appendix even critically to Kant. Thus Anquetil created a bridge between what he regarded as the world's most ancient philosophy (that of the *Oupnek'hat*) and the endeavors and themes of modern philosophy that could not but attract the attention of someone like Schopenhauer.

5. Schopenhauer's Markup (1814–1860)

We now return to the fifth layer that has occupied us to some degree from the beginning: Schopenhauer's markup of his copy of the *Oupnek'hat*. The number of pages that show traces of Schopenhauer's interest is important in both volumes.

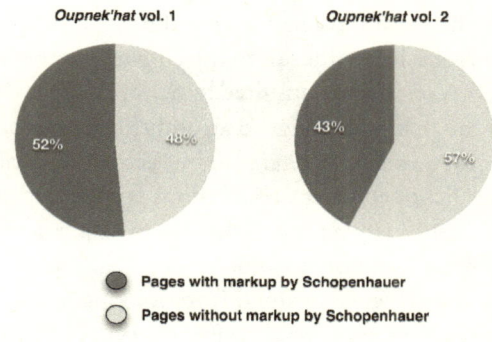

Ratio of *Oupnek'hat* pages with markup by Schopenhauer

Our initial sample, the beginning of the Isha Upanishad (p. 395 of the *Oupnek'hat*'s first volume), has shown that Schopenhauer's markup has several sub-layers. That specific page contained four: (A) notes at the top of the page in deep black ink; (B) notes in the margins in dark grey ink; (C) one note in the margin and an emphasis line in pencil; and (D) several emphasizing lines in deep black ink. The detailed study of these and of additional layers of Schopenhauer's markup in his favorite book is an urgent desideratum. This effort will hopefully include, apart from the high-resolution digitalization of the work, the analysis of different inks, handwriting styles, etc., and the digital markup of all traces of Schopenhauer's interest.

The layers we distinguished in our initial sample relate to physical characteristics. But the same data can be categorized in multiple ways.

Appendix 1

For example, the ink lines on page 395 are related to Schopenhauer's appreciation of the printed text of the *Oupnek'hat*, and double lines indicate that he found some of this text more interesting than what is marked with a single line. The above-mentioned remark in pencil "Ding an sich u. Erscheinung" (thing-in-itself and representation) is also related to Schopenhauer's appreciation of the *Oupnek'hat* text but belongs to a different category since it spells out how Schopenhauer understood it. The three and a half lines at the top of the page that were transcribed by Hübscher point not to the *Oupnek'hat* text but rather to three alternative translations consulted by Schopenhauer. The dark grey ink writing in the margin belongs to an additional category because it furnishes not just a literature reference but actual quotations from an external source. Schopenhauer's conclusions from comparisons of the *Oupnek'hat* with alternative translations (an example of which we saw on p. 5 above) form one more category.

Apart from the categories gained from looking at our initial sample, we have already noted several additional types of Schopenhauer's markup: text that is struck through (like "Deus" and "Gabriel"), text that is identified as commentary ("Gloße"), text that is identified as addition ("additamentum imprudentissimi librarii Islamitici"), cross-references ("p. 15, not. 2"), definitions ("Brahm. Omitto"), and critique. Further types include the philosopher's indexes of technical terms, reminders for research, literature references, cross-references, corrections of Latin style, corrections on the basis of other authors or translations, summaries of other publications (for example of Colebrooke's terminology on the back page of vol. 1 of the *Oupnek'hat*), reflections not directly related to the text, doubts (often in form of question marks), and tentative interpretations.

Schopenhauer's references to and quotations from literature show how eager he was to compare the *Oupnek'hat* to other translations that gradually appeared. This points to the role of evolving orientalism in Schopenhauer's *Oupnek'hat* reception and helps establishing a degree of chronological stratification of Schopenhauer's markup.

Schopenhauer's handwritten references to (or quotations from) other translations in the *Oupnek'hat* show that he made use of a surprisingly broad array of sources.

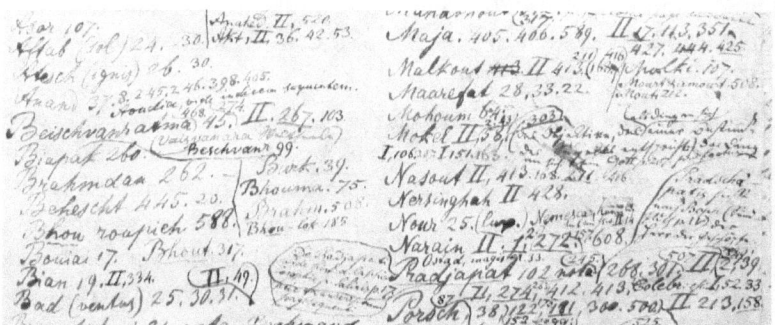

Part of Schopenhauer's index to the *Oupnek'hat* at the back of volume 1

INITIATIONS

After two centuries of neglect, ostracism, obfuscation, and derision, Anquetil-Duperron's *Oupnek'hat* as well as the basis for its translation part, Prince Dara's *Sirr-i akbar*, are beginning to reemerge as works that merit intensive study in their own right. They form crucial junctions in several encounters between East and West. Unlike earlier encounters whose study is difficult or impossible because of the lack of sources, Schopenhauer's discovery of the Upanishads is documented to an extraordinary degree. The most precious source, of course, is the very book Schopenhauer used to read in the evening, that he defended so ardently against other translations purchased at great expense, and that he called the solace of his life and death. The study of its content, of its different strata, and of Schopenhauer's markup will help us understand

Appendix 1

how Schopenhauer arrived at this conviction and how he came to name the Upanishads even before Kant and Plato among the three most important influences on the genesis of his metaphysics of will. Once this *secretum tegendum* really turns into a *secretum legendum*, we might also understand what both Dara and Anquetil meant by "secret" and why Schopenhauer wrote in the preface of the first edition of *Die Welt als Wille und Vorstellung*:

> But if the reader has enjoyed the blessing of the *Vedas*, access to which through the Upanishads to my mind constitutes the greatest advance of our still young century over previous ones (and I expect the influence of Sanskrit literature to have as profound an effect as the revival of Greek literature in the fourteenth century)—if the reader, I say, has already received initiation into ancient Indian wisdom and has been receptive to it: then he will be best prepared to hear what I have to say to him. Then it [the Indian Wisdom as presented in the Upanishads, U.A.] will not strike him, as it strikes many others, as foreign or even inimical, for would it not sound too conceited, I would even like to claim that each of the individual and disconnected utterances that form the Upanishads could be deduced as a consequence from the thoughts I am about to communicate, though conversely my thoughts are certainly not already contained there.[42]

---

[42] » Ist er aber gar noch der Wohlthat der *Veda's* theilhaft geworden, deren uns durch die Upanischaden eröfneter Zugang, in meinen Augen, der größte Vorzug ist, den dieses noch junge Jahrhundert vor den früheren aufzuweisen hat, indem ich vermuthe, daß der Einfluß der Samskrit-Litteratur nicht weniger tief eingreifen wird, als im 14. Jahrhundert die Wiederbelebung der Griechischen: hat also, sage ich, der Leser auch schon die Weihe uralter Indischer Weisheit empfangen und empfänglich aufgenommen; dann ist er auf das allerbeste bereitet zu hören, was ich ihm vorzutragen habe. Ihn wird es dann nicht, wie manchen Andern fremd, ja feindlich ansprechen; da ich, wenn es nicht zu stolz klänge, behaupten möchte, daß jeder von den einzelnen und abgerissenen Aussprüchen, welche die Upanischaden ausmachen, sich als Folgesatz aus dem von mir mitzutheilenden Gedanken ableiten ließe, obgleich keineswegs auch umgekehrt dieser schon dort zu finden ist.« Arthur Scho-

In this important paragraph, Schopenhauer was not writing about "Indian wisdom," the "Vedas," and "the Upanishads" *as we know them* or would like to see them today, but rather the Upanishads *as he knew them*. In other words, he referred to the very Latin *Oupnek'hat* that he so consistently and ardently defended against all translations from the Sanskrit and that he so unwaveringly regarded, from his prime to his grave, as the only genuine expression of "age-old Indian wisdom." Thus Schopenhauer's double claim in the preface of his main work was that the reader *of the Oupnek'hat* would be well prepared to understand his philosophy, and that Schopenhauer's philosophy would in turn provide the key to the *secretum tegendum* of India: its ancient wisdom *as presented in the Oupnek'hat*. In order to understand what Schopenhauer meant by this, more layers will need to be added to the history of his favorite book by future students who download its high-quality scanned version with all of Schopenhauer's notes and marks, study its pages on screen or print them out, gain initiation to its secrets, and contribute to its continuing history by adding ever more layers: their own annotation.

---

penhauer, *Die Welt als Wille und Vorstellung*. Leipzig: F. A. Brockhaus, 1819, pp. XII–XIII.

Appendix 2

Research Perspectives

When Schopenhauer announced his main work to publisher Brockhaus in March of 1818, he wrote that it contains "a supremely coherent train of thought that had hitherto never entered any man's mind"[1] and explained:

> The essence of this train of thought already existed four years ago in my head; but in order to develop it and make it completely clear to myself through countless essays and studies I needed no less than four full years, during which I occupied myself exclusively with this and with directly related studies of other works.[2]

He explained that he had planned to travel to Italy in 1816 but "postponed it for two years because of this work." In the spring of 1817 he finally began to "formulate the entirety in sequence in order to make it comprehensible for others."[3] According to Schopenhauer's own presentation, which we saw confirmed by the notes in his Manuscript Remains, the year 1814 was thus the year of birth of this "train of thought" whose presentation in his main work he already in March of 1818 was to call the fruit of his life. On the basis of these notes we can divide the genesis of his metaphysics of will roughly into three major phases: a

---

[1] »eine im höchsten Grad zusammenhangende Gedankenreihe, die bisher noch nie in irgend eines Menschen Kopf gekommen« (Briefe 29).

[2] »Jene Gedankenreihe war, dem Wesentlichen nach, schon vor 4 Jahren in meinem Kopfe vorhanden: aber um sie zu entwickeln und sie durch unzählige Aufsätze und Studien mir selber vollkommen deutlich zu machen, bedurfte es ganzer 4 Jahre, in welchen ich mich ausschließlich damit und mit den dazu gehörigen Studien fremder Werke beschäftigt habe.« (Briefe 29)

[3] »das Ganze in zusammenhangendem Vortrag für Andre faßlich zu machen« (Briefe 29–30).

Appendix 2

birth phase (spring 1814 in Weimar to late summer 1814 in Dresden); an *elaboration phase* (late 1814 to late 1816); and a *presentation phase* (1817–1818) issuing in his main work published in December of 1818 (see the table on p. 21).

If one accepts on the basis of the facts and arguments first presented in this book that the *Oupnek'hat* was a major inspiration of his conception of will, the illusory nature of multiplicity (*maya*), the importance of the body (the 'city of Brahm' *Brahmapura*) as access point, and the notion of overcoming of will (*fanā*), then various new perspectives open up. The first concerns the evaluation of previous attempts at presentation that stress the "processual" character of Schopenhauer's philosophy. They rely almost without exception on Schopenhauers main work, *The World as Will and Representation*, that is, the outcome of the *presentation phase* of 1817 and 1818 that has so far received very little scholarly attention. The "Copernican revolving turnabout" (kopernikanische Drehwenden) evoked by Spierling and the "crises" stressed by Malter all concern Schopenhauer's systematic presentation of 1818 and not necessarily the "train of thought" that Schopenhauer, according to his own account, had in his head in 1814 and that he then for several years elaborated and "clarified to himself." Whatever one may think about the logical deductions and connections between parts of Schopenhauer's system that were proposed by Spierling, Malter, or Atwell: they are all related to the final product of this drawn-out process that emerged in 1817 and 1818 when Schopenhauer sought to "formulate the whole thing in sequence to make it understandable for others."

However, the historical process of system genesis seems to have gone through rather different "revolutions" and "crises" than the final product of 1818 would have us think. Once one avoids seeing the genesis of Schopenhauer's metaphysics of will through the rear mirror of his completed work and approaches this process not by logical deduction but by historical induction, then a number of important questions arise. Here I shall mention only a few examples. Could various "antinomies," "vicious circles," and "contradictions" that Schopenhauer has been accused of, be due to hitherto neglected influences such as the *Oupnek'hat* and structural problems or apparent fissures caused by them? Could it be possible that Schopenhauer's idiosyncratic understanding of Kant's "thing in itself" (Ding an sich) was influenced by the monistic teaching of the *Oupnek'hat*? Conversely, was Schopenhauer's characteristic interpretation of the *principium individuationis*, inspired as it was by the *Oupnek'hat*'s concept of *maya*, a product of his Kantian, transcendental-idealistic reading of the Latin Upanishads? Is there a connection between Schopenhauer's much-criticized "conclusion by analogy"—that man's inner experience of will is a valid doorway to the essence of all things—and the teachings of the *Oupnek'hat* and *Bhagavad Gita*? Could the problematic ambiguity of Schopenhauer's concept of knowledge (Erkenntnis) be a result of the conflation of Kantian and Platonic elements with the doctrine of the Upanishads and of prince Dara? To which degree did the *Oupnek'hat* and the neoplatonic doctrine of hypostases (along with Plato's doctrine of ideas, Spinoza's modifications, and Blumenbach's view of nature) influence Schopenhauer's conception of the objectification of will and of its levels? Could Schelling's most crucial influence consist in his combination of neoplatonic and mystical elements? Is the difficulty to understand Schopenhauer's theory of salvation (Atwell 1995:160) somehow linked to his dependence on the *Oupnek'hat* and on Prince Dara's conception of askesis and self-abolition (*fanā*)? What role was played in this respect by the discrepancy of the goals of Dara (abolition of ego and awakening to the fundamentally good, divine unity) and of Schopenhauer (insight into the nature of blind, self-mangling will, and overcoming of will)?

The phases of system formation were preceded, as described in the first chapters of this book, by an important period. Hans Zint (1921 & 1954) highlighted the early and dominant experience of a 'better consciousness' which transported young Schopenhauer in a world without subject and object. This opposition between an extraordinary, selfless contemplative knowing and an ordinary one that is driven by self-interest appears to be a basic engine of Schopenhauer's thinking.

Appendix 2

The overall development process, if one chooses to simplify it, appears to be the following. In the beginning there was, as Schopenhauer did not tire to repeat, experience (Erfahrung). The scarce notes and letters of Schopenhauer's youth do not shed much light on this, but they indicate that the young man in nature and art experienced states of consciousness that made him feel "like having entered another world." In his main work he described this kind of experience in various ways, for example:

> That liberation of knowing lifts us out of everything to such a degree, and in such a total manner, as sleep and dream: happiness and unhappiness have vanished: we are no longer the individual, it is forgotten.[4]

This particular state of mind was praised, among others, by Wackenroder (who experienced music in similar depth as Schopenhauer) and by Zacharias Werner as "moments of bliss" (Augenblicke der Weihe). This might form the backdrop of the young man's interest in mystics who confirmed for him the existence and potential permanence of what he was later to call the 'better consciousness.' Already in 1811, Schopenhauer knew at least Jacob Böhme's *Mysterium magnum* so well that he was able to immediately identify specific doctrines of Böhme adopted in Schelling's essay on freedom (HN2:314). But neither Wackenroder and Werner nor Jacob Böhme (who had inspired both of them) furnished cogent explanations for this better consciousness.

Schopenhauer's early acquaintance with the thought and ideals of European mystics appears to be connected with his earliest "philosophy" as described by Wieland's niece in the spring of 1811. According to her, Schopenhauer was already at that early point "filled with philosophical ideas" and "totally devoted to a philosophy" that battles

---

[4] »Jenes Freiwerden der Erkenntniß hebt uns aus dem Allen eben so sehr und ganz heraus, wie der Schlaf und der Traum: Glück und Unglück sind verschwunden: wir sind nicht mehr das Individuum, es ist vergessen« (W1, SW2.233; Z1:254).

against "all inclination, desire, and passion"[5] and appears to be inspired by mysticism and asceticism. This tendency was thus present long before Schopenhauer got acquainted with Upanishadic thought and also long before he read texts attributed to the German mystic Tauler.[6] The study of early influences by Western mystics, though hitherto neglected in favor of philosophical influences, is certainly of great interest.[7]

In 1811, when he was thus already "totally devoted to a philosophy," twenty-two year old Schopenhauer began to study this subject at the university of Göttingen. During his student years in Göttingen and later in Berlin he sought explanations especially in the 'divine' Plato, Schelling, Fichte, and the 'astonishing' Kant. The philosophy of a double consciousness, which is often regarded as Schopenhauers earliest philosophy, was an early (and still not very systematic) explanation model inspired by Plato, Schelling, and Fichte, with Böhme, Plotinus, Neoplatonism, and French enlightenment atheism in the background. Schopenhauer's dissertation, which described under Kantian influence the basic laws of 'empirical consciousness,' was already an attempt at systematic explanation of 'empirical' subject-object based consciousness set on the barely visible but essential backdrop of Schopenhauer's conception of 'better consciousness.' But the young philosopher wanted to find a comprehensive explanation addressing both the blissful instants

---

[5] See pp. 57–58 above.

[6] Robert Heimann (2013) argues in his dissertation that Schopenhauer read Pseudo-Taulerian literature as early as 1813 and that the formation of his system was decisively influenced by such study. While it is possible that Schopenhauer began to study such texts early on, Schopenhauer's first reference in his Manuscript Remains dates from 1817 and Heimann has to admit (p. 247) that "the question why Schopenhauer omitted this source cannot be answered." By contrast, Schopenhauer made from 1814 onward copious notes of his readings of Orient-related sources, mentioned the *Oupnek'hat* prominently in both unpublished and published writings, and as early as 1816 named the Upanishads as the first of three major influences on the genesis of his system.

[7] Of particular interest in this respect are the recent books by Lemanski (2009 & 2011) and Heimann (2013).

of 'better' consciousness that he saw confirmed by mystics and saints, and the 'empirical' consciousness at the opposite pole. This had to be an explanation that—unlike those proposed by Schelling and Fichte—does not transgress the limits of rationality and thus of philosophy.

It was this kind of explanation that Schopenhauer was after when he discovered in the spring of 1814 the *Latin Upanishads*. This encounter happened at a time when Schopenhauer, in part through his contact with Goethe, had already pondered much about art and genius. The book-worm was already familiar with much of Europe's best literature, and his frequent theatre and concert visits had already produced many of the insights that he was to present in the third book of his main work. One can say that at the time of Schopenhauer's discovery of the Upanishads the basis for the third book (Plato's doctrine of ideas, Kant's aesthetics, and a classical/romantic vision of art) was already more or less established. But the magic word that would serve as "open Sesame" to his system and furnish the ultimate basis for his theory of cognition and of art was still missing. As the study of de Cian (2002) shows, Schopenhauer's concept of will at the end of 1813 was still fundamentally different from that of the following summer. As described in the body of our book, it was in the supposedly oldest book of the world, the *Oupnek'hat*, that the philosopher in the spring of 1814 found not only a convincingly formulated doctrine of all-oneness but also a concept of will of cosmic dimensions. Of importance was not only that this will, though appearing as multiplicity (*maya*), forms the singular and eternal essence of everything, but also that, based on Prince Dara's Sufi perspective, its overcoming is consistently advocated as the way to salvation. The *Oupnek'hat* asserted again and again that abolition of will is the only way to break through the illusion of maya and to realize all-oneness, which is how all desire vanishes in one fell swoop. Schopenhauer thus found in the *Oupnek'hat* not only the all-embracing will as foundation of his 'empirical' and 'better' consciousness (affirmation and negation of will identified as the ground of suffering and its annihilation) but also the motto for his ethics of compassion: *tat twam asi*, "thou art that."

The clarification of the implications of Schopenhauer's discovery of will extended, as we saw, from 1814 to the end of 1816. This phase was followed by two years during which Schopenhauer systematized and formulated his insights sequentially in the form of a theory of cognition, a metaphysics of nature, an aesthetic theory, and a system of ethics. These became the four books of his main work.

The genesis of Schopenhauer's system must therefore not be seen in the deformed mirror of his major work as a linear, logical process corresponding exactly to the structure of *The World as Will and Representation*. The influences that can be historically identified are often surprisingly complex, as the example of Neoplatonism shows. It reached Schopenhauer in three ways. The first and most obvious consists in the neoplatonic component of German idealism which in recent years became progressively clearer (Beierwaltes 2004). Its Schellingian strand exerted considerable influence not only on Schopenhauer but also on other German readers of the *Oupnek'hat* such as Görres, Kanne, and Richard Wagner's uncle Adolph Wagner. This path of influence also involved the study of works by Plotinus in the original Greek or in German translation. The second route of neoplatonic influence was linked to Christian mysticism. Writings of authors such as Pseudo-Dionysius, Scotus Eriugena, Nicolaus of Cusa and of course also Meister Eckhart and Jakob Böhme were all influenced in different ways by Neoplatonism (Halfwassen 2004). In the first decade of the 19th century this influence can be seen in Germans such as Schelling, Franz Baader, Zacharias Werner and also in Werner's young friend Schopenhauer. But the third route of influence was far less apparent: the neoplatonic component of the Sufi tradition which had also left its imprint on Prince Dara's works including his interpretation of the Indian Upanishads.

As mentioned in the body of our book, Oriental influences on Schopenhauer have hitherto been portrayed in so distorted a manner that a discussion of earlier views risks degenerating into a long-winded parade of contradictions and absurdities.[8] The sobering main conclusion is that apart from Piantelli (1986) not a single author has hitherto studied the *Oupnek'hat* and made use of the Latin text read by Schopenhauer.[9] What would one say if a specialist of German mysticism asserted that, instead of studying Meister Eckhart's Bible commentaries in their own right, it is sufficient to read the Bible in modern translation, and if the entire guild of scholars followed his advice? In fact Schopenhauer's favorite book had an even more amazing fate. Arthur Hübscher, who contributed much to Schopenhauer studies, documented almost every comma that Schopenhauer scribbled into Kant's works—but he mentioned just two of Schopenhauer's countless handwritten remarks

---

[8] To mention but a few typical views: Dutt Shastri (1938:74–6) celebrates Schopenhauer as an inspired validator of Indian truths and Zimmer (1938:267) claims that his thinking "emerged as a primal realisation from his own chest without the need of any cue from India." Gestering (1995:53) portrays the "Indian roots of Schopenhauer's pessimistic metaphysics" as "peculiar byproducts" (»originelle Nebengebilde«) and as "air-roots" (»Luftwurzeln«) which, "while assisting in fortifying his thought structure from the outside, have no fundamental causative function and are entirely secondary developments (»sein Gedankengebilde von außen zwar festigen helfen, jedoch keine ursächlich fundamentale Funktion haben, sich vielmehr ganz sekundär entwickeln«). Schopenhauer's favorite book, the *Oupnek'hat*, is on one hand called "the most significant book" of Schopenhauer's entire life (Scholz 1996:21) and a "major influence" on his philosophy (Berger 2000:84); but on the other hand it is claimed (Gestering 1995:53) without any basis that Schopenhauer had himself affirmed "that he did not adopt anything fundamental from the Upanishads" (»daß er nichts Grundlegendes von den Upanischaden übernommen habe«).

[9] Even though in several recent books the importance of the *Oupnek'hat* is clearly recognized (Scholz 1996:21, Meyer 1994:115, Cross 2013:4), neither these authors nor Vecchiotti (1969) and Berger (2000, 2004) made use of it, not to speak of Schopenhauer's richly marked-up copy. Instead they invariably refer to sources that at the time of the formation of Schopenhauer's philosophy (or even in his lifetime) were not yet available—which is why such publications generally offer no answer to questions of influence and pertain to the (sometimes very interesting) sphere of comparative philosophy where anything can be compared to anything.

Research Perspectives

in the *Oupnek'hat* (HN5:338)[10] and asserted against all evidence that the influence of this work had begun late: "Later even than the Upanishads, Buddhism appeared to him, once more through publications of third and fourth hand."[11] From this point of view Meister Eckhart's discourses on biblical themes would of course also be "publications of third and fourth hand," relying as they do not on Hebrew and Greek texts but Latin translations. It is obvious that Bible interpretations by Eckhart, Jakob Böhme, or Madame Guyon do not present the "genuine" Bible in "pure" form; but who would on this basis jump to the conclusion that they are therefore worthless and should not be allowed to exert any influence? In Eckhart's sermons, writings by other Christian mystics, and Prince Dara's *Oupnek'hat*, the interpretation of a fundamental sacred text plays an extremely important role, and a fundamentalist fixation on the "genuine" Bible or Upanishads cannot but hinder their understanding. In brief, Schopenhauer's favorite book must find less prejudiced readers who take it seriously in its own right, and I hope that the present book helps opening the door to a thorough investigation of this important source and its multifaceted role not only with respect to Schopenhauer but also to the broader realm of religious and philosophical East-West encounters.

The birth process of Schopenhauer's philosophy described in the body of this book also shows that not a theory of cognition adopted from Kant played the decisive role, as several recent authors claimed, but rather Schopenhauer's discovery of his characteristic conception of will. Deeply and causally connected with this discovery was from the beginning the doctrine of salvation inspired by the *Oupnek'hat*. We have also seen that Schopenhauer's characteristic conception of will— though the terrain was naturally also prepared by reflections such as those of Schelling, Fichte, and Böhme— was born exactly at the time

---

[10] See Appendix 1 here above.

[11] »Später noch als die Upanischaden tritt der Buddhismus an ihn heran, wieder in Veröffentlichungen aus dritter und vierter Hand« (Hübscher 1973:50).

Appendix 2

when he first studied the *Oupnek'hat*, and that the profound influence of this work is the likely reason why Schopenhauer as early as 1816 listed the Upanishads as the first of three major influences on the genesis of his system.

In the vast majority of studies, Kant and Plato figure as decisive influences on the birth of Schopenhauer's metaphysics of will, whereas the Upanishads merely serve as confirmation of earlier insights.[12] As mentioned above, the recent book *Schopenhauer's Encounter with Indian Thought* by Stephen Cross (2013) also subscribes to this "confirmation" scenario. Though it is (in spite of its title) not a study of *Schopenhauer's* encounter with Indian thought but rather the author's comparison of Schopenhauers philosophy and Indian thought as it is known *today*, and though the author states that questions of Indian influence on Schopenhauer must await the "thorough study of his personal copy of the *Oupnek'hat*" (Cross 2013:4), the question of influence constantly and inevitably raises its head. Cross treads the "confirmation" line and states (italics are his):

> While there is little doubt that he [Schopenhauer] was influenced by Indian ideas—although to what extent is at present unclear—this is really to miss the main point. For the Upaniṣadic thought contained in Anquetil's book was important to him primarily because it *confirmed* conclusions regarding the nature of the empirical world that he, following the lead of Kant, had already arrived at in his first published work, *The Fourfold Root of the Principle of Sufficient Reason*. To him the *Oupnek'hat* came not so much as a revelation of ideas that were new as an almost miraculous confirmation, from a remote time and place, to his own insights. To a considerable degree, it was not new knowledge that the *Oupnek'hat* brought to Schopenhauer but confirmation that he was on the right path, the path of ancient and universal truth. (Cross 2013:26–27)

---

[12] See some examples on p. 203 here above.

Research Perspectives

According to Cross there is "little reason to doubt" that Schopenhauer's concept of will grew out of "Kant's teaching of the empirical and intelligible characters" (p. 3). Yet in his conclusions he mentions a most striking similarity between the Indian concept of *śakti* (usually translated as "energy" or "power") and Schopenhauer's "will" and argues that "by a curious chance, the concept of *śakti* may have played a part in the genesis of the doctrine of the will" (p. 177). The "curious chance" refers to Prince Dara's understanding of *maya = ishq* as described by Piantelli which—as explained in our Chapters 6 and 7—is a central feature of the *Oupnek'hat* and a key factor in the genesis of Schopenhauer's conception of will.

Based on the evidence presented in the body of our book, the role of the *Oupnek'hat* appears in a new light: Schopenhauer found the key to his system through the Latin *Oupnek'hat*—though without Kant and Plato (and in addition Schelling, German mystics and probably also Spinoza and Bruno) he would have never understood Anquetil's work the way he did. All of these rays had to simultaneously converge in one man's mind, and that is what happened in 1814. Yet only a single work became Schopenhauer's favorite book: the *Oupnek'hat*.

Moreover, it is frequently asserted that Schopenhauer only used Indian thought as a means of self-presentation or self-glorification. It has become commonplace to air regrets that Schopenhauer's main inspiration of Indian origin was, as it were, poisoned: instead of the "genuine" Sanskrit Upanishads he regrettably used a corrupt translation from Persian. The adduced example of the Eckhart specialist demonstrates the absurdity of such views. As is evident from Schopenhauer's reflections on Greek tragedy, the doctrine of transmigration and many other topics, he showed extraordinary ability in peeling the kernel out of conglomerates of ideas. His penetrating reading of the exceedingly complex Indo-Persian-Latin Upanishads show this brilliantly. This work contained not only excellent presentations of Indian wisdom (for example regarding the insight into the nature of the world through introspection) but also of the essence of Sufi mysticism: the abolition of selfhood (*fanā*) as way to the realization of the true divine essence and unity of everything. The "abandonment of 'I' and 'mine,'" the longed-for ideal of Schopenhauer since his youth, appeared in the *Oupnek'hat* as *nolle* (not-willing) in opposition to *volle* (willing). Was it not logical for an atheist such as Schopenhauer, who understood the "Brahm" of the *Oupnek'hat* as "will," to interpret Dara's and Anquetil's *amor* not as the loving will of a creator God but rather as a blind cosmic energy or urge? As soon as one tries to read the *Oupnek'hat* with Schopenhauer's eyes and studies what he underlined, struck out, and wrote in the margins, his interpretation of the text appears not arbitrary but rather coherent and well-founded. This was *his* interpretation of *Anquetil*'s presentation of *Dara*'s interpretation, and Dara's interpretation was colored by *Vedantic* commentaries and his *Sufi* perspective on texts that are "original" in the sense that they are novel interpretations of age-old Vedic rituals. And for conservative Vedic priests performing rituals and sacrifices in ancient India, the interpretations forming the "original" text of the Upanishads must have seemed not just beside the point but heretical—yet this did not prevent Shankara, Prince Dara, Majer, or Paul Deussen from finding them extremely interesting and profound.

In view of Prince Dara's particular interpretation it was to be expected that Schopenhauer would later criticize other translations and divergent interpretations of the Upanishads. Indeed, until his death in 1860 he stubbornly insisted that only the *Oupnek'hat* contains the pure and genuine wisdom of India. He invested much time and money in India-related books, and it is likely that the numerous alternative Upanishad translations scribbled in the margins of his *Oupnek'hat* volumes are a symptom of gnawing doubts about the reliability of the source that had inspired him so decisively in his youth. Schopenhauer's collection of orientalia, incompletely catalogued by Hübscher (HN5:319–352), illustrates his extraordinary interest in oriental philosophies and religions. Of course the translations of Upanishads from Sanskrit that he studied in the course of four decades failed to pass his *Oupnek'hat* litmus test. He suspected that Sanskrit scholars did not understand their texts any better than high school boys in our schools their Greek texts[13] and complained that their translations barely contain the contours of the "Ur-text's" thought: "Everything is modern, vacuous, bland, flat, destitute of meaning, and occidental: it is europeanized, anglicized, frenchified, or even (which is worst) germanically obfuscated and fogged—that is, it furnishes instead of a clear and well-defined meaning mere words, but ample ones."[14] Even though Schopenhauer was not aware of Prince Dara's Sufi connections, he later on became an avid reader of Sufi texts and also appreciated—as is evident from numerous notes in his *Oupnek'hat* copy and other books in his library—presentations of the doctrines of Vedanta. If one takes into account the idealistic doctrines of Buddhism which influenced vedantic doctrines such as its concept of *maya*, it becomes clear that Schopenhauer—in spite of all problems of communication, interpretation, and understanding—showed pronounced interest precisely in those philosophical trends that had, directly or indirectly, shaped Prince Dara's interpretation of the Upanishads: Sufism, Vedanta, and Buddhism.

With regard to the influence of *Buddhism* we saw that, at the time of the birth of Schopenhauer's metaphysics of will, only articles contained in Klaproth's *Asiatisches Magazin* (borrowed by Schopenhauer in December of 1813) could play a role.[15] In the period between 1814 and 1815 direct Buddhist influence is therefore of minor importance. However, indirect influences were present since Buddhist idealism had substantially influenced Vedanta and had through this back door

---

[13] »so beschleicht mich der Verdacht, daß unsre Sanskritgelehrten ihre Texte nicht sehr viel besser verstehn mögen, als etwan die Sekundaner unserer Schulen die griechischen« (P2 §184; SW5.421; Z10.436).

[14] »Alles ist modern, leer, fade, flach, sinnarm und occidentalisch: es ist europäisirt, anglisirt, französirt, oder gar (was das Aergste) deutsch verschwebelt und vernebelt, d. h. statt eines klaren, bestimmten Sinnes bloße, aber recht breite Worte liefernd« (P2 §184; SW5.422; Z10.437).

[15] See App 1998a. For the history and role of the *Forty-Two Sections Sutra* in early European Orientalism see Chapter 4 of App 2010c; for its versions and textual history in China in particular pp. 223–231.

also found its way into the *Oupnek'hat*. Starting in November of 1815, Schopenhauer studied the first ten volumes of *Asiatick Researches* where he found bits and pieces of information about the huge religion whose ideal *nirvana* consists in the extinction of suffering.[16] From the mid-1820s onward Schopenhauer regarded Buddhism as a striking confirmation of his philosophy, but the concrete influence of specific sources studied by Schopenhauer on his thought has so far received insufficient attention by scholars familiar with the history of 18th- and 19th-century orientalism.[17]

In conclusion I would like to briefly discuss an old chestnut of Schopenhauer critique: the philosopher's *pessimism* and its connection with Buddhism. A recent book that attempts to trace Schopenhauer's "odd" philosophy and conception of will back to his "morbid pessimism" and overblown ideal of happiness (Haucke 2007:206) shall serve as an example. Schopenhauer has long been denigrated as a "pessimist," and Haucke is in good company when he portrays his philosophy as the outgrowth of a pessimistic and depressive character. But as Dörpinghaus (1997) has conclusively demonstrated, Schopenhauer used the term "pessimism" as antithesis of the "optimism" of Leibniz who described our world as "the best of all possible ones" created by a God who claimed that "all was good." Already for young Schopenhauer, by contrast, the world seemed rather to be—as it had been for the gnostics—the work of a demon. But the realization that our world is characterized by suffering is the point of departure not only of Schopenhauer's thinking but also of Buddhism. The first Noble Truth of Buddhism states clearly that "All

---

[16] See App 1998a. Schopenhauer's notes from these volumes are transcribed and translated into English in App 1998b. See also the recent overview of the various phases of Schopenhauer's interest in Buddhism, his major sources, and an English translation of his essay on Sinology in App 2010a.

[17] The above-mentioned article by Moira Nicholls (1999) shows the hazards of analysis of influence without sufficient knowledge of orientalist sources of the period. For an overview of Schopenhauer's major oriental sources and influences see App 2013. For specific case studies see App 2008a (Schopenhauer's view of Tibetan Buddhism) and App 2010a (Schopenhauer and Chinese Buddhism).

is suffering." The second designates "thirst" (*taṇhā*) or "desire" as the fundamental cause of suffering. The third proclaims the possibility of a definitive uprooting of desire and suffering (nirvana), and the fourth indicates the eightfold path to reach this goal. Both for Schopenhauer and for Buddhism, suffering is not something that man merely *has* and can abandon like an exaggerated expectation. Critics like Haucke pathologize Schopenhauer's fundamental insight that the nature of man and the entire world is *will*—an ever coveting and never quenched desire—and that therefore suffering pertains to its essence. But Rudolf Malter was right on the mark when he characterized Schopenhauer's fundamental position in a manner that unmasks such pathologizing views of Schopenhauer's thought as superficial: "We *are* suffering, we do not merely have it; suffering is not just an accidental feature of our existence but rather its essential content."[18]

In the course of his study of Buddhism over four decades, Schopenhauer grew ever more convinced of the similarity of its fundamental doctrines and his own philosophy (App 2010a, 2013). This was a major reason why from the mid-1820s his interest in Buddhist literature grew by leaps and bounds, whereas his passion for other Indian literature gradually diminished—the *Oupnek'hat* of course excepted. The thinker's affinity to Buddhism is already apparent in his excerpts of 1816 from the sixth volume of *Asiatick Researches* where Buddhism's first Noble Truth of suffering ("weight, old age, illness, death") and the definition of nirvana (extinction of suffering) occupied center stage (App 1998b:21). Though this topic exceeds the boundaries of the present book dedicated to the birth of Schopenhauer's philosophy, I deem it important to stress that both Schopenhauer's doctrine and Buddhism can hardly be called "pessimistic." On the contrary: both are in fact fundamentally optimistic since they point to the possibility of a complete overcoming of suffering in one's lifetime.

---

[18] »Wir *sind* das Leiden, wir haben nicht bloß Leiden, dieses ist kein Akzidens unserer Existenz, sondern ihr wesenhafter Gehalt« (Malter 1991:281).

Appendix 2

Just as the negative pole of a magnet is always paired with its positive counterpart, the pessimism (or rather, realism) of suffering in both Schopenhauer and Buddhism is linked to a pronounced optimism of salvation: from Samsara to Nirvana. And the central thesis of this book is that precisely this bipolarity of suffering and its overcoming lies at the heart of Schopenhauer's thought since his youth. It is the fundamental bearing not only of *The World as Will and Representation* but of his entire philosophy: *Schopenhauer's Compass*.

Chronological Table

1788	Birth of Schopenhauer in Danzig
1797–9	Two-year stay in Le Havre, France; study of French
1803–4	Voyages with parents in England, France, Switzerland, Austria; study of English
1805	Death of Schopenhauer's father, Heinrich Floris Schopenhauer
1805–7	Commerce apprenticeship in Hamburg
1807	From December in Weimar; for three months frequent meetings with the poet Zacharias Werner; first familiarity with mystical literature
1807–9	Preparation for university entrance; study of classical languages (Greek and Latin) and literature
1809–11	Study at the University of Göttingen, first as student of medicine. From 1810 participation in lectures on philosophy by Prof. Schulze. Study of natural sciences. Ethnology course with Prof. Heeren with information about Asia and Asian religions
1811–13	Study of philosophy in Berlin, visit of lectures by Fichte and Schleiermacher. Study of works by Kant, Schelling
1813	Redaction of doctoral dissertation on the Fourfould Root of the Principle of Sufficient Reason in Rudolstadt
1813	Doctorate, promotion *in absentia* in Jena in October
1813–14	Late autumn 1813 to May 1814 stay in Weimar. Studies on colors with Goethe. Introduction to Indian antiquity by Friedrich Majer. First borrowing of Asia-related literature: *Asiatisches Magazin* (with German Bhagavat Gita translations by Majer, Buddhist 42-Sections-Sutra translation by Julius Klaproth)

CHRONOLOGICAL TABLE

1814	First study phase of the *Oupnek'hat* from late March 1814. Traces in Manuscript Remains from notes #188; in note #192 first mention of the "method of the Indians"
1814	Move to Dresden in late May; notes in Manuscript Remains from #202
1814	June to July: second study phase of the *Oupnek'hat* (note #213, will is the fundamental problem; liberation from will through better knowledge. First quotations from and references to the *Oupnek'hat*
1814	Summer and fall: purchase of the *Oupnek'hat*. Conception of the core of Schopenhauer's metaphysics of will (notes c. #240–365)
1815	Notes #365–509. Elaboration of the metaphysics of will. Study of histories of philosophy. From November study of *Asiatick Researches*
1816	Publication of the book *Ueber das Sehn und die Farben* (On Seeing and Colors)
1816	Notes #510–631. Study of *Asiatick Researches* volumes until May. During spring: revision of Schopenhauer's understanding of Maya, thoughts about overall architecture of his system. In summer: two-column table of his philosophical system (note #577). Shortly afterwards "confession" about the crucial influence of the *Oupnek'hat*, Plato, Kant (note #623)
1817	Notes #631–707. Study of mystics. Beginning of the redaction of *The World as Will and Representation*
1818	December: publication of *The World as Will and Representation*

Abbreviations

#	Note number in HN1 (*Manuscript Remains*, vol. 1)
Briefe	A. Hübscher (ed.) Schopenhauer, *Gesammelte Briefe* (Collected letters)
Gespräche	A. Hübscher (ed.) Schopenhauer, *Gespräche* (Conversations)
HN	*Der handschriftliche Nachlaß* (*Manuscript Remains*, with number of volume)
HN4b	*Der handschriftliche Nachlaß* (*Manuscript Remains*) volume 4, Part 2
HNB	Handschriftlicher Nachlaß (*Manuscript Remains*) original manuscripts stored in Berlin
NAF	Bibliothèque nationale Paris, Nouvelles acquisitions françaises (with number of manuscript)
P	Arthur Schopenhauer, *Parerga and Paralipomena* (with volume number)
OUP1	A.-H. Anquetil-Duperron, *Oupnek'hat* Vol. 1 (1801)
OUP2	A.-H. Anquetil-Duperron, *Oupnek'hat* Vol. 2 (1802)
Reisen	Arthur Schopenhauer, *Reisetagebücher* (*Travel diaries*), ed. L. Lütkehaus
SW	Arthur Schopenhauer, *Sämtliche Werke* (*Collected Works*) ed. by A. Hübscher (with number of volume)
W	*Welt als Wille und Vorstellung* (*The World as Will and Representation*) (with volume number)
Z	Arthur Schopenhauer, *Werke* (*Collected Works*, Zürich edition of 1977 based on SW)

Bibliography

Anquetil-Duperron, Abraham Hyacinthe. ca. 1752. *Le Parfait Théologien*. Bibliothèque Nationale, Nouvelles Acquisitions Françaises NAF 8858, Fonds Anquetil-Duperron. Paris.

———. 1762. Relation abrégée du voyage que M. Anquetil Du Perron a fait dans l'Inde pour la recherche & la Traduction des ouvrages attribués à Zoroastre. *Journal des Sçavans*: 413–429.

———. 1771. *Zend-Avesta, Ouvrage de Zoroastre*. Paris: Tilliard.

———. 1776. *Anquetil Du Perron, Mitglieds der Akademie der schönen Wissenschaften zu Paris, und Königl. Französischen Dollmetschers der morgenländischen Sprachen, Reisen nach Ostindien, nebst einer Beschreibung der bürgerlichen und Religionsgebräuche der Parsen, als eine Einleitung zum Zend-Avesta, dem Gesetzbuch der Parsen durch Zoroaster*. Übersetzt von J. G. Purmann. Frankfurt a. M.

———. 1776–1777. *Zend-Avesta, Zoroasters lebendiges Wort*. Übersetzt von J. F. Kleuker. Riga: Hartknoch.

———. 1778. *Législation orientale*. Amsterdam: Marc Michel Rey.

———. 1787a. Des Recherches historiques & géographiques sur l'Inde, & la Description du Cours du Gange & du Gagra, avec une très grande Carte. In *Description historique et géographique de l'Inde*, ed. by J. Bernoulli. Berlin: Pierre Bourdeaux.

———. 1787b. *Oupnek'hat, traduit littéralement du persan, mêlé du samskrétam*. In Bibliothèque Nationale: Nouvelles acquisitions françaises NAF 8857, Fonds Anquetil-Duperron. Paris.

———. 1791. Vier Upnekhat, aus dem Samskrutamischen Buche die Upnekhat. In *Sammlung asiatischer Original-Schriften. Indische Schriften*, 269–315. Zürich: Ziegler und Söhne.

———. 1801. *Oupnek'hat (id est, secretum tegendum)*. Bd. 1. Argentorati: Levrault.

App, Urs. 1998a. Schopenhauers Begegnung mit dem Buddhismus. *Schopenhauer-Jahrbuch* 79:35–58.

———. 1998b. Notes and Excerpts by Schopenhauer Related to Volumes 1–9 of the Asiatick Researches. *Schopenhauer-Jahrbuch* 79:11–33.

———. 2003. Notizen Schopenhauers zu Ost-, Nord- und Südostasien vom Sommersemester 1811. *Schopenhauer-Jahrbuch* 84:13–39.

———. 2006a. Schopenhauer's India Notes of 1811. *Schopenhauer-Jahrbuch* 87:15–31.

———. 2006b. NICHTS. Das letzte Wort von Schopenhauers Hauptwerk. In >*Das Tier, das du jetzt tötest, bist du selbst* ...<. *Arthur Schopenhauer und Indien*, ed. by J. Stollberg, 51–60. Frankfurt: Vittorio Klostermann.

———. 2006c. Schopenhauer's Initial Encounter with Indian Thought. *Schopenhauer-Jahrbuch* 87:35–76.

———. 2006d. OUM – Das erste Wort von Schopenhauers Lieblingsbuch. In >*Das Tier, das du jetzt tötest, bist du selbst* ...<. *Arthur Schopenhauer und Indien*, ed. by J. Stollberg, 36–50. Frankfurt: Vittorio Klostermann.

———. 2007. How Amida got into the Upanishads: An Orientalist's Nightmare. In *Essays on East Asian Religion and Culture*, ed. by C. Wittern and L. Shi, 11–33. Kyoto: Editorial Committee for the Festschrift in Honour of Nishiwaki Tsuneki.

———. 2008a. The Tibet of Philosophers: Kant, Hegel, and Schopenhauer. In *Images of Tibet in the 19th and 20th Centuries*, ed. by M. Esposito, 11–70. Paris: Ecole Française d'Extrême-Orient.

———. 2008b. Schopenhauer's Initial Encounter with Indian Thought. In *Schopenhauer and Indian Philosophy: A Dialogue between India and Germany*, ed. by A. Barua, 7–57. New Delhi: Northern Book Centre.

———. 2009. William Jones's Ancient Theology. *Sino-Platonic Papers* 191: 1–125.

———. 2010a. Schopenhauer and China: A Sino-Platonic Love Affair. *Sino-Platonic Papers* 200: 1–160.

———. 2010b. Schopenhauers Nirwana. In *Die Wahrheit ist nackt am schönsten. Arthur Schopenhauers philosophische Provokation*, ed. by Michael Fleiter, 200–208. Frankfurt: Institut für Stadtgeschichte / Societätsverlag.

———. 2010c. *The Birth of Orientalism*. Philadelphia: University of Pennsylvania Press.

———. 2011. *Schopenhauers Kompass*. Rorschach/Kyoto: UniversityMedia.

———. 2012. *The Cult of Emptiness. The Western Discovery of Buddhist Thought and the Invention of Oriental Philosophy*. Rorschach/Kyoto: UniversityMedia.

———. 2013. "Required Reading: Schopenhauer's Favorite Book." *Jahrbuch der Schopenhauer-Gesellschaft* 93: 65–86.

———. 2014. Asiatische Philosophien und Religionen. In *Schopenhauer Handbuch. Leben – Werk – Wirkung*, ed. by Daniel Schubbe and Matthias Koßler, 187–192. Stuttgart / Weimar: J. B. Metzler.

Assmann, Jan. 1998. Hen kai pan—Ägyptens geheime Theologie nach Ralph Cudworth. In *Moses der Ägypter*, 118–30. München: Carl Hanser.

———. 2007. *Religion und kulturelles Gedächtnis*. München: Beck.

Astruc, Jean. 1753. *Conjectures sur les mémoires originaux dont il paroit que Moyse s'est servi pour composer le livre de la Genese. Avec des remarques, qui appuient ou qui éclaircissent ces conjectures*. Bruxelles: Fricx.

Atwell, John E. 1995. *Schopenhauer on the Character of the World: The Metaphysics of Will*. Berkeley: University of California Press.

Baldaeus, Philippus. 1672. *Naauwkeurige beschryvinge van Malabar en Choromandel, der zelver aangrenzende ryken, en het machtige eyland Ceylon ...* Amsterdam: J.J. van Waesberge.

Beierwaltes, Werner. 1991. *Selbsterkenntnis und Erfahrung der Einheit. Plotins Enneade V 3*. Frankfurt am Main: Vittorio Klostermann.

———. 2004. *Platonismus und Idealismus*. Frankfurt am Main: Vittorio Klostermann.

Berger, Douglas. 2000. *The Veil of Maya: Schopenhauer's System theory of falsification: the key to Schopenhauer's appropriation of pre-systematic Indian philosophical thought*. Ann Arbor, Michigan: UMI Dissertation Services.

———. 2004. *The Veil of Maya: Schopenhauer's System and Early Indian Thought*. Binghampton, NY: Global Academic Publications.

Bernier, François. 1688. Mémoire sur le Quietisme des Indes. In *Histoire des Ouvrages des Sçavans*, 47–52. Rotterdam: Reinier Leers.

———. 1699. *Voyages de François Bernier, docteur en médecine de la Faculté de Montpellier: contenant la description des États du Grand Mogol, de l'Indoustan, du Royaume de Cachemire, &c*. Bd. 2. Paris: Chez Barbin.

Blumenbach, Johann Friedrich. 1791. *Über den Bildungstrieb*. Göttingen: Dieterich.

———. 1803. *Specimen Archaeologiae Telluris*. Göttingen: Dieterich.

———. 1806. *Beyträge zur Naturgeschichte*. Göttingen: Dieterich.

Bohinc, Tomas. 1989. *Die Entfesselung des Intellekts*. Frankfurt am Main / Bern: Lang.

Böhme, Jakob. 1843. *Jakob Böhme's sämmtliche Werke*. Ed. by K. W. Schiedler. Leipzig: Johann Ambrosius Barth.

Booms, Martin. 2003. *Aporie und Subjekt. Die erkenntnistheoretische Entfaltungslogik der Philosophie Schopenhauers*. Würzburg: Königshausen und Neumann.

Boulduc, Jacques. 1630. *De Ecclesia Ante Legem*. Paris: Joseph Cottereau.

Brucker, Johann Jacob. 1742–1744. *Historia critica philosophiae*. Leipzig: Christoph Breitkopf.

Bruno, Giordano. 1993. *Von der Ursache, dem Prinzip und dem Einen*. Übersetzt von A. Lasson. Ed. by P. R. Blum. Hamburg: Feliz Meiner Verlag.

Buhle, Johann Gottlieb. 1800–1804. *Geschichte der neuern Philosophie*. Göttingen: Johann Georg Rosenbusch's Wittwe.

Caland, Willem. 1918. *De Ontdekkingsgeschiedenis van den Veda*. Amsterdam: Johannes Müller.

Chardin, Jean. 1711. *Voyages de Mr. le Chevalier Chardin en Perse, et autres lieux de l'orient*. Bd. 5. Amsterdam: Jean Louis de Lorme.

Chenet, François. 1997. Conscience empirique et conscience meilleure chez le jeune Schopenhauer. In *Les Cahiers de l'Herne: Schopenhauer*, ed. by J. Lefranc, 103–30. Paris: Éditions de l'Herne.

———. 1998. *Psychogenèse et cosmogonie selon le Yoga-vāsiṣṭha*. Paris: Collège de France / de Boccard.

Corbin, Henri. 1969. *Creative Imagination in the Sufism of Ibn Arabi*. Princeton: Princeton University Press.

Creuzer, Georg Friedrich. 1819–1821. *Symbolik und Mythologie der alten Völker, besonders der Griechen*. Leipzig & Darmstadt: Heyer & Leske.

Creuzer, Georg Friedrich & Gottfried Hermann. 1818. *Briefe über Homer und Hesiodus, vorzüglich über die Theogonie*. Heidelberg: Oswald.

de Bary, William Theodore. 1958. *Sources of Indian Tradition*. New York and London: Columbia Universiy Press, 1958.

de Cian, Nicoletta. 2002. *Redenzione, Colpa, Salvezza. All'origine della filosofia di Schopenhauer*. Trento: Verifiche.

Decher, F. 1996. Das ›bessre Bewußtsein‹: Zur Funktion eines Begriffes in der Genese der Schopenhauerschen Philosophie. *Schopenhauer Jahrbuch* 77:65–83.

Deussen, Paul. 1897. *Sechzig Upanishad's des Veda*. Leipzig: Brockhaus.

———. 1922. *Die Philosophie der Upanishad's* (Allgemeine Geschichte der Philosophie, 1. Band, 2. Abteilung). Leipzig: Brockhaus.

Diderot, Denis, and Jean le Rond d'Alembert. 1751. *Encyclopédie ou dictionnaire raisonné des sciences, des arts et des métiers*. Vol. 1.

D'Onofrio, Svevo, and Fabrizio Speziale (tr.). 2011. Muḥammad Dārā Šikōh: *La congiunzione dei due oceani (Majma' al-Baḥrayn)*. Milano: Adelphi.

Dörpinghaus, Andreas. 1997. *Mundus pessimus. Untersuchungen zum philosophischen Pessimismus Arthur Schopenhauers*. Würzburg: Königshausen & Neumann.

Dresden, Mark. 1974. On the Genesis of Anquetil Duperron's Oupnek'hat. In *Mémorial Jean de Menasce*, ed. by P. Gignoux, 35–43. Louvain: Fondation Culturelle Iranienne.

Droit, Roger-Pol. 1989. Une statuette tibétaine sur la cheminée. In *Présences de Schopenhauer*, ed. by R.-P. Droit, 201–17. Paris: Grasset.

———. 1997. *Le culte du néant. Les philosophes et le Bouddha*. Paris: Seuil.

Dürr, Thomas. 2003. Schopenhauers Grundlegung der Willensmetaphysik. *Schopenhauer Jahrbuch* 84:91–119.

Dutt Shastri, Prabhu. 1938. Admiration for Schopenhauer. *Jahrbuch der Schopenhauer-Gesellschaft* 25:74–76.

Ernst, Carl W. 2003. "Muslim Studies in Hinduism? A Reconsideration of Arabic and Persian Translations from Indian Languages." *Iranian Studies* 36: 173–95.

———. 2005. "Situating Sufism and Yoga." *Journal of the Royal Asiatic Society* (Series 3, no. 15:1): 15–43.

Faggin, G. 1951. *Schopenhauer, il mistico senza Dio*. Firenze: Tip. Poligrafico Toscano.

Fénelon, François de Salignac de La Mothe. 1698. *Explication des maximes des saints sur la vie intérieure*. Frankfurt am Main: J. D. Zunner.

Filliozat, Jean. 1980. Sur les contreparties indiennes du soufisme. *Journal Asiatique* 268 (3–4):259–273.

Formichi, Carlo. 1913. Schopenhauer e la filosofia indiana. *Jahrbuch der Schopenhauer-Gesellschaft* 2:63–65.

Frank, Othmar. 1808. *Das Licht vom Orient*. Nürnberg: Stein.

Garewicz, J. 1987. Schopenhauer und Böhme. In *Schopenhauer im Denken der Gegenwart*, ed. by V. Spierling, 71–80. München / Zürich: Piper.

———. 1989. Erkennen und Erleben. Ein Beitrag zu Schopenhauers Erlösungslehre. *Schopenhauer Jahrbuch* 70:75–83.

Gautier, Judith. 1964. *Lettres à Judith Gautier*, edited by Léon Guichard. Paris: Gallimard.

Gestering, Johann G. 1986. *German Pessimism and Indian Philosophy: A Hermeneutic Reading*. Delhi: Ajanta Publications.

———. 1995. Schopenhauer und Indien. In *Ethik und Vernunft. Schopenhauer in unserer Zeit*, ed. by W. Schirmacher, 53–60. Wien: Passagen Verlag.

Gimm, Martin. 1995. Zu Klaproths erstem Katalog chinesischer Bücher, Weimar 1804 – oder: Julius Klaproth als 'studentische Hilfskraft' bei Goethe? –. In *Das andere China: Festschrift für Wolfgang Bauer zum 65. Geburtstag*, ed. by H. Schmidt-Glintzer, 559–99. Wiesbaden: Harassowitz.

Gjellerup, Karl. 1919. Zur Entwicklungsgeschichte der Schopenhauerschen Philosophie. *Annalen der Philosophie* 1:495–517.

Glasenapp, Helmuth von. 1955. Schopenhauer und Indien. *Jahrbuch der Schopenhauer-Gesellschaft* 36:32–48.

———. 1960. *Das Indienbild deutscher Denker*. Stuttgart: Koehler.

Göbel-Gross, Erhard. 1962. *Die persische Upaniṣaden-Übersetzung des Moġulprinzen Dārā Šukoh*. Marburg: Erich Mauersberger.

Görres, Joseph. 1810. *Mythengeschichte der asiatischen Welt*. Bd. 1. Heidelberg: Mohr und Zimmermann.

———. 1935. *Gesammelte Schriften, Vol.5: Mythengeschichte der asiatischen Welt*. Köln: J. P. Bachem.

Gregorios, Paulos Mar. 2002. *Neoplatonism and Indian Philosophy*. Albany, N.Y.: State University of New York Press.

Grisebach, Eduard von. 1888. *Edita und Inedita Schopenhaueriana*. Leipzig.

Guignes, Joseph de. 1759. "Recherches sur les Philosophes appelés Samanéens." *Mémoires de Littérature tirés des Registres des l'Académie Royale des Inscriptions & Belles Lettres* vol. 26 Paris: Imprimerie royale, 770–804.

Guyon, Jeanne-Marie Bouvier de la Motte. 1720. *La Vie de Guyon, écrite par elle-même*. Bd. 1,2,3. Köln: J. de la Pierre.

———. 1727. *Das Leben der Madame J.M.B. de la Mothe Guion von Ihr selbst in Frantzösischer Sprache beschrieben, nun aber ins Teutsche übersetzt und in drey Theilen heraus gegeben*. Leipzig: Samuel Benjamin Walthern.

———. 1978. *Die geistlichen Ströme*. Marburg an der Lahn: Edel.

Gwinner, Wilhelm. 1862. *Arthur Schopenhauer aus persönlichem Umgange dargestellt. Ein Blick auf sein Leben, seinen Charakter und seine Lehre*. Leipzig: F. A. Brockhaus.

Hacker, P. 1950. Eigentümlichkeiten der Lehre und Terminologie Śaṅkaras: Avidyā, Nāmarūpa, Māyā, Īśvara. *Zeitschrift der Deutschen Morgenländischen Gesellschaft* 100:246–286.

Halbfass, Wilhelm. 1987. Schopenhauer im Gespräch mit der indischen Tradition. In *Schopenhauer im Denken der Gegenwart*, ed. by V. Spierling, 55–70. München / Zürich: Piper.

Halfwassen, Jens. 1992. *Der Aufstieg zum Einen. Untersuchungen zu Platon und Plotin*. Stuttgart: B.G. Teubner.

———. 2004. *Plotin und der Neuplatonismus*. München: Beck.

Hamilton, Alexander. 1803. Anquetil's Oupnek'hat. *The Edinburgh Review* 2:412–421.

Hankamer, Paul. 1920. *Zacharias Werner. Ein Beitrag zur Darstellung des Problems der Persönlichkeit in der Romantik*. Bonn: Friedrich Cohen.

Harris, R. Baine. 1982. *Neoplatonism and Indian Thought*. Norfolk, Virginia: International Society for Neoplatonic Studies.

Hasrat, Bikrama Jit. 1982. *Dārā Shikūh: Life and Works*. Calcutta: Munshiram Manoharlal.

Haucke, Kai. 2007. *Leben & Leiden. Zur Aktualität und Einheit der schopenhauerschen Philosophie*. Berlin: Parerga.

Hecker, Max F. 1897. *Schopenhauer und die indische Philosophie*. Köln: Hübscher & Teufel.

Heimann, Robert. 2013. *Die Genese der Philosophie Schopenhauers vor dem Hintergrund seiner Pseudo-Taulerrezeption*. Würzburg: Königshausen und Neumann.

Hemsterhuis, François & J. G. von Herder. 1781. Ueber das Verlangen. Von Herrn Hemsterhuis. *Der Teutsche Merkur* (4):97–122.

Herder, J. G. von. 1781. Liebe und Selbstheit. *Der Teutsche Merkur* (4):211–235.

Hitzig, Julius. 1823. *Lebens-Abriss Friedrich Ludwig Zacharias Werners*. Berlin: Sandersche Buchhandlung.

Holbach, Paul Henri (pseud. M. Mirabaud). 1770. *Système de la nature, ou des loix du monde physique & du monde moral*. London.

Huart, C., and L. Massignon. 1926. Les Entretiens de Lahore [entre le prince impérial Dàrà Shikùh et l'ascète hindou Baba La'l Das]. *Journal Asiatique* 209:285–334.

Hübscher, Arthur. 1938. *Der junge Schopenhauer. Aphorismen und Tagebuchblätter*. München: Piper.

———. 1971. *Arthur Schopenhauer: Gespräche*. Stuttgart: Friedrich Frommann Verlag.

———. 1973. *Denker gegen den Strom. Schopenhauer: Gestern — Heute — Morgen*. Bonn: Bouvier Verlag Hermann Grundmann.

———. 1979. Schopenhauer und die Religionen Asiens. *Jahrbuch der Schopenhauer-Gesellschaft* 60:1–16.

———. 1981. *Schopenhauer-Bibliographie*. Stuttgart-Bad Cannstatt: Frommann-Holzboog.

———. 1987. *Arthur Schopenhauer: Gesammelte Briefe*. Bonn: Bouvier.

———. 1988. *Arthur Schopenhauer. Ein Lebensbild*. Mannheim: Brockhaus.

Hübscher, Angelika, and Michael Fleiter. 1989. *Arthur Schopenhauer: Philosophie in Briefen*. Frankfurt a. M.: Insel Verlag.

Hyman, Arthur. 1992. From What is One and Simple only What is One and Simple Can Come to Be. In *Neoplatonism and Jewish Thought*, ed. by L. E. Goodman, 111–35. Albany N.Y.: State University of New York Press.

Izutsu, Toshihiko. 1984. *Sufism and Taoism*. Berkeley: University of California Press.

Jacobi, F. H. 1789. *Ueber die Lehre des Spinoza in Briefen ;an den Herrn Moses Mendelssohn*. Breslau: Gottlob Löwe.

Jalālī Nā'īnī, Muhammad Rizā, and Tārā Chand. 1961. *Upānishād / tarjumah-i Muhammad Dārā Shikūh az matn-i Sānskrīt; bā muqaddimah u havāshī u ta'līqāt u lughatnāmah u i'lām ba-sa'y u ihtimām-i Tārā Chand [va] Sayyid Muhammad Rizā Jalālī Nā'īnī*. Tehran: Taban.

Jones, Anna Maria (ed.). 1799. *The Works of Sir William Jones*. London: Robinson & Evans.

Jones, William. 1771. *Lettre à Monsieur A*** du P*** [i.e. Anquetil du Perron], dans laquelle est compris l'examen de sa traduction des livres attribueés à Zoroastre*. London: Elmisly.

Kamata, Yasuo. 1988. *Der junge Schopenhauer: Genese des Grundgedankens der Welt als Wille und Vorstellung*. Freiburg: Alber.

Kanne, Johann Arnold. 1813. *System der indischen Mythe, oder Chronus und die Geschichte des Gottmenschen in der Periode des Vorrückens der Nachtgleichen*. Leipzig: Weygand.

Kapani, Lakshmi. 1996. Schopenhauer et son interprétation du >Tu es cela<. In *L'Inde inspiratrice. Réception de l'Inde en France et en Allemagne (XIXe & XXe siècles)*, ed. by G. Fussman, 45–69. Strasbourg: Presses Universitaires de Strasbourg.

———. 2002. Schopenhauer et l'Inde. *Journal Asiatique* 290 (1):163–292.

———. 2005. Schopenhauer et le Vedânta. In *Sakyamuni et Schopenhauer: La lucidité du philosophe et l'éveil du Bouddha*, 86–103. Arvillard: Prajña.

———. 2011. *Schopenhauer et la pensée indienne, similitudes et différences*. Paris: Hermann, 2011.

Korfmacher, Wolfgang. 1992. *Ideen und Ideenerkenntnis in der ästhetischen Theorie Arthur Schopenhauers*. Pfaffenweiler: Centaurus.

———. 1994. *Schopenhauer zur Einführung*. Hamburg: Junius.

Koßler, Matthias (ed.). 2008. *Schopenhauer und die Philosophien Asiens*. Wiesbaden: Harrassowitz.

Lanjuinais, Comte de. 1823. Analyse de l'Oupnek'hat. *Journal Asiatique* 2–3:vol. 2: 213–236; 265–282; 344–365 and vol. 3: 15–34; 71–91.

Lemanski, Jens. 2009/2011. *Christentum im Atheismus. Spuren der mystischen Imitatio Christi-Lehre in der Ethik Schopenhauers*. 2 vols. London: Turnshare.

Lenoir, Frédéric. 1999. *La rencontre du Bouddhisme et de l'occident*. Paris: Fayard.

Lorenz, Theodor. 1897. *Zur Entwicklungsgeschichte der Metaphysik Schopenhauers*. Leipzig: Breitkopf & Härtel.

Lütkehaus, Ludger. 1998. *Die Schopenhauers. Der Familien-Briefwechsel von Adele, Arthur, Heinrich Floris und Johanna Schopenhauer*. München: Deutscher Taschenbuch Verlag.

Magee, Brian. 1997. *The Philosophy of Schopenhauer*. Oxford: Clarendon Press.

Mahfuz-ul-Haq, M. 1929. *Majima'-ul-Baḥrain or The Mingling of the Two Oceans, by Prince Muhammad Dârâ Shikûh*. Calcutta: Asiatic Society of Bengal.

Majer, Friedrich. 1802. Das Bhaguat-Geeta, oder Gespräche zwischen Kreeshna und Arjoon. In *Asiatisches Magazin*, ed. by J. Klaproth, Vol.1, pp. 406–53; Vol.2, pp. 105–35, 229–55, 73–93, 454–90. Weimar: Industrie-Comptoir.

———. 1802. Die Verkörperungen des Wischnu. In *Asiatisches Magazin*, ed. by J. Klaproth, Vol.1, pp. 116–38, 221–44, 395–405; Vol.2, pp. 11–70 Weimar: Industrie-Comptoir.

———. 1818. *Brahma oder die Religion der Indier als Brahmaismus*. Leipzig: Reclam.

Malter, Rudolf. 1982. Erlösung durch Erkenntnis. In *Zeit der Ernte*, ed. by W. Schirmacher, pp. 41–59. Stuttgart / Bad Cannstatt: Frommann-Holzboog.

———. 1988. *Der eine Gedanke. Hinführung zur Philosophie Arthur Schopenhauers*. Darmstadt: Wissenschaftliche Buchgesellschaft.

———. 1991. *Arthur Schopenhauer: Transzendentalphilosophie und Metaphysik des Willens*. Stuttgart / Bad Cannstatt: Frommann–Holzboog.

Marchand, Suzanne L. 2009. *German Orientalism in the Age of Empire*. Cambridge: Cambridge University Press.

Merkel, Rudolf. 1945/48. Schopenhauers Indien-Lehrer. *Jahrbuch der Schopenhauer-Gesellschaft* 32:158–81.

Meyer, Urs Walter. 1994. *Europäische Rezeption indischer Philosophie und Religion*. Bern: Peter Lang.

Mirri, E. 1987. Un concetto perduto nella sistematica schopenhaueriana: la 'migliore coscienza'. In *Schopenhauer e il sacro: Atti del Seminario tenuto a Trento il 26–28 aprile 1984*, ed. by G. Penzo, 59–82. Bologna: EDB.

Mischel, Franz. 1882. *Das Oupnek'hat*. Dresden: C. Heinrich.

Mockrauer, Franz. 1928. Schopenhauer und Indien. *Jahrbuch der Schopenhauer-Gesellschaft* 15:3–26.

Mommsen, Katharina. 2014. *Goethe and the Poets of Arabia*. Tr. by Michael M. Metzger. Rochester NY: Camden House.

Morewedge, Parviz. 1992. *Neoplatonism and Islamic Thought*. Albany, N.Y.: State University of New York Press.

———. 1992. The Neoplatonic Structure of Some Islamic Mystical Doctrine. In *Neoplatonism and Islamic Thought*, ed. by P. Morewedge, 51–73. Albany, N.Y.: State University of New York Press.

Mühlethaler, Jacob. 1910. *Die Mystik bei Schopenhauer*. Berlin: Alexander Duncker Verlag.

Müller, Friedrich Max. 1962. *The Upanishads*. New York: Dover.

Nicholls, Moira. 1999. The Influences of Eastern Thought on Schopenhauer's Doctrine of the Thing-in-Itself. In *The Cambridge Companion to Schopenhauer*, ed. by C. Janaway, 171–212. Cambridge / New York: Cambridge University Press.

Olivelle, Patrick. 1998. *The Early Upanisads*. New York / Oxford: Oxford University Press.

Pfeiffer, Franz (ed.). 1851. *Theologia deutsch: Die leret gar manchen lieblichen underscheit gotlicher warheit und seit gar hohe und gar schone ding von einem volkkomen leben*. Stuttgart: K. Fr. Hering.

Piantelli, Mario. 1986. La »Mâyâ« nelle »Upanishad« di Schopenhauer. *Annuario filosofico*:163–207.

Pluquet, Adrien-François. 1757. *Examen du fatalisme*. Paris: Didot & Barrois.

Polaschegg, Andrea. 2005. *Der andere Orientalismus. Regeln deutsch-morgenländischer Imagination im 19. Jahrhundert*. Berlin: de Gruyter.

Pons, Jean François. 1781. Lettre du Père Pons, Missionnaire de la Compagnie de Jésus, au Père Du Halde, de la même Compagnie. In *Lettres édifiantes et curieuses, écrites des missions étrangères*, ed. by C. Le Gobien, Vol.14, 65–90. Paris: G. Merigot.

Postel, Guillaume. 1553. *De Originibus seu de varia et potissimum orbi Latino ad hanc diem incognita, aut inconsyderata historia, quum totius Orientis, tum maxime Tartarorum, Persarum, Turcarum, & omnium Abrahami & Noachi alumnorum origines, & mysteria Brachmanum retegente: Quod ad gentium, literarumque quib. utuntur, rationes attinet*. Basel: J. Oporin.

Riconda, G. 1972. La >Noluntas< e la riscoperta della mistica nella filosofia di Schopenhauer. *Schopenhauer Jahrbuch* 53.

Rizvi, Saiyid Athar Abbas. 1983. *A History of Sufism in India*. Vol. 2: From Sixteenth Century to Modern Century. New Delhi: Munshiram Manoharlal.

———. 1995. *Muslim Revivalist Movements in Northern India*. New Delhi: Munshiram Manoharlal.

Rocher, Rosane. 1978. "Nathaniel Brassey Halhed on the Upanisads (1787)." In *Annals of the Bhandarkar Oriental Research Institute, Diamond Jubilee Volume (1977–78)*. Poona: Bhandarkar Oriental Research Institute, 279–89.

Safranski, Rüdiger. 1987. *Schopenhauer und Die wilden Jahre der Philosophie*. München: Carl Hanser.

Sauter-Ackermann, Gisela. 1994. *Erlösung durch Erkenntnis? Studien zu einem Grundproblem der Philosophie Schopenhauers*. Cuxhaven: Junghans.

Schelling, Friedrich Wilhelm Joseph. 1798. *Von der Weltseele. Eine Hypothese der höhern Physik zur Erklärung des allgemeinen Organismus*. Hamburg: Friedrich Perthes.

Schelling, F. W. J. 1803. *Vorlesungen über die Methode des akademischen Studiums*. Tübingen: Cotta.

Schelling, Friedrich Wilhelm Joseph. 1803. *Ideen zu einer Philosophie der Natur als Einleitung in das Studium dieser Wissenschaft*. Landshut: Philipp Krüll.

———. 1804. *Philosophie und Religion*. Tübingen: I. G. Cotta.

———. 1809. *F. W. J. Schelling's philosophische Schriften. Erster Band*. Landshut: Philipp Krüll.

———. 1834. *Bruno oder über das göttliche und natürliche Princip der Dinge*. Reutlingen: Enßlin.

Schimmel, Annemarie. 1992. *Mystische Dimensionen des Islam*. München: Eugen Diederichs Verlag.

Schirmacher, Wolfgang. 1985. *Insel-Almanach für das Jahr 1985: Schopenhauer*. Frankfurt am Main: Insel Verlag.

Schlegel, Friedrich. 1808. *Über die Sprache und Weisheit der Indier*. Heidelberg: Mohr und Zimmer.

———. 1836. *Friedrich Schlegel's Philosophische Vorlesungen aus den Jahren 1804 bis 1806*. Ed. by C. J. H. Windischmann. Bonn: Eduard Weber.

Schmidt, A. 1986. *Die Wahrheit im Gewand der Lüge. Schopenhauers Religionsphilosophie*. München / Zürich: Piper.

Scholz, Werner. 1996. *Arthur Schopenhauer – ein Philosoph zwischen westlicher und östlicher Tradition*. Frankfurt / Bern: Peter Lang.

Schopenhauer, Arthur. 1819. *Die Welt als Wille und Vorstellung*. Leipzig: F. A. Brockhaus.

———. 1969. *The World as Will and Representation* (2 vols). Translated by E. F. J. Payne. New York: Dover Publications.

———. 1970. *Essays and Aphorisms*. Translated by R. J. Hollingdale. Harmondsworth: Penguin.

———. 1974. *On the Fourfold Root of the Principle of Sufficient Reason*. Translated by E. F. J. Payne. La Salle, IL.: Open Court.

———. 1974. *Parerga and Paralipomena* (2 vols). Translated by E. F. J. Payne. Oxford: Clarendon Press.

———. 1977. *Zürcher Ausgabe. Werke in zehn Bänden*. Zürich: Diogenes Verlag.

———. 1985. *Der handschriftliche Nachlaß*. Ed. by A. Hübscher. München: Deutscher Taschenbuch Verlag.

———. 1987. *Die Welt als Wille und Vorstellung*. Ed. by R. Malter. Frankfurt: Insel.

———. 1988. *Sämtliche Werke*. Ed. by A. Hübscher. Mannheim: Brockhaus.

———. 1988. *Arthur Schopenhauer. Die Reisetagebücher*. Ed. by L. Lütkehaus. Zürich: Haffmans.

———. 1988. *Manuscript Remains in Four Volumes. Volume 1: Early Manuscripts (1804-1818)*. Translated by E. F. J. Payne. Oxford / New York / Hamburg: Berg.

———. 1989. *Manuscript Remains in Four Volumes. Volume 3: Berlin Manuscripts (1818-1830)*. Translated by E. F. J. Payne. Oxford / New York / Hamburg: Berg.

———. 1992. *On the Will in Nature*. Translated by E. F. J. Payne. New York: Berg.

———. 1992. *Arthur Schopenhauer. Der Briefwechsel mit Goethe und andere Dokumente zur Farbenlehre*. Ed. by L. Lütkehaus. Zürich: Haffmans.

———. 1994. *On Vision and Colors*. Translated by E. F. J. Payne. Oxford: Berg.

———. 1995. *On the Basis of Morality*. Translated by E. F. J. Payne. Oxford: Berghahn Books, 1995.

———. 2007. *Il mio oriente*. Ed. by G. Gurisatti. Milano: Adelphi.

———. 2009. *The Two Fundamental Problems of Ethics*. Translated by Christopher Janaway. Cambridge: Cambridge University Press.

———. 2010. *The World as Will and Representation*, vol. 1. Translated by Judith Norman, Alistair Welchman and Christopher Janaway. Ed. by Christopher Janaway. Cambridge: Cambridge University Press.

Schröder, Wilhelm. 1911. *Beiträge zur Entwicklungsgeschichte der Philosophie Schopenhauers mit besonderer Berücksichtigung einiger wichtigerer frühnachkantischer Philosophen (Maimon, Beck, G. E. Schulze, Bouterwek und Jacobi)*. Rostock: Boldt.

Schubbe, Daniel & Matthias Koßler (eds.). 2014. *Schopenhauer Handbuch. Leben – Werk – Wirkung*. Stuttgart / Weimar: J. B. Metzler.

Schwab, Raymond. 1934. *Vie d'Anquetil Duperron*. Paris: Ernest Leroux.

———. 1950. *La Renaissance orientale*. Paris: Payot.

———. 1984. *The Oriental Renaissance: Europe's Rediscovery of India and the East, 1680-1880*. Translated by Gene Patterson-Black. New York: Columbia University Press.

Schwabe, Gerhard. 1887. *Fichtes und Schopenhauers Lehre vom Willen, mit ihren Konsequenzen für Weltbegreifung und Lebensführung*. Jena: Frommannsche Buchdruckerei (H. Pohle).

Sedlar, Jean W. 1982. *India in the Mind of Germany*. Washington, D.C.: University Press of America.

Sengupta, Lalita. 2004. *Contribution of Darashiko to Hindu-Muslim Philosophy*. Kolkata: Sanskrit Pustak Bhandar.

Shayegan, Daryush. 1997. *Hindouisme et soufisme – Une lecture du confluent des deux océans: le Majma 'al-Bahrayn de Dârâ Shokûh*. Paris: Albin Michel.

Siegler, Hans Georg. 1994. *Der heimatlose Arthur Schopenhauer: Jugendjahre zwischen Danzig, Hamburg, Weimar*. Düsseldorf: Droste.

Skinner, David. 2011. "Impertinent Questions with David Cartwright." *Humanities* 32.2 (March/April 2011). http://www.neh.gov/humanities/2011/marchapril/iq/impertinent-questions-david-cartwright.

Hardy, Robert Spence. 1853. *A Manual of Budhism, in its modern development; translated from Singhalese mss.* London: Partridge and Oakey.

Spierling, Volker. 1984. *Materialien zu Schopenhauers ›Die Welt als Wille und Vorstellung‹.* Frankfurt: Suhrkamp.

———. 1987. *Schopenhauer im Denken der Gegenwart.* München / Zürich: Piper.

———. 1994. *Arthur Schopenhauer. Philosophie als Kunst und Erkenntnis.* Frankfurt: Frankfurter Verlagsanstalt.

Stanley, Thomas. 1690. *Thomae Stanleii Historia Philosophiae Orientalis.* Übersetzt von Jean Le Clerc. Amsterdam: Viduam Swart.

———. 1701. *The History of Philosophy: Containing the Lives, Opinions, Actions and Discourses of the Philosophers of every Sect: Illustrated with the Effigies of Divers of Them; The History of the Chal[d]aick Philosophy.* London: W. Battersby.

Steiger, Robert. 1988. *Goethes Leben von Tag zu Tag. Vol. V: 1807–1813.* Zürich / München: Artemis Verlag.

Steiger, Robert, and Angelika Reimann. 1993. *Goethes Leben von Tag zu Tag. Vol. VI: 1814–1820.* Zürich / München: Artemis Verlag.

Stollberg, Jochen (ed.). 2006. *›Das Tier, das du jetzt tötest, bist du selbst ...‹ Arthur Schopenhauer und Indien.* Frankfurt: Vittorio Klostermann.

Strich, Fritz. 1910. *Die Mythologie in der deutschen Literatur von Klopstock bis Wagner.* Halle an der Saale: Max Niemeyer.

Tennemann, Wilhelm Gottlieb. 1798–1819. *Geschichte der Philosophie.* Leipzig: Johann Ambrosius Barth.

Tieck, Ludwig. 1799. *Phantasien über die Kunst, für Freunde der Kunst.* Hamburg: Friedrich Perthes.

Tiedemann, Dieterich. 1791–1797. *Geist der spekulativen Philosophie.* Marburg: Neue Akademische Buchhandlung.

Timm, Hermann. 1974. *Gott und die Freiheit. Studien zur Religionsphilosophie der Goethezeit. Vol. 1: Die Spinozarenaissance.* Frankfurt am Main: Vittorio Klostermann.

Vecchiotti, Icilio. 1985. Schopenhauer im Urteil der modernen Inder. In *Schopenhauer*, ed. by J. Salaquarda. Darmstadt.

———. 1969. *La dottrina di Schopenhauer. Le teorie schopenhaueriane considerate nella loro genesi e nei loro rapporti con la fisosofia indiana*. Roma: Ubaldini.

Volkelt, Johannes. 1900. *Schopenhauer. Seine Persönlichkeit, seine Lehre, sein Glaube*. Stuttgart: Frommann.

Wagner, Cosima. 1977. *Die Tagebücher*. München: R. Piper.

Wagner, Gottlob Heinrich Adolph. 1813. Uebersicht des mythischen Systems. In *System der indischen Mythe, oder Chronus und die Geschichte des Gottmenschen in der Periode des Vorrückens der Nachtgleichen*, 565–611. Leipzig: Weygand.

Walbridge, John. 2000. *The Leaven of the Ancients: Suhrawardi and the Heritage of the Greeks*. Albany, N.Y.: State University of New York Press.

Walravens, Hartmut. 1999. *Julius Klaproth (1783–1835): Leben und Werk*. Wiesbaden: Harassowitz.

Weber, Albrecht. 1850–1865. Analyse der in Anquetil du Perron's Uebersetzung enthaltenen Upanisad. *Indische Studien; Zeitschrift für die Kunde des indischen Alterthums*. 1850: 247–302, 380–456; 1853: 1–111, 170–236; 1865: 1–54.

Weiner, Thomas. 2000. *Die Philosophie Arthur Schopenhauers und ihre Rezeption*. Hildesheim: Georg Olms.

Weiss, Otto. 1907. *Zur Genesis der Schopenhauerschen Metaphysik*. Leipzig: Thomas.

Werner, Friedrich Ludwig Zacharias. 1823. *Die Söhne des Thal's*. Berlin: Sandersche Buchhandlung.

Wilhelm, Karl Werner. 1994. *Zwischen Allwissenheitslehre und Verzweiflung. Der Ort der Religion in der Philosophie Schopenhauers*. Hildesheim / Zürich: Georg Olms.

Wilkins, Charles. 1785. *The Bhagvat-Geeta, or Dialogues of Kreeshna and Arjoon*. London: C. Nourse.

Young, Julian. 1987. *Willing and Unwilling. A Study in the Philosophy of Arthur Schopenhauer*. Dordrecht: M. Nijhoff.

Zimmer, Heinrich. 1938. Schopenhauer und Indien. *Jahrbuch der Schopenhauer-Gesellschaft* 25:266–273.

Zimmermann, F. W. 1986. The Origins of the so-called Theology of Aristotle. In *Pseudo-Aristotle in the Middle Ages*, ed. by J. Kraye, W. F. Ryan and C. B. Schmitt, 110–240. London: Warburg Institute, University of London.

Zint, Hans. 1921. Schopenhauers Philosophie des doppelten Bewusstseins. *Schopenhauer Jahrbuch* 10:3–45.

———. 1954. *Schopenhauer als Erlebnis*. München / Basel: Ernst Reinhardt Verlag.

Index of Names, Places, and Texts

A

Abraham 148
Adam 24, 40, 48, 147, 148, 185, 283
Afghanistan 146
Agra 129, 275
Alcibiades (c. 450–404 BCE) 54
Alexandria 55
Amitabha, jap. Amida, ch. A-mi-tuo) / Omitto Buddha 191, 288, 291, 296
Anquetil-Duperron, Abraham Hyacinthe (1731–1805) 8, 9, 122, 130, 140, 142, 146–161, 163–167, 169, 170, 174, 178, 179, 181–183, 189, 190–192, 202–205, 209–212, 225, 234, 239, 240, 251, 266, 267, 269, 271–274, 276, 277, 279–294, 297, 298, 310–312
    French Upanishad translation. Bibliothèque nationale NAF Fonds Anquetil-Duperron no. 8857 150, 151, 225, 273, 282, 283, 284, 287
    Législation orientale (1778) 149, 274
    Le Parfait Theologien 148
    Zend Avesta (1771) 149, 163, 284
    Oupnek'hat (1801–2) *passim*
archangels Gabriel, Michael and Raphael 210, 296
Asiatick Researches 14, 112, 157, 235–240, 251, 314, 315, 319
Asiatisches Magazin 119, 175–177, 251, 252, 313, 318
Atwell, John 24, 242, 302, 303
Aurangzeb (1618–1707) 129, 280

B

Baader, Franz Xaver (1765–1841) 117, 307
Baba Lal (Baba Jai Lal Ji Ubhi; 1561–1641) 138, 139, 145
Bacchus 72
Baldaeus, Philippus (1632–1672) 148
Bayle, Pierre (1647–1706) 102, 122, 294
    Dictionnaire historique et critique (1702) 122
Beausobre, Isaac de (1659–1738) 158
Beethoven, Ludwig van (1712–1773) 38

Beierwaltes, Werner 175
Benares (Varanasi) 130, 150, 178, 273, 276, 277, 286
Berger, Douglas 182, 204, 228, 241, 308
Bergson, Henri (1859–1941) 258
Berkeley (California) 269
Berkeley, George (1685–1753) 159, 160
Berlin 4, 58, 60–62, 65, 67, 71, 103, 157, 175, 176, 305, 318
Bernier, François (1620–1688) 122, 125, 127–131, 150, 153, 158, 273
Bhagavad Gītā 139, 157, 177, 178, 251, 275, 303, 318
Bible 88, 123, 148, 271, 308, 309
Blumenbach, Johann Friedrich (1752–1840) 47, 48, 49, 50, 51, 52, 303 (1806) 49
    Specimen archaeologiae telluris (1806) 49
Bohinc, Thomas 182
Böhme, Jacob (1575–1624) 16, 17, 31, 35–37, 39, 40, 43, 58, 66, 67, 77–79, 88, 97–99, 102, 103, 105, 111, 113–118, 123, 171, 177, 181, 182, 184, 205, 221, 230, 262, 263, 268, 304, 305, 307, 309
    Mysterium magnum 66, 67, 97, 98, 113, 116, 304
    On Election by Grace 117
Book of Enoch 148
Books of Solomon 151
Booms, Martin 228
Boughton-Rouse, Charles (1747–1821) 284, 290
Brahma 125, 147, 179, 180, 209, 210, 211, 239, 283, 292
Brucker, Johann Jakob (1696–1770) 121, 122, 125, 158, 292
    Historia critica philosophiae (1741-44) 121–122, 125
Bruno, Giordano (1548–1600) 103, 104, 110, 113, 118, 171, 173–175, 208, 213, 221, 240, 246, 311
    De triplici minimo et mensura 175, 208
Buddha 24, 25, 33, 160, 236, 251, 263, 288
Buhle, Johann Gottlieb (1763–1821) 221
Burnet, Thomas (c. 1635–1715) 158
Büttner, Christian Wilhelm (1716–1801) 175

C

Caland, Willem 148
Carey, William (1761–1834) 272, 274

Cartwright, David 5
Chand, Tara 266, 280
Chardin, Jean (1643–1713) 122, 125–127, 150
Chenet, François 75, 276
China 122, 124, 127, 148, 151, 160, 166, 175, 177, 269, 288, 313, 314
Colebrooke, Henry Thomas (1765–1837) 236, 238–240, 284, 290, 296
Collier, Arthur (1680–1732) 160
Corbin, Henri 136
Creuzer, Georg Friedrich (1771–1858) 107, 167, 168, 169
    Symbolik und Mythologie der alten Völker (1819-1821) 167–168
Cross, Stephen 203, 308, 310, 311
Cudworth, Ralph (1617–1688) 158, 294
Cusa, Nicolaus of (1401–1464) 102, 307
Cuvier, Georges (1769–1832) 48

D

da Gama, Vasco (c. 1460–1524) 27
Dara Shukoh (1615–1659) 110, 128–135, 137–147, 149, 150, 153–157,
    161, 164, 167–170, 174, 178, 179, 181, 183, 187, 189, 190–192,
    202–205, 209, 218, 224–226, 228, 230, 240, 242, 246, 248, 249,
    252, 253, 262, 263, 266, 273–277, 279, 280, 283, 284, 286, 288,
    289, 292, 293, 297, 298, 303, 306, 307, 309, 311–313
    Compass of Truth (Risala-i-Haq Numa) 131, 132, 135
    Confluence of Oceans (Majma-ul-Bahrain) 135, 137, 139, 276
Darwin, Charles (1809–1882) 51, 258
de Bary, William Theodore 283
de Blésimaire, Anthime Grégoire 29, 31
de Cian, Nicoletta 19, 69, 247, 306
de Guignes, Joseph (1721–1800) 177, 288
de Nobili, Roberto (1577–1656) 145
de Sacy, Antoine Isaac Sylvestre (1758–1838) 151
Delhi 150, 273
Deluc, Jean-André (1727–1817) 48, 49, 52
Democritus (c. 460–370 BCE) 126
Descartes, René (1596–1650) 127
Deussen, Paul (1845–1919) 141, 143, 144, 152, 153, 189, 193, 194, 230,
    266, 267, 312

Diamond Sutra 16
Diderot, Denis (1713–1784) 122, 124, 158, 246
    Encyclopédie (Article on Asian philosophy) 122, 125
Dionysius Areopagita (c. 500 CE) 16, 17
D'Onofrio, Svevo 139, 276
Dörpinghaus, Andreas 314
Dresden 20, 87, 102, 119, 123, 175, 181, 199, 208, 221, 235, 280, 302, 319
Dresden, Mark 266
Droit, Roger-Pol 181

E

Eckhart, Meister (c. 1260–c. 1328) 24, 25, 307–309, 311
Egypt 37
Empedocles (c. 495–435 BCE) 12
Encyclopédie 122, 125
Epicurus (341–271 BCE) 51, 126
Eriugena, John Scotus (810–c. 877) 16, 118, 307
Ernst, Carl W. 4, 54, 71, 139, 265, 266, 276
Esposito, Monica (1962–2011) V, 9
Eve 48

F

Fénelon, François (1651–1715) 37, 252
Fichte, Johann Gottlieb (1762–1814) 17, 18, 19, 35, 55, 56, 57, 58, 61, 62, 64, 65, 66, 67, 71, 72, 73, 74, 75, 76, 77, 78, 82, 92, 97, 105, 107, 111, 113, 246, 256, 305, 306, 309, 318
    Wissenschaftslehre 55, 71, 73
Forty-Two Sections Sutra 177, 313, 318
Frankfurt am Main 1, 2, 3, 6, 7, 8, 9, 39, 267, 269
Freud, Sigmund (1856–1939) 258

G

Gambarotto, Francesca 267
Gassendi, Pierre (1592–1655) 127
Gay, John (1685–1732) 28
German Theology (*Theologia deutsch*) 17, 24

Gerson, Jean (1363–1429) 294
Gestering, Johann G. 308
Göbel-Gross, Erhard 130, 133, 134, 140, 141, 145, 150, 266, 276–278, 280, 284, 293
God 16, 27, 44, 54, 62, 68, 75, 76, 79, 81, 89, 90, 101–103, 105, 109, 113–117, 123, 126–128, 131–137, 140, 143–145, 147, 148, 151, 152, 154, 158, 159, 169, 170–172, 174, 189–191, 196, 203, 208, 209, 211, 213, 224, 225, 240, 250, 258, 262, 274, 283, 287–289, 296, 312, 314
God (Allah) 110, 169, 191, 203, 209, 224, 288
Goethe, Johann Wolfgang (1749–1832) 2, 6, 35, 36, 47, 52, 101, 102, 107, 173–176, 208, 213, 234, 306, 318
  Faust (Part I) 234
Goettingen 47, 48, 49, 51, 54, 58, 60, 71, 119, 176, 199, 236, 305, 318
Görres, Joseph (1776–1848) 163–167, 204, 249, 307
  Mythengeschichte der asiatischen Welt (1810) 165, 166
  Oupnek'hat review (1809) 164–165
Graul, Karl (1814–1864) 24, 25
Guyon, Madame (Jeanne-Marie Bouvier de La Motte, 1648–1717) 27, 37, 39, 40, 43, 58, 77, 111, 128, 159, 181, 184, 252–254, 256, 262, 309
Gwinner, Wilhelm (1801–1866) 271

H

Hacker, Paul (1913–1979) 145
Halbfass, Wilhelm 204
Halfwassen, Jens 307
Halhed, Nathaniel Brassey (1751–1830) 284, 290
Hamburg 29, 31, 33, 47, 48, 318
Hamilton, Alexander (1762–1824) 150, 284, 290
Hasrat, Bikrama Jit 131, 132, 133, 275, 283
Haucke, Kai 314, 315
Heeren, Arnold Hermann Ludwig (1760–1842) 48, 51, 58, 119, 236, 318
Hegel, Georg Wilhelm Friedrich (1770–1831) 249
Heimann, Robert 305
Hemsterhuis, François (1721–1790) 102, 103, 123, 175, 208
  Oeuvres philosophiques 175

Herder, Johann Gottfried (1744–1803) 101, 102, 163, 176
Hesiod (7th–6th century BCE) 168, 169, 240
Hitzig, Julius Eduard (1780–1849) 35, 36
Hoffmann, E. T. A. (1776–1822) 34
Holbach, Paul-Henri Thiry (1723–1789) 51, 68
    Système de la nature (1770) 51
Huart, Clément 138, 145
Hübscher, Arthur (1897–1985) 2, 8, 19, 77, 193, 203, 267–269, 271, 272,
    296, 308, 309, 312
Hyman, Arthur 132, 135

I

Ibn Arabi (1165–1240) 132, 135–138, 155
India 16, 27, 51, 110, 119, 122, 123, 126, 128–130, 132, 133, 135, 145,
    146, 148, 149, 151, 153, 157, 160, 163, 166, 178, 179, 211, 235,
    252, 275, 276, 294, 299, 308, 312
Irenaeus (d. c. 202 CE) 268

J

Jacobi, Friedrich Heinrich (1743–1819) 17, 75, 101, 102, 174, 175, 208
    Ueber die Lehre des Spinoza in Briefen an den Herrn Moses Mendelssohn
    208
Jahangir (emperor, 1569–1627) 273
Japan 122, 160, 269
Jena 92, 173, 175, 176, 318
Jesus 88, 185, 192
Jings (Chinese classics) 151
John, Saint (evangelist) 114
Jones, William (1746–1794) 149, 157, 164, 239, 269, 284, 290

K

Kabbalah 158
Kamata, Yasuo 20, 203
Kanne, Johann Arnold (1773–1824) 163, 169, 170–172, 204, 249, 307
    Chronus (1813) 169–170

Kant, Immanuel (1724–1804) 4, 5, 16–18, 36, 55, 56, 58, 61, 62, 64, 65, 75–77, 83, 96, 97, 99, 105, 113, 117, 118, 171, 182, 183, 186, 195, 203, 207, 213, 218, 221, 222, 224, 227–229, 231–234, 240, 241–243, 245, 246, 268, 292, 294, 298, 303, 305, 306, 308–311, 318, 319
   Critique of Pure Reason 96
   Metaphysical Foundations of Ethics 76
   Metaphysical Foundations of Jurisdiction 76
   Metaphysical Foundations of Natural Science 76
Kapani, Lakshmi 181, 230
Kashmir 145, 146, 163, 166
Kircher, Athanasius (1601–1680) 127
   China illustrata 127
Klaproth, Julius (1783–1835) 175–177, 313, 318
   Asiatisches Magazin 175–176 (see also under Asiatisches Magazin)
Königsberg 36
Koran 130, 134, 140, 209
Korfmacher, Wolfgang 223
Koßler, Matthias 258
Krause, Karl Christian Friedrich (1781–1832) 67, 117, 235, 236

L

Lanjuinais, Jean Denis (1753–1827) 159–163
La Peyrère, Isaac (1596–1676) 48, 49, 147
Lassen, Christian (1800–1876) 268
Laws of Menu 251
le Clerc, Jean (1657–1736) 121
Le Gentil, Guillaume (1725–1792) 146, 273, 274, 283
Leibniz, Gottfried Wilhelm (1646–1716) 294, 314
Lemanski, Jens 305
Lenoir, Frédéric 181
Lessing, Gotthold Ephraim (1729–1781) 101, 102
Lettres édifiantes et curieuses, écrites des missions étrangères 125
Liber de causis 132
London 28, 48, 283, 284
Lucretius (99–55 BCE) 51, 52

M

Magee, Brian 203
Mahfuz-ul-Haq, M. 138, 139, 276
Majer, Friedrich (1771–1818) 122, 163, 176–181, 312, 318
    Brahma oder die Religion der Indier als Brahmaismus 179–180
Malebranche, Nicolas (1638–1715) 18, 19, 294
Malter, Rudolf (1937–1994) 19, 23, 69, 181, 222, 224, 250, 257, 302, 315
Marchand, Suzanne 157, 167
Merkel, Rudolf 178
Meyer, Urs Walter 204, 308
Mian Mir (Mir Mohammed Muayyinul Islam; 1550–1635) 132, 133
Milton, John (1608–1674) 28
Mischel, Franz 266, 267
Molinos, Miguel de (1628–1697) 128
Moses 38, 147, 148, 208
Mosheim, Johann Lorenz (1693–1755) 158, 292
Muhammad (prophet) 134
Mulla Shah Badakhshi 133, 275
Müller, F. Max (1823–1900) 4, 160, 265, 266
Mumtaz Mahal (1593–1631) 129, 275

N

Neumann, Volker Maria 2
New Testament 130, 146
Nicholls, Moira 13, 314
Nietzsche, Friedrich (1844–1900) 152, 258
Novalis (Georg Philipp Friedrich Freiherr von Hardenberg, 1772–1801) 31, 103, 117

O

Oeningen 48, 50
Oken, Lorenz (1779–1851) 175
    Abriss der Naturphilosophie 175
    Über das Universum als Fortsetzung des Sinnensystems 175
    Über Licht und Wärme 175
Old Testament 146, 147, 148, 149, 155, 163

Olivelle, Patrick 274, 276, 279, 280
Origen (185–254) 123, 158
Oudh (Awadh) 146, 273
Oupnek'hat 3–8, 14, 27, 87, 110, 112, 119, 123, 130, 141–144, 147, 150–154, 158–167, 169–172, 174, 176, 178, 179, 181–183, 185, 187–195, 197, 199, 202–205, 207–215, 217–219, 221, 225, 226, 228–232, 235, 239, 240, 243, 246, 249–251, 253, 254, 262, 265–272, 274, 275–280, 283, 284, 286–289, 291–297, 299, 302, 303, 305–315, 319 (see also Upanishads, *et passim*)

P

Pauthier, Guillaume (1801–1873) 268, 272
Payne, E. F. J. (1895–1983) 8, 189
Persia 110, 126, 127, 146, 149, 160
Piantelli, Mario 5, 141, 182, 204, 308, 311
Plato (c. 428–348 BCE) 4, 5, 16,–19, 54, 55, 58, 72, 77, 79, 83, 103, 106, 107, 109–111, 123, 124, 177, 186, 207, 221, 223, 228, 229, 234, 241, 243, 245, 246, 298, 303, 305, 306, 310, 311, 319
   Philebos 54
   Res publica 79
   Symposion 54
   Timaeus 103
Plotinus (204–270 CE) 105–107, 118, 131, 132, 135, 146, 181, 294, 305, 307
   Enneads 132, 135
Pluquet, Adrien-François (1716–1790) 122, 123, 125, 158
Polaschegg, Andrea 167, 175
Polier, Antoine-Louis Henri de (1741–1795) 176, 181, 251, 290
   Mythologie des Indous 176, 181, 251
Pons, Jean François (1688–1752) 125, 126, 153, 158
Postel, Guillaume (1510–1581) 148
Proclus (412–485) 106, 107, 131, 132
Psalms (Old Testament) 130
Pseudo-Dionysius (5th–6th century) 158, 307
Pythagoras (c. 570–490 BCE) 12, 118, 123, 126

R

Ramsay, Andrew Michael (1686–1743) 37
Regehly, Thomas 9
Rizvi, Saiyid Athar Abbas 131, 132, 276
Röer, Hans Heinrich Eduard (1805–1866) 268, 272
Roy, Rammohun (1772–1833) 240, 268, 272
Rudolstadt 20, 75, 318
Russia 50

S

Saccas, Ammonius (d. 240 CE) 105, 146
Safranski, Rüdiger 182, 203
Sarmad Kashani (1590–1661) 133
Schelling, Friedrich Wilhelm Joseph (1775–1854) 17–19, 36, 39, 52–67, 76, 78, 79, 81, 83, 86, 96–99, 10–105, 107–119, 123, 124, 173, 181–184, 205, 213, 218, 228, 246, 256, 268, 303–307, 309, 311, 318
   Bruno (1802) 103–105
   Ideas about a Philosophy of Nature 52, 54, 55, 56, 57, 183
   Lectures about the Method of Academic Study 58–59
   Of the I as Principle of Philosophy 62
   Of the World-Soul 52, 57, 183
   Philosophical Inquiries about the Essence of Human Freedom (1809) 66, 66–67, 98–99, 112–117, 116, 183, 304
   Philosophical Letters about Dogmatism and Criticism 63, 64
   Philosophy and Religion (1804) 76, 105, 108–115, 183
   private lectures in Stuttgart (1810) 115
Scheuchzer, Johann Jakob (1672–1733) 48
Schiller, Friedrich (1788–1805) 37, 224
Schirmacher, Wolfgang 203
Schlegel, Friedrich (1772–1829) 31, 35, 67, 117, 122–124, 163, 164, 208
   On the Language and Wisdom of the Indians 123, 163, 164, 208
Schleiermacher, Ludwig (1785–1844) 35, 36, 39, 79, 318
Schmidt, Isaac Jacob (1779–1847) 15, 16
Scholz, Werner 182, 267, 308
Schopenhauer Archive 1, 6, 9, 269

INDEX

Schopenhauer, Johanna (mother; 1766–1838) 33–35, 37, 47, 54, 57, 88, 92, 146, 165, 168, 236, 275
Schopenhauer conversations (Gespräche) 35, 58, 190, 247, 257
Schopenhauer works
    Cambridge edition 8, 189
    Fundamental Problems of Ethics (1841) 21, 117, 118, 119, 232
    Manuscript Remains (passim)
    On Seeing and Colors (1816) 21, 319
    On the Fourfold Root of Sufficient Reason (Dissertation; 1813) 21, 92–98, 310, 318
    On Will in Nature (1836) 21, 258
    Parerga and Paralipomena 4, 12, 16, 17, 18, 19, 21, 64, 265, 313
    Senilia notebook 25
    The World as Will and Representation 4, 12, 13, 15, 18–21, 23–25, 31, 43, 44, 62, 83, 94, 97, 112, 172, 181, 188, 189, 194, 195, 203, 217, 222, 227, 228, 233, 238, 241, 243, 246, 250, 255, 259, 262, 263, 302, 304, 307, 316, 319
    Travel diaries (1800, 1803–4) 28
Schorcht, Wilhelmine 57, 69, 84, 247, 304
Schubbe, Daniel 258
Schulze, Gottlob Ernst (1761–1833) 54, 55, 56, 58, 71, 105, 107, 119, 199, 318
    Kritik der theoretischen Philosophie 199
Schwab, Raymond (1884–1956) 157
Sengupta, Lalita 276
Shah Jahan (emperor, 1592–1666) 128, 129, 273, 275
Shankara (early 8th century) 141, 145, 155, 236, 274, 278, 312
Shastri, Dutt 308
Shayegan, Daryush 276
Shiva 209, 210, 211
Siberia 48, 50, 160
Sirr-i akbar (The Great Secret) 130, 140, 145–147, 150–152, 157, 266, 276–278, 280, 282–284, 287, 290, 293, 297
Skinner, David 5
Socrates (d. 399 BCE) 54, 106
Spain 127, 146
Spence Hardy, Robert (1814–1864) 24, 25
Speziale, Fabrizio 139, 276

Spierling, Volker 302
Spinoza, Baruch (1632–1677) 18, 19, 55, 57, 63–65, 101, 102, 103, 105,
    112, 113, 118, 122, 123, 128, 147, 159, 171, 173, 174, 177, 183,
    208, 221, 233, 234, 246, 303, 311
Stanley, Thomas (1625–1678) 121
    Historia philosophiae orientalis (1690) 121
    The History of the Chaldaick Philosophy (1662) 121
Steffens, Henrich (1773–1845) 175
    Beyträge zur innern Naturgeschichte der Erde 175
Stollberg, Jochen 181, 266, 269
Stuttgart 24, 115
Suhrawardi (Shahab al-Din Suhrawardi, 1155–1191) 145
Surat 149
Swiss National Science Foundation 7
Synesius (bishop; c. 373–414) 158

T

Taj Mahal 129, 275
Tauler, John (c. 1300–1361) 17, 252, 262, 305
Tauler (works attributed to) 252, 305
Tennemann, Wilhelm Gottlieb (1761–1819) 105–108, 221
Theology of Aristotle 131, 131–132
Thomas of Kempis 294
Tibet 16, 146, 160, 314
Tieck, Ludwig (1773–1853) 29, 30, 31, 33, 35, 36, 253
Tieck, Ludwig & Wackenroder, Wilhelm Heinrich
    Fantasies about Art for Friends of Art 29–31
Tiedemann, Dieterich (1748–1803) 221
Timm, Hermann 101, 102, 103
Torah 130, 147

U

Upanishads 3–5, 118, 123, 129, 130, 133–135, 137, 139–145, 147, 149,
    151–154, 156, 157, 161, 164, 169, 179, 182, 188, 189, 193, 194,
    203–205, 209, 211, 212, 218, 229–232, 235, 236, 238–240, 243,
    246, 265–268, 271, 272, 274–280, 283, 284, 286–289, 292–295,
    297–299, 303, 305–313 (see also *Oupnek'hat*, et passim)

V

Vecchiotti, Icilio 182, 267, 308
Veda 3, 27, 118, 130, 139, 147–149, 151, 152, 153, 156, 165, 166, 167, 168, 178–180, 208–210, 212, 213, 221, 232, 236, 238, 241, 243–245, 251, 265, 273, 276–277, 283, 286, 298, 299
Vishnu 145, 153, 177, 209, 210, 211
Voltaire (François-Marie Arouet; 1694–1778) 148, 149, 163
   Essai sur les moeurs 148

W

Wackenroder, Wilhelm Heinrich (1773–1798) 29–31, 33, 35, 36, 39, 42, 253, 304
Wagner, Gottlob Heinrich Adolph (1774–1835) 171, 174, 249, 307
Wagner, Richard (1813–1883) 171, 174, 258, 267, 307
Weber, Albrecht (1825–1901) 266
Weimar 20, 34, 35, 37, 43, 57, 77, 101, 102, 119, 173, 175, 176, 181, 221, 302, 318
Weiner, Thomas 227, 250
Werner, Zacharias (1768–1823) 33–44, 60, 77, 85, 103, 110, 111, 115, 117, 175, 249, 253, 304, 307, 318
   The Sons of the Thal 37, 37–43, 60, 61
Wieland, Christoph Martin (1733–1813) 35, 57, 58, 69, 84, 247, 257, 260
Wilkins, Charles (1749–1836) 157, 177

Y

Yijing (Book of Changes) 124, 148
Yogavāsistha 139, 276

Z

Ziegenbalg, Bartholomäus (1682–1719) 145, 148
Zimmer, Heinrich 163, 308
Zint, Hans 69, 195, 303
Zürich 48, 269

Related Books by Urs App

William Jones's Ancient Theology
Sino-Platonic Papers no. 191. PDF, 125 p. Freely downloadable at http://sino-platonic.org/complete/spp191_william_jones_orientalism.pdf

The Birth of Orientalism
Philadelphia: University of Pennsylvania Press, 2010. xviii + 550 p.
ISBN 978-0-8122-4261-4 (hardcover). 2012 book prize of the Académie des Inscriptions et Belles-Lettres, Paris.

Schopenhauer and China
Sino-Platonic Papers no. 200. PDF, viii + 164 p. Freely downloadable at http://www.sino-platonic.org/complete/spp200_schopenhauer.pdf

The Cult of Emptiness
The Western Discovery of Buddhist Thought and the Invention of Oriental Philosophy
Rorschach / Kyoto: UniversityMedia, 2012. 295 p.
ISBN 978-3-906000-09-1 (hardcover)
Wil (Switzerland): UniversityMedia, 2014. 295 p.
ISBN 978-3-906000-12-1 (paperback)

Richard Wagner and Buddhism
Rorschach / Kyoto: UniversityMedia, 2011. 102 p.
ISBN 978-3-906000-00-8

The First Western Book on Buddhism and Buddha
Wil (Switzerland): UniversityMedia, forthcoming 2014
ISBN 978-3-906000-27-5

www.ingramcontent.com/pod-product-compliance
Lightning Source LLC
Chambersburg PA
CBHW021942240426
43668CB00037B/482